# The Discourse of Tourism and National Heritage

# The Discourse of Tourism and National Heritage:

## *A Contrastive Study from a Cultural Perspective*

By

Claudia Elena Stoian

**Cambridge Scholars** Publishing

The Discourse of Tourism and National Heritage:
A Contrastive Study from a Cultural Perspective

By Claudia Elena Stoian

This book first published 2015

Cambridge Scholars Publishing

Lady Stephenson Library, Newcastle upon Tyne, NE6 2PA, UK

British Library Cataloguing in Publication Data
A catalogue record for this book is available from the British Library



ISBN (10): 1-4438-8219-4
ISBN (13): 978-1-4438-8219-4

*To my family*

# TABLE OF CONTENTS

**Part III: The Study**

## Part IV: Conclusions

# LIST OF FIGURES

# LIST OF TABLES

# FOREWORD

## ARSENIO JESÚS MOYA GUIJARRO[1]

The promotion of tourism in an international market is nowadays most often realized by means of the Internet, which has revolutionised the distribution of information. Tourism websites have the functions of informing, advising, promoting and selling. Their success depends on a combination of elements; among the most important are attractiveness and useful design. The discourse of tourism uses several semiotic resources to create meaning and communicate information, exploiting both the linguistic and the visual codes, which have a complex and complementary relation. Their simultaneous use aims to produce a better promotional message and to ensure that the informative and persuasive purposes of tourist discourse are reached. The monument or destination promoted is portrayed by means of language and image, both separately and together, in order to persuade readers to become visitors.

Claudia Elena Stoian's book, *The Discourse of Tourism and National Heritage: A Contrastive Study from a Cultural Perspective,* aims to contribute to the field of online tourism promotion. It presents the multimodal analyses of two sets of websites, institutional and commercial, from three different countries, Romania, Spain and Great Britain. The multimodal approach embraced uses powerful tools, those proposed by Halliday's Systemic-Functional Linguistics and Kress and van Leeuwen's Visual Social Semiotics. The results of the analyses are compared in relation to (1) the organization and layout of the webpages, (2) their content and message, and (3) the visual and verbal strategies used to inform, persuade and direct potential visitors to the promoted destinations.

---

[1] Arsenio Jesús Moya Guijarro is a Senior Lecturer at the Department of English Language and Linguistics, Faculty of Education, University of Castilla-La Mancha, Cuenca, Spain. He has published many articles and books in the fields of Systemic-Functional Linguistics and multimodality. The most recent ones are: *A Multimodal Analysis of Picture Books for Children: A Systemic Functional Approach* (Equinox, 2014), as author, and *The World Told and the World Shown: Multisemiotic Issues* (Palgrave Macmillan, 2009), as co-editor together with Eija Ventola.

The study also explores the way words and images are combined into multimodal acts in order to promote the tourist landmarks.

The book addresses students and professionals in the fields of tourism discourse, online promotion and intercultural communication as it makes explicit the complexity of a website's communication and its relation to cultural and contextual factors. It also identifies the verbal and visual tools that can be used to promote products, assets or landmarks. All in all, the book provides not only theoretical insights, but also practical implications. Last but not least, the study contributes to making us, potential users, aware of the different persuasive techniques that advertisers and promoters may use to fulfil a persuasive function and obtain their ultimate goal of selling. *The Discourse of Tourism and National Heritage: A Contrastive Study from a Cultural Perspective* is a very commendable study, which I strongly recommend to both students and professionals.

*Cuenca, June 2015*

# PREFACE

The present study is a revised and updated version of my PhD thesis in the field of online tourism promotion. It focuses on the national online promotion of UNESCO World Heritage Sites, in two different types of websites–institutional and commercial–from three countries, Romania, Spain and Great Britain. The study analyses the way each country presents its national landmarks and combines various modes to create a virtual brochure with a promotional message from both institutional and commercial standpoints. For this, it studies the organization of the websites and their webpages, as well as the lexico-grammatical and visual features of the promotional messages. The results of the different analyses are interpreted from a cultural perspective.

The theoretical framework for the analysis is Systemic Functional Linguistics. The linguistic text is analysed following Halliday's theory of the metafunctions (1985; 1994; Halliday and Matthiessen 2004). Thus, the analysis focuses on the ideational, interpersonal and textual meanings of the verbal message. The analysis of the visual text applies Kress and van Leeuwen's model (1996; 2006), studying the same types of meanings realized visually.

The results of the different analyses are compared from two perspectives: namely, in relation to a) the types of websites and b) the countries in which they were produced. The comparison between institutional and commercial websites reveals a pattern in which the similarities seem to be related to characteristics typical of web organization and layout, tourist promotion and specific topic, while differences seem to reflect the types of websites and their functions. However, when the websites are compared from the point of view of the different countries, a number of national characteristics of web promotion, common to the two types of websites are revealed. These are further interpreted from a cultural point of view, showing that the findings can be accounted for by the context dimension of cultural variability (Hall 1976; 2000; Hall and Hall 1990). The Spanish and British sets of websites are, in general, consistent with the literature on intercultural communication consulted (Hall 2000; Würtz 2005; Neuliep 2006; Şerbănescu 2007), whereas the Romanian sets do not follow the pattern for the country's usual classification as a high-context culture, but combine features of both low-contexts and high-contexts. The consistencies seem to indicate the stability of Spanish and British cultures.

At the same time, departures from the cultural contextual patterns exist in all the cases analysed. These inconsistencies can be explained by cultural changes and influences brought out by globalization and internal changes in terms of politics, economy and society. They also indicate that cultural patterns can be affected by the medium of communication (Internet) and the context of communication (type of promotion).

The findings from the study emphasize the need for an understanding of multimodality and interculturality in online tourism promotion, especially as applied to creating an image or brand for a country's successful international promotion. They show that Systemic Functional Linguistics offers a useful tool, from both theoretical and practical perspectives, which can be applied to areas like composition of promotional messages, online promotion, tourism discourse and its strategies, or intercultural communication.

*Timişoara, August 2015*

# ACKNOWLEDGMENTS

I am very grateful to a number of persons for their support during my research period.

First of all, I thank my thesis supervisor, Dr. Rachel Whittaker, for her guidance and suggestions. I am grateful for her dedication and time, in spite of her busy schedule.

I am also grateful to the *Sysfling* and *Sys-func* online discussion groups for providing me with the possibility to put forward my doubts related to the linguistic analysis of the texts. My special thanks go to Laura Hlavacka and Michael O'Donnell, for their constant answers, and to Gordon Tucker, for his suggestions and for making me believe more in my analysing skills. I thank also Meriel and Thomas Bloor for including one of my discussed examples in their 3rd edition of *The Functional Analysis of English*. I want to express my gratitude also to Morten Boeriis, Tuomo Hiippala, Geoff Thompson and Gordon Tucker, for reviewing my study, and to Daniel Dejica, Lise Fontaine, Clara Molina, Jesús Moya Guijarro and Mick O'Donnell, for sitting on my exam board. My sincere thanks go to Joseph F. Uddo III for his help in proofreading this book and to the whole Cambridge Scholars Publishing team for making this happen.

I would like to acknowledge the assistance of the World Tourism Organization for providing useful and up-to-date data regarding tourism. I am also indebted to Ciao Romania, Romania Tourism and Turespaña for granting me the copyright permission to use their screenshots in this book.

I also thank all the people, too many to name personally, who have contributed to the development of this paper, in one way or another. My special thanks go to Ainoa Cerezuela, Ciprian Chirilă, Cristi Gașpar, Sorin Gheța, Monica Mitroi, Flavia Munteanu, Elena Petrovici and Cristina Rașcu. I am particularly in debt to Sorin Ciutacu and Carlos Sanz Mingo for their personal encouragement, help with bibliography and proofreading.

Last but not least, I am mostly in debt to my family, especially my husband, mother and brother, who supported me with their love and understanding and helped me overcome the hardest moments.

# PART I:

# INTRODUCTION

# CHAPTER ONE

# INTRODUCTION

The use of the Internet for the promotion of tourism across the world is an ever-growing phenomenon (OMT 2001, 20; Montiel Torres 2002, 539; Plog 2005, 280; Mena 2008, 209; Mocini 2009, 291). Both institutional and commercial entities related with tourism have embraced and adapted this new medium to promote their countries and reach a wide national and international audience (OMT 1999, 34, 58). The possibilities and tools offered by the hypermedia environment are more than favourable for these purposes (Montiel Torres 2002, 539-542).

This chapter introduces the study by presenting its motivation. Then, the study is set into the framework of the field by a succinct description of the present situation of research. Its intended contribution to the field introduced is indicated in a number of research objectives. Finally, the chapter describes the organization of the book.

## 1.1. Motivation for the research

Different motives have contributed to undertaking the research on which this study is based. They are related to the topic, the corpus and the method of research. The choice of online tourism as a topic has been influenced by its frequent presence as an alternative medium to paper or other types of promotion (Antelmi and Santulli 2012, 14). The Internet has become "an indispensable tool" (Perandrea 2011, 1), not only for navigation on and buying from tourist websites, but also for promotion. Both institutional and commercial tourist entities have been influenced in their promotion strategies by the appearance and progressive diffusion of the Internet (OMT 1999; Rodríguez Abella 2011). Its relative novelty means that the body of research in the area, while not small, still leaves interesting questions open.

Online tourism promotion is based on websites (OMT 1999, 30; 2001, 84), which are not only text, but also "conglomerate[s] of images, multimedia, interactive features, animated graphics, and sounds" (Würtz 2005). This complexity indicates that the composition and production of appealing and efficient websites is not an easy task. The task is even more complicated when the websites are created and used in different cultural contexts; their design, content, layout and multimodal communicative acts should be culture-sensitive. Differences in communication styles across cultures "are expected to pose challenges to the ways in which websites communicate their messages most optimally" (Würtz 2005). Considering the complicated task of promoting tourism online in a culturally diverse world, attempts have been made to provide instructions in the form of guides to improve efficiency. Market research companies carry out studies to find out more about people's expectations and perceptions regarding different characteristics, like webpage configurations, designs or messages, with the purpose of improving websites (OMT 2001; Crystal 2004; Shchiglik and Barnes 2004; Steinmetz 2004). Nonetheless, recommendations are only beginning to be formulated and many of these are tentative (Crystal 2004, 15). This study, then, aims to contribute to the field of online tourism promotion with new insights, deriving from the analysis of institutional and commercial websites from the point of view of intercultural communication and offering suggestions as to practical implications.

The countries chosen as online tourism promoters are Romania, Spain and Great Britain. The sample was chosen for a number of reasons. The countries are different as far as tourism is concerned. Romania is a relatively new country in the tourism market. As such, it is trying to distance itself from the bad connotations left by the communist regime, create a distinctive brand and become known to the international world (Morgan and Pritchard 2000, 145; OMT 2005a, 32; Babu *et al.* 2008; Light *et al.* 2009, 234, 235; OECD 2009; Timothy and Nyaupane 2009, 6). Its numbers for 2013[1], compared to those for the other two countries, are very low: 1,715,000 international tourists and 1,438 million dollars income from tourism (OMT 2014, 8). However, it has to be considered that these numbers have grown in the last few years and are expected to keep growing (OMT 2013, 2). In Spain, in turn, tourism is a flourishing industry (Macleod 2004, 23). The country has repositioned itself successfully "as a cultural destination" different from its "bucket and spade cheap beach holiday image", especially after Franco's dictatorship ended (Moilanen and Rainisto 2009, 5; WTO and ETC 2009, 10). The Spanish tourist board has worked at the creation of a brand for almost a century (Macleod 2004, 23; Piñanes Leal 2004, 91). In the 1980s, it finally managed to make Spain the first "supra-brand" (Morgan and Pritchard 2000, 282, 289), mainly due to its consistent logo and associated core

[1] 2013 is the most recent year in the statistics published by the World Tourism Organization (OMT 2014).

values promoted (Morgan and Pritchard 2000, 289; Bartlett 2002, 45). Spain has higher numbers of tourists and is situated in 3rd position in the world for international tourists (60.7 million) and 2nd position in the world, after USA, and 1st in Europe for income (60.4 billion dollars) (OMT 2014, 6). Finally, Great Britain has always been on the market as a top destination (Macleod 2004; Babu *et al.* 2008). The destination's "supra-brand", established in the 1990s, can be promoted on its own or in conjunction with one of the other main brands, i.e. Scotland, Wales, England and London (Morgan and Pritchard 2000, 237). The latest documented data show that Great Britain has fallen several positions in the world's top list of international arrivals and income from tourism, even if the numbers are slightly higher than in the previous years (OMT 2013, 6). The number of tourists for 2013 is 31.2 million and the amount of income is 40.6 billion dollars (OMT 2014, 6).

These different destinations are expected to have different promotional messages. In this study, the differences have been restricted to the countries' multimodal communicative acts by choosing the same language of promotion and the same types of landmarks. English has been chosen, as it is the most widely used language on the Internet, the language of business and tourism (Danet and Herring 2008, 554; Ciutacu 2009, 316; Meyer 2009, 22). This lingua franca status assures international distribution to the promotional message. As for the types of landmarks promoted, those designated World Heritage Sites (WHS) by UNESCO have been selected because they are some of "the world's most visited and heavily marketed tourism attractions" (OMT 2009, 1, 5). Countries frequently use their WHS as a way of becoming visible to tourists (Timothy and Nyaupane 2009, 11) since the UNESCO award is "a highly valued promotional tool for developing tourism" (Timothy and Nyaupane 2009, 11). As the three countries have a large number of WHS[2], the types most visited by international tourists have been selected. These are religious, historic and urban landmarks (Timothy and Boyd 2002, 37, 39, 43; Sharpley 2006, 143; Richards 2007, 17; Timothy and Nyaupane 2009, 10; Steinecke 2010, 188, 189). The examination of webpages dedicated to famous World Heritage Sites from different countries, each with a different background in tourism, can indicate the ways each country promotes its most important destinations–its heritage sites–internationally.

[2] Romania has 7 World Heritage Sites (WHS)–6 cultural and 1 natural, very few compared to the other two countries. Spain has many WHS as it is the 3rd in the world, after China and Italy, and the 2nd in Europe. It has 44 WHS, of which 39 cultural, 3 natural and 2 mixed. Great Britain has 28 WHS (23 cultural, 4 natural and 1 mixed) (UNESCO 2014).

Analysing these sites can also reflect the identity of the countries, as projected in their webs, since the sites are related to their past and reflect their values. The purpose, thus, is to observe the ways top tourist destinations and emerging ones promote their famous landmarks and their identity to the world, paying special attention to verbal and visual modes.

Online tourism promotion can be analysed from different perspectives. The theoretical perspective chosen for this study comes from a school of functional linguistics. As already mentioned, websites are complex as they are built using a number of modes and resources. Systemic Functional Theory (SFT) (Halliday 1985; 1994; Halliday and Matthiessen 2004; Kress and van Leeuwen 1996; 2006), with its perspective on meaning-making in context, has been considered a revealing model for the analysis of websites (Djonov 2005, 46). This model has been chosen to analyse the promotional messages of the corpus collected, from the point of view of how they combine to make meanings. The verbal and visual modes are both analysed in detail, as separate modes, and together, as multimodal acts. This deconstruction attempts to reveal the way each mode contributes to promotion, for a better understanding of the combined message (Hiippala 2013, 1). In this study, the analysis is taken to a further dimension, that of culture, attempting to show differences in the communicative acts, which may be rooted in the country's culture. The way language and image are used to depict people, places and circumstances; present social interactions; and compose a meaningful multimodal act can reflect cultural patterns (Würtz 2005; Stoian 2013a; 2013b; forthcoming). These can also be observed in the design of the websites (Würtz 2005). For the analysis, the cultural dimension chosen is that of context (Hall 1976; 2000; Hall and Hall 1990), since it seems the most relevant to the type of message studied and its function. This study, therefore, proposes SFT for the analysis of websites and attempts to provide more evidence to support those studies that consider it effective for the analysis of digital media. Furthermore, the characteristics revealed can reflect cultural communicative styles. The study, of course, does not intend to reinforce stereotypes, but to interpret the findings in each country's cultural communicative style. It also aims to insist once more that cultural competence is a must in today's business world.

To summarise, the present research study covers many areas (online communication, promotion, tourism, multimodal discourse and intercultural communication) and hopes to bring new insights to each. It conducts a Systemic Functional analysis of online national tourism promotion in order to show the ways World Heritage Sites are presented on the international market. For a more general contribution, different types of websites (institutional and commercial), destinations (less and more popular), landmarks (religious, historic and urban), from different countries and cultures (Romania, Spain and Great Britain) have been chosen. Apart from this, the study includes the possibility to apply the results; it hopes to improve the understanding of the complexity of websites and provide useful information in the form of implications for more effective communication and successful promotion. It targets the creation, production, transmission and understanding of online messages. Many people contribute to these actions: websites designers, managers, copywriters, editors, tourist entities and/or governmental officials, to mention just a few. Understanding the implicit meanings of their choices in building their multimodal messages for intercultural communication would make it easier for them to achieve their different goals. The present work aims to draw specialists' attention and make them aware of the complexity and importance of good communication. The multimodal study of online tourism promotion from a Systemic Functional perspective, then, can help online and tourism writers, designers and/or marketers "develop appropriate communication strategies and design communication channels with a certain degree of cultural sensitivity" (Tsotra *et al.* 2004, 4219).

## 1.2. Previous studies

Tourism, as the world's largest industry (Smith 2001; WTTC 2003), has been studied from various perspectives. Topics like the tendencies of tourism markets (OMT 2003; 2005a; 2008; 2011), tourism products and the factors influencing them (McKean *et al.* 1995; McKercher 1998a; McKercher and du Cros 2002), the impact of tourism (Archer *et al.* 2005) or tourists and their behaviour (Plog 2005), have been thoroughly researched. Special attention has also been paid to different types of tourism, like global (Theobald 2005; Conrady and Buck 2010), national (OMT 2002), rural (Light 2006), nature-based (McKercher 1998b), religious (Richards 2003) or urban (Cazes and Potier 1996; Jansen-Verbeke and Lievois 2002).

A type of tourism that has spread to "all corners of the globe", and its study together with it, is cultural tourism (Richards 2007, 9). Considered an arguably "good" form of tourism for the destination, avoiding many of the pitfalls of conventional tourism while offering additional benefits (Richards 2007, 2), cultural tourism has been investigated in relation to authenticity and globalization (Schouten 2007), its behaviour on the market of different countries (Hughes and Allen 2005) or the types of cultural tourists (Richards 1996; Kemmerling-Clack 1999) and market segments (McKercher and du Cros 2002). The Organisation for Economic Co-operation and Development (2009) has looked at the relationship between tourism, culture and destinations' attractiveness and competitiveness. It has also examined the development of tourism production and distribution in relation to cultural resources, identifying the key factors and policy interventions that can maximise the attractiveness of destinations, as places to visit, live and invest in. Researchers have also focused on heritage tourism (Graham *et al.* 2000; Mckercher and du Cros 2002; Timothy and Boyd 2002; Light *et al.* 2009) and its management by World Heritage Sites (OMT 2009). Heritage assets have been identified, described and classified (Ashworth and Tunbridge 2000; Butler and Boyd 2000; Jansen-Verbeke 2010). Particular attention has also been given to the social implication of heritage tourism (Herbert 1995), its cult and mythicization (Rooijakkers 2002), its consumers (Timothy and Boyd 2002) and their reasons for visiting heritage places, like enhancing learning, satisfying curiosity, growing spiritually, relaxing or getting away from home (Prentice *et al.* 1997; Confer and Kerstetter 2000; Poria *et al.* 2004).

Another important area of research in the tourism field is branding. This has been applied to countries, places and destinations (Kotler and Gertner 2002; Olins 2003; Hemelryk Donald and Gammack 2007; Moilanen and Rainisto 2009; WTO and ETC 2009). It seems that place branding is becoming a theoretical and methodological field in its own right (Hemelryk Donald and Gammack 2007, 169). Several researchers have emphasised the fact that the success of tourism relies on successful image creation (Selwyn 1993; Morgan and Pritchard 1998). There are many reasons for adopting a brand, like competitive advantage (Aaker 1995), differentiation (Evans *et al.* 1995) and/or a special place in consumers' minds (Chacko 1997). Various studies have depicted successful destination brands, such as Scotland (Butler 1998; Moilaren and Rainisto 2009), Great Britain (Morgan and Pritchard 2000) and Spain (Piñanes Leal 2004; Mariottini 2012), pointing out the importance of cultural heritage assets in building destination branding (McKercher and du Cros 2002). Attention has been directed also to new tourism markets represented by countries like Romania, Poland and Bulgaria (Morgan and Pritchard 1998; Light 2006). These examples, together with other studies (Bartlett 2002; Buliç 2002; Anholt 2009), indicate different ways to build destination brands. To become successful, brands should be, most of all, "credible, deliverable, differentiating, conveying powerful ideas, enthusing for trade partners, resonating with the consumer" (Morgan and

Pritchard 2000, 296). Clearly, such complex objectives could be supported by research into ways of improving the message of a country as a tourist destination.

The tourism industry, like almost every field, has been influenced by the Internet era and the research focus has shifted towards "New Tourism" (Poon 1993). The application of information and communication technologies (ICTs) and their impact on tourism have been studied by a number of researchers (Poon 1993; Nijman 1999; Sawhney and Prandelli 2000; Fernández Cavia and Huertas 2009). Montiel Torres (2002) has focused on ICTs and provided the main advantages brought by the Internet to tourist promotion. She has also indicated some requirements for a successful website. She has tested her theory on two Spanish corporative websites, one belonging to the Rural Hotels Association in Andalusia and the other to the county department promoting Malaga. Similarly, Majó and Galí (2002) have analysed the importance of the Internet on tourist information, by briefly presenting various studies regarding webpages of different Spanish tourist boards and agents such as comarcal and city councils and hotels in Barcelona and Cataluña. The Internet has also changed the habits of 21st century tourists (Talón *et al.* 2007; Rodríguez Antón and Alonso Almeida 2009); they increasingly use it to look for information on destinations and/or cultural events (Richards 2003; PEW/Internet 2004 in Janoschka 2004) and to book and buy holidays and/or services (Dwyer 2005; Pyka and Freitag 2010). Tourists' expectations and perceptions are frequently investigated by means of questionnaires or other methods and/or tools in order to help improve websites (OMT 2001; Shchiglik and Barnes 2004; Steinmetz 2004). The identification of consumers' needs makes personalization easier, information being continuously controlled and updated (Buhalis 1998; Steinmetz 2004).

The success of promotion and, obviously, of tourism depends, among various factors, on the website created for the purpose. Various features and/or components have been claimed to make a website successful. These include contents and design (Huizingh 2000; OMT 2001; Montiel Torres 2002); access speed, navigation, interactivity and responsiveness (OMT 2001; Palmer 2002); ease of use (OMT 1999); motivation to purchase (Jeong 2002) or marketing concepts (OMT 2005b). Frequently used in marketing, the AIDA model[3], for example, has been used to study more than 160 Internet presentations of European Regional Destination Management Organisations (IZT and DWIF 2003). The results have showed that the application of the model to tourism websites' design and

[3] The acronyms stand for Attention, Interest, Desire and Action.

structure of information can make them attractive and successful (OMT 2005b, 8). AIDA has also been applied to analyse different tourism campaigns, like Turespaña's[4] 2010 (Mariottini 2012). Other researchers (Mich *et al.* 2003) have studied websites from the perspective of rhetoric with the aim of finding a conceptual basis and a reference outline for the evaluation of website quality.

The discourse of tourism, understood as the particular ways of using language and image to communicate information related to tourism (Thurlow and Jaworski 2010), also plays an important role in promotion and branding. As such, it has received the attention of various researchers, who have focused on the evaluative techniques (Kaltenbacher 2007) used to portray destinations positively (Hiippala 2007), sometimes linking them to tourists' nostalgia (Dann 2005); on its features of specialised discourse (Gotti 1991), its translation (Londero 2006, Mocini 2009) or its diachronic evolution (Antelmi 2011), among many other topics. Frequently, tourism discourse has been seen as promotional discourse and compared to advertising (Henríquez Jiménez 1997; Morgan and Pritchard 2000; Bosh Abarca 2001; Londero 2006; Crişan 2013), its online variant making no exception (OMT 1999). Different tourist materials have been analysed, like travel guides (Mapelli and Santos López 2010), tourist brochures and leaflets (Hiippala 2007; 2013), paying attention to their discursive characteristics (Leech 1996; Juan González 2000; Ruiz and Saorín 2000; Saorín 2001; Moya Guijarro 2006), intertextuality (Antelmi 2011), sensorial techniques (Pérez Vázquez 2011), rhetorical structure (Mongkholjuck 2008) or their moves and generic structure (Ramm 2000; Vimonnan 2003; Toledo Pereira 2006; Calvi 2011).

Interest has been raised also by online materials, mainly represented by various types of websites, such as institutional, produced by tourist boards (Calvi and Mapelli 2010; Rodríguez Abella 2011) or by UNESCO (Navarro and Miotti 2011), and/or commercial (Calvi 2006; Calvi *et al.* 2008). In these cases, the attention has been directed to their discursive and linguistic features (Pierini 2008), their translations into English for an international audience (Pierini 2007; Garzone 2008), their comparison to other websites (Garzone 2009) or their structure as digital genres (Stein 2006; Bateman 2008; 2014; Calvi 2010; Mariottini 2011; Suau Jiménez 2011). *Linguaturismo*[5] (Calvi 2006; 2010; Calvi *et al.* 2008; Calvi *et al.* 2009; Calvi and Mapelli 2011), for example, is an interuniversity research project that focuses on the language of Spanish and Italian tourism

---

[4] Turespaña stands for *Instituto de Turismo de España*, i.e. the Institute of Tourism in Spain or the Spanish Tourist Board.

[5] The project is carried out by a research team from Milan University.

communication. Its purpose is to create an extensive corpus of tourist texts, including websites, and analyse it from interlinguistic and intercultural perspectives. Among various objectives, it aims to provide qualitative and quantitative data regarding the birth, development and eventual fixation of two online genres, institutional and commercial websites. Apart from the research topics presented above, tourism studies have also focused on entire national tourism campaigns (Londero 2006; Santulli 2011; Mariottini 2012).

Research on the discourse of tourism has been affected by the recent shift from language to multimodality, as "the artefacts participating in tourism discourse are inherently multimodal" (Hiippala 2013). The linguistic mode has been studied thoroughly. Its lexical, morpho-syntactical and textual characteristics (Dann 1996; Calvi 2000; Mocini 2009; Moya Guijarro 2013a) contribute to its importance for tourist promotion (Cogno and Dall'Ara 2001; Giordana 2004; Giacomarra 2006; Mariottini 2012). However, the visual mode has only lately started to receive more attention. The analysis of the role of the visual for tourism (Scarles 2004; Garrod 2008; 2009; Jokela 2011) shows that tourism can be understood as a visual practice or gaze (Adler 1989; Urry 1990). Tourism relies on images (Hiippala 2013), as their content (Machin 2004) has a considerable effect on the formation of a destination brand (Molina and Esteban 2006). A number of images from the online campaign carried out by Turespaña's website have been analysed by Garcia Álvarez (2006), who observed that they do not only present reality, but also the values associated to it. Multimodal analysis has proven to provide suitable tools for the study of tourism discourse, as the iconic and verbal codes combine into the construction of the destination's image (Londero 2006; Yui Ling Ip 2008; Rodríguez Abella 2011; Francesconi 2014, Moya Guijarro and González Lanza 2014). This combination has turned into a marketing strategy crucial to create an attractive and desirable image of the place to be visited (Held 2004).

Multimodality provides a useful framework also for the analysis and interpretation of websites. Based on Systemic Functional Theory, multimodal discourse analysis focuses nowadays on digital texts. Halliday's SFL and its core principle of the metafunctions have been extended to other semiotic resources than language for the study of meaning-making. These include visual images (O'Toole 1994; Kress and van Leeuwen 1996; 2006) and their use in scientific texts (Lemke 1998) and education (Jewitt 2006); colour (van Leeuwen 2011); music and sound (van Leeuwen 1999); movement and gesture (Martinec 2000; 2001); films (Martinec 2000; Iedema 2001); and architecture and space (O'Toole 1994;

Stenglin 2004), to mention just a few. Modern semiotic resources, websites have been investigated multimedially in relation to information organization (O'Donnell 1997; Thorlacius 2002; Djonov 2005); thematic analysis (Thibault 2001); levels of information structure on a multimodal text page (Bateman and Delin 2001); literacy (Kress 2003); institutions (Kok 2004); hypermedia (Garzone 2002; Lemke 2002; Bargiela Chiappini 2005) and its (educational) applications (Baldry 2000; Unsworth 2001; Jewitt 2002); digital technology and software (O'Halloran *et al.* 2009; O'Halloran 2011); and/or online virtual worlds (Maiorani 2009).

Promotional tourism discourse and websites have received attention also from the field of cultural research. Culture, understood as a "collective programming of the mind which distinguishes the members of one group or category of people from another" (Hofstede 1991, 4), determines the way people act, the manner in which they relate to others and the way they interpret events happening in the surrounding context (Dumitrescu 2009, 26). This concept, and everything that it implies, have been thoroughly studied from various perspectives–like anthropology (Bernard 1988; Barnard and Spencer 1996; Duranti 2004), psychology (Triandis *et al.* 1985; Triandis 1995; Matsumoto and Juang 2007), sociology (Alexander 2003; Jacobs and Hanrahan 2005), communication (Clyne 1994; Scollon and Scollon 2001; Gudykunst 2005; Kotthoff and Spencer-Oatey 2008), linguistic exchanges in business (Bargiela-Chiappini *et al.* 2007; Guillén Nieto 2007; Dumitrescu 2009; Nardon and Steers 2009), globalization (Jameson and Miyoshi 1998; Wise 2008) or technology (Russo and Boor 1993; Becker and Wehner 2001), among others.

As cultures contain maps of meaning to make the world comprehensible to their members, and these do not carry the same weight in every culture (Lehtonen 2000, 10, 14), frameworks which can be applied to the classification of cultures have been proposed by several researchers in the area (Kluckhohn and Strodtbeck 1961; Hall 1976; Hofstede 1984; 2001; Hall and Hall 1990; Trompenaars 1993; Trompenaars and Hampden-Turner 1998; Schwartz 1992; 1994; House *et al.* 2004; Hofstede and Hofstede 2005; Nardon and Steers 2009). Their models highlight different aspects of societal beliefs, norms, and/or values. Each of them puts forward different cultural dimensions in order to account for cultural variability, and, thus, identify and describe features of particular cultures. The models overlap in some cases, which can only reinforce their utility and possible validity (Nardon and Steers 2009, 9). Nevertheless, they are sometimes criticised for being not very applicable, imprecise or stereotypical, especially in the present globalised world (McSweeney 2002; Light 2003; Dahl 2004; Jones 2007; Cardon 2008).

Among these models, the most important and frequently cited in the realm of intercultural research, despite not being very recent (Gudykunst *et al.* 1988; Clyne 1994; Würtz 2005; Guillén Nieto 2007; Matsumoto and Juang 2007) are those proposed by Hofstede and Hall. Hofstede conceptualised cultural variability in terms of five dimensions: individualism/collectivism, power distance, uncertainty avoidance, masculinity/femininity (1984) and long-term orientation/short-term orientation (2001). His research, considered still valid nowadays (de Mooij and Hofstede 2010, 86) helps people understand cultures using a dimensional approach, as the dimensions are related to concrete differences in attitudes, opinions, beliefs, and behaviours. Hall (1976; 2000; Hall and Hall 1990), in turn, classifies cultures in relation to monochronic/polychronic time, space and high-context/low-context. These models have applicability in real life situations providing a base for cultural awareness and improvement of intercultural situations.

Regarding communication, culture influences discourse and, at the same time, is influenced by discourse (Şerbănescu 2007, 255). As such, discourse is a field frequently studied from a cultural perspective (Barker and Galasinki 2001; Gumperz and Cook Gumperz 2008; Martin and Rose 2008). Special attention has been paid to the relation of language to culture, looking at topics like language use (Kress 1989; Besnier 2004) or translation (de Mooij 2004), especially in intercultural interaction (Gudykunst *et al.* 1988; Carbaugh 2007). This relation has been taken further by the Sapir–Whorf Hypothesis (Sapir 1929; Whorf 1940) and its followers. Also known as linguistic relativity, the hypothesis suggests that speakers of different languages think differently, and that they do so because of the differences in their languages. Their thought processes or their ways of interpreting the world may be different because their language has helped shape their thought patterns. With the 20th century explosion of imaging and visual technologies, the research focus has shifted from language to visual communication (Kostelnick 1995; Mirzoeff 1998; Jewitt and Oyama 2001; Lister and Wells 2001; Würtz 2005).

Promotional discourse, like advertising (Oyama 1999; Hiippala 2012) or tourism (Lewis 2004; Londero 2006; George 2008), including its online variant (Würtz 2005; Calvi and Mapelli 2010), has also been observed culturally and cross-culturally. Producers of campaigns are every day more aware of the need to be culturally proficient. The adaptation of marketing, branding and advertising strategies to the culture of the consumer has been recognised as necessary (Şerbănescu 2007; de Mooij and Hofstede 2010; Hiippala 2012). Culture is said to also influence information processing, perception and categorization (Würtz 2005; de Mooij and Hofstede 2010).

It seems, then, that the focus of research has been mainly on the reception of the message. Not much has been said, instead, about the role of culture in the production of the promotional message (de Mooij 2005; Würtz 2005). Würtz examines cultural variability in the production of online promotion, by identifying the strategies high-context cultures (Hall 1976; 2000; Hall and Hall 1990) call upon in their visual communication on the Internet for marketing purposes. Other researchers have approached the following topics from a cultural point of view: website design (Hu *et al*. 2004; Cyr *et al*. 2005; Faiola and Matei 2005), content (Singh 2005) or usage (Singh *et al*. 2006), some considering Hostede's dimensional model of national culture in their analyses (Marcus and Gould 2000; Sheridan 2001). The models of Hofstede and Hall mentioned above are recommended by researchers as useful tools for examining cultural variability in the production and reception of (online) promotional discourse (Würtz 2005; de Mooij and Hofstede 2010).

## 1.3. Summary and research objectives

Within the frameworks presented above, the present study looks at the way different countries promote several of their national UNESCO landmarks online for an international audience. In brief, the research and its aims are as follows:

1. This study describes the features of two sets of websites from three countries: Romania, Spain and Great Britain. Both sets promote national UNESCO landmarks, one from an institutional standpoint and the other from a commercial one. The research studies the way each country presents its national landmarks and combines various modes to create a virtual brochure containing a promotional message. The analysis takes a Systemic Functional perspective applying the tools provided by Halliday's theory (1985; 1994; Halliday and Matthiessen 2004), in the case of the linguistic text, and by Kress and van Leeuwen's model (1996; 2006), in the case of the visual message. The analysis can indicate the main linguistic and visual strategies used to present and promote the landmarks and the country. The overall meanings built by the organization of the websites and their webpages, as well as the lexico-grammatical and visual features of the promotional messages are expected to

share some similarities, but also to reveal differences. Their identification has a twofold aim: to relate similarities and differences a) to the source of the message, i.e. institutional vs. commercial, and so to the different types of websites, and b) to the culture of the different countries, i.e. Romanian, vs. Spanish vs. British.

2. The results of the study are also observed from a cultural perspective. As the sets of websites analysed are produced in different countries, they can be considered representatives of those cultures. As marker of cultural variability, the dimension of context is studied (Hall 1976; 2000; Hall and Hall 1990) in order to interpret the previous findings.
3. The study also hopes to throw light on this important area, making explicit the way different messages are encoded in the language and image of online communication in international tourism. Results may be applied to training in domains like promotional messages and their composition; online promotion; tourism discourse and its strategies; or intercultural communication.

## 1.4. Organization of the study

The study is divided in four parts. Part I introduces the work, its motivation, the previous studies in the field and the research questions the study aims to answer.

Following this introductory section, Part II sets the theoretical framework of the research in four chapters. Chapter two addresses the field of tourism and focuses on one type, namely, cultural tourism. It also shows the importance destination branding and the Internet have on tourism, paying special attention to the features websites need to be successful. Chapter three is more specific, and presents the particularities of promotional tourism discourse in relation with two of its most frequent modes: language and image. Chapter four introduces the theoretical framework for the multimodal analysis of the websites collected, i.e. Systemic Functional Theory (Halliday 1985; 1994; Kress and van Leeuwen 1996; 2006; Halliday and Matthiessen 2004). Finally, Chapter five adds a new field to the study, cultural variability. It describes studies on the relation between discourse and culture and argues for the appropriateness of the cultural dimension of context dependency (Hall 1976; 2000; Hall and Hall 1990) for the study of online promotional tourism discourse. The research questions deriving from the studies presented close Part II.

Part III presents the study. The methodology followed in the research is described in Chapter six, including the design of the study, the collection and presentation of the data and the method of analysis of its linguistic and visual components. The following chapters provide the results of the analyses and the comparison between types of promotion and countries. Chapter seven presents and discusses the results of the analyses for the institutional set of websites, while Chapter eight refers to the commercial set. Chapter nine focuses on the results from two perspectives: the type of websites (institutional vs. commercial) and country (Romanian vs. Spanish vs. British), and interprets them from the cultural dimension of context.

Finally, Part IV is dedicated to the conclusion of the research study. Chapter ten summarises the main findings, highlighting their practical implication for the field of online tourism.

The work also contains an Appendix that includes the detailed linguistic analyses of the texts belonging to the selected webpages. For reasons of space, only the most important part of the analyses is included in the Appendix.

# PART II:

# THEORETICAL BACKGROUND

# CHAPTER TWO

# TOURISM

Travel has become an important part of people's lives in the present society. To travel, in order to see new places, meet new people and live new experiences, has turned into a lifestyle for many. Due to this, tourism represents "the largest form of temporary migration in the world" (Timothy and Boyd 2002, 1). It is also claimed to be the largest industry in the world (Timothy and Boyd 2002, 1; Theobald 2005, 6) and the world's biggest or second biggest business (McKercher and du Cros 2002, 26). Taking into consideration its dramatic expansion over the past years, tourism is expected to continue growing as societies become more mobile and more prosperous (OECD 2009, 9).

Tourism can be defined as "the activities of visitors, persons travelling to and staying in places outside their usual environment for up to 12 months for leisure, business, pilgrimage, etc." (Theobald 2005, 17). According to Schouten (2007, 29), "the core of the tourism industry is the commodification of escapism, the commercial answer to the longing of humankind for another reality beyond the dull and grey of the everyday experience". In other words, tourism is "all about selling dreams" (Schouten 2007, 29). The nature of tourism is complex, since tourism is essentially a commercial activity, which involves the consumption of experience and entertainment and which cannot be easily controlled due to its demand-driven character (McKercher and du Cros 2002, 26-28).

This chapter starts by describing the concepts of cultural and heritage tourism. Secondly, it explores destination branding and its importance for tourism promotion. Then, it focuses on tourism on the Internet. Finally, it points out the characteristics of successful websites.

## 2.1. Cultural tourism

There are various forms of tourism, such as beach, sport, adventure, nature, urban or conference tourism, to mention just some of the World Tourism Organization's (WTO) top ten most important and/or dynamic tourist products (OMT 2001, 236). Cultural tourism is also on the list. It can be understood as a trip to other places than the usual residence of people interested in knowing other cultures by contemplating cultural resources, mainly related to history or art (Rodríguez Antón and Alonso Almeida 2009, 153). The International Council of Monuments and Sites, following WTO's directives, goes into further detail and considers it "a movement of persons, essentially for a cultural reason", such as study trips, festivals or other cultural events, visits to places and monuments, and pilgrimage (Santana Talavera 2003, 37). It can, then, be said that cultural tourism is, first of all, a tourism activity in which the cultural assets of a destination are presented and/or offered for tourists' consumption (McKercher and du Cros 2002, 9).

Until fairly recently, cultural tourism was seen as just another niche in the market. This gradually changed; cultural landmarks began to attract more tourists and make the difference between destinations. Nowadays cultural tourism has spread to all corners of the world and is believed to be a mainstream, mass tourism activity (McKercher and du Cros 2002, 135; Richards 2007, 9). This can be due to several reasons, such as more income, a higher level of education, the effects of media and movies, technology and/or globalization (Timothy and Boyd 2002, 10). Extremely popular, cultural tourism is one of the largest and fastest growing global tourism markets (OECD 2009, 10) and a major source of economic development for many countries (McKercher and du Cros 2002, 19). WTO states that almost half of the international tourism is cultural (Rodríguez Antón and Alonso Almeida 2009, 153). More people are looking for a greater variety of activities and unique holiday experiences, associating holiday not only with relaxation, but also with rediscovery and personal development (Morgan and Pritchard 2000, 122-123). With a long tradition, starting with the Grand Tour of the English aristocracy in the 17$^{th}$ and 18$^{th}$ century, culture is a tourist resource that has "a vivid present and a promising future" (Steinecke 2010, 185). The combination of tourism and culture is, thus, extremely successful. The two seem to have a mutually beneficial relationship that can strengthen the attractiveness and competitiveness of destinations, regions and countries in a crowded global marketplace (OECD 2009, 3).

Cultural tourism is considered to encompass both heritage tourism, which is related to artefacts of the past, and arts tourism, which is represented by contemporary cultural production (Richards 2001, 5). The World Tourism Organization defines heritage tourism as "an immersion in the natural history, human heritage, arts, philosophy and institutions of another region or country" (Timothy and Boyd 2002, 1). It "typically relies on living and built elements of culture and refers to the use of the tangible and intangible past as a tourism resource" (Timothy and

Nyaupane 2009, 1). The most important attractions visited by tourists are "traditional" attractions, such as monuments, museums and galleries (Richards 2007, 16). Interest seems to be stirred also by historic cities and monuments, archaeological sites and ancient monuments, cathedrals and churches or castles and palaces (Richards 2007, 17; Timothy and Nyaupane 2009, 10; Steinecke 2010, 185-189). They become even more interesting if they carry the UNESCO label, which is a highly valuable promotional tool (Timothy and Nyaupane 2009, 11). These last heritage assets are World Heritage Sites, i.e. places around the world internationally recognized by UNESCO for their outstanding value as natural and cultural treasures (Harms 2010, 113), and encompass many of the world's most important cultural and natural heritage places. They represent some of "the world's most visited and heavily marketed tourism attractions" (OMT 2009, 5).

## 2.2. Destination branding

The success of a tourism destination depends on a variety of factors. These can range from natural attributes to clever competitive strategies, effective marketing campaigns, creativity and product innovations or dynamic national carriers (Poon 2010, 161). Since all tourism involves the consumption of experiences and products (Urry 1990), cultural heritage assets must be transformed into cultural tourism products. For this, they are usually "manipulated and packaged" to be easily consumed by the public (Eden 1990 in McKercher and du Cros 2002, 28). The information received by tourists prior to the visit, in terms of type, quality and veracity, is said to shape their expectations of the asset and their behaviour while visiting it (McKercher and du Cros 2002, 8). Heritage assets should be both unique, in order to attract and compete on a globalized market, and universal, in order to appeal to different visitors (Nuryanti 1997 in Timothy and Boyd 2002, 11).

These contradictory requirements are mainly due to the globalized market of today's societies. The world is said to have become borderless as a result of many political, economic, technological and informational developments. The global marketplace is common to all people, who, no matter where they come from, tend to "desire the same products and lifestyles" (Levitt 1983 in Morgan 2005, 348). On this market, the tourist attraction is, in terms of exports, simply another product embedded in a network that spreads overseas with the purpose of being sold (Macleod 2004, 6; Sharpley 2006, 16). All countries compete for tourists within the global tourism market, where movement is increasingly easy and accessible. According to Urry (2008, 157), a global public stage has emerged upon which all countries "have to appear, to compete and to mobilise themselves as a spectacle in order to attract large numbers of visitors". In order to differentiate themselves from their competitors, countries or destinations adopt branding. By this, they try to have a prominent place in consumers' minds (McKercher and du Cros 2002, 155).

A brand can be defined as "a name, term, design, symbol, or any other feature that identifies one seller's goods or services as distinct as those of other sellers" (American Marketing Association in Hemelryk Donald and Gammack 2007, 46). It is considered "a compilation of customer expectations, the service culture and the product (experience) delivered to the customer" (Moilanen and Rainisto 2009, 122). Customers are expected to perceive relevant unique added values that match their needs most closely (Hemelryk Donald and Gammack 2007, 51). The ability to sustain these values in the face of competition contributes to the brand's success (Morgan and Pritchard 2000, 280). In the case of tourism, the characteristics of a destination brand can be summarized as follows, according to Buncle's definition (2003 in WTO and ETC 2009, 9). A destination brand represents the sum of people's perceptions about a place, which emotionally influence their attitudes towards that destination. It reflects the enduring essence of the place and the combination of its core characteristics that make it distinctive and memorable. A brand exists in the eyes of the beholder and, due to this, it has to be credible and real as it cannot be manufactured. The branding process, thus, consists of the way in which a destination nurtures, develops and presents its core characteristics to its main public. This establishes, reinforces and sometimes, changes the destination's reputation. The destination brand, however, can only be "an approximation of the 'true' spirit of the place" (Hemelryk Donald and Gammack 2007, 174). Sometimes, it even modifies the destination's image in order to be closer to the consumers' desires (Mariottini 2012, 106).

A destination has to identify its assets, build on them and promote them in a way that differentiates it from other destinations (WTO and ETC 2009, 9). There are various types of assets used in destination branding strategies, but cultural and heritage ones are predominant (McKercher and du Cros 2002, 155). There are many possible heritage assets, as presented in the previous subsection, but not all of them have potential for tourism (McKercher and du Cros 2002, 32; Timothy and Boyd 2002, 31). The tourism potential of an asset and, thus, of a country, frequently depends on the policies and strategies portraying and promoting a favourable brand image. The groups most responsible for these are usually national and local governments, tourist boards, travel agencies, environmental groups, other private companies and/or public-private partnerships (Morgan and Pritchard 2000, 277; Poon 2010, 162). As stated by Anholt (2009, x), "understanding, measuring and even managing the 'nation brand' is one of the primary tasks of responsible governments and businesses". Their ultimate goal is to promote and "sell" the country's image to a vast international public formed by ordinary consumers as well as highly informed tour operators (Anholt 2009, i).

## 2.3. Tourism on the Internet

One of the best ways to create a country brand is by means of tourism promotion on the international market (Piñanes Leal 2004, 91). In order to influence choice and increase consumption, different promotional instruments can be used as marketing strategies, such as guidebooks, travel literature, advertisements or websites (Antelmi and Santulli 2012, 14). These usually create and enhance a positive image, emphasizing special features, in order to stir the consumers' curiosity (Giacomarra 2005 in Antelmi and Santulli 2012, 14).

Destination branding, marketing and the entire tourism industry have, in recent years, been influenced by technological advancements. The impact of technology, mainly the Internet, has been "dramatic and far-reaching", fundamentally revolutionising the distribution of information and changing the manner in which tourism is promoted and purchased (Morgan and Pritchard 2000, 314; OMT 2001, 11; Sharpley 2006, 157; Mocini 2009, 28). Destinations are now marketed commercially to a global audience, to whom the Internet presents a window to the world. If they do not appear on the Internet, they risk remaining "off-the-pace" (WTO and ETC 2009, 29). The Internet is not a trend, but a recognized new channel of promotion, commercialization and distribution (Montiel Torres 2002, 542). It has become an almost universal marketing tool (OECD 2009, 11) and a global communication network (Steinmetz 2004, 245; Danet and Herring 2008, 553), obviously for the part of the world connected to it (Majó and Galí 2002, 400). Its scope is global and its services, like the World Wide Web, are easily accessible from all over the world (Janoschka 2004, 1). Highly used (OMT 1999, 25) and spectacularly growing (OMT 2001, 20), the Internet has also brought about new dimensions of communication. It has created a sort of globally open universal platform to communicate and present information (OMT 2001, 11). The user can search all over the world the product needed for her/his particular necessity (OMT 1999, 154).

In the tourism industry, the Internet is said to have become the major agency in the world, as it is the most frequently used tool for tourism promotion (Calvi 2006, 50; Perandrea 2011, 28, 30). There is an increasing use of the Internet to obtain information, planning, booking and buying tourism products and services (OMT 2001, 20; Montiel Torres 2002, 539; Plog 2005, 280; Mena 2008, 209; Mocini 2009, 291). According to Pyka and Freitag (2010, 8), more than half of all European travellers use the Internet as information source for their trips. Its use for online booking seems even more frequent. The travel and tourism sector has become the type of product that sells the most on the Internet (OMT 2001, 17). Those who use the Internet to organize their trip outnumber those who do not and their numbers are expected to keep growing (PEW/Internet 2004 in Janoschka 2004, 45; Pyka and Freitag 2010, 8). Even in the case of cultural tourists, the Internet is one of the main sources of information, close after personal recommendations from friends and family. Guidebooks have not been affected by the Internet as they remain the most important source of published information, whereas tour operators' brochures and tourist board information are little used (Richards 2003, 150; 2007, 17-18). The online tourism sector continues to grow, regardless of the world crisis (Marcussen 2006; Perandrea 2011, 10). The World Tourism Organization describes the ideal relation between tourism and the Internet perfectly (OMT 2001, 11), briefly presented in the following lines. The user wants to travel to an unknown destination and starts planning her/his trip. S/he is faced with the problem of buying a product without first seeing it. The Internet comes with the solution by providing immediate access to necessary information on destinations all over the world, information more varied and detailed than the one previously available. Apart from that, it gives the user the possibility to reserve in a quick and simple way.

Various characteristics lead to its success in the tourism sector. Mainly, the Internet offers a global market available for every country and every business, no matter its size, 24 hours 7 days a week with few administrative costs (OMT 1999, 52; Timothy 2002, 161; Lipman 2008, 22; Rodríguez Antón and Alonso Almeida 2009, 63; Perandrea 2011, 6). It presents many opportunities for tourism enterprises, intermediaries, and destination managers to expand markets and improve efficiencies in product delivery and communications management (Frew 2000 in Dwyer 2005, 538). The Internet is cheaper than real distribution and marketing and promises continuous growth, both in size and importance (OMT 1999, 31). The tourist information can be composed as an always available electronic brochure, which can be continuously updated and even adapted to the different types of users for greater efficiency (Majó and Galí 2002, 399; Steinmetz 2004, 244). The effectiveness of online-distributed information can be measured by all kinds of tools (Steinmetz 2004, 244). The Internet also offers the possibility to visualize a priori the tourist attraction (OMT 2001, 254). Apart from these, the simplicity and variety of online offers, the possibility to see other people's opinions or the competitive prices also contribute to the Internet's success (Perandrea 2011, 10). Due to its interactive nature, the Internet combines features of mass communication and interpersonal communication; the message addresses a mass audience and, at the same time, allows a reciprocal exchange between sender and receiver via email or newsgroups (Pierini 2007, 85). To sum up, the Internet is very much used, as it is more practical, considering both function and content. It is easier to use and its access costs are less expensive, while its speed is higher (OMT 2001, 11; Pierini 2007, 85). The advantages of using the Internet for tourism promotion are global access in time and space, high number of users, reduced costs, aesthetic resources, more adapted messages and products, updated electronic brochures, flexible and dynamic information, better services, interactivity and interpersonal communication (Montiel Torres 2002, 539-542).

The Internet has influenced not only the distribution of information or the processes of marketing and purchase, but also tourists' expectations and behaviours. Nowadays, access to information on trips and tourism is taken for granted. The users planning a trip investigate the destination online. As information is available anywhere at any time or place, they are increasingly mobile (Lipman 2008, 22). They have become knowledgeable and, thus, demanding, as they are computer literate and want both quality and value (Lipman 2008, 20; Rodríguez Antón and Alonso Almeida 2009, 148). Users are more independent than ever because they do not necessarily need advice or intermediaries; they just surf and select (OMT 1999, 54, 80; Lipman 2008, 20). It seems users like to organize their trips by themselves, considering it entertaining and practical (OMT 1999, 81). The organization of the trip and all that this implies is, then, part of the tourist experience.

In order to keep up with the technological progress of information and all the related changes, many of them mentioned above, the public and private tourism sectors have adapted. They have rapidly understood the potential to promote and sell products online. They have accepted the Internet as a new medium of distribution to get to tourists all over the world (OMT 1999, 34, 58). There is an adaptation movement from government departments to public and private agencies in order to deliver the message (Lipman 2008, 21). As the market is globally open, every company, regardless of its size and location, can compete and sell in the entire world (OMT 1999, 154-155; Timothy 2002, 161; Steinmetz 2004, 244; Rodríguez Antón and Alonso Almeida 2009, 63). The Internet offers to promotional entities the possibility to provide information and booking services to a high number of users at a relatively low price and, at the same time, save a lot of money in the production and distribution of leaflets and other traditional activities, like information desks (OMT 2001, 11).

### 2.3.1. Websites

The public and private tourism sectors are represented online by websites, mainly those belonging to institutions, companies and tour operators. From a technical perspective, a website is "a group of webpages or hypertext mark-up language (HTML) documents housed within the same WWW domain" (Djonov 2005, 112). The proliferation of websites started in the early 1990s (Thorlacius 2007, 65). Nowadays, almost every tourist board and/or travel company has a website, as it is considered that no business could survive without one (Rheem 2010, 299). On the World Wide Web, there are thousands of websites dedicated to destinations. Some of them are exploited commercially, while others are just present online, being developed by different types of governmental institutions and tourist boards responsible with destinations' management (OMT 1999, 30; 2001, 84). Sometimes, institutions collaborate with the private sector and their websites contain links to private travel agencies in order to help tourists and provide them with the necessary information (OMT 2005a, 33).

The cultural tourism sector makes no exception and is present on the Internet with specific websites. There is even a growing number of Internet sites which offer tourists the possibility to package cultural sites and events with accommodation and travel (OECD 2009, 55). Their main aim is twofold: attract clients from all over the world (OMT 1999, 51) and, simultaneously, contribute, together with advertisements, to the creation of a destination brand (Antelmi and Santuli 2012, 14). The websites related to tourism vary depending on their function. Perandrea (2011, 30) proposes three types: those related to the organization of tourism, intended for the booking and buying of tickets and services–which contain descriptions of the services offered, prices and instructions for booking; those of direct advertising like advertisements or catalogues; and those webpages containing information of interest for tourism–which describe places and infrastructures, contain maps and blogs or offer tourists the possibility to exchange opinions. Put simply, websites can be informational (providing information about any aspect of tourism), promotional (belonging to tourist boards and promoting a destination area) and commercial (belonging to intermediaries and service providers) (Pierini 2007, 85). However, it is difficult to have a clear-cut classification of websites, as they are very diverse and rapidly changing (Calvi 2006, 52).

Tourism websites should have certain characteristics in order to be successful. They should provide an image and atmosphere coherent with the identity of the destination and its brand (OMT 1999, 133; Miller 2011, 89). The design, presentation, images, texts, functionality and other characteristics should serve the purpose of the website and its owner (OMT 1999, 139; 2005b, 23; Miller 2011, 89) and gain the users' confidence as trustworthy (OMT 2005b, 13; Miller 2011, 228). They should be entertaining and informative, encouraging users to repeat (Morgan and Pritchard 2000, 324). They should come in various languages even if English is the dominant language on the Internet (Danet and Herring 2008, 554). The design of a website should be animated and attractive in order to maintain users' interest and be remembered (OMT 1999, 131, 139; 2001, 94; Morgan and Pritchard 2000, 324). Webpages, considered the basic building blocks of websites (Nielsen 2000), play a crucial role in the presentation of any websites' content organisation and navigational options (Djonov 2005, 112). The home page, the first thing users see, should be attractive, should establish the websites' identity and mission and clearly communicate the site's content, structure and navigational options, providing a positive image of the destination (OMT 2001, 113; Djonov 2005, 113; Miller 2011, 229). The message and content should be simple, clear and adequate for the targeted users and their necessities (OMT 2001, 94; 2005b, 13; Majó and Galí 2002, 400; Miller 2011, 79). The appearance of each webpage is important, as it is experienced visually by users. For this reason, information should not be confusing or disorganized, but rather transmitted in innovative and interesting ways (OMT 1999, 133; 2001, 113). The content presented should be true, updated, precise, relevant, detailed and interesting (OMT 1999, 131, 139, 140; 2001, 94; Morgan and Pritchard 2000, 324).

Turning to the navigation of websites, this should be intuitive, in the service of content, offering easy and quick ways to get to important sections (OMT 2001, 94; 2005b, 9; Majó and Galí 2002, 400; Miller 2011, 85). Users can become frustrated and leave the page, if they have to click through several pages to reach relevant information (Morgan and Pritchard

2000, 324; Crystal 2004, 47). This can be avoided by including a link to the home page, a list with the main content on each page, a map or index of the page, submenus or search tools (OMT 2001, 115-117). Multimedia features should be used moderately as their purpose is not to get in the way of presenting the message or lower the functionality of the site, but to add value (OMT 1999, 131, 139; 2001, 94; Miller 2011, 79). Websites should also be interactive and include search bases, trip planners, virtual leaflets and tours, transactions services, spaces for forums and messages and/or customers services (OMT 1999, 131; 2001, 114, 115; 2005b, 14, 24, 25; Morgan and Pritchard 2000, 324). Finally, they should be easy to find on the Internet by means of search tools and services (OMT 1999, 131; 2001, 94; 2005b, 18).

In other words, it seems that websites should behave as any other product on the market, i.e. inform, attract and induce purchase (Morgan and Pritchard 2000, 326). Despite the fact that the tourist product is different from other products, as it has a heterogeneous, intangible and temporal character and needs to be presented by various types of information (OMT 2001, 237-238; Yui Ling Ip 2008, 4), websites should follow the AIDA concept, used in products marketing (OMT 2005b, 8). The initials stand for: Attention, Interest, Desire and Action, all of which are made possible by the characteristics presented above. These features can belong to any website, including those dedicated to cultural tourism. In particular, these should contain general information on the tourist asset, its history and related stories, guided tour data and/or information about different events, accommodation and the destination place in general (OMT 2001, 254).

To conclude this chapter, cultural tourism destinations need a brand or a place in the possible tourists' minds. They are successful if they can satisfy users' thirst for information and persuade them that the place promoted, its heritage assets and everything related to it are worth the time and money they could spend on visiting it (OMT 1999, 25). Information and persuasion take place on the Internet, which is said to have become the major agency in the world, having the functions of informing, advising, promoting and selling products (Perandrea 2011, 30). The creation of Internet platforms to provide information on cultural attractions and events is therefore extremely important, particularly to reach international markets (OECD 2009, 55). Websites have become a necessary condition for the promotion of tourist products. However, it seems that a website is not enough if it does not reflect the quality of the offered product, i.e. attractive, reliable, true and updated (Montiel Torres

2002, 540-542). The design of a website, whose pages are considered electronic brochures or advertisements (Montiel Torres 2002, 541), is not just a matter of graphic images or computer techniques (Majó and Galí 2002, 408). In order to be successful, it needs a combination of strategies related to areas such as communication, public orientation or marketing, to mention just a few.

In this study, the analysis of websites related to cultural tourism will examine these different strategies. The research focuses on cultural tourism. It analyses the websites related to several UNESCO World Heritage Sites, in particular religious, historical and urban assets from three different countries: Romania, Spain and Great Britain. The websites are both institutional and commercial.

# CHAPTER THREE

# PROMOTIONAL TOURISM DISCOURSE

Promotion is an important part of branding and marketing. It is used to draw attention to something or to inform somebody of something, usually by exaggerating facts or appealing to emotions (Dyer 1982, 3). In the tourism sector, promotion is even more vital than in other industries, as the product is a service, characterised as "intangible, inseparable, variable and perishable" (Morgan and Pritchard 2000, 10). On the one hand, following Calvi (2006, 22), there is the promotional activity carried out by institutions (national and/or regional agencies, local entities) with the aim of configuring the tourist image of a place, pointing out its attractiveness for different types of tourists and their necessities. Even if these messages do not appear to be advertisements, their promotional aim is very strong (Bhatia 2004, 73). On the other hand, there is the commercial advertising carried out by travel agencies and/or other service producers and destined to the direct sale of tourist products and services (Calvi 2006, 22). For the potential tourist, "promotion *is*[1] the product"; s/he decides to go on a holiday "purely on the basis of symbolic expectations established promotionally through words, pictures, sounds and so forth" (Morgan and Pritchard 2000, 10). This is closely related to the fact that tourism promotion is, ultimately, about "selling dreams and aspirations" (Morgan and Pritchard 2000, 46).

The organizations involved in the tourism business usually have mixed goals: to inform, persuade and/or induce action, the degree of each depending from case to case (Morgan and Pritchard 2000, 7; Bhatia 2004, 62; Bloor and Bloor 2007, 141). These are in line with the AIDA principle, briefly mentioned in the previous chapter: attract Attention, create Interest, foster Desire and inspire Action (Holloway 2004, 265). It seems, therefore, that the skill in tourism marketing "lies in creating the perceived value of the product, in packaging it and in promoting the

[1] The authors' italics.

experience in a way which gives an organization a competitive edge" (Morgan and Pritchard 2000, 10).

The relation between tourism and its discourse is strong and inseparable. Tourism discourse has become an important tool for presenting and promoting destinations (Mocini 2009, 2). It informs, describes, promotes, advertises, persuades and manipulates (Crişan 2013, 943). Like any other promotional discourse, tourism uses multiple semiotic resources in meaning-making (Hiippala 2007, 2). It usually exploits to the maximum the linguistic code and its interaction with other modes, especially the visual one (Londero 2006, 249; Bloor and Bloor 2007, 114; Cook 2008, 113). Tourism discourse includes, thus, the particular ways of using language and image to communicate information (Thurlow and Jaworski 2010). The choice of a holiday depends, many times, on how well the destination was promoted or on how persuasive the message was. This means it is important to create unique destinations and magical settings, or "heavenly destinations images" (Crişan 2013, 943), by referring to history, culture and beautiful scenery (Morgan and Pritchard 2000, 279).

This chapter focuses on the particularities of promotional tourism discourse. First, it describes the ways tourist products and/or services are promoted online. Then, it focuses on the two most frequent modes of tourism promotion: language and image.

## 3.1. Online tourism promotion

Online promotion, like any act of online communication, can be considered a type of computer-mediated communication. As such, it is an asynchronous form of communication, having the characteristics of monologue-oriented mass communication, as the message is accomplished in the relation one-to-many (Janoschka 2004, 2). It is modelled by the characteristics of the medium of its creation and distribution, which is electronic, global, and interactive (Crystal 2004, 18, 24). Various other factors, like social and cultural ones, can influence online communication, either carried over from other media or internally generated in computer-mediated environments (Herring 2003, 625).

From a generic perspective, webpages[2] can be considered specific cases of "emergent digital genres" (Posteguillo and Pique in Calvi 2011,

[2] The terms "website" and "webpage" are sometimes used as synonyms in the literature consulted. From a compositional and technical point of view, websites are composed by various webpages, as indicated in Chapter two. This lack of difference does not, however, affect the claims made here.

21), having institutional variants, created by public entities, and commercial ones, owned by companies. They can also be interpreted as macrogenres due to the multiple contents they can include. As tourist genres, the characteristics of webpages can be summarised as follows: their format or diffusion medium is the Internet; their functions are to inform, advise, persuade, promote an image and/or sell a product, they are usually consulted before and after the trip; and their textual typologies are varied–descriptive, expositive, narrative, instructive, argumentative, and/or conversational (Calvi 2006, 55). Their structure usually goes from the most general to the most specific, i.e. from general information about a place or asset to the description of its most important element(s) and, then, to the description of something even more specific (Toledo Pereira 2006, 177 following Ramm 2000). Several pieces of information are considered necessary in the composition of a promotional tourism message: the name of the tourist attraction; its background and description details; and/or its services and contact data (Mongkholjuck 2008).

Websites, apart from carrying advertisements in different sections of their pages, are used as advertising or promotion instruments themselves (Singh and Dalal 1999, 50; Janoschka 2004, 2). This is obvious in the case of travel agencies' or tour operators' websites, which have also the buying option. The same can, however, be said about websites belonging to institutional or national tourist boards. By presenting a destination, they actually promote it, even if there is no booking or purchasing offer. Non-profit making as they are, institutions can use persuasive techniques of commercial advertising (Dyer 1982, 5). Similarly to tourist brochures, websites may be considered to have a dual function (Hiippala 2007, 10). On one hand, they provide the tourists with information about the destination and its surroundings, possible activities and so on (Valdeón 2009, 23; Hiippala 2013, 6). On the other hand, they are a form of marketing and advertising, encouraging people from everywhere in the world to come and visit that particular destination (Hiippala 2013, 6). Following Delin (2000, 123), the aim of advertising may not just be to persuade someone to purchase a particular product or service; it may be a complex or longer-term aim that does not include purchasing at all, but rather the improvement or transformation of a brand's image. This brand can refer to a destination or a country. The tourist website can be more promotional and, thus, more successful, if it is constructed following the AIDA marketing model, mentioned previously. The World Tourism Organisation (OMT 2005b, 8) applies the model to websites and provides several pieces of advice. In order to get the users' Attention, the home page is expected to present a general vision of the website; to provide logos, attractive photos and special offers; to emphasize the unique characteristic(s) of the regions; and to indicate ways to communicate with the organization. The users' Interest is stirred by attractive descriptions, photos and sound and by complete practical information on boarding and trips within the region, including maps and itineraries. Desire can be stimulated by means of attractive descriptions of what one can do and see and some information on accommodation. Finally, Action can be induced by indicating possibilities for interaction and booking.

Attracting the users' interest and calling them to action can be accomplished by different modes and methods. The webpage as a text is considered a multisemiotic entity resulting from the interplay of various resources, such as language, usually written and sometimes spoken; pictorial, mainly images and/or icons; graphic, particularly layout and typographic features; and acoustic elements like sounds and music (Pierini 2007, 88). Apart from these, webpages contain accompanying texts presented by means of hypertexts (Rodríguez Abella 2011, 158). Hypertext links, the most fundamental structural and specific property of the Web, represent the jumps that users can make if they want to move from one page or site to another (Crystal 2004, 202; Bolaños Medina *et al.* 2005, 137). The cross references via links can expand to webpages existing on the site, to other websites or, even, to software applications (Djonov 2005, 5). Websites, thus, generate meaning multimodally, by the totality of verbal and non-verbal signs, in order to enhance the effectiveness of their messages (Crystal 2004, 9; Danesi 2004, 259; Janoschka 2004, 123; Pierini 2007, 88; Rodríguez Abella 2011, 158). Their evolution is inevitably linked to that of technology, leading to changes like macroscopic organization of the page, multimodal interaction or hypertextual suggestions. The sum of these factors responds to the new demands of rapid and immediate satisfaction, which require access facility and favour fragmentation (Santulli 2011, 99). The alternative instruments provided by technology, together with various interactive and multimodal possibilities, design different techniques of commercialization, which, in their turn, can create "the distinctive and attractive image that seems to be so important for a country in order to position itself positively in the consumers' mind and to differentiate itself from others" (Mariottini 2012, 106).

As the tourist product and/or service cannot be inspected before, the design of websites and their content have great influence on tourists' final decision. They are meant to inform, orientate potential tourists, and, ultimately, persuade people into visiting the destination or buying the product promoted (Mongkholjuck 2008, 30; Yui Ling Ip 2008, 12). It has to be taken into account that the tourist product combines material elements, like landscape, art works and tourist systems, with ideal aspects linked to tourists' expectations, their conception of the trip and the entertainment's social valorisation (Calvi 2006, 18). It is considered that tourism discourse "directs expectations, influences perceptions and thereby provides a preconceived landscape for the tourist to 'discover'", "the directed landscape" becoming the real one (Weightman 1987, 230). In order to be successful marketing tools, websites rely on highly selective language, images and/or other resources, which present only the positive and attractive sides of the potential tourist experience (Yui Ling Ip 2008, 12) and appraise the destination (Hiippala 2007, 2; Mocini 2009, 154). The power of language and image is used to shape tourists' opinion and way of looking (Calvi 2006, 19), contributing to the persuasive nature of promotional materials (Yui Ling Ip 2008, 4). The discourse of tourism has a "complex physiognomy, reflecting the heterogeneity that characterizes this professional sector and the variety of the components that intervene in the description of the tourist product" (Calvi and Mapelli 2010).

## 3.2. Language and tourism promotion

The aim of promotional tourism websites is informative-persuasive (Gotti 2008, 32; Mongkholjuck 2008, 19; Mocini 2009, 2; Calvi and Mapelli 2010). They can be placed alongside a continuum ranging from informational to commercial (Hiippala 2007, 10), oscillating between information transmission and persuasion (Calvi 2006, 25). Mainly, these websites inform tourists about places to visit, services to use or events to attend, and persuade them to visit the place. The multimodal presentation of the tourist message is an excellent strategy for this, since it is based on various forms of representation of verbal and visual dimensions (Mariottini 2012, 110).

The verbal dimension of the promotional message is very important, as tourism needs a language to construct reality in positive terms and convert a place in a tourist destination (Calvi and Mapelli 2010). In order to attract tourists, a destination has to demonstrate how it is different from other destinations, providing the reasons that make it worth been visited (WTO and ETC 2009, 10). As such, the linguistic message should highlight the destination's best assets and identify them in "a highly competitive global marketplace, in which people's awareness of different destinations is limited, their attention span short and the competitive 'noise' very loud" (WTO and ETC 2009, 11). Apart from this, it should manipulate, adjust and present the tourist product in a way that can be easily consumed by the tourist (McKercher and du Cros 2002, 27). It seems that "most tourists want to have their experience controlled and are amenable to have the asset presented in a way that facilitates easy consumption" (McKercher and du Cros 2002, 36). This may be due to the fact that most tourists may visit an asset only once in their lifetime and consequently wish to get the most out of the experience, without losing time with unessential elements (McKercher and du Cros 2002, 36-37). Another reason can be the limited level of knowledge of most people visiting the destination (McKercher and du Cros 2002, 38; OECD 2009, 52). Tourists are eager and curious, but at the same time, they are not experts in the history of art and culture. They just want to see something impressive, gain new impressions and be informed in an entertaining manner (Steinecke 2010, 191). They are mainly driven by a combination of atmosphere, local culture and history (Richards 2003, 147; 2007, 16). There is no guarantee that the message is received in the desired manner since tourists' ability to comprehend cultural assets varies (McKercher and du Cros 2002, 157).

According to McKercher and du Cros (2002, 122-127), there are various interrelated ways to transform cultural heritage assets into cultural tourism products. This means the asset should tell a story, as it has little meaning on its own, since the world is full of beautiful places and old buildings. Stories should inspire people's imagination and not be a mere description of the destination (WTO and ETC 2009). The message should thus be creative, as tourists want to discover not only dates and names, but also human dramas. It should also be exciting because entertainment is an important part of most experiences. The tourist experience should be participatory, since participation enhances the experience for the visitor. The transformation of an asset into an attraction can be carried out by different tactics, such as mythologizing the asset, building a story around it, emphasizing its otherness, showing a direct link from past to present and/or making it triumphant, spectacular, fantastic, fun, light and/or entertaining (McKercher and du Cros 2002, 127-134). Obviously, the tactic(s) chosen depend(s) on a combination of factors related to physical and emotional characteristics of the asset, the management goal, the desired experience to be provided or the existing knowledge (McKercher and du Cros 2002, 134).

Three main functions of the tourist message can be pointed out: to inform, persuade and direct (Calvi and Bonomi 2008, 183; Calvi 2011, 35). These functions are present, up to a certain degree, in all tourist texts, influencing the discursive strategies and the used linguistics structures (Calvi 2011, 36). In the tourism field, there is a high demand of information (Calvi and Bonomi 2008, 183) to satisfy the practical and cognitive necessities (Calvi 2011, 35). Information can be practical, as it is necessary in trip decision-making and planning, and can refer to infrastructure, schedules, maps or weather (OMT 2001, 238; Calvi 2006, 33; Molina and Esteban 2006, 1050; Calvi and Bonomi 2008, 183). It can also be related to cultural, historical and artistic aspects, such as description of the most important monuments and views of the location that set up the attractiveness of a tourist destination and motivate people to visit it (Saorín 2001, 336; Molina and Esteban 2006, 1051-1052; Calvi and Bonomi 2008, 183). The informative sequences are descriptive and expositive, usually objective and impersonal (Bosch Abarca 2001, 329; Santulli 2010, 27; Calvi 2011, 35, 37). Narration of facts is sometimes used to present the history of a destination (Santulli 2010, 27; Hiippala 2013, 91). These sequences should allow the potential tourist to "know a priori" the place or asset promoted (Montiel Torres 2002, 544). Apart from informing, they direct the gaze of the tourist, shaping it by pre-established itineraries and aesthetic judgments presented in an assertive manner (Calvi 2006, 35; Mapelli and Piccioni 2011, 64; Pérez Vázquez 2011, 307). The message tends to be as suggestive as possible since the tourist product is intangible (Bosch Abarca 2001, 328).

The communication of tourist information is more or less persuasive. The tourist product should be presented and described as attractive (Montiel Torres 2002, 544; Mocini 2009, 100), as the core of tourism is to "mystify the mundane, to amplify the exotic, minimize the misery, rationalize the disquietude, and romanticize the strange" (Mason 1994 in Schouten 2007, 30). According to Rooijakkers (2002), there is a need for "social fiction", for "mythomania" around traditions, rituals, and customs, in other words, for the cult of heritage. This is usually done by cognitive and emotional manipulation, whose purpose is to cause "doing" (Mocini 2005, 160; 2009, 26). Tourists expect illustrated, lively and emotionally touching presentations, rather than dry data, numbers and facts (Steinecke 2010, 192). Undoubtedly, one way to motivate them is the evocation of sensations (Pérez Vázquez 2011, 308). They are not interested in getting a complete and systematic overview, but rather look for "the extraordinary, the typical or the superlative" (Steinecke 2010, 192). As such, sightseeing should include all senses, not just the intellect, facilitating sensual and emotional experiences (Steinecke 2010, 192, 194; Pérez Vázquez 2011, 297). In order to manipulate, address the senses and, ultimately, persuade, the language is often argumentative (Reiss 1983 in Bugnot 2006, 22; Hiippala 2013, 7), containing evaluative resources and other expressions full of connotative values (Bosch Abarca 2001, 329; Calvi 2006, 19; Mocini 2009, 26; Calvi 2011, 35).

Apart from informing and trying to persuade, the tourist message directs and guides the tourists' steps. It contains directives to follow during the trip, with the purpose of orienting tourists' gaze and behaviour (Calvi 2006, 35; Molina and Esteban 2006, 1050; Calvi and Bonomi 2008, 183). They can be presented as recommendations or suggestions, leaving more freedom to the audience. For this, any direct address is avoided; impersonal forms, recommendation verbs or conditional constructions being preferred instead (Calvi 2011, 35). Directives can also appear as instructions and present sequences of actions (Calvi 2011, 35). Explicit or implicit, the instructional sequences appeal to the reader by modal or opinion markers in order to mitigate the propositions and other rhetorical resources (Bosch Abarca 2001, 329). For tourists, they are a way of touching, listening, tasting, and, above all, of direct seeing (Mocini 2009, 27).

In the tourism industry, language plays, thus, an important part in the transmission of knowledge and information required by tourists, in the promotion of places, in the creation or re-creation of tourist identities and, also, in inducing certain behaviours (Calvi and Mapelli 2011, 1). The message develops on various levels, such as cognitive (make know), sensorial (make see) and advisory (make do), establishing an asymmetrical communication with an evident didactic component (Moirand 2004, 152 in Santulli 2010, 27). Usually constructed in assertive language, it represents facts logically (Mariottini 2012, 110). Apart from the characteristics presented so far, the linguistic message can contain features of specialized discourse, like compound nouns and semi-technical vocabulary consisting of verbs which serve to situate or describe a site or words from fields such as history, gastronomy, entertainment or online communication (Saorín 2001, 337; Calvi 2006, 17; Pierini 2007, 89); brevity, density and nominal style (Gotti 1991; Londero 2006, 249); present tense and personalization (Pierini 2007, 89) or place and time adverbs, past tense, material and relational processes (O'Toole 1994, 231). The message has also many features of advertising, such as heavy use of specific adjectives to stress the high quality of the proposed destination (Saorín 2001, 337); superlative language and words to refer to idyllic places (Saorín 2001, 337; Calvi 2006, 17; Pierini 2007, 89) or cultural connotations (Gotti 1991). Frequent strategies are: tourist implication and inclusion, giving the client the impression of finding him/herself directly in the destination (Calvi 2006, 2, 44); direct appellation (Pierini 2007, 89; Calvi 2009, 210); content organized on obligatory moves, such as general description including main characteristics of the place(s) to visit and descriptions of attractions, and optional moves like how to get there or further information (Saorín 2001, 337). Being transmitted online, the language can also have features typical of online communication like virtual orality (use of questions, imperatives and deixis) or light style (tendency to use short, simple sentences) (Pierini 2007, 89). The discourse moves between an objective style, typical of technical discourse and characterized by nominalizations and specialized terms, and a dynamic and modalized register, with a strong implication of the interlocutor (O'Toole 1994, 231; Calvi 2011, 40). Online promotional tourism discourse seems, therefore, to be quite hybrid and combine different features coming from promotional, specialized or online communication fields.

## 3.3. Image and tourism promotion

As mentioned before, websites combine mainly verbal and visual codes in the composition of their messages. This simultaneous use of the two codes ensures a better message, as the possibilities of both systems are exploited. Thus, "the significant use of space and colour, peculiar to visual language, can be combined with the abstraction typical of verbal language (Rodríguez Abella 2011, 172). Even if images are sometimes considered secondary to language, the relationship between image and text is never one of illustration, clarification or supplement used to make the text look prettier or more informative (Myers 1994, 136). Instead, images have a clear argumentative dimension, playing an ever-increasing role (van Leeuwen 2005, 16), sometimes placing the text in second place (Viallon 2004 in Calvi 2011, 31). A growing tendency to replace language with visual symbols has been observed lately (Thorlacius 2007, 66), especially in the virtual space of computer screens (Bolaños Medina *et al.* 2005, 128). Visual icons are useful and simple means of anchoring texts and catching or directing users' attention to specific areas of importance (Thorlacius 2007, 68). They can also be associated to different products, services and/or destinations, contributing to the creating of a "*visual*[3] brand" (Hiippala 2007, 25).

Tourism promotion makes extensive use of images to portray products and/or services. Regardless of the language's informative or persuasive function, the image of a destination in the tourists' minds is created and influenced particularly through visual modes of communication (Molina and Esteban 2006). Images play an important role in convincing people to visit a place; by "acting as stimuli to the readers' minds", these help "build

[3] The authors' italics.

new schemata and reinforce the relevant existing schemata" (Yui Ling Ip 2008, 8). Images can also "give shape and meaning to the anticipation, experience and memories of travelling" (Rojek and Urry 1997, 179). Language alone may not be sufficient for all this, since the space reserved for text is often limited. A picture, instead, may be worth a thousand words, as it possesses better representational qualities than language (Hiippala 2007, 22). Images have a dual function: referential (typical of any message) and expressive (meant to make an impression on the viewer) (Rodríguez Abella 2011, 172). They can persuade, instruct or warn (van Leeuwen 2005, 120), to mention just some of the many possible purposes pictures can have. Seeing may be more suggestive than description and narration. The visual dimension communicates, in an empirical and emotional manner (Mariottini 2012, 110), highly selective and positive aspects (Yui Ling Ip 2008, 8). It seems then that promoting and, ultimately, selling a destination is immersed in the language of visuals (Scarles 2004, 45).

The preference for images may be due to the fact that people believe more what is illustrated, especially if it is a photograph (Myers 1994, 136). The truth or authenticity potential of photography is related to the idea that seeing is believing (Kuhn in Lister and Wells 2001, 89). Photographs are considered as having a simple and obvious meaning, since they depict reality (Myers 1994, 136; Rose 2001, 87). They seem formed by nature and not by the hand of the photographer (van Leeuwen 2005, 171). According to Rose (2001, 87), "unlike any other visual technology, there is a sense in which the camera is an instrument that records what was in front of its lens when the shutter snapped". This can imply that they are a source of objective and disinterested fact (Lister and Wells 2001, 89) and do not lie (Myers 1994, 136). But, in fact, they can, as they "can be framed and altered and cropped, and can subsequently be manipulated in all sorts of ways and put to all sorts of uses" (Rose 2001, 87), depending on their purposes and interests (Lister and Wells 2001, 65). Webpages select, shape and structure elements of the physical environment in order to reflect mental images, belonging to photographers, their clients or tourists (Rojek and Urry 1997, 189). Pictures are never transparent windows to the world; they rather interpret the world and display it in very particular ways (Rose 2001, 5). In the case of digital images, even if they look like photographs, "the people, places and things they show may never have existed before the lens of the camera" (van Leeuwen 2005, 171). Manipulation, to use a term enclosing the strategies mentioned above, can be performed in pictures by means of modality and salience (Hiippala 2007, 24). Various interplays of dimensions, like colour saturation or depth, can present images as more lifelike or more abstract and their elements as more or less important (Hiippala 2007, 24). Just using photo-editing software, various actions can be operated, such as amplifying the beauty and desirability of the scenery, leaving out unfavourable conditions, adjusting brightness or contrasting colour (Yui Ling Ip 2008, 8-9). Also the presence and depiction of humans can be manipulative. In many photos encountered in tourism promotion, humans are totally absent or are used as icons of otherness. However, there has been an increasing focus on human representation lately (Calvi 2011, 31), probably for the sake of identification.

It seems, thus, that images, of whatever kind, are not natural or neutral (Rose 2001, 5; Anthonissen 2003, 301; Hiippala 2007, 22), but completely coded cultural artefacts (Lister and Wells 2001, 89). They are ideological and socially constructed, like any other mode of discourse (Rojek and Urry 1997, 189; Anthonissen 2003, 301). Lifelikeness or reality depends "on the context of situation and culture, the producers of the image and the intended audience" (Hiippala 2013, 38). Pictures usually reflect the photographers' and/or producers' cultural values and attitudes (Rojek and Urry 1997, 190). Following Kress and van Leeuwen (1996, 45), it can be said that pictorial structures do not simply reproduce the structures of reality; they rather produce images of reality which are bound up with the interests of the social institutions within which the pictures are produced, circulated and read. They reproduce and enhance society's preferred images, while appearing to present entirely accurate representations (Rojek and Urry 1997, 183). Pictures provide a "privileged representation" of a landscape or an asset, to which tourists are implicitly invited to adapt (Santulli 2010, 29). Viewers are then involved in the construction of a range of messages (Myers 1994, 136), bringing previous knowledge or competencies into play (Lister and Wells 2003, 63). Together with the photographer or producer, they engage in "a mutually reinforcing social process of constructing and altering images of places and experiences" (Rojek and Urry 1997, 189).

To sum up, tourism promotion takes place nowadays mainly online. Promotional tourism websites actually construct the image of a country (Garzone 2009, 32). Following Garzone (2009, 32), it can be said that they provide basic information about a country, offering users elements to decide whether they are interested or not. They also give users an idea of the attractions to visit and things to do in the destination. At the same time, due to their multimedia and multimodal properties, they guide the users' gaze and actions through the destination's nature, history, culture, leisure practices, sites and sights (Garzone 2009, 32). Practically, websites intend to "make see", by means of description and images, "make know", by narration and practical information, and "make do", by means of advice (Santulli 2011, 98). The persuasive force that drives tourists towards destinations and cultural assets is achieved through a set of discursive and linguistic strategies. Both the verbal and visual modes play their part in the communication of the message, complementing each other in the manipulation of the user. Verbal descriptions and their displays of photographs represent that very special form of communication typical of the tourism industry (Mocini 2005, 160). As perfectly summarized by Dann (1996, 2), "via static and moving picture, written texts and audiovisual offerings, the language of tourism attempts to persuade, lure, woo and seduce millions of human beings, and, in so doing, convert them from potential into actual clients".

The present study looks at the way all these strategies are used in the multimodal representation of each website chosen, describing their linguistic and visual promotional tourism discourses.

# CHAPTER FOUR

# MULTIMODAL DISCOURSE ANALYSIS

All communication is inherently multimodal, as various semiotic systems complement each other in the creation of the meaning of a single discursive phenomenon (Royce 1998, 26; Matthiessen 2007, 1; O'Halloran 2011, 6; Andersen and Boeriis 2012, 1). According to Jewitt (2009, 1), with reference to the study of multimodality,

> "the starting point is to extend the social interpretation of language and its meanings to the whole range of representational and communicational modes or semiotic resources for making meaning that are employed in a culture–such as image, writing, gesture, gaze, speech, posture".

Multimodal discourse, referring as it does to discourse that relies on more than one mode of communication (Bloor and Bloor 2007, 8), requires for its production and reception a semantic and formal interrelation of all the present sign repertoires (Stockl 2004, 9). Two of the most common modes of communication, i.e. verbal and visual, have a complex and complementary relation (Stockl 2004; Moya Guijarro and Pinar Sanz 2007; Moya Guijarro 2013b), as writing names what would be difficult to show, whereas image shows what takes too long to read (Kress 2010, 1). Following Barthes' theory (1977, 39-41), words can anchor images, elucidating their meaning, and images can anchor words by illustration. Text and image complement each other, being fragments of a more general syntagm (Moya Guijarro 2014). As such, they provide different, but semantically related information, each adding value to the meaning of a message (Djonov 2005, 2).

Nowadays, discourse relies even more on multimodal resources, as modern technology enables access to visual information easily (Bloor and Bloor 2007, 8) and increases the ease with which two or more modes and media can be combined in the creation of texts (Djonov 2005, 2). As stated by O'Halloran *et al.* (2010, 2),

> "the ongoing revolution in multimedia design and digital technology within contemporary society at large has led to a proliferation of multimodal documents (using media such as graphics, digitized photographs, audio and video texts, contemporary digital media, in particular web-based media, and three-dimensional virtual objects)".

The move from page to screen realizes a different compositional relationship between image and writing; image usually dominates the space on the screen, while writing becomes a visual element, making textual meaning beyond its written content (Herring 2003, 612; Jewitt 2004, 184). The screen, as a new semiotic entity, seems to be organized by the logic of image, which dominates the ordering, shape, appearance and uses of writing (Kress 2003, 48, 136). This means that all elements on the screen are treated as visual entities; their appearance and placement matter (Kress 2003, 65). As multimodal communicative acts on screen, websites are primarily text and picture based. They may transmit their content just by written information or in combination with pictures, animations, illustration, even short films or commercials, and sound (Janoschka 2004, 48). These semiotic resources and their interactions afford "new forms of informational and design complexity" (Lemke 2002, 299), allowing multiple reading paths (Kress and van Leeuwen 2006, 204). Like other websites, promotional tourism websites take advantages of multimodal opportunities, relying heavily on the careful use of words and images to inform and persuade tourists, providing the essential information for helping them decide what places to visit, as presented in the previous chapters.

The analysis of multimodal discourse starts from the premise that traditional (linguistic) patterns of textuality have been fundamentally distorted by the new technologies such as the Internet and mobile phones (Blommaert 2011, 132). Linguistic analysis alone is no longer enough. A visual analysis or an analysis of other modes, depending on the communicative act, is needed in order to totally describe the multimodal contemporary sign. A theory that encompasses this complexity of modes is the Systemic Functional Theory (SFT). Providing a social semiotic approach to discourse analysis, it "focuses on meaning-making as a social process which both constitutes and is affected by the socio-cultural context in which it occurs" (Djonov 2005, 18). The basic assumption is that every piece of communication has three main functions: "1) to engage our attention and interest, 2) to convey some information about reality, and 3) to structure these into a coherent textual form" (O'Toole 1994, 5). The SFT main principles can be applied to study any semiotic system, like language, image, sound, action, and their interaction in multimodal texts. As such, it can also be used to study websites (Djonov 2005, 46).

This chapter briefly summarizes the main features of SFT. It presents the tools for analysing the websites' linguistic component, following Halliday's theory of the metafunctions (1985; 1994; Halliday and Matthiessen 2004). Then, it moves to the visual component and describes the analytic tools proposed by Kress and van Leeuwen (1996; 2006).

## 4.1. Theory of metafunctions

Halliday (1985; 1994) and Halliday and Matthiessen (2004) proposed, explained and developed the theory of the metafunctions for the analysis of meaning-making in linguistic discourse. As pointed out by Halliday, "the notion of metafunction is simply an attempt to capture the relationship between the internal forms of the language and its use in contexts of social action" (Thibault 1987, 607). The principle at the base of Systemic Functional Linguistics sustains that language, like any semiotic system, simultaneously fulfils three communicative functions: ideational–the way the experience of reality is constructed in discourse; interpersonal–the grammatical choices that enable people to enact their complex and diverse interpersonal relations; and textual–the internal organization and communicative nature of a text (Halliday and Matthiessen 2004, 5).

### 4.1.1. Ideational metafunction

The ideational metafunction focuses on the ways the patterns of experience are logically related. It also expresses meaning about the world (Eggins 2004, 254), being concerned with specifying how language users' experience of reality, material and symbolic, is constructed in discourse. This metafunction can be further classified into logical and experiential.

#### 4.1.1.1. Logical metafunction

According to Halliday (1994, 216), the logical component of the linguistic system represents "the functional-semantic relations that make up the logic of natural language". This component is used to establish and interpret the relation between clauses in a message. There are two systemic dimensions that provide the functional framework for the description of clause complexes (Halliday 1994, 216). A CLAUSE COMPLEX is "the grammatical and semantic unit formed when two or more clauses are linked together in certain systematic and meaningful ways" (Eggins 2004, 255). When there is only one clause, the term used is CLAUSE SIMPLEX (Eggins 2004, 256). In written language, clause boundaries are usually indicated by full stops.

The first dimension is the SYSTEM OF INTERDEPENDENCY or TAXIS, which describes the relations between clauses linked into a clause complex. It offers two options: PARATAXIS and HYPOTAXIS. Parataxis defines the relation between two independent elements of equal status, one initiating and the other continuing. Hypotaxis, on the other hand, represents the relation between a dependent clause and a dominant one. The clauses are not equal; the dominant one can function alone, while the other cannot. The dependent clause can be also non-finite (Halliday 1994, 216-225; Eggins 2004, 258-270).

The second dimension of the logical function is the LOGICO-SEMANTIC SYSTEM, which applies to linked clauses. This includes a wide range of logico-semantic relations between a primary and a secondary member of a clause complex linked in a sequence. The relations can be grouped in EXPANSION and PROJECTION and can be encountered in both types of TAXIS.

In the case of expansion, clauses develop on previous meanings. The secondary clause expands the primary one, by means of ELABORATION, EXTENSION and ENHANCEMENT. In elaboration, one clause expands another by techniques such as restating in other words, specifying in greater detail, commenting or exemplifying. These elaborations can be further classified into: exposition, exemplification and clarification. In the category of extension, one clause extends beyond another clause by adding a new element, giving an exception or an alternative. The categories of extension are addition and variation. As for enhancement, one clause embellishes another by qualifying it with some circumstantial feature of time, place, manner, cause or condition. These circumstances can be further characterized as: temporal, spatial, manner, cause and conditional (Halliday 1994, 225-238; Eggins 2004, 270, 278-284).

Regarding projection, the secondary clause is projected through the primary clause, which instates it as a LOCUTION or as an IDEA. The clauses indicate that someone or something said or thought something. Both speech and thought can be presented as quoted or as reported (Halliday 1994, 216, 251-260; Eggins 2004, 270-275).

#### 4.1.1.2. Experiential metafunction

The experiential metafunction is concerned with how reality is represented. As stated by Halliday (1994, 106), "language enables human beings to build a mental picture of reality, to make sense of what goes on around them and inside them". The grammatical system by which this is achieved is TRANSITIVITY. This system is involved in the construction of the experiential domain related to "the flux of 'goings-on' as configurations of a process, the participants involved in it, and the circumstances attendant on it" (Matthiessen and Halliday 2009). The transitivity system construes the world of experience into a manageable set of process types. Each process type provides its own model or schema for construing a particular domain of experience as a figure of a particular kind (Halliday and Matthiessen 2004, 170).

The transitivity system proposes a number of types of processes, participants and circumstances. MATERIAL PROCESSES are processes of doing, expressing that some entity does something, undertakes some action. They are not necessarily concrete and physical events; they can also be abstract doings and happenings. The participants associated with these processes are usually ACTOR, the constituent of the clause doing the action, and sometimes GOAL, the constituent to whom the action is extended (Halliday 1994, 110-111; Eggins 2004, 215-218). MENTAL PROCESSES refer to what goes on in the internal world of the mind and can express AFFECTION/REACTION, COGNITION or PERCEPTION. The participants involved are SENSER, the conscious participant that feels, thinks or perceives, and PHENOMENON, representing what is felt, thought or perceived by the conscious participant (Halliday 1994, 112-119; Eggins 2004, 225-233). Another important type of processes is RELATIONAL. This category refers to the relationship set up between two entities. It can be either ATTRIBUTIVE or IDENTIFYING. In the case of attributive relational processes, an entity has some quality ascribed or attributed to it. The entity is referred to as CARRIER and the quality as ATTRIBUTE. In identifying relational processes, some thing, person, etc. has an identity assigned to it. Now, the clause is not about ascribing or qualifying, but about defining. The participants are TOKEN, standing for what is being defined, and VALUE, the one that defines. Both types of relational processes can be further classified in INTENSIVE, those that assign a relationship; CIRCUMSTANTIAL, those that encode meaning about circumstantial dimensions; and POSSESSIVE, those that reflect ownership and possession (Halliday 1994, 119-138; Eggins 2004, 239-248). Taking the description into further detail, both material and relational processes can appear in causative constructions. Another participant is added, an agent making or causing something. In CAUSATIVE MATERIAL PROCESSES, an AGENT causes an Actor other than her/himself to carry out the action. In the case of CAUSATIVE RELATIONALS, an ATTRIBUTOR causes the Carrier to have an Attribute ascribed or an ASSIGNER makes the Token take a Value (Eggins 2004, 224, 248-249).

Apart from these main types of processes, other, less central, processes are recognized, which are considered to share some characteristics with the main ones. BEHAVIOURAL PROCESSES, considered halfway between mental and material processes, refer to typically human physiological and psychological behaviour. They have an obligatory participant, typically conscious, the BEHAVER (Halliday 1994, 139-140; Eggins 2004, 233-235). VERBAL PROCESSES, in turn, are considered midway between mental and relational. They are verbs of "saying" and are related to the transfer of messages through language. The participants involved in this type of processes are SAYER–the one responsible for the verbal process, RECEIVER–the one to whom the saying is directed, VERBIAGE–the content of what is said or the name of the saying, and TARGET–the entity targeted in the process of saying (Halliday 1994, 140-142; Eggins 2004, 235-237). The list of process types ends with EXISTENTIAL PROCESSES. Located in between relational and material processes, they express the mere existence of an entity without predicating anything else of it. The only obligatory participant involved in this type of processes is called EXISTENT and may be a phenomenon of any kind or an event (Halliday 1994, 142-144; Thompson 1996, 79-101; Eggins 2004, 238).

The PARTICIPANTS presented above are considered direct. There are also some indirect or oblique participants, which can be grouped under the labels: BENEFICIARY and RANGE. The Beneficiary is the one to whom or for whom the process is said to take place. It can be further classified in RECIPIENT (the participant to whom goods are given to) and CLIENT (the participant for whom services are done). This type of participant appears in material and verbal processes and, occasionally, in relational ones (Halliday 1994, 144-146; Eggins 2004, 220-221). The other oblique participant, sometimes difficult to distinguish from Goal, Range, is the element that specifies the range or scope of the process. It is not a real participant, but merely adds specification to the process. A Range can appear with all types of processes except existential (Halliday 1994, 139-149; Thompson 1996, 100-104; Eggins 2004, 217-220). Not all these participants must be realized, sometimes they are not necessary or they are implied, i.e. "unactualised, but understood" (Downing and Locke 2006, 126).

Regarding CIRCUMSTANCES, they "essentially encode the background against which the process takes place" (Thompson 1996, 104). Following Halliday's model (1994, 149-161), the main types of circumstances are: EXTENT (distance and duration), LOCATION (point in place and time), MANNER (means, quality and comparison), CAUSE (reason, purpose and behalf), CONTINGENCY (condition, concession and default), ACCOMPANIMENT (commutation and addition), ROLE (guise and product), MATTER and ANGLE. Their use and choice "depends on the level of description needed by the writer of the clause" (Matthiessen and Halliday 2009).

### 4.1.2. Interpersonal metafunction

Apart from representing experience by logical relations, the clause is simultaneously organised as an interactive event involving language users. The interpersonal metafunction is concerned with the social relationships between the participants represented within, and interacting through the text, and their attitudes regarding its subject matter. In the act of communicating, language users adopt particular speech roles. By this, they assign the audience a complementary role (Halliday 1994, 68). The most fundamental roles in any exchange are giving (and taking) or demanding (and being given). The commodities exchanged can be information and/or goods-and-services. When what is being demanded is information, "language is the end as well as the means, and the only answer expected is a verbal one". The clause is then a PROPOSITION. In the case of goods-and-services, "the exchange commodity is strictly non-verbal: what is being demanded is an object or an action, and language is brought in to help the process along". The clause takes on the form of a PROPOSAL (Halliday 1994, 68-71). These possible combinations lead to four basic speech roles: giving information, demanding information, giving goods-and-services and demanding goods-and-services. Their usual labels are: statement, question, offer and command. These are closely associated with particular grammatical structures; statements are expressed by declarative clauses, questions by interrogatives and commands by imperatives (Thompson 2004, 47). Real discourse is not however so clear-cut, variations can occur in these typical correlations.

The clause as exchange develops by means of Mood[1]. This is its principal grammatical system and refers to the overall structure of the clause. The clause has two functional constituents: MOOD, which functions to carry the argument, and RESIDUE, which can be left out or elided. The MOOD element of the clause is constituted by SUBJECT and FINITE. The Subject, a nominal group, realises the thing by reference to which the proposition can be affirmed or denied. It provides the person or thing in whom is vested the success or failure of the proposition, i.e. what is held responsible. As for the Finite element, it has the function of making the proposition finite. Expressed by a verbal group, it represents something that can be argued about, bringing the proposition down to earth. This can be done by PRIMARY TENSE, MODALITY and POLARITY. Primary tense anchors the proposition by reference to time; it can be present, past or future. Modality, however, makes reference to the judgement of the speaker, regarding probabilities and/or obligations. It can be further classified into MODALIZATION–in the case of propositions, and MODULATION–in the case of proposals. Modalization involves the expression of probability and/or usuality and refers to the speakers' attitudes towards what they are saying, whereas Modulation expresses obligation and/or inclination and refers to the speakers' judgements or attitudes about actions and events. Both can have various degrees: low, median or high. As for polarity, this classifies the verbal operators in either positive or negative (Eggins 2004, 151-154, 174-183; Halliday and Matthiessen 2004, 111-121, 143-151).

Regarding the other functional constituent of the clause, the Residue, this is constituted by PREDICATOR, COMPLEMENT and ADJUNCT. Present in all major clauses, except elliptical ones, the Predicator is realized by a verbal group minus the temporal or modal operator. It fills the role of specifying the actual event, action or process being discussed. It also adds time meaning other than that of the speech event and specifies various other aspects or phases and the voice of the clause. The Complement, typically expressed by a nominal group, is the non-essential element of the clause, a participant somehow affected by the main argument of the proposition. As for the Adjunct, this is usually realized by an adverbial group or prepositional phrase. It can be defined as the element that contributes some additional, but non-essential, information to the clause. There are various types of Adjuncts, such as CIRCUMSTANTIAL, MODAL and CONJUNCTIVE. Among them, the only ones located in Residue are Circumstantial Adjuncts. They add

[1] "Mood" is used to describe the overall structure of the clause, while "MOOD" is used to refer to the constituent of the clause.

ideational content to the clause by expressing some circumstances related to the process represented. Modal Adjuncts, instead, are located in the MOOD structure and add interpersonal meaning to the clause, as they are somehow connected to the creation and maintenance of the dialogue. These can be further classified into MOOD ADJUNCTS, which are associated with the meanings constructed by polarity, modality, temporality and mood, and COMMENT ADJUNCTS, which express the speakers' attitude to the proposition as a whole. Finally, Conjunctive Adjuncts are not considered to be in the Mood structure. They contextualise relationships with some other portion of the text, adding textual meaning (Eggins 2004, 155-172; Halliday and Matthiessen 2004, 121-133).

### 4.1.3. Textual metafunction

The textual metafunction, the third and final strand of meaning made in the clause, is concerned with the creation of text, particularly, "with the presentation of ideational and interpersonal meanings as information that can be shared by speaker and listener in text unfolding in context" (Matthiessen and Halliday 2009). Moreover, it "enables the clause to be packed in ways which make it effective given its purpose and its context" (Eggins 1994, 273). One way of doing this is through the system of Theme[2].

The system of Theme accounts for the coherence and internal organization of a discourse either by organizing the initiation of the clause or by directing the attention of the receiver of the message to the parts the sender wishes to emphasize (Dejica 2005; 2006). It is realized through a structure in which the clause falls into just two main constituents: THEME and RHEME. The Theme is the element that serves as the starting point for the message; it is what the clause is going to be about, in some way. It is represented by the first experiential constituent in the clause. Rheme is the part of the clause in which Theme is developed (Eggins 2004, 273-275; Halliday and Matthiessen 2004, 64-67). Practically, everything that is not Theme is Rheme. These constituents are usually associated with given and new information, since "we typically depart from the familiar to head towards the unfamiliar" (Eggins 2004, 275). So, Theme usually contains familiar or given information (information which has already been mentioned somewhere in text or is familiar from the context), while Rheme contains unfamiliar or new information (Halliday 1994, 59). These associations, however, are not always the case. Language users "can

[2] "Theme" stands for the system constructing the textual meaning, whereas "THEME" stands for the functional element in the Thematic structure.

always decide, for particular purposes, to give an informational prominence to a content already known or mentioned, by presenting it as the Rheme of the utterance" (Lombardi Vallauri 1995, 359).

Theme can be further classified into simple Theme, when it contains only one element, the first experiential element in the clause, and multiple Theme, when it includes several elements. These elements preceding the experiential Theme are restricted. They can be: textual–signal how clauses are linked together and give cohesion to the text, and/or interpersonal–convey the writer's point of view on the message. When all these Themes appear simultaneously in the clause, their typical ordering is textual, interpersonal and experiential (Thompson 1996, 156-160; Halliday and Matthiessen 2004, 68, 79-87).

The Theme choice may be unmarked or marked, depending on the type of clause (declarative/non-declarative) and the writers' purposes. When Theme choices are the most typical or usual ones, the Theme is unmarked and considered to carry the lowest degree of new information (Westergaard 1986 in Manoliu-Manea 1994, 230). This happens when the Theme position is occupied by a Subject (in a declarative clause), Finite (in an interrogative), Predicator (in an imperative) or WH-element (in a wh-interrogative) (Eggins 1994, 295). Atypical or unusual Theme choices, instead, are marked THEMES. The most common are Adjuncts and Complements (in declaratives) and dependent clauses (in clause complexes) (Eggins 1994, 296-297; Halliday and Matthiessen 2004, 73-79). Marked Themes tend to bring in new information and thus, to be double salient, both topically and informationally (Westergaard 1986 cited in Manoliu-Manea 1994, 230). Markedness, however, can only be determined in context, as pointed out by McCabe (1999, 85). This can mean that there is always a "degree of markedness"; some Themes can be more marked than others, as for example Adjuncts, which are considered somewhat marked. Also, depending on context and purpose, some unmarked Themes may carry a certain degree of markedness or a marked Theme may be attenuated (Thompson 1996, 144-146).

The selection and identification of an individual THEME of a given clause "is not in itself particularly significant" (Dejica 2010, 22). What plays an important part in organizing a text and in providing a point of orientation for a given stretch of language is "the overall choices and ordering of Themes" (Dejica 2004, 49). THEME choices work together through a text to signal its underlying coherence and its method of development. THEMATIC DEVELOPMENT (Fries 1983) refers to "the way Themes interact with each other and with Rhemes in order to provide continuity in discourse and to organize the text" (McCabe 1999, 169).

There are different Thematic patterns (Daneš 1974) showing how the message unfolds and how Thematic elements succeed each other. THEME RE-INTERATION or CONTINUOUS PATTERN maintains the same Theme over several clauses, providing the message with a clear focus. Thematic shifting can be achieved cohesively by Thematic progression, either by a ZIG-ZAG PATTERN or by a MULTIPLE-THEME PATTERN. In the case of the zig-zag or linear pattern, an element or several elements from the Rheme portion of each clause becomes the Theme of the following clause. This gives the text a sense of cumulative development as it builds on newly introduced information. In the multiple-theme or split pattern, the Rheme of one clause introduces a number of different pieces of information, each of which is then picked up and made Theme in subsequent clauses. This pattern often provides the underlying organising principle for a text (Eggins 1994, 302-305). Thematic development seems to perform several functions, such as signal the maintenance or progression of "what the text is about" at a certain point; specify or change the framework for the interpretation of the following clause(s); point out the boundaries of sections in the text and show what the speaker considers to be the useful or important starting point (Thompson 1996, 165-173).

To sum up this section on the metafunctions, clause complex systems provide language users with structural resources to construct logical connections between experiential events (Eggins 2004, 256). They work alongside the experiential structures of transitivity, involving the logical chaining together of experientially related meanings and allowing, thus, language users to express ideational meanings as they turn the world into text. By means of transitivity and clause complex choices, language users express experiential meaning about participants, processes and circumstances and logically link these into coherent, semantically sequenced packages (Eggins 2004, 295). These choices are actively decided so as to represent reality or experience in a particular way. Their study can explain how the topic of the text is constructed, by developing and shifting to a number of experiential phases. Simultaneously with representing experience, interpersonal meanings are made. The systems of Mood and Modality are fundamental to understand the interpersonal relationships between interactants and the text producers' relation with the content of the text. Their study can, thus, uncover the interpersonal relationships expressed in the text. A close look at the grammatical choices language users make and the role they play in discourse can indicate the social creation and maintenance of hierarchic, social-cultural roles (Eggins 2004, 187). The successful construction of a text, however, involves more than just expressing sequences of content full of interpersonal relations. This content is expressed in a way which makes clear its relationship to the prior text and which signals the part of the text more or less important to the understanding of the overall text (Eggins 2004, 194). The thematic organisation of the clause is the most significant factor in a text's development. The selection of Themes guides the reader throughout the unfolding message. The analysis of the thematic structure and development of a text can point out its texture and organisation. It can also show the way in which the language user makes clear the nature of her/his underlying concerns and priorities (Whittaker 1995a; 1995b; Halliday and Matthiessen 2004, 105). The study of texts, by applying the theory of the metafunctions, can then simultaneously indicate: the experience represented and the way it is logically connected; the relation between the participants in the communication and their social and cultural roles; and the organisation of the message and the information prioritized by its creator.

## 4.2. Visual design theory

The theory presented above has been applied to other semiotic resources, such as visuals. As they represent the place where meaning is created and contested (Mirzoeff 1999, 6), they can be powerful and seductive in their own right (Rose 2001, 10). Every image, apart from representing the world, plays a part in some interaction and, accompanied or not by language, constitutes a recognizable kind of text (Jewitt and Oyama 2001, 140; Pinar Sanz 2006, 136). Kress and van Leeuwen used Halliday's metafunctions to study visual communication and provided a "grammar" of visual design, proposing a number of analytical tools for interpreting visual language. They consider that "the visual has to serve several communicational (and representational) requirements, in order to function as a full system of communication" (Kress and van Leeuwen 1996, 42). As such, visuals simultaneously fulfil the same three main metafunctions: ideational, interpersonal and textual. In the case of images, they are called representational, interactive and compositional functions.

### 4.2.1. Representational function

The representational function refers to the way experience is encoded visually. In visual language, "reality" is presented through NARRATIVE and CONCEPTUAL STRUCTURES. In the same way as simple or complex clauses in language, these structures can appear individually or together, in the last case embedding takes place. The distinction between major and minor processes in visuals is determined "by the relative size and conspicuousness of the elements" (Kress and van Leeuwen 2006, 107-109).

Narrative structures present unfolding actions and events, processes of change and transitory spatial arrangements. According to Kress and van Leeuwen (2006, 59), they always contain a vector, i.e. a depicted element which forms an oblique line and indicates directionality. Depending on the vectors used and participants involved, narrative structures can be built by different processes. In the case of ACTION PROCESSES, the vector is formed by a depicted element or an arrow and starts from a participant, called ACTOR. The action can be non-transactional, including only the Actor, or transactional, presenting also the GOAL, the participant towards which the vector is directed. Some transactional processes can be bidirectional, meaning that each participant interchanges the roles of Actor and Goal, as INTERACTORS. Another type of processes, REACTIONAL, depicts a vector formed by the direction of the glance of one or more participants, called REACTERS. This structure can also be non-transactional, when the glance is directed towards something outside the picture frame, and transactional, when the glance is directed towards another participant, PHENOMENON. SPEECH and MENTAL PROCESSES present dialogue or thought balloons to link the speakers or thinkers to their speech or thought. The participants represented in speech processes are SAYER and UTTERANCE, while those in mental processes are SENSER and PHENOMENON. Finally, CONVERSION PROCESSES, common in the representation of natural events, refer to a chain of transactional processes, where the third participant, RELAY, is Goal with respect to one participant and Actor with respect to another (Kress and van Leeuwen 2006, 63-70). Apart from processes and participants, narrative structures contain also secondary participants, CIRCUMSTANCES. They are related to the main participants by ways other than vectors. They can be left out without changing the narrative pattern, though that would imply loss of information. Visual circumstances can be: LOCATIVE–which relate participants to SETTING; MEANS–which indicate the tools used in action processes; and ACCOMPANIMENT–which present participants not linked by a vector (Kress and van Leeuwen 2006, 72).

CONCEPTUAL STRUCTURES, the other constituents of the representational system, present participants in terms of their class, structure or meaning. They can be CLASSIFICATORY, ANALYTICAL and SYMBOLICAL. Classificatory processes relate participants to each other; at least one participant plays the role of SUBORDINATE with respect to at least one other participant, SUPERORDINATE. They are further divided into covert taxonomies, when the Superordinate is not shown or named, and overt ones, when it is shown. Analytical processes, on the other hand, relate participants in terms of part-whole structure, the POSSESSIVE ATTRIBUTES representing the parts and the CARRIER, the whole. They have a wide array of types and can be further classified into UNSTRUCTURED, which do not present a Carrier, or EXHAUSTIVE and INCLUSIVE, the former ones represent the Possessive Attributes of a Carrier exhaustively, while the latter leave much of the Carrier unaccounted for. The list can be continued by TEMPORAL, realized by time lines; SPATIO-TEMPORAL, applicable to charts; TOPOGRAPHICAL, representing physical spatial relations, and, finally, TOPOLOGICAL, showing logical relations between participants. The last case of conceptual structures, SYMBOLICAL PROCESSES, describes what a participant is or means. It can be ATTRIBUTIVE, in which case two participants are involved, i.e. the Carrier–the part whose meaning or identity is established in the relation, and the SYMBOLIC ATTRIBUTE–the part that represents the meaning or identity itself. It can also be SYMBOLIC and have only one participant, the Carrier, whose meaning and identity are not conferred, but rather derived from its own qualities (Kress and van Leeuwen 2006, 79-113).

### 4.2.2. Interactive function

The interactive meaning in visuals refers to the "things we can do to or for each other with visual communication and with the relations between the makers and viewers of visual 'texts' which this entails" (Kress and van Leeuwen 1996, 119). According to Kress and van Leeuwen (1996, 114), visual communication builds and maintains different relations between participants, such as the ones between REPRESENTED PARTICIPANTS (the subject of the visual communication, like depicted people, places and things). Another relation is between INTERACTIVE PARTICIPANTS (the real people involved in the act of communication through images, such as producers and viewers) and concerns the things these do to or for each other through images. There can also be a relation between these different types of participants, which presents the interactive participants' attitude towards the represented participants.

Producing an image involves a choice of IMAGE ACT, SOCIAL DISTANCE, and POINT OF VIEW. The image act is identified according to the direction of the gaze of the represented participants, towards the viewer or not. When the represented participants look directly at the viewer, the image is a DEMAND. This type of picture is used to address the viewer and to demand something from him/her, as if establishing an imaginary relation with the participants represented. On the other hand, when there is no gaze contact between participants, the viewer becomes the subject of the look and the represented participant(s) the object(s). In this case, the image is an OFFER. It addresses the viewer indirectly by presenting the represented participants impersonally as items of information or objects for contemplation. The choice of image act suggests different relations between participants; they can engage with, or detach from, others, depending on their communicative power (Kress and van Leeuwen 2006, 116-124).

SOCIAL DISTANCE, another choice the producer of an image has to make, is related to the SIZE OF FRAME, which can be CLOSE-UP, MEDIUM or LONG, suggesting thus different relations between represented participants and viewers. The distances between people depend on their social relations and determine how much of the represented participants is in the viewers' field of vision. Social relations can be established also between objects, buildings or landscapes, as social distance is not restricted only to humans (Kress and van Leeuwen 2006, 124-129).

Images can present the relations between participants also through POINT OF VIEW or PERSPECTIVE. There are two types of images: SUBJECTIVE, when the viewer can see only from a particular point established and imposed by the image producer, and OBJECTIVE, in which case the viewer is disregarded and the image presents all there is to know about the represented participants (Kress and van Leeuwen 1996, 136). Different types of angles, like HORIZONTAL or VERTICAL, suggest different relations between participants. The horizontal angle can be FRONTAL, encoding involvement, or OBLIQUE, encoding detachment. The vertical angle can present represented participants from a HIGH position, giving power to interactive participants, from a LOW one, assigning power to represented participants, or from an EYE LEVEL position, keeping an equal relation between participants (Kress and van Leeuwen 2006, 133-143).

MODALITY is also present in the visual interpersonal metafunction, playing an important part. As in language, it has to do with the reliability of the message. Following Kress and van Leeuwen (1996, 161), "visuals can represent people, places and things as though they actually exist in this way or as though they do not (as imaginary)"; the decision depends on social and cultural factors. In images, Modality is constructed by a complex interplay of markers, such as colour saturation, differentiation or modulation; contextualization; representation; depth; illumination and brightness[3]. In all these cases, the point of highest Modality does not coincide with the extremes, but is somewhere in between (Kress and van Leeuwen 2006, 154-166).

### 4.2.3. Compositional function

The compositional function presents "the way in which representations and communicative acts cohere into the kind of meaningful whole we call 'text'" (Kress and van Leeuwen 1996, 181). Kress and van Leeuwen (1996, 183) consider that the representational and interactive meanings of pictures are related to each other through three interrelated systems: INFORMATION VALUE, SALIENCE and FRAMING. Not restricted to single pictures, they apply also to composite visuals (visuals that combine text, image and/or other graphic elements) and their layouts, as is the case of the websites studied.

The way in which elements are arranged in a text attributes them a particular information value. This is related to three main "zones" of the image: left and right; top and bottom; and centre and margin. They do not have to appear as separate, but they can be combined. When the composition is structured along the horizontal axis, the information is divided between left and right. The information value assigned to the left side is that of GIVEN, in which case the viewer is assumed to be familiar with the information and to accept it as a point of departure for the message. The right side is reserved to NEW INFORMATION, to something that is not known by the viewer or needs special attention. Information can also be structured along a vertical axis, i.e. top and bottom. The information placed in the upper section is presented as essential, visualising the "promise of the product", and is considered IDEAL, whereas that at the bottom is more specific and practical, visualizing the product itself and is called REAL. In the case of centre-margin alignment, the centre presents the nucleus of information, while the margins are similar and subservient to the centre (Kress and van Leeuwen 2006, 179-201).

SALIENCE, another important system in the composition of meaning, is used to create a hierarchy of importance among elements, presenting some of them as more important or attractive than others. It can be indicated by visual clues such as size, sharpness of focus, tonal and colour contrast, placement in the visual field, perspective and specific cultural factors (Kress and van Leeuwen 2006, 201-203). The elements in a picture

[3] For more details, see Kress and van Leeuwen (2006, 160-163).

or page can be either connected and joined together or disconnected and marked off from each other. This is realized by FRAMING, particularly by frame lines, discontinuity of shape or by empty space between the elements. Connection can be further emphasized by vectors (Kress and van Leeuwen 2006, 203-204).

Visual design, then, follows the same three-layered patterns of meaning as language. Narrative and conceptual structures describe the types of processes, participants and circumstances in the image. Simultaneously, interactive meaning is built in the image by the choices of image act, social distance and point of view. The reliability of the message is indicated by the interplay of modality markers. The combination of the representational and interactive meanings into a coherent whole is realized by means of information value, salience and framing. These systems confer special features to information. The study of images and other visuals can show the ways image producers, at the same time, visually construct experience and depict reality; create relationships between participants, either represented or interactive or both; and compose and communicate meaning, prioritising certain elements in favour of others.

To summarise the chapter, multimodal discourse analysis regards the message as a multimodal communicative act. Systemic Functional Theory provides one of the theoretical frameworks that can be adopted for the analysis of such an act. Within this framework, the theory of the metafunctions proposes the existence of a three-layered meaning: ideational, interpersonal and textual. This meaning is said to exist in every multimodal communicative act. As such, Halliday (1985; 1994) and, later, Halliday and Matthiesen (2004), describe the application of the metafunctions theory to language, whereas Kress and van Leeuwen (1996; 2006) refer to its application to visuals. These models can be used to analyse the language, the image and the layout of any message, including websites. Their study can indicate the way experience, relations and content are constructed linguistically and visually.

The present study applies the models presented above to analyse both the language and image of the selected websites. It also looks at the way these two modes combine to create a meaningful, informative and persuasive message.

# CHAPTER FIVE

# CULTURE

Promotion and other marketing tools, no matter their instrumental aim, are communicative acts. As such, they are cultural representations and can offer narratives about possible ways to live, refer to identity and related issues and/or appeal to people's image, happiness and fulfilment (Tomlinson 2002, 32). Communication is considered "an integral part of culture", with which it goes "hand in hand" (Peace Corps 2011, 75). It both presumes and constitutes social realities, since people, while communicating, engage in a meta-cultural commentary; they say things about themselves, their relationships, their feelings, actions and/or situations explicitly and implicitly (Carbaugh 2007, 168). Culture is omnipresent in people's lives and in the society they live in. According to Fornäs (1995, 1),

> "we are human by understanding and interpreting what we perceive, that is, by constructing symbols where something stands for something else. Symbols make it possible to think of what is not present, and thus to reflect upon the past and plan the future, to explore the other(s) and speculate about the unknown. By collectively shaping such symbolic patterns we construct a world and give ourselves specific positions in it".

Furthermore, this construction is not a transparent reproduction, but rather a symbolically coded reconstruction, which is never identical with what it depicts or points at (Fornäs 1995, 134).

Culture can be defined as "an accumulated pattern of values, beliefs, and behaviours, shared by an identifiable group of people with a common history and verbal and nonverbal symbol systems", which "has a direct influence on the physical, relational, and perceptual environment" (Neuliep 2006, 20-21). This pattern or "way of living", either conscious or unconscious, is transmitted from one generation to another (Matsumoto and Juang 2007, 10; "Cross Cultural Business Management" 2014, 32). It can be related to themes, such as orientations to life and beliefs; values and principles; perceptions of role relationships; behavioural rituals, conventions and routines; communication norms and conventions; or formal and informal institutions (Spencer-Oatey 2005; 2008, 52; "Cross Cultural Business Management" 2014, 32). Some of them, like, for example, physical manifestations, are considered objective elements of culture, while social norms, customs, attitudes, values and other non-physical aspects are seen as subjective (Triandis 1972; Matsumoto and Juang 2007, 46). Culture, then, exists in every individual, due to the processes of socialization and enculturation, as a set of psychological norms, attitudes, values and beliefs, which is strongly related to his/her cognition, emotions, personality and judgments of morality and their framing or representation (Moscovici 1981; 1998; Matsumoto and Juang 2007).

Culture is characterized by the following features: socially shared and constructed, since it is based on social interaction and creation; prescriptive, as it prescribes the kinds of behaviour considered acceptable in society; communication facilitator, as it makes communication easier between members of the same group; learned, since it is not inherited genetically, but acquired; arbitrary, because it is created by people and not dictated by natural laws; subjective, as different cultures have different ideas about the same object; internalized, since it is perceived as natural, as part of people/nations' character; enduring, because it is passed from generation to generation; cumulative, since it is based on hundreds of years of accumulated circumstances; and dynamic, as it is constantly changing and adapting itself to new situations and new sources of knowledge (Trompenaars and Hampden-Turner 1997, 24; Rose 2001, 6; Matsumoto and Juang 2007, 10, 65, 482; Dumitrescu 2009, 26, 28; "Cross Cultural Business Management" 2014, 33). Furthermore, culture can be influenced by various factors, such as population density, affluence, technology and/or context (de Cillia *et al.* 1999, 154; Lehtonen 2000, 12; Bloor and Bloor 2007, 26; Matsumoto and Juang 2007, 13; van Dijk 2009, 10), to name just a few.

This chapter focuses first on the interdependent relation between culture and discourse, mainly looking at the verbal and visual components. Then, it introduces the concept of cultural variability and presents the features of one of the most important cultural dimensions, context dependency (Hall 1976; 2000; Hall and Hall 1990). It also argues for the appropriateness of this dimension for the study of online promotional tourism discourse, proposing a possible link between context dependency and the linguistic and visual representations of the metafunctions.

## 5.1. Culture and discourse

Culture, as a set of practices, is primarily concerned with the production and exchange of meanings between the members of a society or group (Hall 1997, 2). Meanings, explicit or implicit, conscious or unconscious, can be conveyed through different types of discourses and modes (Rose 2001, 6; Dumitrescu 2009, 32). The context of culture represents the general context that gives meaning to culturally recognized activities (Lehtonen 2000, 10; Şerbănescu 2007, 134). People do not participate in communication as blank slates; they bring their socio-culturally shared knowledge, historical knowledge, understandings, assumptions, personal experiences, emotions and communicative resources to any particular communicative task (Halliday 1978; Martin 1992; van Dijk 2009). The choices made on the level of culture are realized in configurations of context-of-situation variables, i.e. in the field, tenor and mode of discourse (Eggins and Martin 1997).

As far as semiotics is concerned, culture can be understood as the way people communicate, by means of representations of culture, such as language and visual images (Lawes 2002, 253). As observed by Kress and van Leeuwen (2001, 112), semiotic resources have been produced "in the course of social/cultural/political histories–histories which of course keep going on" and, as such, are bearers of meaning (Djonov 2005, 73). Similarities and differences between societies and cultures mean similarities and differences in representation and meaning (Kress 2010, 8). A text, regardless of its form and mode, "is a sociological encounter through which the meanings that constitute the social system are exchanged" (Halliday 1978, 139). It mirrors society and, at the same time, takes part in its formation (Fornäs 1995, 134). The exchangers, both producers and receivers, are not isolated individuals, but members of groups, institutions or cultures which share meaning; in other words, they are products of culture (Dyer 1982, 13; Barker and Galasinki 2001, 63; Matsumoto and Juang 2007, 267). The choices they make to construct discourse and reality carry their values, beliefs, in a word, their culture, as "the construction of any representation of 'reality' is necessarily selective, entailing decisions as to which aspects of that reality to include and how to arrange them" (Barker and Galasinki 2001, 65). Ideologies are then formulated, reproduced and reinforced by semiotic resources and practices (Barker and Galasinki 2001, 65). The viewing of different semiotic systems "'from above', from the vantage point of the context of culture in which they operate" shows that these "complement one another in the creation of meaning" (Matthiessen 2007, 1).

Language, as the dominant mean of communication, plays an important role in any culture. It represents a powerful tool for creating, maintaining, and celebrating culture and social relationships (Mithun 2004, 137). It constitutes "the prime means of an individual's acquiring knowledge of the world, of transmitting mental representations and making them public and intersubjectively accessible" (House 2007, 11). Simultaneously, language acts as a means of "categorizing cultural experience, thought and behaviour for its speakers" (House 2007, 11). Culture can be understood by exploring the way meaning is symbolically produced through the signifying practices of language within material and institutional contexts, as indicated by Barker and Galasinki (2001, 3). It seems, then, that language, situational and cultural systems are all fundamentally interconnected (Halliday 1985, 11; Kress 1989, 5; Martin 1992; Clyne 1994, 6; House 2007, 11; Matsumoto and Juang 2007, 262). Language and meaning are always social in character and there can be no private language (Wittgenstein 1953 in Barker and Galasinki 2001, 35). Language is considered a resource, a complex set of potentialities for meaning-making, which is validated by social situations and cultures. These, in turn, are themselves to be understood as meaning-making resources (Halliday 1985, 11; Coupland 2011, 142). This is due to the "systematic relation between the social environment, on the one hand, and the functional organisation of language on the other hand" (Halliday 1985, 11). The cyclical nature of the relationship between culture and language suggests that no culture can be fully understood without understanding its language, and vice versa (Matsumoto and Juang 2007, 262).

As mentioned before, regularities are culture-specific for all modes (Kress 2003, 68), the visual being no exception. Visuals also represent and contribute to culture, as they bear meaning. Visual communication is "not transparent and universally understood, but culturally specific", since it is formed in and produced by particular cultures (Kress 2003, 68; Kress and van Leeuwen 2006, 4). Visual means of communication are rational expressions of cultural meaning as they are usually related to the interests of the societies where they are produced, circulated and read (Lister and Wells 2004, 64; van Leeuwen 2005, 23; Kress and van Leeuwen 2006, 45). Photographs, for example, as emphasized in Chapter three, are often considered "a source of objective and disinterested facts", but they are not; they are rather "complexly coded cultural artefacts" (Lister and Wells 2004, 64), simultaneously denoting and connoting shared meanings (van Leeuwen 2005, 37). Visual cultural meanings can be indicated, among many others, by design conventions, elements' placement, saliency or colours (Kostelnick and Hassett 2003; Kress 2003; Kress and van Leeuwen 2006; Hemelryk Donald and Gammack 2007; Hiippala 2007).

Tourism discourse, like any discourse, is both cultural representation and production. Carrying strong cultural connotations (Mocini 2009, 100), it can be considered a representation of social reality (Hiippala 2007, 35). Producers, copywriters and/or promoters tend to be selective about the reality they portray, and so present the values and ideals most familiar to them (Dyer 1982, 12). The context of culture and its value systems define, then, the content of tourist texts (Hiippala 2007, 35). The elements presented are usually culturally salient and refer to important buildings, like religious places and museums, or to generally accepted truths about the distinctive features of that particular culture (Therborn 2002, 39; Hiippala 2007, 35). Apart from representing their producers' culture, tourist texts are directed towards an audience. The marketing of the destination or asset can be different around the globe, having in mind different speech styles and listening habits or specific audience expectations (Lewis 2004, 125). This means that the initial text can be adapted to the audience's cultural expectations and values.

Since culture influences discourse and, at the same time, is influenced by discourse (Şerbănescu 2007, 255), as stated above, it can be related to the metafunctions presented in Chapter four. The links between them can be highlighted as follows. As experience is encoded differently by means of linguistic and visual systems, the experiential meaning denotes people's beliefs, biases, and ideas about the world. The logical meaning further points out how these systems are logically related and coherently put together. An exploration of these systems may reveal a great deal about the worldview expressed and its organization. The interpersonal meaning, on the other hand, refers to people's interactions and evaluations and the way they establish and maintain social links. The study of these links can indicate the type of people interacting, the values they have, the society they inhabit or the culture they share. Finally, the textual meaning shows how information is organized and focused. Its study can, thus, show which meanings are prioritised and what is considered new in particular social and value systems (Stoian 2015).

## 5.2. Cultural variability

World cultures are not alike; they resemble, differ from and reciprocally influence each other (Şerbănescu 2007, 134). The resemblances between cultures consist of the objective realities of the surrounding world, like people, houses or mountains; universal truths, like the fact that life ends;

humans' inherent similarities, whether physical or psychical; humans' universal activities, like sleeping or eating; and their answers to exterior stimuli, such as laughing or getting angry. Cultural differences, however, are not random, but result from the geographical, social, cultural, economic, political, religious and historical backgrounds in which communities, groups or nations developed. Differences depend also on humans' subjective interpretation of various exterior elements and relations, on their perception of exterior stimuli (Şerbănescu 2007, 134-5). All this leads to particular cultural patterns, which, in turn, determine a certain way of life and interpretation of reality (Şerbănescu 2007, 135).

Cultural variation and its parameters can be captured by various cultural dimensions and models, such as high-context//low-context (Hall 1976; 2000; Hall and Hall 1990), individualism/collectivism (Hofstede 1985), or humane orientation (House *et al.* 2004). National culture groups seem to operate within a common framework, having similar values, knowledge and behaviour. Even if there are exceptions, it is still possible "to make reasonably accurate statements (generalizations)" about the characteristics of a particular culture (Peterson 2004, 23). The classification of a culture, according to one dimension or another, is not a "precise diagnostic", but a general framework for the understanding and interpretation of certain social behaviours (Şerbănescu 2007, 154). As generalizations, the dimensions of cultural variation can also help predict the individual and social behaviours of the members of a culture. At the same time, they offer a unitary base for the explanation of differences among persons from different cultures (Şerbănescu 2007, 154).

Cultural dimensions can be situated on a cultural continuum (Hofstede *et al.* 2002, 40; Şerbănescu 2007, 153). Although clear distinctions exist between the extremes of the continuum, no culture is considered to exist at either extreme. Deviations from the main cultural pattern can occur in certain contexts and situations, since cultures are "dynamic, continuously developing, and evolving" (Barker and Galasinki 2001, 124; Besnier 2004, 95; Neuliep 2006, 45) and are influenced by different factors (Şerbănescu 2007, 155). These can be geographical, historical, religious, economic, social, political, technological, contextual and situational, or related to humans' uniqueness (de Cillia *et al.* 1999, 154; Lehtonen 2000, 12; Şerbănescu 2007, 155; Dumitrescu 2009, 123). Cultures are inherently changing, constantly adapting to new situations, absorbing elements from all directions, and transforming themselves in the course of history (Besnier 2004, 95). It can be said that all modern nations are "culturally hybrid" (Hall 1994, 207) and "multidimensional" (Hofstede *et al.* 2002, 126), as they are "integrated and related in new spatio-temporal terms" (de

Cillia *et al.* 1999, 155) due to globalization, on one hand, and localization, on the other (de Cillia *et al.* 1999, 155; Bloor and Bloor 2007, 140).

All cultural dimensions can show cultural features and particularities in certain aspects and domains, but, for the present study, context (Hall 1976; 2000; Hall and Hall 1990) has been selected as most relevant to the type of message studied and its function. It can be related to the metafunctions presented in Chapter four, as their analysis can reveal characteristics of different dimensions. At the same time, cultural dimensions can predict patterns in communication (Şerbănescu 2007, 255).

### 5.2.1. Context

Despite not being very recent, one of the most popular, extensively used and important cultural dimensions (Gudykunst *et al.* 1988, 56; Würtz 2005; Guillén Nieto 2007, 96; Peace Corps 2011, 78) is context, as proposed by Hall's model of cultural variability (1976; 2000; Hall and Hall 1990). It seems that, following Würtz (2005), "communication patterns today still resonate with the cultural dimensions proposed decades ago". The context dimension is considered broader and more encompassing than other dimensions (Gudykunst *et al.* 1988, 39), as it influences many aspects of intercultural communication.

Context refers to the situation, background, or environment connected to an event, a situation, or an individual (Würtz 2005). It represents a "set of assumptions (drawn from general knowledge, perception, previous communication, etc.)" (Spencer-Oatey 2008, 327) used in the production and interpretation of communicative acts. In other words, context is the information that surrounds an event and, as pointed out by Hall and Hall (1990, 6), is inextricably bound up with the meaning of that event. The elements that combine to produce a given meaning usually depend on culture. Hall suggests that meaning and context should be considered together with the language code systems, i.e. elaborated and restricted (Bernstein 1971), in order to come to an understanding of communication. He claims that cultures can be differentiated along a dimension of contextualization and can be situated in relation to one another through the styles in which they communicate. As such, Hall proposes two types of culture: high-context and low-context. In brief, contextual dependency is either high or low, depending on the degree to which members of a culture rely in their communication on experiences, expectations and background information shared with the members of the same culture (Şerbănescu 2007, 141; "Cross Cultural Business Management" 2014, 49). This classification can explain how communication is conveyed and perceived

(Würtz 2005) and can provide a framework for the understanding of cultural variability in communication styles.

### 5.2.1.1. High-context cultures

According to Hall and Hall (1990, 6), a high-context communication or message is one in which most of the information is already part of shared knowledge, while very little is in the coded, explicit, overtly transmitted part of the message. In restricted code systems, much of the information is contained in the nonverbal part of the message, whereas the verbal part is secondary. Members of high-context cultures imply messages through that which is not uttered, as they are especially sensitive to nonverbal contexts of information, which include the physical (geographical location of the interaction), social (relationships between interactants) and psychological/perceptual contexts (attitudes, motivations and cognitive dispositions of interactants). Thus, they have less need to be explicit and so rely less on words and more on nonverbal communication in order to convey meaning, knowledge being situational and relational. It seems that people carry within them highly developed and refined notions of how most interactions will unfold and how they will behave in particular situations. Within this context, some elements are expressed indirectly or not at all, since meaning is assigned on the base of shared experiences and expectations, which leads to inferences and contextual predictions. As a consequence, information is not linearly organized, emotions are central, the messages are neither strongly structured nor focussed on their content. Thinking is considered to be deductive, from general to particular. The large amount of additional information the message needs is what high context refers to. Without context, the message could not be properly understood (Hall 2000; Würtz 2005; Neuliep 2006, 58-61, 320; Şerbănescu 2007, 141-143; Peace Corps 2011, 78-81; "Cross Cultural Business Management" 2014, 49).

### 5.2.1.2. Low-context cultures

At the other end of the cultural continuum are situated low-context cultures. These are just the opposite; more exactly, "the mass of the information is vested in the explicit code", as explained by Hall and Hall (1990, 6). They rely on elaborated code systems; messages are explicit and clear, words being used to convey the main part of information. The members of low-context cultures depend much less on nonverbal clues and more on the explicit verbal code in order to create and interpret meaning. Due to this, communication within these contexts involves the transmission of direct, explicit and highly structured messages; the linear organization of text in logical arguments; and the focalization of information and details. Thinking is seen as inductive, from specific to general. In low-context cultures, thus, the words and their meanings can be separated from the context in which they occur. What is said is what is important, and not how and/or where it is said (Hall 2000; Würtz 2005; Neuliep 2006, 58-61, 320; Şerbănescu 2007, 141-143; Peace Corps 2011, 78-81; "Cross Cultural Business Management" 2014, 49).

In conclusion, culture has an enormous influence on people's lives. It influences their language, their perceptions of the surrounding world, their behaviours and attitudes, the structures of their homes, their systems of education, government, and/or health (Matsumoto and Juang 2007, 469). By means of the discourse they use, people are transformed into agents of their culture. They embody the essence of the culture and, at the same time, they reinforce it. It is almost impossible to send a message without any cultural content, as it is impossible to receive one without filtering it culturally (Peace Corps 2011, 75). Both cultural universals and differences influence communication (Spencer-Oatey 2008, 52), its production and interpretation. It seems, then, that people of different cultures structure the world around them differently, at least in the discourse they use to describe that world (Matsumoto and Juang 2007, 267). Cultural variability is evident in the styles of communication (Lewis 2004, 130).

This is true also for promotion. Its discourse reflects the socio-cultural context of culture (Montes Fernández 2007, 220). Its study can, therefore, show cultural patterns of communication. These can be predicted by various cultural dimensions, such as context (Hall 1976; 2000; Hall and Hall 1990). Context dependency can, thus, be related to Halliday's metafunctions and their application to visual design (Stoian 2015), since the overall organization of discourse and its logical composition, the reality presented and the relation between its producers and receptors can indicate the preference for a certain context of communication.

The present study investigates to what extent the chosen websites belong to a particular type of context and whether they are consistent with their cultural classifications. Intercultural communication research has focused on the cultures under discussion here from the context dimension perspective, classifying them as follows: Romanian and Spanish cultures are seen as high-context (Şerbănescu 2007, 149, 305), whereas British culture is considered low-context (Neuliep 2006, 60, 78; Şerbănescu 2007, 143).

# SUMMARY AND RESEARCH QUESTIONS

To conclude this overview of the theories the present study draws on, it is clear that cultural tourism represents an important type of tourism. Both institutional and commercial entities participate in the promotion and branding of cultural heritage assets. This promotion is carried out by multimodal messages frequently presented via the Internet. Websites combine different types of semiotic resources, mainly words and images, to create a discourse of tourism that informs, persuades and guides the tourist. Online promotional tourism discourse can be studied multimodally from a Systemic Functional (SF) perspective, since Halliday's metafunctions can be applied to the linguistic message and Kress and van Leeuwen's visual tools can be used for the visual message. Analysed within the SF framework, the techniques used to create this type of discourse can reveal particular communication patterns. Such patterns of meaning, in turn, belong to a cultural system, which can be investigated from the point of view of one of Hall's cultural dimensions, that of context.

Within this framework, the present research studies a number of websites from three different countries. Encompassing both institutional and commercial variants, it analyses their multimodal message and layout. The concerns presented in the introductory part, regarding online tourism promotion, and the theoretical frameworks considered have led to the formation of the following general question:

***How do different countries promote their national World Heritage Sites online for an international audience?***

This general question is broken down into a number of specific Research Questions:

1. What similarities and differences can be found between the institutional and the commercial promotion of the same landmarks?
2. Do the three countries–Romania, Spain and Great Britain–use similar and/or different multimodal communication strategies to promote their national landmarks in an online environment?

3. Can the results of the analysis of online national promotional messages, including their language and image, be accounted for from the point of view of the cultural dimension of context?

Before turning to the analyses, Chapter six presents details of the corpus and a concise picture of the methodology of the study, based on the background presented here.

# PART III:

# THE STUDY

# CHAPTER SIX

# METHODOLOGY

This chapter presents the methodology followed in the research study, regarding its design, collection and presentation of data, and method of analysis of the linguistic and visual components.

## 6.1. Research design

The study analyses two sets of websites: one institutional and the other commercial. They are produced by Tourist Boards and agencies that promote World Heritage Sites online. Their webpages have been analysed from a Systemic Functional perspective following Halliday's model (1985; 1994; Halliday and Matthiessen 2004) for the written text and Kress and van Leeuwen's model (1996; 2006) for the visual. The results of the linguistic and visual analyses have been compared from different approaches.

## 6.2. Data collection

To select the corpus, a number of search criteria have been followed. English has been set as the language of promotion since the focus of the study is on the ways different countries and landmarks are promoted internationally using this lingua franca. It was decided that the World Heritage Sites (WHS) should come from different fields (religious, historic and urban destinations) and different regions of each country. The purpose has been to select for analysis important landmarks, which represent those that receive the largest number of visitors. It was thought that different regions should be included to cover possible diversity in the landmarks' features and their promotion. The analysis of more than one item per website aims to obtain a broader view and discover if there is a particular promotional pattern related to the site. The collection of the corpus followed a slightly different pattern in the two sets.

### 6.2.1. Methodology for the collection of the institutional corpus

The selection process for the institutional corpus has been simple, as the search looked for the websites belonging to each country's national Tourist Board. The webpages promoting the three WHS selected from the beginning, i.e. religious, historic and urban, have been chosen. As the focus has been on those particular pages as presentation cards, no links directing to other webpages or information on the landmark have been followed.

### 6.2.2. Methodology for the collection of the commercial corpus

The process in this case has been more complicated as there are many travel agencies and/or tour operators promoting the WHS chosen, but few promoting all three. Also, most of the tour operators offer tours, transport and accommodation, but only a few describe the place promoted, a problem encountered by other researchers (Perandrea 2011, 2). Travel guides or any other websites without commercial aims have been disregarded. The selection process used the Google search engine and has taken the results generated by the word "visit", followed by the name of the religious landmark. The first agency to appear has been checked also for the historic and urban landmarks. The agency fulfilling these criteria–advertising all the three items–has been selected. The same procedure has been followed for each country. The preference for a sole tour operator promoting all the three landmarks instead of one tour operator for each landmark aimed to ensure the commercial corpus was similar to the official one. This would permit comparison between the corpora; they promote the same national landmarks to users, the difference being their nature: institutional vs. commercial.

## 6.3. Corpus

The corpus consists of two sets of websites, institutional and commercial, as already explained. Each set contains three websites from different countries: Romania, Spain and Great Britain. These countries differ with respect to the field of tourism, as explained in Chapter one. Romania is a relatively new country in the tourism market whose number of visitors is expected to grow (Morgan and Pritchard 2000, 145; OMT 2005a, 32; 2013, 2; Babu *et al.* 2008; Light *et al.* 2009, 234, 23; OECD 2009; Timothy and Nyaupane 2009, 65). Spain, on the other hand, has repositioned itself successfully "as a cultural destination" (Moilanen and

Rainisto 2009, 5; WTO and ETC 2009, 10), whereas Great Britain has always been on the market as a top destination (Macleod 2004; Babu *et al.* 2008).

Every website includes three webpages, each introducing a different national World Heritage Site. Their complete or partial screenshots[1] are presented in the analysis section. Other details can be checked on the actual websites, which have not changed since the collection of the corpus, except in the case of the British institutional and commercial websites, which have been partially modified, and the Spanish institutional website, which undergoes periodical renewal and has been adapted considerably since 2011 when the data was collected. The corpus may be characterised briefly as follows: the field is tourism, particularly World Heritage Sites; the medium is the Internet; the modes are text, image and/or video clip; the language is English; the communicative purpose is to inform and persuade; the sender of the message is a body, either a Tourist Board or a tour operator; and the addressee is the general international public, who may be interested in gathering information, planning a trip and/or buying tours or travel packages.

### 6.3.1. Description of the institutional corpus

The institutional corpus contains the following websites: Romanian Tourism (romaniatourism.com), Spain Info (www.spain.info) and VisitBritain (www.visitbritain.com). These belong to the national Tourist Boards of the countries chosen: for Romania, RoNTO–the Romanian National Tourist Office; for Spain, Turespaña–*Instituto de Turismo de España*; and for Great Britain, VisitBritain–the national tourism agency. As such, they act as promotional tools on a global market. Their names suggest the idea of information on the country. They have an ideal position on Google, as they appear the first on the list of results. The Romanian Board has a different representative for every language and, thus, a different website. This means that the content is not the same, varying according to the promoter and the audience speaking the language. The Spanish and British Boards, instead, have the same websites for all the languages they offer; their webpages are just translated and adapted into various languages. The types of World Heritage Sites chosen were the most visited by international tourists, i.e. religious, historic and urban landmarks (Timothy and Boyd 2002, 37, 39, 43; Sharpley 2006, 143;

[1] Every effort was made to get permission to use the webpages in this publication. When copyright was not granted, an impression of the structure of the page has been included so that the reader can follow the analyses.

Richards 2007, 17; Timothy and Nyaupane 2009, 10; Steinecke 2010, 188, 189). These are: for Romania, the Monastery of Horezu, the Dacian Fortresses of Orastie Mountains and Sighisoara; for Spain, the Royal Monastery of San Lorenzo el Escorial, the Alhambra and Santiago de Compostela; and for Great Britain, Canterbury Cathedral, the Tower of London and Edinburgh.

### 6.3.2. Description of the commercial corpus

The commercial websites are: Ciao Romania (www.ciaoromania.co.uk), Spain Day Tours (www.spaindaytours.com) and Evan Evans Tours (www.evanevanstours.co.uk). These work in the countries mentioned and offer tours to visitors; they are tour operators that both promote the landmarks and offer the possibility to buy a tour. They are not only present online, but also have a physical address and office. The Romanian operator has several variants for different languages, with the tours translated. The languages are English, Italian, French and German. The Spanish and British tour operators present their website almost exclusively in English, though there are a few tours described in a language other than this lingua franca. The Spanish website has a few options of Portuguese tours, while the British website has both Spanish and Portuguese. The landmarks chosen correspond to those of the institutional corpus as explained. However, on the commercial pages, they are presented in conjunction with other sites, as they form part of a tour. If the landmark appears in several tours, the same text is used for its promotion.

The corpus, then, represents important tourism websites that promote their country, owned by both Tourist Boards and commercial tour operators. In this way, the study gives a picture of the strategies chosen by the different stakeholders in the world of tourism.

## 6.4. Method of analysis

Each website is presented by its home page since this is its representative; it is the first element users get access to and plays a decisive role in the decision to visit the site (Garzone 2009, 36). The sites are described from the point of view of content, layout and marketing tools. The webpages describing the landmarks chosen are then studied, paying special attention to their layout, text and image. A brief description of the visual-organizational composition of the entire webpage has been included before the actual multimodal analysis of the message to set the context, providing the background of the message and helping readers situate the analysis that follow. As Lemke (2002, 310 based on Arnheim 1956) says, it is "the salient structure which guides the eye in its traversals across the page". For the same reasons, each text and image are first described briefly and then analysed. Due to their length, only the most important parts of the actual analyses are included in the Appendix. The theoretical terms have been signalled following the conventions in the SFL field: small caps and/or capitals, for an easier reading.

### 6.4.1. Linguistic analysis

The selection of text for the linguistic analysis is different in the two corpora. In the institutional corpus, the entire text included in the webpage has been analysed since it shows the particular way each country presents the landmark and represents the promotional method of the national Tourist Board. The webpage is meant to be the landmark's identity card for the users visiting the site. In the commercial corpus, however, the entire text appearing on the webpage has not been considered for analysis, as it advertises a tour of different landmarks, which are not the object of discussion in this paper. This means that only the text referring to the particular World Heritage Site chosen has been analysed.

First, text length was counted using the Word Tool contained in the Microsoft Office Pack. For syntactic elaboration and complexity, the ratio of number of words to the number of sentences and/or clauses and the ratio of number of clauses to the number of sentences have been calculated using the instruments proposed by Wolfe-Quintero *et al.* (1998).

The linguistic analysis is organised following Halliday's proposal of metafunctions (1985; 1994; Halliday and Matthiessen 2004) and has looked at each function individually. For the analysis of the ideational metafunction, logical and experiential meanings have been dealt with as follows. The logical analysis has characterized the texts from the point of view of distribution of types of clauses: clause simplexes and complexes. The clauses with a realized verb, either finite or non-finite, as well as a few constructions, such as preposed attributives, elliptical clauses or minor clauses have been analysed. Embedded clauses have not been considered as they operate at another rank in the text. The clause complexes have been analysed for tactic and logico-semantic relations. The analysis, then, has quantified the types of clauses and their relations. The transitivity analysis has considered each clause and has looked at its processes, participants and circumstances. The participants considered have been the landmark, the visitor/client and the Tourist Board/tour operator; the other possible participants have been excluded since they are not relevant for the purpose of the analysis. The embedded clauses have been marked and placed separately, as can be observed in the analysis included in the Appendix.

Regarding the interpersonal analysis, this has investigated only independent clauses since dependent clauses usually have the same mood choice as the clause they depend on (Thompson 2004, 48). The unit of analysis is the independent conjoinable clause complex, which consists of an independent clause together with all hypotactically related clauses and words that are dependent on that independent clause (Fries 1995). Even if not analysed, the hypotactic clauses have been signalled. The focus of the analysis has been on mood structure, types of Subjects, Finites, Adjuncts, modality, polarity, mood choices and speech roles.

Finally, the textual analysis has also examined only independent conjoinable clause complexes, as this seems to be the optimal method for showing Thematic progression (Thompson 1996, 166; McCabe 1999, 73). The initial part of the clause up to the first experiential constituent has been considered Theme for the unit of analysis. In the case of fronted dependent clauses, these have been taken as Theme, as the point of departure for the whole complex. The analysis includes the types of Themes, their status, composition and their Thematic progression.

### 6.4.2. Visual analysis

The written text is almost always accompanied by an image representing the landmark. There are two exceptions, in the Romanian and Spanish commercial sets. Sometimes, the landmark is illustrated by several images. In this case, the first image has been analysed as the most representative of the tourist landmark, considering that the copywriter chose to place it in a prominent position as the first picture users see. The visual analysis follows Kress and van Leeuwen's model of visual design (1996; 2006) and has observed the expression of the metafunctions in the visual representation of the landmarks. For the representational function, the analysis has looked at represented participants, processes and circumstances; in the case of the interactive function, at image act, social distance, perspective, angle and modality markers; and in relation to the compositional function, at information value, salience and framing.

For reasons of space, only the most important part of the analyses is included in the Appendix. Chapter seven and eight provide the results and their discussion for each metafunction mentioned above in both modes, the former refers to the institutional corpus, while the latter deals with the commercial one. This format was decided in order to allow readers to see the whole picture that comes out of the numerous different meaning-making strategies used by the web designers and their copywriters. Readers may consult details in the Appendix, without the complete analyses preventing them from seeing the patterns that emerge. Finally, in Chapter nine, the similarities and differences between the two corpora are discussed and related to their cultural contexts.

# CHAPTER SEVEN

# INSTITUTIONAL CORPUS: RESULTS AND DISCUSSION

This chapter presents the results of the multimodal analyses of the webpages belonging to the institutional corpus. Each set starts with a description of the websites' home page in order to contextualise the analyses and discussions to follow. The chapter focuses on the webpages considered and presents a two-layered analysis: linguistic and visual. The linguistic analysis uses several subheadings to guide reading, i.e. Overview, Logical, Experiential, Interpersonal and Textual; they are not meant for analysis subdivision as overlaps of areas occur. The linguistic and visual analyses are then summarized from the perspective of the multimodal act they compose.

The institutional websites present Romania, Spain and Great Britain to the world. As their promotion is institutional, the Tourist Boards depict the countries from an official perspective. This section refers to the three institutional websites considered: Romanian (Romania Tourism), Spanish (Spain info) and British (VisitBritain). Their webpages are: for Romania, the Monastery of Horezu, the Dacian Fortresses of the Orastie Mountains and Sighisoara; for Spain, the Monastery of El Escorial, the Alhambra and Santiago de Compostela; and for Great Britain, Canterbury Cathedral, the Tower of London and Edinburgh.

## 7.1. Romanian set of institutional webpages

The Romanian National Tourist Office (http://romaniatourism.com/) has a relatively short and vertically organised home page. In it, three main areas can be clearly distinguished: header, main body and footer. The header has the form of a visual and can be further divided in three vertical zones. The first one contains a logo and a slogan, on the left, and the technical contents and search button, on the right. The logo contains the word "Romania", written in green and partially covered by a green and blue leaf. Green can imply the forest and blue the sky, in a word nature–

one of the most popular advertising themes (Delin 2000, 67). This is confirmed by the slogan, which emphasises the natural facet of Romania: "explore the Carpathian garden" (Romania Tourism 2011). The user is addressed directly, by the imperative, and exhorted to "explore", verb that can have both physical and mental implications. The naming of Romania as "the Carpathian garden" highlights, as mentioned, the connection with nature, but also adds a mystic, exotic and paradisiacal sense; "Carpathian" sounds remote and also exotic, probably unknown to many of the users, whereas "garden" implies paradise-like surroundings. The various tones of green that spread out like beams on the page are also linked to the concept of "nature". The navigational menu is composed by: "Home", "Site Map", "Special Offers", "Links", "Maps", "About Us" and "Contact us". The focus seems to be on navigational directions, interactive details and transactional information. The identity of the Tourist Board looks important, as its data are highlighted repeatedly.

The second section of this first part is a rectangular box which contains the contents of the website displayed horizontally: "About Romania", "Regions & cities", "Main attractions", "Special interest", "Trip planner" and "Images". These are in larger print and in capital letters and refer to information related to the country and not to the website. Special importance is attached to general information on the destination, whereas the particular information necessary for planning a trip is presented as secondary. The last section is organized horizontally, placing a picture on the left, as given information, and a text on the right, as new information, maintaining the same green. The keeping of the same colour provides continuity to the message. The picture presents a lake and a hiker, projected on an impressive view of mountains peaks. The choice of mountains can be related to the Carpathians mentioned in the slogan. The picture becomes a visual on which three words in different colours and shapes are added: "culture", "authenticity" and "nature". Their colours and position draw them into the users' attention. The text on the right presents the picture as the "photo of the month" and describes hiking in the "Retezat National Park" briefly.

The main body of the webpage is set on a white background as a separate piece of information. It is divided in three columns to make reading easier (Garzone 2009, 38). The first one develops the keywords presented in the image, each preceded by a picture aimed to represent them visually, i.e. the roof of the Romanian Athenaeum for "Cultural Romania", the Merry Cemetery for "Authentic Romania" and pelicans in the Danube Delta for "Natural Romania". They function as links to other webpages of the website which develop that particular topic. In case the user is not sufficiently interested by this left column, s/he can watch some "Romania travel videos" or follow the Tourist Board on socialization networks. The second column is the widest one and is where the Tourist Board's message appears. First of all, it welcomes the user and specifies the aim of the site: "assist travellers". Then, in two paragraphs, it describes briefly Romania and identifies several of its attractions, such as the medieval towns in Transylvania or the Black Sea. The end of the message is clearly signalled by another welcome to Romania and a signature of the Tourist Office. The layout can be associated to an official letter from the Tourist Board to the users, a sort of invitation letter. This may add reliability and veracity to the message as it comes from an official voice. The message is addressed directly to the website's users by an impersonal and professional entity. The column continues by detailing the contents from the menu bar; it actually repeats all the contents and presents their sub-contents with direct links. Even if probably aimed to offer a detailed view of the contents of the website, this can be repetitive and redundant for users, who can find them at the beginning of the home page. The last column, on the right, starts with a map of Europe, which locates Romania and situates users. This map, together with other elements, like the "Welcome" message, the aim of the site, the picture of the Athenaeum and the visual, is what users see first when accessing the website and what builds their first impression. The first message seems to be quite iconic and visual. After the map, there are some links to special offers and promotions, hotels and varied information related to "Entry Formalities" or "Upcoming Tours". At the end of the column, a number of quotations present "what travel guides say about Romania", guides like that of "The Lonely Planet". These are probably aimed to convince users, to offer them, once again, the reliable voice of the official and independent expert.

The last section of the home page is short and contains the footer. In green, like the header, it frames the main body and indicates the end of the page. It contains a horizontal list of some contents related to the website and mentioned in the header, like "Home" or "Links". This is another instance of possible redundant information, as mentioned before. It can, however, be handy, as users do not have to scroll up to the beginning in order to get "Home". The home page of the Romanian institutional website follows some of the patterns proposed by WTO in accordance with the AIDA marketing model (OMT 2005b, 8), described in the Theoretical Background in Chapter three. The users' Attention seems to be drawn by the book, by aspects like the logo and slogan, the general presentation of the website, the attractive photos, the unique characteristics of the country signalled by keywords, the special offers link or the possibility to communicate with the Board. Interest is stirred by descriptions, photos and maps, whereas Desire is stimulated by the possibility to do diverse things and by the opinions on Romania provided by various travel guides. Information on boarding and trips in the region is indirectly indicated by links to specialised subsections. Action is induced by the possibility to contact the Board; there is no link to booking.

### 7.1.1. The Monastery of Horezu in the institutional corpus

A webpage dedicated entirely to the Monastery of Horezu does not exist. The Romanian Tourist Board prefers to put all the World Heritage Sites (WHS) belonging to Romania together in a subsection with the same name, part of the section "Main attractions" indicated in the menu bar. This can be more appealing for users, as they know what they are looking at from the beginning. The WHS status is displayed proudly, like an emblem or mark of the expert (UNESCO) that validates the asset's potential. It seems an objective quality, as it does not come from the possible subjective Tourist Board, but from others.

The webpage presenting the Romanian WHS keeps the same header of the home page without the visual. Following the layout of a regular page, it is organized in two columns. The left one is marginal and short and provides navigational and practical information. The navigational bar of the section "Main attractions" displays its contents in list form. This can reiterate the website's attractions and offer quick and easy ways to get to important sections (OMT 2001, 94; 2005b, 9; Majó and Galí 2002, 400; Miller 2011, 85), but it can also affect readability and ease of use (Rodríguez Abella 2011, 161). An advertisement on flights is placed next, named suggestively "From the world to Romania". The right column is much wider, longer and occupies almost the entire screen. Dedicated to general information, it first introduces the World Heritage Sites in Romania and then presents each in more detail. As the page is quite long, various links are provided for users to access the desired WHS without wandering blindly through the webpage. For the same reason, each landmark has at the end a "Top" link to redirect users at the top of the page. The information value of this left-right placement presents the content and advertisement as given information and the actual description as new information (Kress and van Leeuwen 2006, 179).

The Monastery of Horezu is the first one on the list of WHS. Not longer than a screenshot, the layout imitates a regular page, with a title followed by a text. The first part of the message looks like an identity card of the monument, written in italics and offering information regarding its location, nearby large town and telephone number. The second part contains a text and a picture forming a communicative act, as can be seen in Fig. 7-1. The text is placed on the left and stands for given information, while the image, situated on the right and embedded in the text, depicts new information and can be interpreted as an illustration of the text. The picture, however, is presented as a different element, even if part of the same whole, since it is framed. The framing and its colours on the white background make it salient. Users' attention falls first on the salient elements of the message: the title, the practical information and the picture.

Fig. 7-1 The Monastery of Horezu institutional webpage

**The Monastery of Horezu**

*Location: Walachia - Southern Romania*
*Nearby large town: Ramnicu Valcea (27 miles east)*
*Nearest train station: Ramnicu Valcea*
*Telephone: (250) 860.071*

Founded in 1690 by Prince Constantine Brancoveanu, the monastery of Horezu is a masterpiece of the '*Brancovenesti*' style. Renown for the richness of its sculptural detail, the treatment of its religious compositions and its painted decorative works, the monastery houses precious collections of frescos and icons dating from the end of the 17th century and beginning of the 18th century.

The *Hurezi School* of mural and icon painting established at the monastery in the 18th century had a profound influence on religious art and architecture in the Balkan region.

The monastery museum, housed in the princely residence, features masterpieces of Brancovenesti art: icons, books, embroideries, silver collections and an interesting library of old books containing approximately 4,000 volumes. Overnight accommodation available.

TOP

*Source*: Romania Tourism (2011)

### 7.1.1.1. Linguistic analysis[1]

*Overview*. The text analysed forms part of the second section of the message mentioned above. It is organised in three paragraphs, each of them being dedicated to a different topic. The first one specifies the reasons for the Monastery's fame, the second one refers to the Hurezi School of mural and icon painting, while the last paragraph presents one of the Monastery's attractions, its museum.

*Logical*. The text describing the Monastery is quite short with long, syntactically developed and complex sentences. These are organized in clause complexes by hypotaxis-elaboration. The dependent clauses, always non-finite, add details to the information presented and, at the same time, make the message more compact (Gotti 2008, 94). Details are always added as secondary and never as embedded, a technique that seems to focus on them instead of hiding them within the clause structure. The syntax of the message looks entangled since the hypotactic non-finite clauses act as non-defining relative clauses and are placed salient in the text. They are either fronted ("*Founded in 1690 by Prince Constantine Brancoveanu*, the monastery of Horezu is a masterpiece of the 'Brancovenesti' style") or interpolated ("The Hurezi School of mural and icon painting *established at the monastery in the 18th century* had a profound influence on religious art and architecture in the Balkan region") (Romania Tourism 2011). Their purpose probably is to draw attention to the noun focused and to be as detailed as possible about it. The nouns elaborated this way refer to the topics of the three paragraphs mentioned. There is no instance of parataxis, the focus on elaboration by details being further emphasised. The pattern of the paragraphs is similar: in the same clause, the text introduces the topic and then describes it by various details.

*Experiential*. The transitivity system is built mainly by relational clauses. The processes are usually attributive and situate the Monastery in the real world, by providing location details regarding its contents ("the monastery *houses* precious collections of frescos and icons") and the placement of its museum ("[the monastery museum is] *housed* in the princely residence"). They also describe it as "a masterpiece of the 'Brancovenesti' style", an exaggeration typical of advertising discourse repeated several times to impress users. The other two components referred to by the text are also identified: the Hurezi School of mural and icon painting as having profoundly influenced the art in the Balkan region

---

[1] As mentioned earlier, each webpage has three sections: linguistic, visual and multimodal.

and the Monastery museum as containing a library of 4,000 volumes. As can be noticed, connotative words are once again used. The few instances of material processes focus on historical facts regarding the Monastery and its school, like “found” and “establish”; their antiquity is thus emphasised. There are a large number of circumstances compared to the few cases of material process. The circumstances are varied and provide a detailed background. The locative circumstances are the most predominant and situate the action both in time, “in 1690”, and place, “in the Balkan region”. The other types contribute to the praise of the Monastery and refer to the causes of its fame, “the richness of its sculptural detail”, and its “profound” manner of influence.

Among the participants observed in the analysis (i.e. landmark, visitor and Tourist Board), the only one present is the landmark and its components. It is slightly more often realized than implied in the frequent role of Carrier, the entity described, as for example in “*the monastery of Horezu* is a masterpiece of the 'Brancovenesti' style”. This is expected, as the text is about the Monastery; it has also been predicted by the high number of relational attributive processes. The absence of the visitor and the Tourist Board makes the message sound more impersonal and more centred on the landmark.

*Interpersonal.* The text is composed only by declaratives. The statements present information as fact and, so, reliable. The Mood component is mainly represented by Subject and Finite. The place of the Subject is usually occupied by the Monastery and its attractions, the Hurezi School and the museum. Attention is thus drawn to the topic of the text. The only construction placed in Subject position besides the building is “overnight accommodation”. This practical information, “Overnight accommodation available”, does not seem to fit into the text, considering the type of information presented so far. There is no mention of the visitor or the Tourist Board. There is nothing to prepare the users for this sudden practical information, highlighted by its placement in the clause. Probably for this reason, the clause is elliptical and indirect. Accommodation is available, that is the information provided; the rest is up to the users, who can investigate by themselves. The Finite is fused and usually refers to the present, like “features” and “is”. The attributes of the monastery and its components are presented as generic and timeless. The past tense only mentions the influence the Hurezi School had in the area, contributing to the fame of the Monastery and increasing the necessity to see such famous landmark. There is no modality or polarity. This emphasises the presentation of information as statements of fact (Mocini 2008, 160).

The Residue component of the mood is complex and contains all its elements. Adjuncts are infrequent, and when they appear, they are circumstantial, like "in the Balkan region". This is not expected considering the number of circumstances in the transitivity system. It can only mean that they are expressed in the numerous hypotactic clauses, which have not been analysed for mood. The information presented as principal does not contain many background details; these are included in the subordinate clauses. This can indicate that the spatial and temporal background is secondary to the characterization of the landmark.

*Textual*. The Themes in the text are simple and varied; there is little difference between marked and unmarked ones. Reduced non-defining relative clauses are placed in first position in the role of preposed attributives that add information to the Subject, in this case, the landmark. They emphasise the foundation of the monastery, "*Founded in 1690 by Prince Constantine Brancoveanu*, the monastery …", and the reasons for its fame, "*Renown for the richness of its sculptural detail, the treatment of its religious compositions and its painted decorative works*, the monastery …", as they are enhanced and conspicuous. Preposed attributes are associated with tourism and advertising (Thompson 2004, 163); they postpone the activation of the Subject in discourse and increase the reader's expectation regarding the landmark promoted (Moya Guijarro 2006). This technique is used by the copywriter "to introduce a large quantity of information in the initial part of the sentence", directing the focus on the landmark advertised (Moya Guijarro 2003, 146). Other interesting types of Themes are those containing interpolation, which also add details, by non-defining relative clauses again, about the date of establishment of the School, "The Hurezi School of mural and icon painting *established at the monastery in the 18th century* had a profound influence …", or the place where the museum is housed, "The monastery museum, *housed in the princely residence*, features masterpieces …". The focus seems, thus, to be on temporal and spatial locations and causal circumstances, which create a symbolic scenery for the users (Calvi 2011, 78). Unmarked Themes are expressed only by participants, e.g. "the monastery museum" included in the last example above. The unmarked Themes contribute to the objectivity of the message (Francis and Kramer-Dahl 1991, 354). Except for linear progression, all the other possible patterns are equally present. The Monastery is focused by repetition, whereas its components seem developed cumulatively ("the monastery houses precious *collections of frescos and icons* […] *The Hurezi School of mural and icon painting* [...] had a profound influence on religious art and architecture in the Balkan region. *The monastery museum* […] features masterpieces of Brancovenesti art …"). The only new Theme draws the attention to overnight accommodation, probably in the Monastery, to highlight it as an attraction or a facility. This possibility can raise the interest of the landmark and add to it a personal touch: users can spend the night in the Monastery complex and have a different experience from the normal visit. The message seems organized, but the fronted Themes, the interpolations and the new Theme make coherence unclear and the flow of ideas disrupted and difficult to follow.

The results of the linguistic analysis are presented in Table 7-1.

**Table 7-1 Institutional Monastery of Horezu: Lexico-grammatical summary**

| Clause complex | Transitivity | Mood | Theme |
|---|---|---|---|
| short<br>+ complexes<br>(2 cl.)<br>only expansion<br>only hypotaxis<br>only elaboration<br>+ non-defining rel | + relational<br>+ attributive<br>= intensive &<br>circumstantial &<br>possessive<br>only mental percept.<br>+ realized participants<br>(little dif.)<br>only landmark<br>only land. (realized)<br>only landmark<br>(implied)<br>+ Carrier (landmark)<br>- visitor<br>- promoter<br>various Circs.,<br>+ location, = time &<br>place | = mood &<br>residue<br>+ complex<br>residue<br>+ landmark as<br>Subject<br>only fused<br>Finite<br>+ present<br>only Circ.<br>Adjuncts<br>- modality<br>- polarity<br>only declarative<br>+ full decl.<br>only statements | almost =<br>unmarked &<br>marked<br>only simple<br>only particip. as<br>Theme<br>almost =<br>multiple &<br>continuous<br>patterns & new<br>Themes |

### 7.1.1.2. Visual analysis

The image depicts the Monastery complex from the inside. The building, situated on the right, is not fully or centrally captured. This picture is not the typical one chosen as representative of the Monastery of Horezu; a shot including the entire religious monument is more frequent. It is constructed on a conceptual structure, which presents reality by means of unstructured analytical processes. The Monastery of Horezu, as a whole, is the Carrier, whereas its different parts and surrounding elements, like the green areas and alleys, constitute its Possessive Attributes.

Another structure, this time secondary, is constituted by the Possessive Attributes of the background, i.e. the sky, trees, the nun and other human figures. The presence of human figures confers reality to the picture.

Presented as an offer, the picture is there for observation and contemplation. It is depicted subjectively, like any other picture. The shot is close and medium, depending on the point of focus. The Monastery is in the close shot, whereas another building appears at medium distance. The horizontal angle is oblique; the Monastery is depicted from a lateral frontal angle. The stairs seem to be one of the accesses into the Monastery. The same angle also characterises the other building. Regarding the vertical angle, it is eye level. This can be the reason why the Monastery is depicted from the visitor's perspective, someone who is preparing to enter the building. It seems to show what the visitor would actually see if s/he were there in that place. The relation created is one of closeness and equality. The landmark is, however, out of reach. The visitor may come closer and see the entire Monastery. The modality markers support the idea of reality, the idea of a possible visitor taking the picture. All of them show medium modality, except for illumination and brightness, which tend towards low modality, as if modified in order to make the building more salient.

The compositional structure seems to have no informational value organization; the elements are presented apparently without following any compositional layout. There are, however, salient framed elements that draw the attention of the viewer to a particular visual element. The lateral front of the Monastery is salient, due to its colour, size and closeness. The nun can also be considered salient, due to the black contrast on the white or grey background. Her inclusion in the picture and her saliency inform us that the Monastery is occupied by nuns. The Monastery and the other building from the back look also framed by the blue of the sky and the green of the grass.

The characteristics of the picture are summarised in Table 7-2:

**Table 7-2 Institutional Monastery of Horezu: Visual summary**

| Representational | Interactive | Compositional |
|---|---|---|
| simple<br>conceptual structure<br>unstructured analytical<br>monastery & background<br>(Carrier)<br>component & surroundings<br>(Possessive Attributes)<br>+ humans | offer<br>close & medium shot<br>subjective<br>oblique horizontal angle.<br>eye level vertical angle<br>+ medium modality<br>markers | - information structure<br>monastery & nun<br>(salient)<br>diff. buildings of<br>monument (framed) |

### 7.1.1.3. Multimodal act

To sum up, the Monastery of Horezu is presented in an apparently objective, transparent and impersonal way. This is emphasised by the absence of the Tourist Board and the visitor. The focus of the text is on the description of the Monastery and its components as attractive and influential. The marked and interpolated Themes, the high number of attributive processes and their connotative attributes indicate, however, some subjectivity. The focalization on the landmark's fame and antiquity and its qualitative description highlight its attractiveness and aim to convince users. The Romanian word, "Brancovenesti", kept in the text to name the style of the Monastery and its art, adds mystery and makes users wonder what it means. They may be interested enough to learn more. The picture illustrates the text and seems to present the Monastery as it is. It provides users with a view of the interior of the landmark, as if this is what they would see if they were there. This subjective view is mainly emphasized by its close shot, eye level angle and absence of details. The building of the Monastery is depicted only by its access stairs; users do not get to see how it looks like as a whole. The connotation of the stairs and the limited view of the building can be understood as an invitation to go in and discover it.

The multimodal communicative act mainly informs and illustrates, as it anticipates to the users what is there to see. Persuasive argumentation is indirect and backgrounded. The description of the Monastery focuses on its components, architectural details or paintings, in few words on "Brancovenesti" art, its fame and its international influence. This is the uniqueness of the landmark. Interestingly, though, the Monastery appears as a museum and not as a religious sanctuary; religion is never mentioned except for the name of the landmark and the nun in the picture. This cumulative aspect is aimed to add attractiveness; users can go to the Monastery of Horezu, see its church, visit its museum and sleep over. This is the indirect experience proposed by the Romanian Tourist Board.

## 7.1.2. The Dacian Fortresses of the Orastie Mountains in the institutional corpus

The section dedicated to the Dacian Fortresses of the Orastie Mountains is situated last on the list of Romanian World Heritage Sites. It follows the same layout as the one discussed previously: a title, a short identity card, a text and a picture, as indicated by Fig. 7-2.

Fig. 7-2 The Dacian Fortresses of the Orastie Mountains institutional webpage

**Dacian Fortresses of the Orastie Mountains**

*Location: Transylvania - Central Romania*
*Nearby large town: Hunedoara (15 miles northeast)*

Dating from the 1st centuries B.C. and A.D. and strewn from Orastie to Retezat Mountains, the Dacian and Roman fortresses recognized by UNESCO as World Heritage Sites are an archeologist's delight. Built as a defense ring around the capital of the Dacian kingdom, Sarmizegetusa, they indude the ruins of the fortresses at **Banita, Capalna, Costesti - Blidaru, Costesti - Cetatuie, Luncani - Piatra Rosie,** as well as pre-Roman Dacian capital **(Sarmisegetuza)**.

The fortresses show an unusual fusion of military and religious architectural techniques and concepts from the classical world and the late European Iron Age. The six defensive sites, the nudeus of the Dacian Kingdom, were conquered by the Romans at the beginning of the 2nd century A.D.; their extensive and well-preserved remains stand in spectacular natural surroundings and give a dramatic picture of a vigorous and innovative civilization. At Sarmisegetuza you can still see the remains of the forum and the elliptical brick and stone amphitheatre where gladiator shows were held.

Hiking enthusiasts can enjoy the trails in the nearby Retezat National Park, the oldest in Romania (established 1935). Covering 95,000 acres of pristine forests, alpine meadows, peaks, and some 80 glacial lakes, the area was designated as a UNESCO Biosphere Reservation and provides unforgettable hiking experiences among its peaks, valleys, rivers and gorges.

**Note:** The area is best explored during the summer season with proper hiking equipment and directions.

*Source:* Romania Tourism (2011)

### 7.1.2.1. Linguistic analysis

*Overview*. As in the previous Romanian webpage, the text is divided into three paragraphs: the first describes the cultural asset by setting it in time and presenting its components; the second takes the characterization into further detail and highlights the ruins that can still be seen. The third paragraph changes the topic announced in the title and introduces another attraction in the area: Retezat National Park, the park depicted in the picture from the header of the home page. It even includes a note with advice on when to visit the area. The inclusion of various landmarks may aim to stir users' curiosity and convince them that the area offers more than one attraction. But, it can also distract them from the main topic, the Dacian Fortresses, and, thus, confuse them.

*Logical.* The text presenting the Dacian Fortresses of the Orastie Mountains is medium long and syntactically developed. Its complexes of three and four clauses make the text complex and difficult to read, as for example in "*Dating from the 1st centuries B.C. and A.D. and strewn from Orastie to Retezat Mountains*, the Dacian and Roman fortresses *recognized by UNESCO as World Heritage Sites* are an archeologist's delight" (Romania Tourism 2011). The high number of appositions ("Hiking enthusiasts can enjoy the trails in the nearby Retezat National Park, *the oldest in Romania*") and non-defining relative clauses, most of them non-finite, as underlined in the first example above, also raises complexity. So much detail makes the information load too high for a single unit. Clause complexes are slightly more frequent than simplex. They are composed by both hypotaxis and parataxis, in almost equal numbers. Hypotaxis elaborates on the information presented, adding different details, like the temporal and spatial extent of the fortresses ("*Dating from the 1st centuries B.C. and A.D. and strewn from Orastie to Retezat Mountains*, the Dacian and Roman fortresses [...] are an archeologist's delight"). Parataxis, on the other hand, develops the text by extension as it adds similar information, e.g. "the area was designated as a UNESCO Biosphere Reservation *and* provides unforgettable hiking experiences among its peaks, valleys, rivers and gorges". This can lighten a little the compact text and make it easier to read.

*Experiential.* Relational processes are the most frequent in the text. The fortresses are equally identified and described, especially in terms of circumstances. They are identified as showing "an unusual fusion of military and religious techniques and concepts from the classical world and the late European Iron Age" or as including "the ruins" of various fortresses. Described as "an archaeologist delight", the fortresses are also situated in time, "dating from the 1st centuries B.C. and A.D.", and place, "strewn from Orastie to Retezat Mountains". Their ruins are presented as still "standing in spectacular natural surroundings". The other attraction in the area, Retezat National Park, is also described mainly by relational processes. Identified as "covering 95,000 acres of pristine forests, alpine meadows, peaks, and some 80 glacial lakes" and providing "unforgettable hiking experiences", it is attributed the designation of "UNESCO Biosphere Reservation". This award certifies its qualities and makes it more interesting. The inclusion of numbers and the enumeration of all the fortresses assign objectivity to the message. This is further indicated by the instances of material processes. They present historical data related to the past of both the fortresses and the park. Mental processes also appear a few times and are related to the visitor; s/he can "see" some ruins, like the forum or the amphitheatre, and, at the same time, "enjoy" the trails in the park. Here is the moment in the text when the two objectives in the area are united as a sole one, by means of the visitor, who is promised both knowledge and amusement. These types of processes make the experience more real (Barker and Galasinki 2001, 71). The background information is provided mainly by locative circumstances, which create the scene and situate the events in time, "at the beginning of the 2nd century A.D.", and place, "at Sarmisegetuza". There are also several instances of other types of circumstances, which point to past roles of the fortresses, "as a defense ring around the capital of the Dacian kingdom, Sarmizegetusa", and to the best way to explore the park, i.e. "with proper hiking equipment and directions".

The participants observed are more realized than implied. The landmark is much more present than the visitor, whereas the promoter is totally absent. The fortresses are more realized, being involved in a variety of roles, from Actor ("and [*their extensive and well-preserved remains]* give a dramatic picture of a vigorous and innovative civilization") to Phenomenon ("At Sarmisegetuza you can still see *the remains of the forum and the elliptical brick and stone amphitheatre where gladiator shows were held*"). Their most frequent role is, however, that of Carrier, as the entity described in the text, e.g. "*their extensive and well-preserved remains* stand in spectacular natural surroundings". The park and its hiking trails, on the other hand, are referred to as Identifier and Goal, as they identify the area, "and [the area] provides *unforgettable hiking experiences* among its peaks, valleys, rivers and gorges", and can be explored by visitors, "*The area* is best explored during the summer season with proper hiking equipment and directions". The visitor is rarely present in the text; s/he is both expressed and implied in almost equal instances. When realized, the role is that of Senser, s/he is the one who can "see the remains" and "enjoy the trails". When implied, the role is that of Actor, indirectly suggested as explorer of the area by a passive construction, which is shown in the previous example. Users are addressed directly, by a second person pronoun, in order to involve them and make them feel close (Garcia Álvarez 2006, 83). They are also referred to by a more general term, as "hiking enthusiasts", which probably aims to identification.

*Interpersonal*. The text presents information only by declaratives. As statements, these are to be considered and interpreted as such, as fact. The Mood element contains mainly Subject and Finite, except for two cases of Subject ellipsis ("the area was designated as a UNESCO Biosphere Reservation and *[ø]* provides unforgettable hiking experiences among its peaks, valleys, rivers and gorges"). The fortresses occupy the position of Subject more frequently than the park or the visitor. This is expected, as it is the topic of the text. Taken together, the attractions of the area (the fortresses and the park) are always placed in Subject position, with the exception of the visitor who also appears twice. The Finite is almost with equal frequency both fused, "provides", and expressed, "was", and is mainly in the universal present. The generic message is balanced by the Finites expressed by passivization and modalization. Passivization draws attention to the Subject, whereas modalization mitigates the assertive message. The modal "can" is related only to visitors and presents information as possibility or offer. The visitors have the possibility to see the remains of the forum and enjoy the trails of the nearby park; they can explore the area and verify the facts by themselves. The little modality and the absence of polarity make information more evident (Mocini 2009, 160).

The Residue is complex and includes many Circumstantial Adjuncts, like "among its peaks, valleys, rivers and gorges", though this is surprising considering the high number of relational processes. They contribute to the complexity of the text since they add length to the phrase (Banks 2002, 7). The only instance of Mood Adjunct, the adverb "still", highlights that, even if very ancient, several remains can be seen. It appears in the clause that addresses users directly and it may reflect the intrusion of the voice of the writer in the text. This intrusion can be felt also in the end, in the last sentence, i.e. "Note: The area is best explored during the summer season with proper hiking equipment and directions". The note may be possibly understood as advice from the expert Tourist Board who suggests the best time and way to explore the area. This construction reminds users of the structure of guidebooks (Calvi 2006, 36).

*Textual*. The text contains mainly unmarked and simple Themes, expressed by participants. Their nominalised form, e.g. "The six defensive sites, the nucleus of the Dacian Kingdom", makes the message read as objective (Francis and Kramer-Dahl 1991, 354). There are also many instances of marked and enhanced Themes, in which case, preposed attributives are placed in Theme position, as found in the text on the Monastery of Horezu. The degree of markedness is high as there are even two coordinate dependent clauses as Theme, e.g. "*Dating from the 1st centuries B.C. and A.D. and strewn from Orastie to Retezat Mountains, the Dacian and Roman fortresses recognized by UNESCO as World Heritage Sites* are an archeologist's delight". The Theme in this particular case contains an interpolation, being almost two lines long. Although detailed and informative, this can be confusing, like too much information in a structure. Cohesion is achieved by the frequent continuous Thematic pattern. The risk of sounding redundant and boring seems to be solved by Subject ellipsis and synonyms like "the Dacian and Roman fortresses", "they", "the six defensive sites" or different components like "their extensive and well-preserved remains". Also the introduction of new Themes contributes to this diversity. Totally new Themes draw attention to the place of Sarmisegetuza or to the hiking enthusiasts, shifting the focus from the fortresses. The shift of topic can also disrupt the message or assume that readers know that new piece of information.

The lexico-grammatical summary of the text is presented in Table 7-3.

**Table 7-3 Institutional Dacian Fortresses of the Orastie Mountains: Lexico-grammatical summary**

| Clause complex | Transitivity | Mood | Theme |
|---|---|---|---|
| medium long<br>+ complexes (2 & 3 cl.)<br>only expansion<br>almost = hypotaxis & parataxis<br>almost = elaboration & extension<br>+ non-defining relatives<br>+ apposition | + relational<br>= identifying & attributive<br>+ circumstantial<br>mental, perception & affection<br>+ realized particip.<br>+ landmark<br>+ landmark (realized)<br>+ landmark (implied)<br>+ Carrier (landmark)<br>expressed Senser, implied Actor(visitor)<br>- promoter<br>various Circs.,<br>+ location, = time & place | = mood & residue<br>only complex residue<br>+ landmark as Subject<br>almost = fused & expressed Finite<br>+ present<br>+ Circ. Adjuncts<br>only modalization<br>- polarity<br>only declarative<br>only statements | almost = unmarked & marked<br>+ simple<br>+ participants as Theme<br>+ continuous progression |

### 7.1.2.2. Visual analysis

The picture chosen as representative for the Dacian Fortresses depicts some ruins, probably those of the amphitheatre mentioned in the text. The aerial and panoramic image provides users with a bird's eye view, which can aim to include the entire ruins and transmit a clear and general message. Part of a conceptual structure, the process is symbolic attributive; the ruins, as Symbolic Attributes, stand for the Carrier, the Dacian Fortresses. The fortresses cannot be represented as they are, since they do not exist anymore. The analysis can go further and indicate a secondary narrative structure. The white channel crossing the grass can form a non-transactional action. In this case, the ruins, the only participants in the picture, act as Actors, as if they just stand there.

Presented for contemplation, the picture is a close shot that depicts the ruins from frontal and panoramic high angles. The objectivity of the panoramic and aerial angle is counterbalanced by the involvement indicated by the close and frontal shot. The high angle gives power to users to look down on the ruins, as if the past can be seen from the power of the present. Users have also the power to imagine how the construction looked like approximately two thousand years ago. The modality markers depict the image as possible; the low markers seem to work together in order to emphasise the ruins, by means of colour saturation, contextualization or illumination.

The visual composition can be seen as structured along the dimensions of centre-margin; the channel and grass are central and the amphitheatre surrounds them, as if backgrounded. This is counterbalanced by its salience and framing, which emphasise its importance. The construction should probably, be considered as a whole. Table 7-4 includes the visual characteristics of the image.

**Table 7-4 Institutional Dacian Fortresses of the Orastie Mountains: Visual summary**

| Representational | Interactive | Compositional |
|---|---|---|
| complex<br>conceptual structure<br>symbolic attributive<br>fortresses (Carrier)<br>ruins of amphitheatre<br>(Symbolic Attributes)<br>narrative vector: ruins (Actor) | offer<br>close shot<br>subjective<br>frontal horizontal angle<br>panoramic high vertical<br>angle<br>+ low modality markers | centre-margin<br>ruins (salient)<br>ruins (framed) |

#### 7.1.2.3. Multimodal act

The multimodal act dedicated to the Dacian Fortresses of the Orastie Mountains presents a general view of the landmark. The text describes the fortresses from an apparently objective perspective. The pieces of information are introduced impersonally as facts and are backed up by various details, like the names of the fortresses or dates. It seems the message is descriptive and focused on the landmark until the point when enough information has been given to convince users. It is then, toward the end of the text, when it addresses users directly in order to establish a dialogue and make them feel important (Garcia Álvarez 2006, 83). They should be further impressed by the possibility to see such ancient sites today. The focus is shifted to a possible visit. If the ruins are not sufficiently interesting, a famous and special park situated nearby is introduced to convince users of a definitely enjoying experience. Taking a walk and hiking can attract users as they are rated as the most popular activities during vacation (Steinecke 2010, 188). Several features seem to indicate implied subjectivity, like the connotative attributes, the indirect interference of the copywriter, the association of visitors to perception and affection verbs or the modalized possibilities. The picture completes the message and maintains the general perspective of the verbal mode. The salient ruins stand for the fortresses and impress users by the lack of any further representation or detail. The involvement proposed seems to leave users the freedom to mentally construct a more real image, in which the ruins are replaced by the original constructions. It also confirms the antiquity of the landmark and stirs users' curiosity.

The message is mainly informative and is built around two main important aspects, aimed to seduce, i.e. history and nature. The landmark is ancient and important for the history of the country, not only from an archaeological perspective. The fact that parts of it can still be seen shows a relation between past and present and brings into the present the remains of mythic Dacian constructions mixed with Roman amphitheatres and forums. The park places the visit in "spectacular natural surroundings". The message seems quite clear: surrounded by nature and spectacular hiking trails, users can live a unique experience and try to imagine how the fortresses looked back in the 1st century BC.

### 7.1.3. Sighisoara in the institutional corpus

The section introducing the historic city of Sighisoara is a little bit longer than the previous ones, as can be observed in Fig. 7-3.

Fig. 7-3 Sighisoara institutional webpage

**Historic Centre of Sighisoara**

*Location: Transylvania - CentralRomania*
*Nearest train station: Sighisoara*
*www.RomaniaTourism.com/Sighisoara.html*

Founded by German craftsmen and merchants known as the Saxons of Transylvania, Sighisoara is a fine example of a small, fortified medieval town which played an important strategic and commercial role on the fringes of central Europe for several centuries.

Sighisoara, one of the most beautiful towns in the heart of Transylvania, looks today much as it did 500 years ago. This medieval town was also the birthplace of Vlad Dracula - nicknamed Vlad Tepes (Vlad the Impaler) - ruler of Walachia from 1456 to 1462. It was he who inspired Bram Stoker's fictional creation, Count Dracula. His house is just one of the many attractions here. Others include the Church on the Hill, with its 500-year old frescos; the Church of the Dominican Monastery, renown for its Renaissance carved altarpiece, baroque painted pulpit, Oriental carpets and 17th-century organ; and the Venetian House, built in the 13th century.

Among the most striking attractions is the 210-feet high Clock Tower (Council Tower), built in the 14th century, where each day a different wooden figure emerges from the belfry on the stroke of midnight. The tower was raised in the 13th and 14th centuries when Sighisoara became a free town controlled by craft guilds, each of which had to finance the construction of a bastion and defend it during wartime. The fortification walls, built in the 14th and 15th centuries, were up to 50-feet high and featured 14 defense towers. Most of the old structure and 9 of the defense towers can still be admired today... (more details)

*Source:* Romania Tourism (2011)

It has the same structure as the others; the only difference is that it offers a further link, to the same website, for a more detailed description of the city. If intrigued by this first part, users can choose to access it. If accessed, a webpage presenting a guide to the city appears. The words chosen for the link, "more details", are not very convincing and do not directly invite users to action. As there is no call to action, the Tourist Board seems to leave more freedom to users. The text contains also other links to various elements, like "Saxons of Transylvania" or "Clock Tower"; the majority lead to the page specially dedicated to the city, mentioned earlier.

### 7.1.3.1. Linguistic analysis

*Overview*. In line with the other texts, the information is organised in paragraphs. The first one briefly describes the city, in order to attract attention, the second describes its history and names some of the attractions, whereas the last paragraph focuses on only one attraction, the Clock Tower and its history.

*Logical.* The text presenting the Romanian city of Sighisoara is medium long, syntactically developed and complex. The long sentences, of up to four clauses, can be too complicated for many readers to follow, for example "The tower was raised in the 13th and 14th centuries when Sighisoara became a free town controlled by craft guilds, each of which had to finance the construction of a bastion and defend it during wartime". They are mainly organized in clause complexes. There are a large number of clause simplexes, like "His house is just one of the many attractions here" (Romania Tourism 2011). This may balance the complexity and make the message clearer. The relation between clauses is mainly one of hypotaxis-elaboration. Information is added, like in the other texts in this set, by reduced non-defining relative clauses, e.g. "The fortification walls, *built in the 14th and 15th centuries*, were up to 50-feet high". Their high number indicates a tendency to compact information (Gotti 2008, 94). To this end, there are many appositions that postmodify nouns ("Sighisoara, *one of the most beautiful towns in the heart of Transylvania*, looks today …"). Again, the text can become difficult to follow, due to compactness. A few instances of parataxis extend information by means of addition, as for instance in "The fortification walls, […], were up to 50-feet high *and* featured 14 defense towers".

*Experiential*. The text mainly presents information by relational processes, as expected from the type of text. The identifying and attributive processes have the same frequency and present Sighisoara and its attractions to the users. Identified as "the birthplace of Vlad Dracula ruler of Walachia from 1456 to 1462", the city houses several attractions like "the Church on the Hill", "the Venetian House" or "the Clock Tower". The description of Sighisoara as "a fine example of a small, fortified medieval town", which "looks today much as it did 500 years ago", is linked to its past and the history of the craft guilds. The identifying relational processes seem to be used to depict the city in the present, whereas the attributive ones tell its past. The material processes, like "found" and "build", are also numerous and refer to historical facts related to the city, its towers and fortification walls. By these, the message becomes more objective (Barker and Galasinki 2001, 71). There is also an instance of mental process, which highlights that "most of the old structure" "can still be admired today", as if addressing users. There are a large number of circumstances, as predicted by the number of material processes; location represents once again the most numerous type. The contextualization of events is done mainly in time and specifies the dates of construction of different attractions, such as "in the 13th century", making the description more authentic. The other types of circumstances found, like extent in time, "during wartime", and cause, "for its Renaissance carved altarpiece, baroque painted pulpit, Oriental carpets and 17th-century organ", are rare.

The participants observed are more realized than implied, as in all the texts so far. The landmark is more frequently realized than the visitor, whereas the promoter is not present at all. When realized, the landmark plays the role of Identifier, as the text identifies the attractions of the city, e.g. "the birthplace of Vlad Dracula". Interestingly, in the rare cases when it is implied, the landmark changes the role and is referred to as Goal, as the entity on which several actions were performed in the past, e.g. "[*the city* was] Founded by German craftsmen and merchants". This can mean that, even if the city appears to be the Subject of description, it actually is the product of others' actions. Considering all the instances, Sighisoara and its attractions play various roles in almost equal proportions, i.e. Goal, Carrier and Identifier, as expected from the processes' analysis. The visitor appears only once in the role of a generic Senser; s/he is implied by a passive construction as the possible admirer of the city ("Most of the old structure and 9 of the defense towers can still be admired today …"). This can sound like an indirect invitation. Generality makes the experience atemporal and valid for everybody (Banks 2002, 6). The absence of the promoter highlights the objectivity and impersonality of the message.

*Interpersonal*. The mood in the text on the city of Sighisoara is declarative, like in the other texts in the set. Information is presented as fact; there is no room for negotiation. The number of Mood and Residue components is equal. The Mood component is built by Subject and Finite, except for one instance of Subject ellipsis. The Subject is mainly Sighisoara, its attractions and components. In a few other cases, the Subject position is occupied by one of the city's most famous associations, Vlad Dracula. The Finites are usually fused, like "is" and "featured", providing a generic tone to the message (Banks 2002, 6). The tense expressed is almost equally balanced between present and past, as there is a combination between the description of Sighisoara today and in the past. The past seems to be used to enchant; the combination of Vlad Dracula, the bastion and fortification walls can add mystery or suspense to the city. At the end of this mysterious description of the past, the present is used again to highlight that this is real and that some pieces of evidence, for example ruins, "can still be admired today". The last clause is the only instance of modalization in the text; the user is offered the opportunity to admire the past. The lack of modality and negation confer to the message the feature of straightforward evidence (Mocini 2009, 160).

The Residue is always complex as it contains its usual elements. The Adjuncts are more varied than in the other texts. The Circumstantial ones, part of the Residue, are not very numerous, which is unexpected given the high number of material processes and circumstances encountered. Probably, the background information is provided in the secondary clauses and not in the main ones considered for the mood analysis. The Mood Adjuncts, part of the Mood element, seem to indicate the copywriter's interference in the text by adding judgements to the information presented. The adverb "just" intensifies the presence of many other attractions in the city; Dracula's house is only one of them. The adverb "still", on the other hand, highlights the fact that, even if the constructions are from the 14$^{th}$ and 15$^{th}$ centuries, part of them exists in the present. There is also a Conjunctive Adjunct, outside both Mood and Residue components, which adds cohesion to the text and links Sighisoara to the birthplace of Vlad Dracula, e.g. "This medieval town was *also* the birthplace of Vlad Dracula".

*Textual*. This text is different from the other texts in the Romanian institutional set, in that it is mainly built by unmarked Themes, which contribute to the objectivity of the message (Francis and Kramer-Dahl 1991, 354). Participants are usually placed in Theme position, presenting the city or its attractions and components as a point of departure for the message, as for instance in "*Most of the old structure and 9 of the defense towers* can still be admired today". The only instance of marked Theme is the first clause, where Sighisoara is preceded by an attributive clause indicating its founders. This marked and enhanced Theme can be used to contextualise the city, "founded by German craftsmen and merchants". Users' attention is drawn also to other elements in Theme position, like "Vlad Dracula" and "the fortification walls", by enhancement or interpolation. The repetition of the landmark in Theme position is balanced by synonyms and part-whole relations, like "this medieval town", "among the most striking attractions" or "the fortification walls". Thematic choices are varied by the use of linear progression, which is as frequently used as the continuous pattern. It picks up new elements from Rhemes, like "Vlad Dracula" or "attractions", and constructs the message cumulatively ("His house is just one of the many *attractions* here. *Others* include the Church on the Hill …").

**Table 7-5 Institutional Sighisoara: Lexico-grammatical summary**

| Clause complex | Transitivity | Mood | Theme |
|---|---|---|---|
| medium long<br>+ complexes<br>(3 cl.)<br>only expansion<br>+ hypotaxis<br>+ elaboration<br>+ non-defining<br>relatives<br>+ apposition | + relational<br>causative constr.<br>= identifying &<br>attributive<br>+ intensive<br>many material<br>only mental percept.<br>+ realized<br>participants<br>+ landmark<br>only landmark<br>(realized)<br>+ landmark (implied)<br>almost = Goal &<br>Carrier & Identifier<br>(landmark)<br>only Senser (only<br>implied) (visitor)<br>- promoter<br>various Circs.,<br>+ location, + time | = mood &<br>residue<br>only complex<br>residue<br>+ landmark as<br>Subject<br>+ fused Finite<br>almost = present<br>& past<br>+ Circ. Adjuncts<br>only<br>modalization<br>- polarity<br>only declarative<br>only statements | + unmarked<br>+ simple<br>+ participants as<br>Theme<br>= continuous &<br>linear patterns |

### 7.1.3.2. Visual analysis

The image chosen to represent Sighisoara depicts the Clock Tower, accompanied by Dracula's nearby house, both mentioned in the text. The Tower is easily recognizable and so recalls the city to viewers. The structure is again conceptual, unstructured analytical. The city is the Carrier, while the Clock Tower and the house of birth of Vlad Dracula are the Possessive Attributes. The elements depicted are representative for the city and can be considered symbols. Apart from these buildings, several persons appear in the picture as part of the city, as visitors. This confers a human touch and makes the picture more real and so reliable. It is as if the photographer is there among them, taking the picture and going towards the tower. The viewers may even identify with the visitors.

Regarding the interactive metafunction, the picture is once again an offer, presented from a subjective perspective. Both social distance and angles can be regarded in two ways, depending on the monument focused. If the tower is considered, the shot is medium and the angles are frontal and low. If Dracula's house is considered, the shot is close and the angles are oblique and low. The focus of the picture seems, however, to be on the tower, as it is more famous and recognisable than the house, which looks like any other. The relation created is medium close and involved. The buildings are positioned as more powerful, standing there majestic in front of the viewer/visitor. The interplay of the modality markers, which tend to be medium, presents the picture as real. The exception is the lack of a detailed contextualization, which contributes to the subjective perspective.

The picture follows no compositional structure; it just presents the buildings as they are. This makes it more real, as if not prepared in advance. The tower and the house stand out and are salient due to their colours. The tower looks even framed by the blue of the sky and the yellow of the house. The eye seems to follow the path to the tower and stop on it, especially on its clock and roof.

**Table 7-6 Institutional Sighisoara: Visual summary**

| Representational | Interactive | Compositional |
|---|---|---|
| simple<br>conceptual structure<br>unstructured analytical<br>city (Carrier)<br>Clock Tower, Dracula's house & visitor (Possessive Attrib.)<br>+ humans | offer<br>close & medium shot<br>subjective<br>frontal & oblique<br>horizontal angle<br>low vertical angle<br>+ medium modality markers | - information structure<br>tower & house (salient)<br>tower (framed) |

### 7.1.3.3. Multimodal act

The description of Sighisoara is built around the idea that the city retains the appearance it had in the past, as if time had stood still. Referred to from the beginning of the text, this medieval appearance signals to the users the possibility to experience something special. The past is further combined with legend in order to attract. The name of Dracula adds mystery to the city; the possibility to visit his house stirs curiosity and instigates to action, as if it would be possible to enter another world.

Described as a "beautiful" city, Sighisoara has many attractions to offer. Each of them is briefly described by the details that make it unique in order to augment the attractiveness of the place. The presentation of a group of attractions makes web users more interested (Jansen-Verbeke and Lievois 2002, 94). The attention moves from general to particular and focuses on one of "the most striking attractions", the Clock Tower. This is described in relation to its history and function. The fact that most of its structure can be still admired nowadays contributes to the special experience offered by Sighisoara. This presentation aims to convince by its objectivity and impersonality. Verifiable information on the city is enumerated in order to provide a complete picture. Backed up by data, the attractions are mainly related to the past. The persuasive argumentation is hidden in the story-like atmosphere, the numerous attributes, the Mood Adjuncts or the affection process "admire". This indirectness is suggested also by the wordings of the link to further details. The picture comes to attest the uniqueness of the city by illustration. It is subjective, not presenting a general panoramic view, but focussing on the main attractions presented by the text, the Clock Tower and Dracula's house. The close shot and the presence of people engage the users and make them identify with the tourists depicted.

The communicative act primarily presents and illustrates. Users are informed about the main attractions, which are enumerated like a must-see list. They are invited indirectly to step into the past and admire them. The proposal seems to be special and to guarantee intrigue and enjoyment.

### 7.1.4. Discussion of the Romanian set of institutional webpages

The Romanian institutional website states its aim and identity clearly from the beginning, i.e. help travellers who want to visit or to find more information about Romania. This statement seems to add more reliability to the content to follow. The choice of words and the layout of the initial message situate users in need for help and the Tourist Board in position of the expert counsellor willing to help. The content and navigational options are communicated by two menu bars and detailed later on, towards the end of the home page, with the danger of sounding redundant. The short, attractive and transparent home page prefers a composite structure with self-contained blocks of information, mostly arranged on columns. It appears to develop more on the logical level, as it introduces the users to the general content of the site (Garzone 2009, 36). The reading of this fragmented information can be guided by the red titles and the pictures breaking the monotony of the page (OMT 2001, 113). The webpage dedicated to the World Heritage Sites (WHS) in Romania does not follow the layout of the home page, except for the header. Its design gives more attention to navigational aspects so that they offer easy and quick ways to get to important sections (OMT 2001, 94; 2005b, 9; Miller 2011, 85), preventing users from wasting time. The sections of the webpage analysed are arranged traditionally: title, text and picture, following the layout of typical printed pages of text (Lemke 2002). They are, however, short, as if the printed material is adapted to fit computer screens (Garzone 2009, 50). This can be risky because big blocks of text can result unattractive and difficult to read and can require a greater mental effort from users than other forms of transmitting information (OMT 2001, 113); users can leave the page if not sufficiently curious or interested. Sites with great content, but little design sensitivity, may not always work (Morgan and Pritchard 2000, 325).

The message seems to be transmitted mainly verbally, as the main information is provided textually by topics and words, chunks of texts being favoured over pictures. The interactive aspect is also kept to minimum; the few options of the home page to check offers, read expert opinions or access links to social networks and videos are reduced to only a link to an airline association on the WHS webpage. The Romanian institutional website does not seem to take the most advantage of "the affordances offered by the hypermedia environment" (Garzone 2009, 41).

The aim of the message is informative; it introduces the attraction, presents its background and describes it. Its sections present cultural, historical and artistic details about the three landmarks proposed; various components build their attractiveness. The components of the landmark and the attractions chosen seem also to orient the users' view, as if shaping it by pre-established must-see's and aesthetic judgments (Calvi 2006, 35; Mapelli and Piccioni 2011, 64; Pérez Vázquez 2011, 307). Persuasion is most of the time indirect. Hidden in an objective, factual and impersonal description, the narration of events from ancient history or the allusion to the legend of Count Dracula raises users' interest. They can be attracted by the possibility to live a moment in the past or to confirm the reality of a myth. From an AIDA perspective, Attention is stirred by the title and the photo, whereas Interest is maintained by the short visiting card and the presentation of information. Desire is stimulated indirectly by the possibility to see the items described. The call to Action is almost absent, except for the implied suggestion offered by the link to more information from the message dedicated to Sighisoara; practical and transactional details are almost inexistent.

The language of the sections analysed reflect the predominant informative purpose. The texts seem well structured to fulfil their goals as they are medium long, complex, syntactically elaborated and organized in short paragraphs. They usually develop by clause complexes; hypotactic relations link the clauses in dependent ways in order to present the details as subsidiary to the main message. Thus, information is provided as secondary and compacted by the reduced non-defining relative clauses, a technique frequently encountered in tourism and advertising discourse (Gotti 2008, 94). The relational processes focus on description and presentation and situate the landmarks circumstantially in time and place. As indicated by Table 7-7, material processes are sometimes used to present the historical facts objectively and situate them spatially and temporally. The landmark and its components appear mostly in the role of Carrier as the entity described and characterised in Subject/Theme position. The visitor is absent, except for several indirect implications as generic Senser, as the one who sees, enjoys or admires. The role chosen for the visitor and the words indicating it are quite connotative, as if trying to persuade in an indirect, but sensory way. The Tourist Board does not appear at all; the message is transmitted in an impersonal tone. The dominance of statements, the little modality and the absence of polarity contribute to the intended objectivity of the message and confer it further factual and evident characteristics (Mocini 2009, 160). The preference for fused and present Finites projects the message as generic and timeless (Banks 2002, 6). The focus on the landmark is emphasised by the regular choice of a continuous Thematic pattern. Nonetheless, the landmark shares protagonism with various spatial and temporal details that accompany it in frequent marked combinations for a more conspicuous and dramatic attention (Greenbaum and Nelson 2002, 212).

**Table 7-7 Romanian set of institutional websites: Lexico-grammatical summary**

| System | The Monastery of Horezu | The Dacian Fortresses of the Orastie Mountains | Sighisoara |
|---|---|---|---|
| Clause complex | short<br>+ complexes (2 cl.)<br>only expansion<br>only hypotaxis<br>only elaboration<br>+ non-defining relatives | medium long<br>+ complexes (2&3cl.)<br>only expansion<br>almost = hypotaxis & parataxis<br>almost = elaboration & extension<br>+ non-defining rel. | medium long<br>+ complexes (3 cl.)<br>only expansion<br>+ hypotaxis<br>+ elaboration<br>+ non-defining relatives<br>+ apposition |

| System | The Monastery of Horezu | The Dacian Fortresses of the Orastie Mountains | Sighisoara |
|---|---|---|---|
| | | + apposition | |
| Transitivity | + relational<br>+ attributive<br>= intensive & circumstantial & possessive<br>only mental percep.<br>+ realized particip. (little dif.)<br>only landmark<br>only landmark (realized)<br>only landmark (implied)<br>+ Carrier (landmark)<br>- visitor<br>- promoter<br>various Circs.,<br>+ location, = time & place | + relational<br>= identifying & attributive<br>+ circumstantial<br>mental, perception & affection<br>+ realized participants<br>+ landmark<br>+ landmark (realized)<br>+ landmark (implied)<br>+ Carrier (landmark)<br>expressed Senser, implied Actor (visitor)<br>- promoter<br>various Circs.,<br>+ location, = time & place | + relational<br>causative constr.<br>= identifying & attributive<br>+ intensive<br>many material<br>only mental percep.<br>+ realized participants<br>+ landmark<br>only landmark (realized)<br>+ landmark (implied)<br>almost = Goal & Carrier & Identifier (landmark)<br>only Senser (only implied) (visitor)<br>- promoter<br>various Circs.,<br>+ location, + time |
| Mood | = mood & residue<br>+ complex residue<br>+ landmark as Subject<br>only fused Finite<br>+ present<br>only Circ. Adjuncts<br>- modality<br>- polarity<br>only declarative,<br>+ full<br>only statements | = mood & residue<br>only complex residue<br>+ landmark as Subject<br>almost = fused & expressed Finite<br>+ present<br>+ Circ. Adjuncts<br>only modalization<br>- polarity<br>only declaratives<br>only statements | = mood & residue<br>only complex residue<br>+ landmark as Subject<br>+ fused Finite<br>almost = present & past<br>+ Circ. Adjuncts<br>only modalization<br>- polarity<br>only declarative<br>only statements |
| Theme | almost = unmarked & marked<br>only simple<br>only participants as Theme<br>almost = multiple & continuous patterns & new Themes | almost = unmarked & marked<br>+ simple<br>+ participants as Theme<br>+ continuous progression | + unmarked<br>+ simple<br>+ participants as Theme<br>= continuous & linear patterns |

The visual message illustrates the verbal one; the pictures appear to present the landmarks as they really are. The inclusion of humans contributes to an impression of reality and reliability. It can also serve as persuasive technique to make users identify with them and become also part of the frame, i.e. visitors. This is further suggested by the close and medium shots that engage users. The images are offered for contemplation and present the landmarks as Carriers by means of conceptual structures. These are focused by saliency and framing. The absence of a particular preference for horizontal and vertical angles or for information structures can indicate the spontaneity of the pictures; they are not premeditated or modified, but seem to be chosen randomly to represent the Monastery, the Clock Tower and Dracula's house. This is not so clear with the ruins of the Dacian fortresses, which seem retouched in order to impress. Table 7-8 presents a summary of the analysis of the Romanian set.

**Table 7-8 Romanian set of institutional websites: Visual summary**

| System | The Monastery of Horezu | The Dacian Fortresses of the Orastie Mountains | Sighisoara |
|---|---|---|---|
| Representational | simple<br>conceptual structure<br>unstructured<br>analytical<br>monastery & background (Carrier)<br>component & surroundings (Possessive Attrib.)<br>+ humans | complex<br>conceptual structure<br>symbolic attributive<br>fortresses (Carrier)<br>ruins of amphitheatre (Symbolic Attrib.)<br>narrative vector: ruins (Actor) | simple<br>conceptual structure<br>unstructured<br>analytical<br>city (Carrier)<br>Clock Tower, Dracula's house & visitor (Possessive Attributes)<br>+ humans |
| Interactive | offer<br>close & medium shot<br>subjective<br>oblique horizontal angle<br>eye level vertical angle<br>+ medium modality markers | offer<br>close shot<br>subjective<br>frontal horizontal angle<br>panoramic high vertical angle<br>+ low modality markers | offer<br>close & medium shot<br>subjective<br>frontal & oblique horizontal angle<br>low vertical angle<br>+ medium modality markers |
| Compositional | - information structure<br>monastery & nun (salient)<br>diff. buildings of monument (framed) | centre-margin<br>ruins (salient)<br>ruins (framed) | - information structure<br>tower & house (salient)<br>tower (framed) |

To summarise, the communicative act in the Romanian institutional set is dominated by written text; the visual just highlights important points (Anthonissen 2003, 302). Both modes seem to be consistent with the informative aim of the message. From an objective and impersonal position, the verbal discourse describes, whereas the visual illustrates. The persuasive aspect is hidden in the description of the landmarks. The information is intended to be accurate and detailed so that users know what to expect if they visit. The following of the same layout and organization appears to add consistency to the aim and force to the institutional message. Romania is worth visiting, as it offers the possibility to admire unique paintings and constructions, to follow the steps of Dacians and Romans, to hike in a biosphere reservation among alpine meadows and glacial lakes or to experience a medieval atmosphere charged with myths and legends. These play around the key concepts presented initially in the home page: culture, authenticity and nature. The indirect proposal of the Romanian Tourist Board is one of fascination and enjoyment in a varied destination.

## 7.2. Spanish set of institutional webpages

The Spanish official tourism portal (http://www.spain.info/) has a short vertically organised home page. Apart from the header and footer, it has two main sections; they are easily recognisable due to their bright colour against the black background. The header, which is short, provides the possibility to choose from many languages and gives a number of links to different aspects of the website. The information offered is quite varied; the menu provides specific data on how to plan a trip ("Before you travel"), general information on Spain and the Tourist Board ("About Spain", "About us"), navigational details regarding the site's architecture ("Web map") and interactive contact information ("Newsletter", "Contact").

The first main section is taken up by a still from a video. This is the first thing users see when accessing the website. The video shot is used as a visual, since it contains also written elements. The visual depicts six men looking directly at the user; they are clearly players in the Spanish national team of basketball. The written text restates the identity of the group and highlights, by the existential construction, that "there is only one thing they like more than basketball: Spain" (Spain.info 2011). If played, the video shows basketball players, like Paul Gasol or Ricky Fernandez, saying what they like about Spain and recommending things to do. Sportsmen are used to promote the country; national icons give their image to a campaign in order to make it more believable, more interesting and better known, both for the national and international audience. Their relaxed and smiling posture and their placement facing the users make the message closer, more direct and less formal. The only written text is the existential clause mentioned before, which is placed in the left bottom part of the visual. It seems handwritten and introduced by an asterisk, as if it were a note or an explanation, probably of the picture of the men, as discussed before. There is no mention of the aim of the website or the Tourist Board.

Individual words appear, though, in the visual, disrupting the image of the basketball players. At the top left, the contents of the website, "Home", "Come", "Discover", "Enjoy", "Taste" and "Experience", are displayed horizontally. The direct address to the users by placing imperatives in the menu bar seems an interesting way to establish an initial dialogue and to exhort them to discover the website. The different colours of the words make them salient. There are five words and their meanings are related to emotions, they seem to refer to the five senses; the words appeal to emotion in order to attract the viewer. In other words, the message invites users to discover Spain through their five senses. On the same horizontal line, but to the right, there is the search box permitting users to go directly to the desired item. The last element in the visual is situated in the bottom right and contains half of a sun, whose rays are directed towards the players. Within the sun, there is the Tourist Board's logo and the campaign's slogan. This is the only visible element related to the Tourist Board. The abstract design of the logo, the work of the artist, Miró, known as the "sun of Miró", contains several circles, which remind users of the colours of the Spanish flag and the black of a bull-ring (Morgan and Pritchard 2000, 289), a black asterisk and the word "ESPANA". Next to it, the slogan "I need Spain" is personal and related to senses, as is the entire message so far. It stirs users' curiosity and urges them to find out the reasons for needing Spain. The first personal pronoun makes the phrase even more salient, as it is not directed to users and makes them wonder who this "I" refers to. It can stand for the Tourist Board, even for the sportsmen. Users are probably expected to identify with it. All these elements in the visual are salient and easily observable, due to their colours, position and form. The message here is built multimodally, by image, text and audio, so that the impact is guaranteed.

There is a clear division between the two vertical main sections in the page. A black strip follows the visual and contains four topics: "Spanish National Parks", "World Heritage Cities", "Wine Routes" and "Shopping in Spain". Each is accompanied by a small image representing the words, for example the national parks have an eagle or the wine routes a grape. This can imply a focus on multimodal communication–text and image as part of the same message. There is also a red strip, containing only the word Spain, written in white as if by hand, clearly emphasising that everything there is about Spain. Next, the other most important section on the home page is organised vertically in two columns, as typically in web writing (Garzone 2009, 38). The one on the left, wider and itself divided in two, provides users few ideas to start with. They are developed on the five topics mentioned in the visual. Each topic contains several links, laid out as a list, to tempt users. For example, under the heading "Come", the following ideas are included: "Seville for you", "Autumn break in Vitoria" or "Tarragona, a World Heritage city". They seem quite varied and promotional. After exploring the five topics, interactive information is presented by a list with some "Channels", like "Learning Spanish" or "Accessible Tourism", and a box with the most important searches, probably of other users. Another box invites users directly to take part and talk about their experiences in Spain or to connect to social networks and other multimedia tools. These show that the site is not limited to present information about the country; it frequently interacts with users regarding usual real-life situations, like learning a foreign language or communicating by social networks. The use of past tourists as a model makes information more reliable and their implication in promotion serves as marketing. The human aspect is also emphasised, as if their opinions and experiences matter to the site and to others. As for the right column of this section, it has more practical and interactive links, such as "Youtube Spain Channel", the possibility to win a trip to Spain and some advertisements for accommodation, resorts or senior holiday programmes.

The footer contains four links displayed horizontally: "Before you travel", "Weather", "Reserve accommodation on-line" and "Brochures", all related to specific information for a possible journey. If needed, "Brochures" can provide more detailed information on various Spanish destinations. Each link is accompanied by a symbol, like the sun for weather and a leaflet for brochures, relying, once again, on multimodal communicative acts. At the bottom of the page, outside the frame of the footer, on the black background exactly like the header, there is a text describing in few words the identity and aim of the owner of the website, Spain.info. This is the only place where the name of the Spanish Tourist Board appears.

Several features of the AIDA model can be recognised in the home page (OMT 2005b, 8). Attention is caught by the large picture of the basketball team. The abstract logo and the persuasive slogan have the same purpose. Several pictures indicate attractive characteristics, like national parks, heritage sites or wine routes. The navigational bar presents varied links to practical, navigational and interactional sections, but none to general information about the destination, the site and its content. Even if the information regarding the website's content is not obvious from the beginning, it becomes clearer in the second screenshot. Interest and Desire appear to be achieved simultaneously by the video, the sportsmen and the phrase related to them, the numerous ideas regarding visits and landmarks and the link to accommodation. These ideas are presented telegraphically, without any description to raise the interest and lead to desire, except their connotative wording. Maps and itineraries are also absent. The imperatives in the second navigational bar, like "discover" and "enjoy", and the interactive possibilities can incite to Action. More practical or commercial variants are non-existent.

### 7.2.1. The Monastery of El Escorial in the institutional corpus

The webpage introducing the Royal Monastery of San Lorenzo de El Escorial is constructed on the same vertical layout as the home page–picture at the top, text at the bottom. This advertising layout proposes the text and the practical data as real information, as needed to be known in order to get to the ideal information and visit the promised landmark. The large visual composed by the picture of the landmark comes after the header, which is the same as the one from the home page. Other elements composing the visual are: the word "Conoce" (discover), the navigational menu with the website's contents, the title in a bilingual version, the logo, the search box, the back button and a road map which gives the position of the Monastery. The use of maps makes information more complete (OMT 2001, 115) and gives geographical locations. The presence of the Spanish words facilitates a clearer identification of the cultural asset promoted, especially when accompanied by the English translation. They also confer an exotic touch to the messages (Garcia Álvarez 2006, 73).

The visual is followed by the textual section structured in two columns, like the initial home page; as if general information acts as given information and practical information as new. This alignment can indicate that the information on the landmark exists and is already known; what is new and interesting is the way to get there and visit it. The left side column contains the most important information and is further divided in three horizontal parts, separated by lines, as indicated in Fig. 7-4.

Fig. 7-4 The Monastery of El Escorial institutional webpage

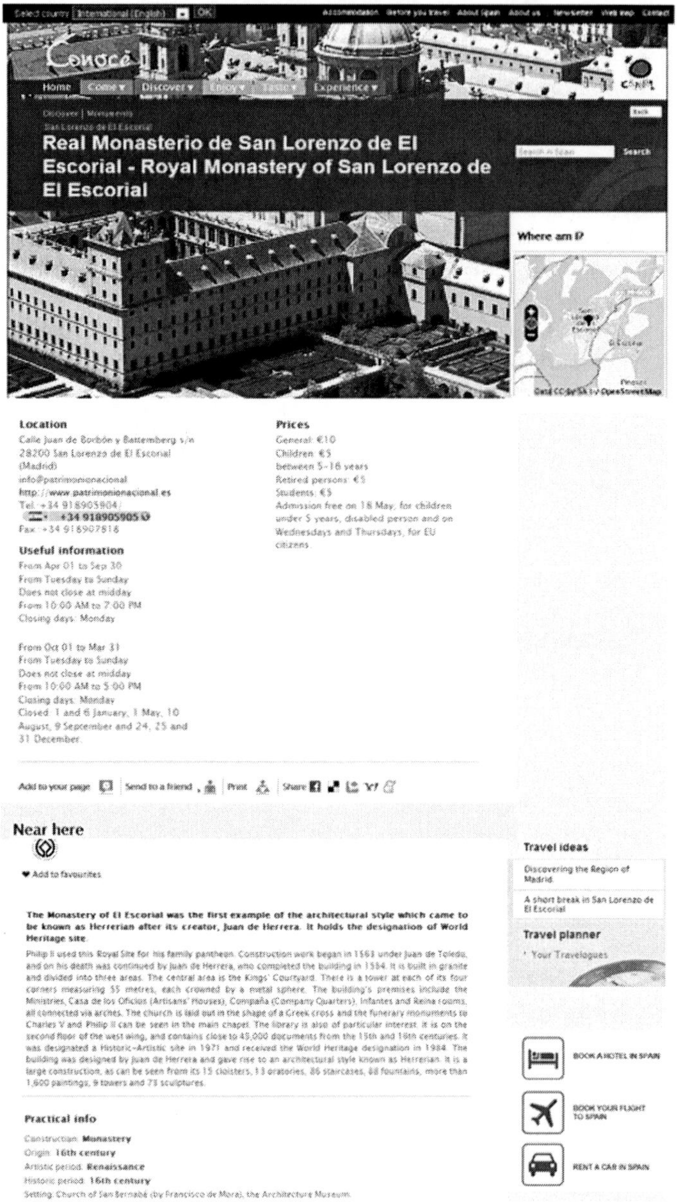


*Source:* Spain.info (2011)

The first part includes the logo of the UNESCO World Heritage Sites, a caption briefly describing the Monastery and a medium long text building on the description. The second section contains "Practical information" on the Monastery, regarding the type of construction, origin or artistic period. It appears like a technical identity card, since it is presented as a list and not as a text, and can be scanned for important details by those users not willing to read the longer text. Following the same layout, the last section of the verbal part offers more practical information necessary for the visit, like location (address, website and telephone), timetable and prices. The right-hand column is rather short and contains links to travel ideas in the area, like short breaks to the city where the Monastery is situated and links to booking accommodation and transport in Spain. The bottom of the webpage is interactive and offers the possibility to send the page to a friend, print it or share it online. The message does not stop here, but links are provided to nearby attractions, accommodation, restaurants, tourist offices and cultural visits, probably with the aim of convincing users by means of combined attractions. Furthermore, users can become members of a forum and/or join the Tourist Board in the promotional mission by sharing the webpage with others on the worldwide web.

Users' attention is drawn by numerous salient and framed elements. The salient ones are: the title, the image, the word "Conoce" (discover) in the visual, the caption in the text and the titles in the practical information section. The framed elements, instead, contribute to the fragmentation of information, presenting the navigational bars, the left side of the page and the section called "Near here" as separate and different from the main message.

#### 7.2.1.1. Linguistic analysis

*Overview.* The text analysed is part of the first horizontal section mentioned above and has been chosen for reasons explained in the Methodology chapter. The caption introduces the Monastery as the first example of Herrerian architectural style and as a World Heritage Site. The medium long text focuses on the Monastery's history, construction and components.

*Logical.* It is medium elaborated and medium complex due to the relatively high number of clause simplexes ("Philip II used this Royal Site for his family pantheon") and the low number of embedded clauses ("The Monastery of El Escorial was the first example of the architectural style *which came to be known as Herrerian after its creator, Juan de Herrera*"). The clause complexes are, though, more frequent and develop by both parataxis and hypotaxis, with a slight preference for the first. In the case of parataxis, the message extends by adding new information, as for example in "The church is laid out in the shape of a Greek cross *and the funerary monuments to Charles V and Philip II can be seen in the main chapel*" (Spain.info 2011). In hypotactic relations, information is elaborated by non-defining relative clauses that add more details to the description, like "There is a tower at each of its four corners *measuring 55 metres, each crowned by a metal sphere*". The pattern in the text is usually to introduce a component of the Monastery and develop it by adding information, which can sometimes be further elaborated by a non-defining relative clause, e.g. "Construction work began in 1563 under Juan de Toledo, *and on his death was continued by Juan de Herrera, who completed the building in 1584*". Information seems, thus, to be added rather than compacted.

*Experiential*. The Monastery of El Escorial is presented mainly by relational processes. It is usually identified, in different circumstances, by verbs such as "lay out" or "connect" ("The church *is laid out* in the shape of a Greek cross"). The presentation of its possessions or of what it "include[s]" and "contain[s]", as for example in "The building's premises include *the Ministries, Casa de los Oficios (Artisans' Houses), Compaña (Company Quarters), Infantes and Reina rooms*", plays also an important part in the Monastery's identification. Occasionally, the Monastery is characterised by various attributes like "particular interest" or "large construction". Material processes are also frequently used, as in "Construction work *began* in 1563 under Juan de Toledo", to present facts and details about the landmark objectively (Barker and Galasinki 2001, 71). There are few instances of other types of processes. The mental process "see" is used in the impersonal construction "as can be seen from" to convey validity and to testify ("It is a large construction, *as can be seen from* its 15 cloisters, 13 oratories, 86 staircases, 88 fountains, more than 1,600 paintings, 9 towers and 73 sculptures"). The construction reminds users also of a real tour, as if exemplifying certain facts and attractions presented. The existential process has the same purpose; it points to the composition of the central area called "Kings' Courtyard". The information is completed by background details, which are quite numerous despite the fact that the main process type is relational. Frequently used, locative circumstances focus more on temporal location than on spatial. The temporal specify different dates related to the Monastery's construction and its awards, "It was designated a Historic-Artistic site *in 1971*", whereas the spatial connect certain components in space, "It is *on the second floor of the west wing*". Few cases refer to the way in which the

Monastery is built and divided and to its functions, as for example in "It is built *in granite* and divided *into three areas*" and "Philip II used this Royal Site *for his family pantheon*". The text does not seem to focus on descriptions to refer to the landmark, but on circumstances; identifying relational processes provide spatial coordinates, whereas circumstances are centred on temporal location.

As expected, the landmark is the most present participant in the text. It is usually expressed and plays, almost in equal proportions, the role of Identified ("*The central area* is the Kings' Courtyard") and Goal ("*The building* was designed by Juan de Herrera"), roles already anticipated by the processes' analysis. It seems the landmark and its attractions are not only the topic of description, but also the past object of different actions, as indicated by the previous example. The possible visitor is never addressed or expressed. S/he is implied as a general Senser by the impersonal construction mentioned before; s/he can be the one to perceive and verify the information presented. The Tourist Board is totally absent, maybe because the text is intended to be an objective and impersonal description.

*Interpersonal*. The text dedicated to the Monastery of El Escorial is built by declaratives. The preferred speech role is the statement; the information about the Monastery is presented as such, as fact. The Mood component frequently has in Subject position the landmark, as the most important component of the clause. Passive forms contribute to the focus on the landmark, as for example in "*It* is built in granite". There are some instances of Subject ellipsis, which can be explained by the high number of clauses related by extension-addition ("It is on the second floor of the west wing, and *[ø]* contains close to 45,000 documents from the 15th and 16th centuries"). These can lead to a compact and cohesive message. The possible visitor is never placed in Subject position, which is expected, considering that s/he is not even overtly expressed in the text. The types of Finites place the action mainly in the present, e.g. "is" and "contains", as if assigning universality to the landmark (Banks 2002, 6). The past is, however, frequently used to describe the history of the Monastery and to provide historical associations, e.g. "was" and "gave". The Finites are usually fused, "is", as typical of generic messages (Banks 2002, 6), even though there are some cases when they are expressed by passive forms, "was designated", and modalization, "can be seen". Modality and polarity are scarcely used in the text. Because of this, information appears as evidence (Mocini 2009, 160). The only instance of modalization is expressed by the modal "can" and refers to the possibility or opportunity to confirm the details presented.

The Residue element is more numerous than the Mood, probably due to ellipsis. It is complex and includes all its usual components. The types of Adjuncts found are not varied; the majority are Circumstantial, "There is a tower *at each of its four corners*", and add meaning to the experiential aspect of the text, as predicted by the high number of circumstances. They also contribute to the length of the clauses (Banks 2002, 7) and, thus, to the complexity of the text.

**Table 7-9 Institutional Monastery of El Escorial: Lexico-grammatical summary**

| Clause complex | Transitivity | Mood | Theme |
|---|---|---|---|
| medium long<br>+ complex (3 cl.)<br>only expansion<br>almost =<br>parataxis &<br>hypotaxis<br>+ extension<br>+ non-defining<br>relatives<br>+ non-finite<br>clauses<br>+ apposition | + relational<br>+ identifying<br>+ circumstantial<br>existential<br>only mental percep.<br>+ realized particip.<br>+ landmark<br>only land. (realized)<br>+ landmark (implied)<br>+ Identified (land.)<br>only implied as<br>Senser (visitor)<br>- promoter<br>+ location, + time | + residue<br>only complex<br>residue<br>only landmark as<br>Subject<br>+ fused Finite<br>+ present<br>+ Circ. Adjuncts<br>only<br>modalization<br>- polarity<br>only declarative<br>+ full decl.<br>only statements | + unmarked<br>+ simple<br>+ participants as<br>Theme<br>+ continuous<br>progression |

*Textual*. The linguistic message develops usually by unmarked Themes, expressed by participants, like "*The library* is also of particular interest", indicating an objective message (Francis and Kramer-Dahl 1991, 354; Gotti 2008, 79). The only marked Theme has the form of a temporal circumstance and refers to the death of the Monastery's first founder ("and *on his death* was continued by Juan de Herrera"). Even if simple Themes dominate, there are several instances of multiple ones. Used to link ideas, the textual Themes, like "and", make the text more cohesive. The Thematic pattern is mainly continuous; the focalization is on the monument, as in "*The library* is also of particular interest. *It* is on the second floor of the west wing and *[it]* contains close to 45,000 documents from the 15th and 16th centuries". Instances of other types of development break this repetitive pattern. The multiple pattern introduces the Monastery's main areas: the King's Courtyard, the church and the library, which are further described ("It is built in granite and [it is] divided into *three areas*. *The central area* is the Kings' Courtyard. [...] *The church* is laid out in the shape of a Greek cross […]. *The library* is also of particular interest)". Attention is drawn to several new Themes, like "Philip II" or "the funerary monuments to Charles V and Philip II", which are further developed both continuously and cumulatively. These names are indicative of a glorious past when Spain dominated the world and had an empire on which the sun never set. As such, they can attract and impress. The text seems, thus, focused, elaborated and structured. However, the pronoun "it" and the noun phrase "building" are used rather excessively and can sometimes create confusion, their referent being ambiguous.

### 7.2.1.2. Visual analysis

The large photo representing the Monastery of El Escorial is taken from a panoramic and lateral high perspective. It does not encompass the entire monument, but just a part of its constructions and gardens. The representation seems hard to distinguish since the red rectangular box covers part of it and makes it look fragmented. Due to this, it may be difficult to identify the building as part of the Monastery. The representational structure is conceptual, since there is no vector to indicate action. The type of visual process is analytical; the elements in the image can be related in terms of part-whole structure. The Carrier is the Monastery as a whole, whereas the Possessive Attributes are represented by its different constructions and gardens. Since the way the parts fit together is not clearly presented, the analytical process can be considered unstructured. This is the only process represented; thus, the picture type is simple.

The image is presented to the viewer as an offer, as an object of contemplation. The shot is close, as if viewers are standing near the Monastery, so near that they cannot capture it entirely. As such, the perspective is subjective. This can be counterbalanced by the panoramic view, usually associated with objectivity (Matthiessen 2007, 57). The horizontal angle is oblique; the picture is not taken from the front, whichever that is. The vertical angle is high, probably to complete the close shot and enlarge the perspective. The relation established between participants is close, but detached; close enough to impress and attract, the Monastery gives the viewer the power to look down at it. Maybe the power is one of choice, the choice to look and go inside the frame. The modality markers oscillate between low and medium, presenting the picture as naturalistic up to a certain point. The Monastery is not represented completely and in the distance, as on a postcard, but very close and engaged, with a colour saturation and illumination that tends towards low modality. The lack of contextualization and the fragmented representation can also indicate low modality. The digitalisation of the picture can be indicated by the red strip, which draws attention to the name of the building. It stirs viewers' interest regarding what is behind the rectangular box and what the picture looks like as a whole. The picture could have been taken from a plane and with a high zoom. The possibility is, however, quite remote. The image producer seems to leave the reality of the picture aside and emphasise its impact on the viewer; the picture may impress by size, closeness and grandeur. It can also imply a sense of uniqueness, as the viewer will never see the monument from that position in real life.

As can be seen in Fig. 7-4, the picture does not follow any evident structure of information. The salient Monastery occupies the entire picture.

**Table 7-10 Institutional Monastery of El Escorial: Visual summary**

| Representational | Interactive | Compositional |
|---|---|---|
| simple<br>conceptual structure<br>unstructured analytical<br>monastery (Carrier)<br>component & garden<br>(Possessive Attributes) | offer<br>close shot<br>subjective<br>oblique horizontal angle<br>high vertical angle<br>= low & medium modality markers | - information structure<br>monastery (salient)<br>- framing |

### 7.2.1.3. Multimodal act

Long well-known as a cultural tourist destination (Precedo Ledo *et al.* 2007), the Monastery of El Escorial is presented multimodally by a layout which reminds users of advertising visual arrangements. The picture is presented as the promised product or the dream world. This is represented as the Monastery of El Escorial captured from a general, panoramic and detached position. The objective perspective is balanced by the visual appeal to senses. The Monastery is expected to stir interest and astonish by its size, placement and impressiveness. The impression of realism, the interplay of full colours and the uniqueness of the shot further play with the viewers' perception. On the other hand, the text is presented as describing the promised product. In fact, it presents a detailed account of the religious landmark, as if to compensate for the visual lack of detail caused by the red strip and the close shot. The information presented about the Monastery is true, objective, generic, timeless, impersonal and reliable. The landmark is shown as it is in the present, photographically, without any manipulation or interference from the Tourist Board, as if the facts are left to speak for themselves. The "postcard painting"-like (Calvi 2006, 36) description goes from general to particular and focuses on several of the Monastery's constructions, like the Kings' Courtyard, the church, the funerary monuments and the library. As if enumerated on a list of must-sees, each of them is briefly identified in terms of architecture, composition or function, in other words, its unique characteristics that build the attractiveness of the landmark. The characteristics are testified as real by the inclusion of historical dates and numbers. The data also shows the Monastery's relation to a glorious history and its still present grandeur. The historical facts act as identifiers that define the Monastery and its components and aim to impress and draw users' attention. The components of the Monastery are connected by various spatial details; their position seems to build a mental description of the landmark, more specific than the one in the picture.

The communicative act mainly informs. The picture introduces the monument by a general caption and indirectly appeals to senses and perceptions. Once users are attracted by the picture, the text comes to convince them of the monument's grandeur, as presented in the picture, by a detailed, impersonal and objective description. The lack of any instructional, interactional or commercial detail can further emphasise the apparent objectivity of the message; this is the monument and there is no lucrative aim to describe it in other ways than it actually is. The Tourist Board plays no part, except as communicator of the message. The same can be said about the visitor; s/he is just a mere spectator, neither appealed to nor involved in by the text.

### 7.2.2. The Alhambra in the institutional corpus

Following the same layout like the previous described page, the webpage introducing the Alhambra is composed on a vertical axis by a visual and a verbal section. The text contains both general and practical information. Attention is drawn to the already typical salient elements of the Spanish webpages: the picture, the logo, the navigational menu, the practical information and the travel ideas. Several differences exist, though, in the layout, but none significant. The visual contains additionally a "Current events" section, which can be very practical for users. A particular event can add a plus to the users' desire to visit the cultural asset. The most important difference is the possibility to book on the spot; the operation is easy for users, as they only have to follow the link. It acts as a persuasive tool since it instigates users to action, to "book". It may also indicate that the landmark is famous and crowded and needs previous booking.

Fig. 7-5 The Alhambra institutional webpage[2]

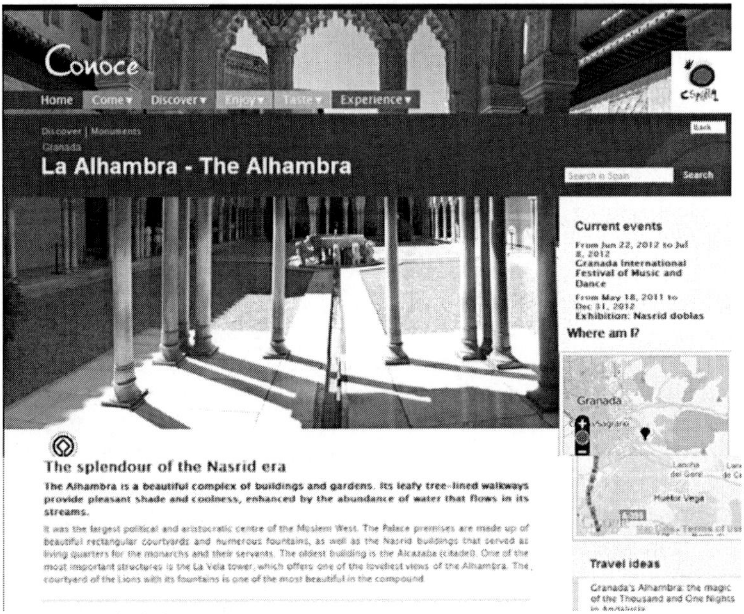


*Source:* Spain.info (2011)

### 7.2.2.1. Linguistic analysis

*Overview.* The section analysed starts with a caption that immerses users in an ancient and exotic atmosphere. The Alhambra is described as a complex of buildings and gardens strongly related to an Arabian past.

*Logical.* Rather short, the text is elaborated and complex. The clause simplexes, like "The Alhambra is a beautiful complex of buildings and gardens" (Spain.info 2011), are slightly more numerous than the complexes, which are linked only by hypotaxis-elaboration. The main clause introduces a topic on which it elaborates in the next clause, by non-defining relative clauses, as for example in "One of the most important

---

[2] For reasons of space, this Figure does not contain the header, footer and practical information sections, which are similar to the one presented by the webpage on the Monastery of El Escorial.

structures is the La Vela tower, *which offers one of the loveliest views of the Alhambra*". Different pieces of information seem to follow each other.

*Experiential.* The Alhambra is presented by means of relational processes, mainly identifying. They identify the landmark as "the centre of the Moslem west" and name several of its components, such as "the Nasrid buildings" or "the courtyard of the Lions". In a few cases, the landmark is described by what its components provide or offer, like "pleasant shade and coolness, enhanced by the abundance of water that flows in its streams". The only attributive process characterizes Alhambra as "a beautiful complex of buildings and gardens". The landmark and its attractions are totally focused since they are the only participant represented in the text. Always overtly expressed, it mainly has the role of Identified ("*It* was the largest political and aristocratic centre of the Moslem West"), as expected from the high use of identifying relational processes. This use, together with the absence of material processes, can explain the lack of background information; there are no Circumstances in the text. The landmark is described by what it stands for and by what it offers and not by its location in a particular time and space.

*Interpersonal.* The mood structure of the text is built up by declaratives acting as statements. In the same way as in the text on the Monastery of El Escorial, information is presented as such, as fact, as observation. There are the same number of Mood and Residue components, probably due to the dominance of declaratives and the absence of ellipsis. In the case of Mood, the Subject position is occupied, throughout the entire text, by the landmark and its components, e.g. "*The oldest building* is the Alcazaba (citadel)", the focus being more than evident. The Finites are usually fused, like "was" and "provide", as there are no passive or modalized forms. These build a more notional and generic message (Banks 2002, 6). The most frequent tense is the present, (e.g. "is"), the Alhambra being described as it is at the moment, picture-like. The present tense and the relational processes seem to confer to the landmark a static and eternal nature. The Residue is complex, but it contains no Adjunct. The writer appears not to interfere in the message transmitted, as there are no Adjuncts, modalization or negation. This adds more assertiveness and evidence to the factual nature and truth-value of the statements.

*Textual.* There are unmarked and simple Themes, always realized by the landmark and its attractions, for instance "*Its leafy tree-lined walkways* provide pleasant shade and coolness". Unmarkedness implies the presentation of observable monuments from an objective perspective (Francis and Kramer-Dahl 1991, 354; Gotti 2008, 79). The flow of the message is assured by Thematic progression. Introduced in the Rheme of the first clause ("The Alhambra *is a beautiful complex of buildings and gardens*"), the complex of buildings and gardens is divided in several Themes, like "the palace premises" or "the courtyard of Lions", which are carried throughout the text by means of a multiple pattern. This pattern is, though, not very clear and can make the message, not only incohesive, but also incoherent; different pieces of information seem just placed together in a telegraphic list, without any connection except the topic. Though the topic contributes to provide certain cohesion, the different attractions are presented as known to the readers, when in fact they are not.

The results found in the analysis of the text on the Alhambra are summarised in Table 7-11.

**Table 7-11 Institutional Alhambra: Lexico-grammatical summary**

| Clause complex | Transitivity | Mood | Theme |
|---|---|---|---|
| short<br>+ simplex<br>only expansion<br>only hypotaxis<br>only elaboration<br>+ non-defining relative clauses<br>1 non-finite clause | + relational<br>causative constr.<br>only identifying<br>only intensive<br>- mental<br>only realized particip.<br>only landmark<br>only land. (realized)<br>- implied<br>+ Identified (land.)<br>- visitor<br>- promoter<br>- circumstances | = mood & residue<br>only complex residue<br>only landmark as Subject<br>+ fused Finite<br>+ present<br>- Adjunct<br>- modality<br>- polarity<br>only declarative<br>only statements | only unmarked<br>only simple<br>+ participants as Theme<br>+ multiple progression |

### 7.2.2.2. Visual analysis

Similarly to the picture representing the Monastery, the image of the Alhambra seems to be cut in half by the red wide line with text. It depicts one of the Alhambra's "most beautiful" components, as the text describes it later, the courtyard of the Lions. Taken from the interior, the picture is representative for the Alhambra, as the courtyard has become a symbol for the whole complex, as a verbal synecdoche. The view is limited, but impressive. It is made up of an unstructured analytical process; it presents the courtyard as Carrier, and the columns, fountain, statues and pavement as Possessive Attributes. The sky is the Possessive Attribute of a limited landscape. There are also some visitors at the back, on the left side of the image. They may be watching the fountain and creating a narrative structure. However, as neither the vector nor the people are clearly depicted, this structure has not been considered in the analysis. Human figures are unusual in the images analysed, excepting the Monastery of Horezu and Sighisoara in the Romanian set presented before. Their presence may make users identify and join the group. The representational analysis can go even deeper and see the fountain as a Symbolic Attribute for the courtyard of the Lions, which in turn, can stand for the entire complex of the Alhambra. Nevertheless, the main process in the complex and connotative picture seems to be the unstructured analytical.

As an offer, the picture is presented for contemplation. The shot depends on the object contemplated; if the focus is on the columns, the shot is close, whereas, if it is on the fountain, the shot is middle. The perspective is subjective, as the view is limited to a frontal eye level angle. The markers of modality indicate a medium towards real modality. The picture seems real; the viewers can be standing there under the columns looking at the fountain, entering the court to move towards the fountain. However, the marker of representation has a low modality degree, probably to address the senses. The image may be intended to impress by involvement; the feeling of experience offers the viewer the impression of being in the middle of the things, inside the courtyard, with the fountain within reach. This shows how the photographer can use images of reality that carry different meanings; instead of a panoramic general Alhambra, s/he prefers a close and more real fountain.

The compositional unity of the picture representing the Alhambra is structured around centre-margins informational zones. The fountain is in the centre, depicted as the most important element, or the star of the tour, and the columns, pavement and sky are the margins, as background to the fountain.

The visual analysis of the picture presenting the Alhambra is included in Table 7-12.

**Table 7-12 Institutional Alhambra: Visual summary**

| Representational | Interactive | Compositional |
|---|---|---|
| complex<br>conceptual structure<br>unstructured analytical<br>courtyard & landscape (Carrier)<br>columns, fountain, statues, pavement & sky (Poss. Attr.) | offer<br>close & medium shot<br>subjective<br>frontal horizontal angle<br>eye level vertical angle<br>+ medium modality markers | centre-margin<br>fountain (salient)<br>- framing |

### 7.2.2.3. Multimodal act

In the webpage dedicated to the Alhambra, the top of the page continues to represent the dreamed world in the same way as in the case of the Monastery of El Escorial. The picture reflects the concept closely. Presented from within the complex, it shows what tourists can see once they reach the courtyard. This technique seems to project them directly inside the courtyard, as if the tourists have stopped, before moving towards the fountain, to take a picture. Their picture would most probably look like this one. The excitement raised by the closeness and reality of the image can encourage users to experience the view for themselves. This subjective and partial view of the Alhambra can further stir users' curiosity about a more general image of the complex. It seems the rest of the Alhambra is left for them to discover.

The text contributes to this discovery as it presents the landmark briefly. Moving from general to particular, the presentation lists a number of attractions of the Alhambra. All are presented by facts which assign them particular characteristics: the gardens–"leafy tree-lined walkways", "pleasant shade and coolness" and streams of water; the Nasrid buildings–Muslim, different, exotic; the Alcazaba–"the oldest building"; the La Vela tower–"one of the most important structures" which "offers one of the loveliest views of the Alhambra"; and the courtyard of the Lions, represented in the picture–"one of the most beautiful in the compound". It seems the selection of the attractions is done subjectively in order to present the appeal of different parts of the complex; their uniqueness contributes to the uniqueness of the Alhambra. The presentation of these attractions evolves in an apparent objective, transparent, true and impersonal way. Nonetheless, the subjective voice of the picture seems to be carried also in the text and concealed by its factual presentation. The discourse is sometimes qualitative, but not very descriptive; attractions are just compared to others in terms of antiquity, importance or appearance, and presented by relational processes. They lack any spatial, temporal or architectural detail. They are just enumerated randomly, as if items of a must-see list. The lack of detail and circumstantial arrangement does not permit the creation of a mental scene of the place to visit. However, the belonging to a Muslim past and a glorious era, the resonance of the Spanish exotic words, the pleasant gardens and the attractions presented can play with the senses. Imagination can build its own scenery, probably one resembling "One Thousand and One Nights" tales. The landmark proposes something different to visit, something related to the architecture and life habits of the Muslims living in "Al-Andalus" during a famous dynasty, the Nasrid one. The characteristics of the Alhambra can turn the visit into an exotic experience; visitors can live in a remote and oriental atmosphere for several hours.

The message is presented as informative. The focus is not on details and dates, but on the importance of the landmark's components. The uniqueness and importance of each component presented is aimed to persuade users that the Alhambra is worth seeing. The overtly persuasive picture and the exotic character address the senses and intensify the need for experience.

### 7.2.3. Santiago de Compostela in the institutional corpus

The webpage presenting the city of Santiago de Compostela follows the same vertical layout as the others analysed, i.e. picture, text and practical information. There are certain differences, which can be due to the different type of cultural asset promoted, since the promotion of a city is not the same as the promotion of a monument. The picture in the visual, for example, is not alone, but it is interchanged with others depicting the main attractions of Santiago. The word "Conoce" (discover) has been replaced by "Ven" (come), which, apart from indicating that the city is not part of the same subsection of the website, invites users to visit. The message is more overt and stronger. The text is even shorter than the previous ones, but has a link not found in the other pages analysed, which opens showing detailed guide-like information on the city. This can help users not feel overwhelmed by too much information; if they are curious after reading the short introduction, they can click the link and find out more. They are called to action by the interactive link of "see more".

The information following the text does not maintain the same layout as the other webpages, as can be seen in Fig. 7-6. The city is modelled to fit exactly what users are looking for, like "Cultural Santiago de Compostela", "Santiago de Compostela with children" or "Shopping in Santiago de Compostela". These multifacets of the city are presented as links; users can choose what exactly to read according to their needs and desires. The organization of information on certain topics can make them feel special, as if receiving tailor-made proposals created especially for them, as announced in the subtitle "Santiago de Compostela for you". In the same way as in the home page, a black rectangular follows these personified possibilities and contains several keywords accompanied by symbols, like "Santiago Cathedral" or "Final stop on the Camino de Santiago". A city map is inserted for further consultation, together with a link to weather forecast.

The last horizontal section on the webpage proposes more possibilities regarding the things one can do in Santiago, focusing on topics like "Practical information", "Visit" or "Sleep", which can be used to organize a trip. Changes are operated also on the right column of information; a "don't miss" list is added to highlight the monuments to visit, such as Santiago de Compostela Cathedral or the Galician Contemporary Art Centre. Another list indicates towns close to Santiago that can also be visited. As can be noticed, there is much more information on the landmark than in the other webpages. This aims to guide the users' sights and steps. The general information about the various attractions is not presented as a text, but as different items, like the practical one so far. Users are addressed directly and have the freedom to choose which link to follow. The repeated use of "you" confers a personal touch. Attention is drawn visually by the salient elements that indicate the important aspects, like the title, picture, short presentation card, different sections and city map.

Fig. 7-6 Santiago de Compostela institutional webpage[3]

*Source:* Spain.info (2011)

[3] This Figure presents only the first part of the webpage, as the entire one is quite long.

### 7.2.3.1. Linguistic analysis

*Overview.* The Spanish Tourist Board uses a very short text to describe the city of Santiago de Compostela. It encourages the users to discover the city and provides several reasons for it, like the number of visitors or its historic centre. Other reasons to go to Santiago are promised to be discovered, if a link is followed.

*Logical.* The text is unelaborated and simple, as its clauses are short and organised in clause simplexes, for example "see more" (Spain.info 2011). The only instance of clause complex is built by hypotaxis-elaboration ("Millions of people from all over the world come to this city every year, *many of them reaching the end of the Way of Saint James pilgrimage route*"); a non-defining relative clause explains why the city is visited by "millions of people from all over the world". The simplicity of the message is varied by a few embedded non-finite clauses, like "This is not the only reason *to come*, however", which slightly compact the information presented. This type of message, concise, simple and to the point, can be used on purpose not to confuse or bore users and stir their curiosity. Firstly, users are presented with something easy to digest, then, if curious or determined, they can further discover more about Santiago.

*Experiential.* The text presenting the Spanish city combines different processes: material, relational and mental. Material processes are more frequent and refer both to the past and future visitors "com[ing]" to the city and to the users "read[ing] more" information. Relational processes identify the city as "a World Heritage Site" and highlight that this is not the only reason to visit it. There are few mental processes, which are directed to the users and encourage them to "discover the main reasons" to visit Santiago. Regarding the participants, all the ones considered (i.e. landmark, visitor and promoter) are present in the text, in contrast to the situation in the other texts in the Spanish institutional set. The landmark is more realized than the other participants and always overtly expressed. It has several roles, like Goal ("Discover *Santiago de Compostela, the capital of the Region of Galicia*"), Carrier ("*Its historic centre* has been designated a World Heritage Site by the UNESCO") and Identified ("*This* is not the only reason to come, however"), as there are few processes and none stands out as being more frequent, though Goal is slightly more numerous. Almost as frequent as the landmark, the visitor is slightly more expressed than implied. When referred in general, by "people", the visitor is depicted as Actor, e.g. "*Millions of people from all over the world* come to this city every year", whereas, when directly mentioned, by "you", the visitor becomes Senser, e.g. "Here *you* can discover the main reasons to visit Santiago". This can suggest that the user is first a Senser, one that wants to discover more information, and then, s/he can become an Actor and identify with the "millions" who already visited Santiago. The promoter appears only once and not as the Tourist Board, but as the website. Suggested by a hyperlink, "see *more*", it directs users to more information; it plays the role of Goal, the entity that has to be discovered by users. Further details related to spatial and temporal location are provided. Spatial circumstances locate the city in relation to the pilgrimage route, known as the Way of St. James, "Millions of people from all over the world come *to this city* every year, many of them reaching the end of the Way of Saint James pilgrimage route", and the user in relation to the source of information, "*Here* you can discover the main reasons to visit Santiago". The temporal circumstance situates the massive visiting "every year" and assigns the feature of continuously visited destination to the city of Santiago, as indicated in the example above.

*Interpersonal.* The preferred mood is declarative. The clauses, acting as statements, present information about Santiago and refer to the reasons for visiting it as facts. The imperative mood is also used, mainly to invite users to "discover" Santiago, in all its meanings, both as "find out more" and as "visit". The user is, thus, directly addressed and instigated to act. The Subject position is occupied by the landmark, e.g. "*Its historic centre* has been designated a World Heritage Site by the UNESCO", and the visitor, e.g. "Here *you* can discover the main reasons to visit Santiago", with a slight preference towards the latter. This is not expected, as the text is about the city and the participant analysis has not shown a clear preference for the visitor. This can mean that the text is visitor-oriented. Always in the present, the Finites are expressed by negation and modalization. Negation, "is not", is used to emphasize the idea that there are more reasons to visit Santiago than the fact that its historic centre is a UNESCO World Heritage Site. The modal "can" ("Here you *can* discover the main reasons to visit Santiago") completes the message and proposes the possibility to discover other reasons directly by surfing the website and clicking on the link provided. These instances of negation and modalization mitigate the assertiveness and universality of the message.

The predominant part of the mood structure is the Residue, probably due to the imperatives. It is complex and contains many Circumstantial Adjuncts, like "to this city" and "every year", which add experiential meaning to the text. The only instance of Conjunctive Adjunct, placed outside the Mood structure, is highlighted by its position at the end of the clause, "This is not the only reason to come, *however*". The contrastive Adjunct "however" links the message to the previous one, by bringing another point of view. It also emphasises the existence of other reasons to visit Santiago, contributing to the argument.

*Textual*. The Themes are usually unmarked, e.g. "*Its historic centre* has been designated a World Heritage Site by the UNESCO", as if the text is presenting an objective message. The only marked Theme, expressed by the deictic "here" in "*Here* you can discover the main reasons to visit Santiago", highlights the important role played by the Tourist Board's website in informing users. This website and not another is the place where the main reasons to visit Santiago can be found. Cohesion is maintained by a linear Thematic progression, which provides the text with a cumulative development, as for example in "Millions of people from all over the world come *to this city* every year. *Its historic centre* has been designated a World Heritage Site by the UNESCO". The Themes introduced as new draw users' attention. The Theme "Millions of people" (included in the previous example), an exaggeration typical of promotional discourse, emphasises the fame of the city and testifies that the city is worth visiting. "Here", the other new Theme, has just been discussed as the deictic used to orientate users.

Table 7-13 presents the lexico-grammatical features of the text.

**Table 7-13 Institutional Santiago de Compostela: Lexico-grammatical summary**

| Clause complex | Transitivity | Mood | Theme |
|---|---|---|---|
| very short<br>+ simplexes<br>only expansion<br>only hypotaxis<br>only elaboration<br>1 non-defining relative<br>+ non-finite clauses | + material<br>+ identifying<br>+ intensive<br>only mental percep.<br>+ realized particip.<br>+ landmark<br>+ land. (realized)<br>only visitor (implied)<br>+ Goal (landmark)<br>= Actor & Senser (visitor)<br>only Goal (promoter)<br>only location, +place | + residue<br>only complex residue<br>+ visitor as Subject<br>+ expressed Finite<br>+ present<br>+ Circ. Adjuncts<br>only modalization polarity<br>+ declarative<br>+ statements | + unmarked<br>only simple<br>+ participants as Theme (little difference)<br>+ linear progression |

#### 7.2.3.2. Visual analysis

As mentioned in the description of the webpage, a number of pictures rotate to depict representative monuments and attractions, like Santiago de

Compostela Cathedral, Rua Porticada, Plaza de las Platerias Square, the Way of Saint James Pilgrims and Botafumeiro ceremony in the Cathedral. These may be used to show what users will see when they reach that particular place. They may also function as a way to express several grouped opportunities to see in the same city. They reinforce each other and produce a sense of excitement (Yui Ling Ip 2008, 7). The first picture to appear has been chosen for the analysis, as explained in the Methodology chapter. This is an image of one of the emblematic landmarks of Santiago de Compostela, its Cathedral, which bears the city's name. Just as the other pictures analysed, it is also constructed by a conceptual structure. The unstructured analytical process presents the Possessive Attributes, i.e. the cathedral, the surrounding buildings and the sky, as parts of the Carrier, i.e. city. The picture is simple, but, like the case of the picture of the Alhambra, the Cathedral can also be seen as a Symbolic Attribute which stands for the city.

This image is similar to the previous ones analysed in that it is presented for contemplation as an offer. The perspective is subjective; the Cathedral is seen from a point of view chosen by the photographer. The shot is medium, whereas the angles are oblique and low towards eye level, depending on the element focused. The Cathedral and its towers seem the main elements of the image. The relation established by the interactive function is rather detached and medium distant. The vertical angle, the colours and the light present the Cathedral as powerful, standing tall and imposing. Viewers are mere observers; they can, though, go closer and change the medium distance into a closer one. The picture could be taken from a hotel window or from the terrace of a building. This is supported by the modality markers that present the picture as realistic. Apart from the contextualization marker, which is low because there is little indication of context, the other markers build a medium modality. The picture is similar to those usually seen in postcards. The sunbeams touching the buildings and the reddish sky, probably at sunset, give it a romantic air.

**Table 7-14 Institutional Santiago de Compostela: Visual summary**

| Representational | Interactive | Compositional |
|---|---|---|
| simple<br>conceptual structure<br>unstructured analytical<br>city (Carrier)<br>cathedral, buildings & sky<br>(Possessive Attributes) | offer<br>medium shot<br>subjective<br>oblique horizontal angle<br>low vertical angle<br>+ medium modality markers | centre-margin<br>cathedral (salient)<br>- framing |

The information value in the picture of Santiago is distributed along a centre-margin structure; the Cathedral stands in the middle surrounded by the other elements. This placement makes the Cathedral salient. The sunbeams and its height contribute to its saliency.

### 7.2.3.3. Multimodal act

To summarise, Santiago de Compostela is promoted multimodally, like the other landmarks. The picture portrays one of the best-known attractions of the city, Santiago de Compostela Cathedral; the view on the city is restricted to this option. The Cathedral stands imposing, within visual reach. Both the picture and the text seem to function on the same principle; they partially present the reasons to visit the city. The picture depicts only the Cathedral and not in its totality. Users are expected to go closer and discover. The text also shows only two reasons. Users are expected, again, to click and read. It can, then, be said that curiosity is doubled and stirred multimodally.

The text is not centred on the city of Santiago de Compostela and its attractions, but on the reasons to visit it. The promotional message is clear from the beginning; the first word of the text, "discover", has a double function. First, it refers to the motivational factors of the trip (Calvi 2006, 43). Then, in a direct and individual manner, it addresses users and instigates them to discover Santiago cognitively and materially. The text interacts with users and, as such, communicative immediacy is created (Janoschka 2004, 121) to facilitate the persuasive transmission of the message. The city's perpetual fame among people all over the world is meant to testify that it is worth visiting. The informational message is combined with a more interactional one in order to persuade. Facts are presented by impersonal and objective constructions as reliable data. The presentation focuses on two reasons: pilgrimage and heritage, as if they are the ones that give the city its unique character. There is no description of the city or any of its attractions. The aim can be to provide objectivity to the message or to stir users' imagination. It can also signify a lack of imposition; users are free to explore for themselves and form their own opinion on Santiago. The interactional part emphasises the existence of other reasons to visit the city, which can be further consulted. Finally, the instructional construction calls to action; it asks users to discover for themselves further information. Negation and deixis contribute to the prescriptive procedural tone.

The informational, interactional and instructional parts complement each other and transmit a clear promotional message. The text has various features that make it resemble an advertisement, like the big and romantic picture of an impressive Cathedral; the short and concise text; its structure and syntax; the repetition of the entire name of the city; and the colloquial and oral language. The parallelism between picture and text reinforces the characteristics of the message and guarantees its transmission. Colloquial, involved and anchored in the present of promotion, the text seems to promote not only Santiago, but also the website.

### 7.2.4. Discussion of the Spanish set of institutional webpages

The Spanish institutional website is characterised by attractive and interesting webpages with a creative and modern design, full of colours that interplay and lead to strong combinations which stand out against the black background. The reading path seems to be guided by colour, size and links, characteristics considered useful in web design, as visitors look more than read (Stein 2006, 4; Miller 2011, 83). The transmission of the message is mainly visual, as it relies on well-marked blocks of information, impressive visuals, a connotative navigational bar and short segments of text. The verbal information is short, fragmented by the numerous links and mainly presented in columns, in compliance with "the golden rules of web writing" (Garzone 2009, 38). The connotative aspect seems to be more important than the rational one, more attention being paid to attracting the tourist than providing information (Garzone 2009, 36). The cultural connotative picture from the home page, the unclear navigational menu and the absence of any statement of purpose and identity information from the website support this.

Apart from images and text, information is transmitted also by interactive links, which address users directly and instigate them to see the contents of the website, check several travel ideas, book accommodation or transport, share opinions on various forums and participate in the promotion of Spain. Their telegraphic and connotative wording can increase users' enthusiasm about the landmark and make them feel eager to go and experience by themselves. This high degree of interactivity and interpersonality seems to go together with the little amount of information and text, a combination typical for websites (Garzone 2009, 50).

All the Spanish webpages follow the same structure: header, visual, main body and footer. The webpages maintain the attractiveness, the connotation and the clear design of the home page. The difference is that they are not as symbolic and telegraphic, but contain also small chunks of text that describe and promote the landmark. They are user-oriented, as they are short and screen centred. The scroll down is limited to two, maximum three screens, as recommended in web design (Miller 2011, 18).

Each screenshot communicates a separate and independent message and all contribute to the whole; the visual represents the landmark promoted, whereas the main body describes it. Their layout reminds readers of the type used in magazine advertisements and marketing oriented websites (Myers 1994): the product, in this case, the landmark, is presented as a promise by a big colourful picture, in the top section of the page, while the text is presented as real information and describes the product, in the bottom section. The practical information attached to the text gives the instructions necessary to get the product. The entire communicative act seems built around the idea of contrast–emotive vs. factual; unity becomes secondary (Kress and van Leeuwen 2006, 186).

The message transmitted by the Spanish Tourist Board is informative. The general and practical data provide a complete picture of the landmark; users have enough information to visit the landmark. The practical information is presented separately from the main text and highlighted by different visual tools. This leaves freedom to users; if they only want to find out about the landmark, but are not interested in visiting it, they can skip the practical information, since it is clearly indicated. The focus is more on information transmission than on description, as if providing a visiting card. Persuasion is hidden in numbers and comparisons, so that the message sounds objective, factual and impersonal. Emotional manipulation can, however, be observable in the landmarks' evocation of a glorious imperial and exotic past. The tone in the webpage dedicated to Santiago is more overtly persuasive, promoting both the landmark and the website, by a message which reminds of the language of advertising. Recommendation is also indirect, the travel ideas can orient users in the area, as they indicate several things to do and see. This is reflected also in the page's transactional aspect since users are not usually offered the possibility to book directly on the spot. They have to click on several pages before getting to the actual booking, a process that can make them abandon the quest (Morgan and Pritchard 2000, 324; Crystal 2004, 47). All transactions are directed to exterior organizations and agencies; the website has no commercial aim.

These different types of information seem to follow the AIDA model. The general information draws users' Attention, by the coloured visual and the bilingual title, and captures their Interest, by the short presentation. The instructional information is used to incite Desire. The practical data call users to Action. The focus seems to be more on Action, even if this is not overtly stated. The structure of the webpages reflects these various types of details; the webpages identify the name of the attraction, set its background, describe it, provide service information and further contact information, similarly to paper tourist brochures. The webpage dedicated to Santiago of Compostela is once again an exception and its structure is different; it only identifies the attraction and leaves the other details for users to discover.

The lexico-grammatical characteristics of the texts presenting the Spanish landmarks, summarized in Table 7-15, indicate the aims presented above. The texts are quite different; the Monastery is described in relation to its components, their characteristics and spatial relations with a clear predominance of data; the Alhambra is presented as exotic and its components are related to their unique characteristics, whereas the city of Santiago is argued as a place worth visiting. Certain preferences can though be observed. The texts appear as concise as they are short, medium elaborated and complex. Information develops by clause simplexes, aiming probably at a clear, simple and easy to process message. In the rare cases of clause complexes, the clauses elaborate on previous meaning by adding various details to complete information. The facts are presented by identifying relational process, as the focus is more on the transmission of information than on description. The landmark, the usual participant, plays the role of Identified and occupies the position of Subject/Theme, implying a focused topic for the text. The visitor and the Tourist Board are absent as there is no indication of any possible visit. It seems the information presented about the landmarks is purely informative; the interlocutors of the message are absent as if, apparently, this is not directed to anybody. Generic and universal, information is stated as true as indicated by the dominant statements. Objectivity is emphasized by Thematic unmarkedness. The message can sometimes seem incohesive, as though pieces of information are placed together without any connection except the topic. The Thematic development, though, makes information flow. There is no common pattern in the texts, but a preference for a cumulative development exists. Differences from this classification are frequently encountered in the text dedicated to Santiago, as expected due to its different topic and more persuasive message. Its message is visit-oriented and mitigated by the expression of possibility. It depicts reality by material processes, in which the general visitor plays the role of Actor and the city that of Goal. The visitor is addressed directly and invited to "discover" Santiago and, implicitly, the website.

**Table 7-15 Spanish set of institutional websites: Lexico-grammatical summary**

| System | Monastery of El Escorial | The Alhambra | Santiago de Compostela |
|---|---|---|---|
| Clause complex | medium long<br>+ complexes (3 cl.)<br>only expansion<br>almost = parataxis & hypotaxis<br>+ extension<br>+ non-def. relatives<br>+ non-finite clauses<br>+ apposition | short<br>+ simplex<br>only expansion<br>only hypotaxis<br>only elaboration<br>+ non-defining relative clauses<br>1 non-finite clause | very short<br>+ simplexes<br>only expansion<br>only hypotaxis<br>only elaboration<br>1 non-defining relative<br>+ non-finite clauses |
| Transitivity | + relational<br>+ identifying<br>+ circumstantial<br>existential<br>only mental perception<br>+ realized particip.<br>+ landmark<br>only land. (realized)<br>+ landmark (implied)<br>+ Identified (land.)<br>only implied as Senser (visitor)<br>- promoter<br>+ location, + time | + relational<br>causative constr.<br>only identifying<br>only intensive<br>- mental<br>only realized participants<br>only landmark<br>only land. (realized)<br>- implied<br>+ Identified (landmark)<br>- visitor<br>- promoter<br>- circumstances | + material<br>+ identifying<br>+ intensive<br>only mental percep.<br>+ realized particip.<br>+ landmark<br>+ landmark (realized)<br>only visitor (implied)<br>+ Goal (landmark)<br>= Actor & Senser (visitor)<br>only Goal (promoter)<br>only location, + place |
| Mood | + residue<br>only complex residue<br>only landmark as Subject<br>+ fused Finite<br>+ present<br>+ Circ. Adjuncts<br>only modalization<br>- polarity<br>only declarative<br>+ full decl.<br>only statements | = mood & residue<br>only complex residue<br>only landmark as Subject<br>+ fused Finite<br>+ present<br>- Adjunct<br>- modality<br>- polarity<br>only declarative<br>only statements | + residue<br>only complex residue<br>+ visitor as Subject<br>+ expressed Finite<br>+ present<br>+ Circ. Adjuncts<br>only modalization polarity<br>+ declaratives<br>+ statements |
| Theme | + unmarked<br>+ simple | only unmarked<br>only simple | + unmarked<br>only simple |

| System | Monastery of El Escorial | The Alhambra | Santiago de Compostela |
|---|---|---|---|
| | + participants as Theme<br>+ continuous progression | + participants as Theme<br>+ multiple progression | + participants as Theme (little dif.)<br>+ linear progression |

The subjective visual mode counterbalances the objectivity of the verbal one. Vividly coloured, the pictures are more persuasive than informative. The Monastery is expected to convince by its size, observed from an aerial perspective; the Alhambra by its closeness and reality, whereas Santiago by its impressive Cathedral.

**Table 7-16 Spanish set of institutional websites: Visual summary**

| System | Monastery of El Escorial | Alhambra | Santiago de Compostela |
|---|---|---|---|
| Representational | simple<br>conceptual structure<br>unstructured analytical<br>monastery (Carrier)<br>component & garden (Possessive Attributes) | complex<br>conceptual structure<br>unstructured analytical<br>courtyard & landscape (Carrier)<br>columns, fountain, statues, pavement & sky (Poss. Attr.) | simple<br>conceptual structure<br>unstructured analytical<br>city (Carrier)<br>cathedral, buildings & sky (Possessive Attributes) |
| Interactive | offer<br>close shot<br>subjective<br>oblique horizontal angle<br>high vertical angle<br>= low & medium modality markers | offer<br>close & medium shot<br>subjective<br>frontal horizontal angle<br>eye level vertical angle<br>+ medium modality markers | offer<br>medium shot<br>subjective<br>oblique horizontal angle<br>low vertical angle<br>+ medium modality markers |
| Compositional | - information structucture<br>monastery(salient)<br>- framing | centre-margin<br>fountain (salient)<br>- framing | centre-margin<br>cathedral (salient)<br>- framing |

The images chosen are clear and representative of the landmarks. They are built by conceptual structures and composed by unstructured analytical processes in which the Monastery, the courtyard and the city play the role of Carriers, as indicated in Table 7-16. The picture of the Alhambra and Santiago seems even more subjective, since they are taken from the interior. The modality markers indicate real pictures, which are offered for contemplation. Nevertheless, their strong colours, clear focus and inclusion into a visual can indicate digitization with the aim of addressing and stimulating the senses. The shot is close or medium, hoping to engage users. The oblique horizontal angle situates, however, the landmarks outside their worlds. The interactive function seems to engage users, but as outsiders, so that they become curious and turn into insiders. Power relations do not seem important, since there is no preferred vertical angle. The composition further emphasises the importance of the main items depicted. The wide red stripe across the page highlights the need to find out the part of the picture that lays beneath and involves users. The pictures depicting the Spanish landmarks seem, thus, to give more importance to perception than to cognition. In language, perception verbs make experience real and communicative efficiency better (Pérez Vázquez 2011, 310); the same can be said about these pictures.

The Spanish institutional website seems, then, not to have a consistent pattern of presentation for its content, except for the layout. The textual message adapts to each landmark according to its characteristics, without following any particular structure or model. This can make the website less intuitive, but, at the same time, maintain a surprise element for users. The message of the webpages analysed is mainly articulated visually (Anthonissen 2003, 302); the big visual draws attention to the representation of the landmark, while the fragmentation of the written message points to different types of information. Reduced to a minimum, the actual presentation of the landmark is brief and concise with the aim of awakening curiosity and avoiding boredom. Both modes inform; one by facts and the other by senses. Sometimes connotative and indirectly persuasive, the entire message presents Spain as related to a glorious imperial past, as influenced by Muslim occupancy, as visited by millions of pilgrims or as awarded by UNESCO. This is the uniqueness of Spain and what makes it worth visiting. However, the effect of the message seems diminished by the absence of an overt promoter and/or addressee.

## 7.3. British set of institutional webpages

The home page introducing the British Tourist Board's website, whose updated version can be checked at http://www.visitbritain.com/en/EN/, is organised vertically; information flows in separated blocks on a vertical axis against a white background. The blocks containing both text and image are laid out on a horizontal axis, with the image on the left, as given information, and the text on the right, as new. The images seem to present something already known, whereas the texts bring in details to describe them. The numerous and various parts compose a quite long home page, which requires many scroll downs. This organization of the page with too much detailed information on varied topics displayed on a long layout can confuse and even bore users, who may leave the page (Morgan and Pritchard 2000, 83; Miller 2011, 83).

The most important part of the message seems to be the first one to appear on the page, as it is foregrounded, popping out from the page. It contains text that explains what the website is about, after users have scanned the coloured images on the screen. This section can be further separated in three zones: the upper one includes, on the left, the Tourist Board's logo and the present campaign's slogan, and, on the right, the search box and the option for language. Both the logo and slogan play with the colours of the British flag: white, blue and red. VisitBritain's logo looks like a present wrapped in blue paper, with the red and white lines resembling a ribbon. The name of the Board is quite direct and significant, as it contains the keyword "visit"; the exhortative message is present from the beginning. The campaign's slogan, "GREAT BRITAIN You're invited" (VisitBritain 2011), uses different text fonts and types; the word "great" in capitals is salient and framed in a red box. It seems to play with some of the adjective's connotations: large in size, excellent, well, famous, admirable, expert and/or something that provokes enthusiasm. In italics and imitating handwriting, the phrase "you're invited" addresses the user directly and invites her/him to Britain. The country seems to be offered as a well-known and desirable gift that can stir enthusiasm and make the user feel good. The expert Board addresses the users personally and directly, by "you're invited", making them feel involved and important. The personal pronoun treats users as individuals, not as members of a group. The invitation is to visit Britain; not any Britain, but the "GREAT" one. Thus, the Board assures a successful trip. A closer relation can make the message more compelling. For this, the invitation is emphasised and humanised via audio mode by a sound track that can be heard in the background, in which different voices repeat the phrase. The voices come from a video that will be later on commented briefly. Regarding the search box, this helps users find a place, landmark or hotel quickly, without having to browse the entire page, and tries to respond directly to their needs. Different languages permit people from all over the world to visit the websites; non-speakers of English can read in French, Spanish, Chinese, Russian and some other languages.

Below this, the second zone displays the contents of the websites in horizontal order, as if enumerated. If clicked, each of them is further classified around that particular topic, offering direct links to the information offered. The navigational menu provides different types of information: general, regarding the destination and country–"Destinations & maps", "Things to do" or "About Britain"; practical, enabling users to plan a trip by themselves–"Accommodation", "Transport" or "Travel tips"; and transactional, providing users with the possibility to become real tourists–"Special Offers". The placement of the navigational bar at the top of the webpage helps the user take in the content of the website rapidly (Djonov 2005).

The real message comes in the last part of this first section, presenting the text on the left and the pictures on the right. They are linked by a car, which, curiously, goes backwards from the pictures to the text. It can stand for movement, trips, and, due to its colours, for the Tourist Board itself. The association can be car–movement–Tourist Board–Britain. As the car offers transport, so the Tourist Board helps to make the trip happen. As in the slogan, the text[4] exploits different text types and fonts. "Welcome To Britain" stands out to receive users; the word "Britain" refers to both country and Tourist Board. They are further assured that everything they need is on VisitBritain.com by a message in the same tone of closeness and colloquialism as the slogan. The use of the complete name for the site emphasises the idea of the expert. It can also be a marketing tool (Bolaños Medina *et al.* 2005, 134) to make the name memorable, as a sort of advertising repetition. The small images on the right depict representative buildings: Windsor Castle, the Millennium Centre, Edinburgh Castle and the London Eye. They serve to introduce links to the regional or local Tourist Boards of England, Wales, Scotland and London. The layout seems to imply that if users read the text and visit the website, they can see the landmarks depicted in the pictures.

The second section of the home page consists of a huge visual composed of: a picture of a landscape, a short title, several links, interactive operations like "share" or "embed" and a map. The map localizes the exact landmark depicted and orientates users spatially. The British flag appears again in the final part of the visual. Several visuals rotate here, all connected to the keywords: "Music", "Countryside",

[4] "Welcome To Britain If you're planning days out or holidays in the UK, looking for hotels or accommodation on UK travel, attractions or events, VisitBritain.com has everything you need" (VisitBritain 2011).

"Sport", "Shopping" and "Heritage", each in turn part of the construction "X is GREAT Britain", where "X" stands for the keyword. This part seems to provide several reasons for Britain's greatness, like entertainment, nature or history. Other reasons are presented by the next section in a video. This is where the voices heard in the moment of accessing the website come from. Named "invitation", in the same line with the campaign's slogan, it shows several famous British people, like Dame Judi Dench, Rupert Everett, Twiggy, Dev Pattel and Jamie Oliver, recommending aspects about Britain and saying "you're invited". The video can be a successful tool as information and persuasion may become more effective through images and sound than through text, since seeing and listening are less demanding than reading. Apart from this, the use of celebrities to promote a country is similar to that of sportsmen encountered in the Spanish institutional home page; it confers reliability to the Tourist Board and its message, as they build on the reasons for Britain's greatness. Celebrities can also provide a link with foreigners, creating interest via people they know and encouraging their continuation in the website to search for more information. They represent different domains, probably to present varied recommendations and to reach a wider audience. Their voices can even diminish the confusion raised by the amount of information on the home page and help its processing and selection.

From the video onwards, the page continues to flow vertically, but in two columns. Customary for web writing, column organisation facilitates an easier reading (Garzone 2009, 38). For example, the video is on the left, accompanied by a board in the colours of the flag, on the right. The board, like the menu placed outside restaurants, presents the link to the "Best of British special offers". It seems the left column is concerned with information about Britain, while the right side contains more interactive information on different discounts, deals and blogs. General information is, thus, presented as old information, whereas interactive and practical information is visually signalled and introduced as new and important. Persuasion seems to follow a pattern, from left to right; this is Britain, already known to the world, and the way to visit it is for users to discover.

The next sections, placed in the left column and spanning more than twelve screenshots are informative; they present a representative picture, on the left, and a small caption that contains a title, a short description and several tips for visiting, on the right. The presentation of images as information taken for granted and of texts as glossing the image is a quite innovative technique (Kress 2003, 136). For example, the picture of a Harvey Nichols' store is accompanied by the title "Leisure & entertainment"; a text which points the fame of the British stores and names some of them; and several links, like “Department stores” or “Markets”. The purpose may be to offer as much information as possible in order to show professionalism and convince users to visit Britain by various methods. The attempt to offer a complete picture leads, however, to repetition and redundancy; some of the topics, celebrities or popular UK attractions are repeated. Repetition can, indeed, emphasise a topic, but it can also tire the user.

The final section of the home page, framed and made to stand out like the first one, returns to the information related to the website, as if closing the initial message. The footer presents the Tourist Board’s partners, those already mentioned by the small pictures at the beginning. It also offers the possibility of subscription to its newsletter so that it maintains posterior contact with users interested in Great Britain. This can be useful for the creation of databases and the monitoring of past users. It has links to other sections of the website like “Legal”, “About VisitBritain”, “VisitBritain Shop” or “Site Map”, links that provide data about the Tourist Board, transactional information and navigational help.

To summarize, the home page of the institutional website belonging to the British Tourist Board seems to indicate the AIDA marketing model (OMT 2005b, 8). It presents a general vision of the website in order to get Attention. For the same reason, it includes a suggestive logo, a persuasive slogan, a video with celebrities, and several attractive photos, which represent the main keywords as unique British characteristics: nature, heritage and entertainment. The “Special offers” section is included also to draw attention and convince by practical information. No information about the way to get in touch with the Board is provided. Interest is stirred by the multimodal chunks of information, the video and the practical information on the right side of the page. The description of attractions and accommodation is general and not centred on the visitor; it presents them, without explicitly pointing what the visitor can do. Desire seems to be left in the background; the focus is on the description and that should stimulate the desire to visit. As for Action, this is induced by links to possible ways to interact and book, like “Need advice” or “Discounts and deals” sections.

### 7.3.1. Canterbury Cathedral in the institutional corpus

The webpage presenting Canterbury Cathedral contains the same header as the home page, except the introductory message related to the website and its accompanying small pictures.

Fig. 7-7 Canterbury Cathedral institutional webpage

*Source:* VisitBritain (2011)[5]

The link to the home page and the existence of the same menu make navigation on the website easy and intuitive (OMT 2001, 94; 2005b, 9); the website seems consistent and coherent. As can be seen in Fig. 7-7, the webpage also follows the same vertical two columns layout; the left part presents information about the Cathedral, while the right one advertises

[5] As mentioned in Chapter six, when copyright was not granted, an impression of the structure of the webpage has been included so that the reader can follow the analyses.

the website's store and several tours to Canterbury offered by different agencies. Their short advertisements present general information about the product and transactional details related to prices. This commercial aspect is useful for users as it gives them the possibility to book instantly. It can also be considered a marketing trick; users have no time to consider the offer; they just feel curious and enthusiastic and buy, without second thoughts.

Finally, the bottom section links this webpage to other webpages in the website according to what other people viewed. This is a good tactic to direct users' visual attention to other landmarks in case this one has not convinced them. Similarly to the home page, it can, however, distract the user with too many possibilities. The link to others can also give a sense of sharing and belonging to a group of people, those interested in the Cathedral or in Great Britain. The footer is the same as in the home page, with links to collaborators and to other information related to the site.

The column presenting the Cathedral has a vertical layout; the title announces the topic, the subtitle and caption introduce particular features of the cultural asset and the main body presents more information on the topic. This top-bottom structure resembles that of a usual page (Lemke 2002). It is in the body where multimodality intervenes; an image and a text are placed together in the same visual field as a single communicative act. The act follows the same horizontal axis proposed by the home page in the case of multimodal chunks of information. Various elements are presented as salient in order to attract the users' attention, such as the title, subtitle, caption and some words or hyperlinks, like Canterbury Cathedral, London or "Must see & do". Framing indicates the distinctive short paragraphs of the text.

#### 7.3.1.1. Linguistic analysis

*Overview*. The text dedicated to Canterbury Cathedral does not present only this religious monument. The copywriter chooses to talk about the area of Canterbury and all its religious assets: Canterbury Cathedral, the Church of St Martin, St Augustine's Abbey and Christ Church Cathedral. "Clustered opportunities" (Jansen-Verbeke and Lievois 2002, 94) are assumed to have a higher tourist attraction. The desire to offer as many details as possible in order to persuade, encountered in the home page, is present here also. The reason for this choice may be due to the World Heritage status of the Cathedral; this is not assigned only to the church, but also to the other named buildings, as if forming a religious complex. The text focuses on the importance of Canterbury and its Cathedral for the

Church of England. The Cathedral is projected in distant time by links to the past, especially to Thomas Becket and pilgrimage. The other churches are introduced briefly with an emphasis on the possibility to see their ruins even nowadays. Apart from these short descriptions, there is also a "must see & do" section that adds further details about attractions in the area, like "Canterbury Tales Experience". Once again, the objectives presented, even if interesting, have nothing to with Canterbury Cathedral. The possibilities can capture users' interest, but can also distract them from the main topic of the text, Canterbury Cathedral, as already discussed in the Romanian institutional set. The text can even sound incoherent, as the title announces a topic which is not totally respected.

*Logical.* The text is medium long and syntactically developed. It is constructed by an almost equal number of clause simplexes and complexes. As such, the text is medium complex. The clause simplexes present information in a compact form, due to the relatively high number of defining relative clauses, which bring additional details, like "His shrine became one of the most visited in the Middle Ages by pilgrims *travelling the Pilgrims' Way from London and Winchester*" (VisitBritain 2011). The clause complexes, in turn, are usually built by two clauses linked by hypotaxis-elaboration. The main clause introduces information, like the different churches in the Canterbury area, and elaborates on it by adding different details, like date of construction or past function, as for example in "Another important church is the Church of St Martin just outside the city's medieval wall, *half of which survives today*". This pattern can be observed in the description of other churches than the Cathedral, the actual topic of the text. Canterbury Cathedral, however, is presented more by parataxis-extension-addition, e.g. "Canterbury Cathedral was founded in AD597 *and* is the Mother Church of the Anglican Communion"; various new pieces of information are put together by juxtaposition. The instances of parataxis and hypotaxis are almost equal, the same as the number of clause simplexes and clause complexes, which can indicate that the text follows no strict pattern; it rather combines the types of clauses and their tactic and logico-semantic relations.

*Experiential.* The main process found in the text analysed is relational. As the main purpose is to inform, the text develops via description. Canterbury Cathedral is mainly identified, by means of relational processes, as "the Mother Church of the Anglican Communion" or "the site of the Archbishop Thomas Becket's martyrdom in AD1170". The majority of the identifying relational processes are intensive, as can be observed from the examples. There are also some instances of attributive relational which characterize the ruins of St Augustine's Abbey as "impressive site", present Canterbury Cathedral's components as possessions or locate in time the Church of St Martin. The landmark impresses by its identity and what it stands for rather than by its attributes and characteristics. The aim of this can be objectivity. The text depicts reality also by means of material processes, other markers of objectivity (Barker and Galasinki 2001, 71). Quite numerous, they refer to the historical details of the landmarks, such as foundation and building, in other words, to facticity (Barker and Galasinki 2001, 71). Material processes are, though, mainly carried out by the possible visitor and suggest several actions like "step back in time" or "visit". The same purpose, that of guiding the visitor, explains the only mental process used, i.e. "see". The experiential meaning seems to follow a pattern: relational processes refer to the Cathedral and other nearby attractions, while material processes relate to possible visitors' actions. The details are brought in mainly by circumstances that locate the action in place, "in the area", and time, "in the 4th century". Spatial and temporal location is expected as the text is aimed to present, explain and orient to various sights (Fries 1995; Ramm 2000). The other instances of circumstances are quite varied, providing information related to manner, "with colour"; role, "as a Roman church"; extent, "for nearly five centuries" and cause, "because of its location just outside the city centre". Other circumstantial details about location are provided also by circumstantial relational processes, like "locate" or "survive".

The participants considered for the analysis, i.e. the landmark, the visitor and the promoter, are more realized than implied. The landmark, including not only Canterbury Cathedral, but also the other attractions chosen by the Tourist Board, like St Augustine's Abbey or Canterbury West Gate Towers, appear more frequently than the (possible) visitor. More realized than implied, the Cathedral is mainly given the role of Goal, of the entity on which others performed actions, like founding ("*Canterbury Cathedral* was founded in AD597"). The landmark's participant role can be considered unexpected, as relational processes are more frequent than material ones. Quite close in numbers, though, the landmark plays also the role of Carrier ("*It* has a perpendicular nave, 12th-century Gothic choir, stunning stained glass windows and a Romanesque crypt") and Identified ("*The Cathedral* is the site of the Archbishop Thomas Becket's martyrdom in AD1170"), roles initially expected. This can mean that the landmark is presented more in relation to action (past, present or future) than to identification and qualification. Almost equally implied and realized, the visitor appears rarely. S/he plays the role of Actor, of the one performing an action on the landmark, like "*you*'ll find many important religious buildings and monuments in the area". This is, however, the case in the beginning and the end of the text. In the main body, the landmark is dominant, having no relation with the visitor. It seems the landmark is introduced to the visitor, then, it is presented as it is, so that, finally, it can be acted upon. Users appear in two forms: as "you" and as "visitors", both having a persuasive aim. The second person personal pronoun captures users' interest and addresses them personally as individuals and not as parts of mass audience (Mongkholjuck 2008, 27). Even if the general term is more neutral (Pérez Vázquez 2011, 302), it makes users identify with it and see themselves in that particular situation (Calvi 2011, 78) ("many *visitors* miss St Augustine's Abbey because of its location just outside the city centre"). The pragmatic marker "just" makes the clause more real and oral, specifying the location of that particular situation (Molina and Romano 2012, 18-19). Promotion seems to be done by action, not by appearance, probably to give dynamism to the message and instigate users to visit. The landmark and the visitor are the only participants; the promoter or the Tourist Board does not appear at all. The absence of an overt promoter voice can aim to give the impression of a neutral and objective message produced by an expert and professional Tourist Board with no intent to manipulate.

*Interpersonal.* The mood structure in the institutional text promoting Canterbury Cathedral is mainly declarative. This means the speech roles are statements asserting facts. Information is presented as true historical facts in accordance with the aim of the message ("Canterbury Cathedral was founded in AD597"). This contributes to the impression of a professional and neutral message. The subjective voice is hidden in the presentation of Canterbury. An exception is the exclamation included which emphasizes Canterbury Cathedral's antiquity presented in the previous example, "(that's over 1,400 years ago!)". The copywriter's voice intervenes in the text, as an aside indicated by the parenthesis, to calculate how many years have passed since the foundation of the Cathedral and to point them out to the user with an exclamation mark. There are also several instances of imperative mood, which invite users to "step back in time" and "see". The copywriter/promoter comes closer to users as s/he addresses them directly, from the beginning, by the exclamation indicating personal contact. This allows the professional and expert voice to further suggest, advise, invite and even command.

The Mood component is mainly composed by Subject and Finite. The Subject position is almost always occupied by the landmark, which is expected, as it is the topic of the text. Rarely, the most important place in the clause is occupied by the visitor. Once, s/he is addressed directly by the personal pronoun "you". As mentioned earlier, the message is personal; you, not anybody else, are the one to find many religious buildings in the area. The other element of the Mood component, the Finite, is usually fused and refers to present, like "is" and "has". The fused forms indicate the message as more notional and generic (Banks 2002, 6), whereas the present makes it timeless and universal. There is also a modalized Finite, which is the only instance of future in the text. The construction can be interpreted as an offer, since it is addressed directly to users and anticipates what they "will find" in Canterbury: a number of religious buildings and monuments. Credibility is assigned to the offer (Calvi 2011, 82). There is no instance of negation, except the construction "not to miss". It can be considered a piece of advice or a suggestion for the users; Christ Church Cathedral is something they should not miss. The lack of modality and polarity invests the message with the authority of straightforward evidence (Mocini 2009, 160). The authority and reliability of the Tourist Board is undisputed.

The Residue component appears more frequently than the Mood, due to the instances of imperatives. It is complex, as it contains Predicators, Complements and Adjuncts. The Adjuncts are only circumstantial and add information to the experiential meaning and not to the interpersonal one.

*Textual.* The text presents the religious landmark usually by unmarked and simple Themes. Unmarkedness leads to an objective and complete message with no room for mediation (Francis and Kramer Dahl 1991, 354). Participants are usually in Theme position, the focus being on information. They are referred to by their complete names, as part of a marketing message (Bolaños Medina *et al.* 2005, 134). Their expression as nominalization, as for example in "Another important church" and "The ruins of this once great abbey", implies the presentation of observable facts from an objective detachment (Francis and Kramer Dahl 1991, 351). There is only one instance of marked Theme. The dependent clause in Theme position, "Probably built as a Roman church in the 4th century", is enhanced and expressed by a preposed attributive that premodifies and adds information. Antiquity is once again highlighted, being made conspicuous by fronting St Martin's date of foundation. The few instances of multiple Themes, in turn, add textual meaning to the message and make it more cohesive, by using the textual Theme "and".

The Thematic development is complex, combining different patterns. The message introduces two new Themes, the Cathedral and the possible visitor, linked by a textual Theme ("*Canterbury* has been a key location for the Church of England for nearly five centuries *and you*'ll find many important religious buildings and monuments in the area"). These two participants are presented both as new, interesting and important, and as linked. This initial clause provides the topic of the text: "many important religious buildings and monuments". The section on Canterbury Cathedral develops both continuously and linearly; the focus is maintained on the Cathedral and the message develops cumulatively. The other religious buildings are introduced as new Themes and constructed linearly ("Many visitors miss *St Augustine's Abbey* because of its location just outside the city centre. *The ruins of this once great abbey* are an impressive sight"); the copywriter probably wants to introduce more monuments and be brief. The "must see & do" section, bringing in new Themes, draws the users' attention to proposals, like "the Canterbury Tales Experience". As some of them are processes in the imperative mood, like for example "see" and "visit", the aim can also be to instigate users to action. The Thematic development provides a clear focus (usually the landmark) and, at the same time, builds on newly introduced information. Its cohesion can be disrupted by the high number of new Themes. Slightly dominating over the other types, they can make the text difficult to follow and rather confusing.

The linguistic analysis of the institutional text presenting Canterbury Cathedral is summarised in Table 7-17.

**Table 7-17 Institutional Canterbury Cathedral: Lexico-grammatical summary**

| Clause complex | Transitivity | Mood | Theme |
|---|---|---|---|
| medium long<br>almost =<br>complexes &<br>simplexes (2 cl.)<br>only expansion<br>almost =<br>hypotaxis &<br>parataxis<br>+ elaboration<br>+ non-defining<br>relatives<br>+ defining clauses | + relational<br>+ identifying<br>+ intensive<br>many material<br>only mental percep.<br>+ realized particip.<br>+ landmark<br>+ land. (realized)<br>almost = landmark &<br>visitor (implied)<br>+ Goal, then Carrier<br>& Identified (land.)<br>Actor (visitor)<br>- promoter<br>+ location, + place | + residue<br>only complex<br>residue<br>+ landmark as<br>Subject<br>+ fused Finite<br>+ present<br>only Circ. Adj.<br>only<br>modalization<br>- polarity<br>+ declarative<br>+ statements | + unmarked<br>+ simple<br>+ participants as<br>Theme<br>almost = new<br>Themes &<br>linear &<br>continuous<br>patterns |

### 7.3.1.2. Visual analysis

The image included in the webpage, presented in Fig. 7-7, does not follow the way the text was organized, i.e. presenting various monuments; it only shows Canterbury Cathedral, the landmark announced by the title. The one chosen by the Tourist Board as representative is frequently associated with this religious cultural asset.

Quite small, it is built on a conceptual structure. It provides a visual representation of the Cathedral and presents its upper part, as observed from one of its laterals. By unstructured analytical processes, several Possessive Attributes, like different parts of the Cathedral (towers) and its surrounding elements (sky and trees), are depicted. Their Carriers, i.e. the cathedral and the landscape, are not presented totally. The picture is complex; the process related to the Cathedral seems the main one, as it is more detailed and focused.

The photo appears as an item of information and contemplation. The perspective is subjective, as the Cathedral is depicted from a particular point of view. The shot is close; the viewer cannot see the entire building. The horizontal angle is oblique; the picture is probably taken from one of the building's frontal sides. The vertical angle is low; the building stands tall in front of viewers. The relation created is close; the viewers are involved, but, at the same time, detached, probably because the Cathedral is presented as having power. The Cathedral is looking down to the viewers majestically; they can contemplate it, closely, but just partly, as their eyes cannot take it in entirely. The modality markers are mainly low, which can indicate a digitally modified picture or, maybe, just one taken by an unprofessional photographer from a too close angle. The predominant colour is ivory and there is little colour saturation, differentiation and modulation. Ivory can make the building more salient, as it stands on a blue background (the sky), accompanied by a green lateral (the tree). The contextualization and representation are also low; there is little detail, regarding both the surroundings and the building itself. The illumination and brightness markers are, though, medium towards normal, depicting the shades left by the towers.

The composition of the picture of Canterbury Cathedral indicates no particular information value. It presents just a conglomerate of elements, in no particular order. In fact, the Cathedral occupies the entire picture, leaving no room for anything else. This makes it salient and focused. It can also be considered framed by the setting.

The results of the visual analysis are presented in Table 7-18.

**Table 7-18 Institutional Canterbury Cathedral: Visual summary**

| Representational | Interactive | Compositional |
|---|---|---|
| complex<br>conceptual structure<br>unstructured analytical<br>cathedral & landscape (Carrier)<br>tower, sky + branches (Possessive Attributes) | offer<br>close shot<br>subjective<br>oblique horizontal angle<br>low vertical angle<br>+ low modality markers | - information structure cathedral (salient)<br>- framing |

### 7.3.1.3. Multimodal act

To sum up, Canterbury Cathedral is presented by a multimodal communicative act, a picture and a text. They seem to form a unitary act as the picture is embodied in the text. This layout may be associated to mental schemata; people usually have a mental image of a certain monument or place to visit, without knowing too many details about it. The text brings new information and describes the picture, giving shape and reality to the mental image. The picture is intended as realistic, even though its features seem to be modified in order to depict a particular position and impress users. Its closeness also contributes to this. The lack of details further stirs users' imagination, as if inviting to find them out. In the same line, the text does not provide many details about the Cathedral. Its focus is on general data, probably because it describes various landmarks. Usual for descriptions, the present is used to "eternize the peculiarities and beauties of the asset" (Calvi 2011, 81), as if they were permanent characteristics (Şimon 2014, 90). The description is impersonal, neutral and objective, as indicated by the preference for unmarked and nominalised Themes (Francis and Kramer-Dahl 1991, 354; Gotti 2008, 79), the presence of several semi-technical words, like Romanesque (Saorín 2001, 339), the little use of attributive processes or the absence of perception verbs (Pérez Vázquez 2011, 307) and the promoter voice. Facts are presented as true and transparent, considering the dominance of statements (Vanderveken 1990, 108; Myers 1994, 46) and the few instances of modality, negation and imperatives (Mocini 2009, 160). All this confers greater credibility to the transmitted ideas (Pérez Vázquez 2011, 307). The Tourist Board becomes an expert professional with no intent to manipulate.

The message is rather informative as the user is presented what is there to see. This is changed towards the end into more instructional and exhortative, by the "must see & do" section. The presentation of information is followed by instigation to action. The Tourist Board seems to be talking to the user and appeal to its senses, recreating the experience of 14th century England by means of the Canterbury Tales. Users are promised they will experience something different. The special and unique characteristics building up the image of the Cathedral seem to be its antiquity and its relation to history and religion. Even if the two modes seem different, the picture–close and subjective, and the text–impersonal and objective, they complement each other in order to persuade users that Canterbury Cathedral is worth visiting.

### 7.3.2. The Tower of London in the institutional corpus

Fig. 7-8[6] shows the webpage dedicated to the Tower of London.

Fig. 7-8 The Tower of London institutional webpage

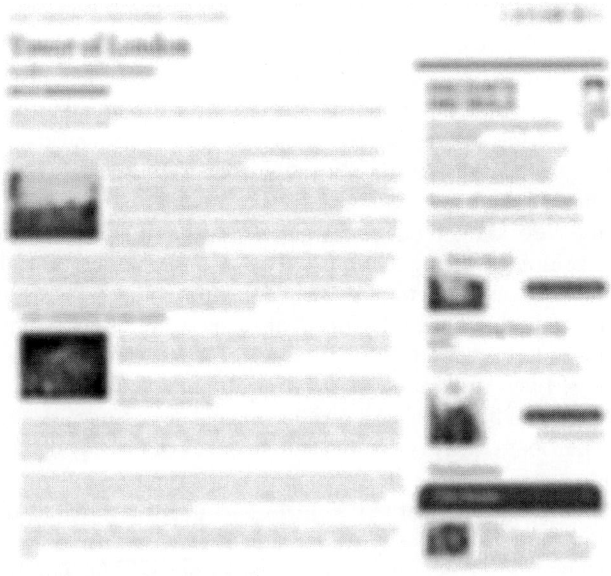

*Source*: VisitBritain (2011)

As can be seen, it follows the same layout as the one presenting Canterbury Cathedral. Briefly, the webpage has the same header and

[6] The header and footer of the webpage have not been included in Fig. 7-8, for reasons of space. They are the same as those in Fig. 7-7.

footer, is vertically organised in two columns and combines image and text on a horizontal axis. It also maintains the interactive section of discounts and deals. The difference is that its message is longer and further divided in two parts: one refers to the Tower of London and the other to the Ceremony of the Keys. Both are identically constructed by a text organised in short paragraphs and a picture embedded in it. The page contains also a direct link to the commercial side of the website, which provides more information regarding the tickets for the Ceremony. The salient elements, like the title, subtitle, introductory caption, pictures and the hyperlinks contained in the actual texts, are meant to capture viewers' attention.

### 7.3.2.1. Linguistic analysis

*Overview.* As just explained, the message dedicated to the Tower of London has two parts. Like in the text dedicated to Canterbury Cathedral, this text does not focus only on one topic. In this case, the addition does not refer to another monument in the area, but to a ceremony that takes place in the monument described. The Ceremony of the Keys is the locking of the Tower of London and is presented as an attraction not to miss. The text referring to the Tower focuses on its history and its main attractions, like the Crown Jewels or the Yeoman Warders. The part dedicated to the attractions goes into further detail and presents the Ceremony of the Keys throughout a text separated from the main one by a subtitle. This resembles the text on the Tower both in layout and in structure, containing even a photo. The attraction receives as much attention as the main cultural asset. This dual focus is not as surprising as in the case of Canterbury Cathedral because the Ceremony takes place inside the Tower. Even if it were not, it has a title indicating the topic to follow, so users cannot be surprised by a sudden change of topic.

*Logical.* The long text is syntactically developed and complex, presenting up to three clauses per sentence, as for example in "During a visit to the Tower you can see Britain's most precious treasure-The Crown Jewels, stand on the execution site of 3 English queens and explore the legends of this world-famous landmark" (VisitBritain 2011). It is built mainly by clause complexes; the number of clause simplexes is, however, high. These present information compacted by means of postmodification through apposition, defining relative clauses and non-finite clauses, as in "The Tower of London has a colourful history *dating back to the 11th century*" or "Don't miss your chance *to watch this fascinating tradition* on your trip to Britain". The tactic system is mainly composed by parataxis, such as "The Chief Yeoman Warder then meets his military escort (members of the Tower of London Guard), *and* together they lock the main gates of the Tower"; equal clauses are linked together by extension-addition. Information is added, extending on the previous message and providing orality to the message. There are also some instances of hypotaxis. In the part dedicated to the Tower, the message develops especially by elaboration on previous information. Different details are added as secondary information given on the Tower or its Beefeaters, frequently by non-finite clauses ("*Spanning over 900 years of British history*, the Tower of London was built by William the Conqueror *to protect London and assert his power*"), which contribute to the complexity of the text. The section related to the Ceremony of the Keys, in turn, expands by enhancement and presents circumstantial details related to time, cause-condition and manner, probably to situate the narration, like for example "*As they pass*, all of the Tower's guards salute the Keys". The text contains not only expansion, but also projection. By means of locution, the clause introduces a legend related to the Tower of London and its ravens ("legend has it *the Tower will fall, along with the Kingdom, if the ravens ever leave the site*"). The voice telling the ravens' legend may be used to mystify the cultural asset and intensify its attractiveness.

*Experiential.* The transitivity system of the text is quite varied. In contrast to the text dedicated to Canterbury Cathedral, material processes are predominant. As markers of objectivity and facticity (Barker and Galasinki 2001, 71), they refer mainly to the Ceremony of the Keys; they present the way it happens and what the Keys actually do every night by processes like "emerge", "lock" and "retrace one's steps". They also provide details regarding the Tower of London, its founder or purposes ("build", "protect"). Material processes are even related to possible visitors, as they point out various actions to be performed, like "explore" or "visit". Visitors are, however, more associated to mental and behavioural verbs, such as "see" and "stand". The text not only presents facts, but also describes. Usually, relational processes assign to the Tower various functions, such as "royal palace" or "prison"; possessions, like "colourful history"; and circumstances, e.g. "over 900 years of British history". The Tower is also identified as "one of the most famous fortified buildings in the world", whose visit can offer "a millennium of British history in one day", a strategy of exaggeration encountered frequently in advertising discourse (Crişan 2013, 946). There are also instances of verbal processes, which bring into the text other voices, like those of the guards. Their voices can give to the legend more authenticity and reliability, as they are experts on the Tower. The setting of the narration is composed by various types of circumstances, like time extent, "since the 1600s"; accompaniment, "along with the Kingdom"; manner, "without fail" and cause, "due to the popularity of the ceremony". The most frequent are location circumstances, as expected, which situate the action both in time, "during a visit to the Tower", and place, "on the execution site of 3 English queens".

The participants involved are much more frequently realized than implied. The landmark, consisting of the Tower and its attractions, is the most frequent one, as expected since it is the topic of the text. It plays the role of Goal, the entity on which action is performed, like in "*the Tower of London* was built by William the Conqueror". There are almost as many representations of the landmark as Carrier, as the one described and characterized, as for example in "*The Tower of London* has a colourful history". The visitor, however, is not very frequent, compared to the landmark. It is more implied than expressed, even if the difference is not very great. S/he is expressed as Senser, as the one who sees the attraction ("*you* can see Britain's most precious treasure-The Crown Jewels"), and implied as possible Actor ("For details on how to apply for tickets, *[you]* visit the Tower of London-Ceremony of the Keys"). Relating this to the role of Goal played by the Tower, the visitor is not the one performing the action on the Tower and its attractions. The promoter is not included at all in the text; its absence creates an illusion of neutrality and objectivity.

*Interpersonal.* The text introducing the Tower of London and its Ceremony of the Keys is built mainly by declaratives. Thus, information is presented as fact, as reliable assertions, in the form of statements, indicating, once again, no manipulative intention. There are some imperatives, by which the possible visitors are guided during the visit. They are indicated what to see and experience directly, "look out for" or "don't miss your chance".

The Mood component contains usually both Subject and Finite; there are however some cases of Subject ellipsis, like "This exceptional heritage site is a great day out and *[ø]* holds daily exhibitions and events throughout the year", which adds cohesion to the text. The text presents a varied interplay of Subject variants. The Tower of London occupies the Subject position more frequently than the other participants, but not as frequently as expected, considering the topic of the text. This is due probably to the fact that it shares protagonism with the Chief Yeoman Warder and the other guards involved in the Ceremony of the Keys. The Ceremony per se appears in Subject position quite rarely, the focus being on its characters. This can indicate a preference for narration rather than description. The visitor also appears many times in the main position in the clause, compared to the landmark. When expressed, the visitor is directly involved as an individual entity by "you". Differently from the text on Canterbury Cathedral, practical information related to the visit of the Tower and the tickets to the Ceremony is placed in Subject position twice to draw attention to it ("*Tickets to the Ceremony of the Keys* are free"). The Finites, the other component of Mood, are mainly fused and refer to present tense, like "is" and "holds", information being presented as general and timeless. The past is rarely used; it appears only to present the story of the only time in history when the Ceremony was not held ("was", "fell", "sent"). The list of tenses is completed by instances of present perfect, which signal changes over time, as in "it *has been* a royal palace, a prison, an execution site, an arsenal, a mint, a keep for wild animals and jewel house", and future, which anticipates and gives more credibility to the visit, as in "You'*ll* also *see* the Beefeaters" (Calvi 2011, 82). There are also instances of expressed Finites, usually in the case of modality. The modals are linked to the visitor as mitigators of the prescriptive voice (Mapelli and Piccini 2011, 68). More frequent, modalization is indicated by "can" and "will". The modal "can" is associated with the possibilities visitors have during a visit, like "see artefacts from every part of this remarkable history" or "see Britain's most precious treasure–The Crown Jewels", presented to them as offers. The modal "will", in turn, anticipates the things visitors will do and see, like "the Beefeaters". The instance of modulation, expressed by "must", recommends users to ask in advance for the tickets for the Ceremony, highlighting the popularity of the attraction ("Tickets to the Ceremony of the Keys are free, but due the popularity of the ceremony, you *must* apply in writing at least 2 months in advance"). Negation is present only once, e.g. "*Don't* miss your chance to watch this fascinating tradition on your trip to Britain", and emphasizes the suggestion of not missing the Ceremony.

Regarding the Residue component, this is usually complex, as it contains all its elements. There are several instances though, in the part dedicated to the description of the Ceremony, when it is expressed only by a Predicate, like "but they *stood up*", "*dusted themselves down*" or "and *carried on*". This is probably to present the happenings as successive and give speed to the action. The Adjuncts are almost always circumstantial, as expected from the high number of circumstances in the transitivity system. They add experiential meaning to the message, as in "The shock and the noise of the bombs sent the group flying *to the floor*".

*Textual.* Theme is frequently unmarked and simple; data is left to speak for itself, as in "*The Tower of London* has a colourful history". It is predominantly expressed by participants, the focus being informational.

Quite frequently, processes act as Theme and shift the focus to instruction and interaction, as they guide the tourists' steps ("*Look out* for the famous black ravens in the grounds of the Tower"). There are, however, a number of cases of marked and multiple Themes. In the case of multiple Themes, the textual element is usually present to add textual cohesion, "and", or to present a contrast, "but". The only case of interpersonal Theme places a negative Finite in the imperative mood in Theme position to strongly suggest that users should not miss the chance to see the Ceremony ("*Don't* miss your chance to watch this fascinating tradition on your trip to Britain"). Regarding the marked Themes, Adjuncts are placed in first position in order to locate action in time, "during a visit to the Tower", and to provide several causes that may influence the visit, like "due the popularity of the ceremony"; their placement makes them more conspicuous and dramatically focused (Greenbaum and Nelson 2002, 219). Marked are also the cases when non-finite clauses are placed in Theme position, premodifying the Subject, like "*Spanning over 900 years of British history*, the Tower of London …". The technique is frequently encountered in tourist and advertising texts (Thompson 2004, 163). This enhanced Theme is the opening of the text. In this way, attention is drawn to the importance of the Tower for the British history and to its antiquity.

The Thematic development combines patterns in almost equal proportions. The Theme is mostly carried continuously, maintaining the focus of the text and the attention of the user on "the Tower", "you" or "the Chief Yeoman Warder". Following a linear pattern, new information is introduced to the text and the message is developed cumulatively elaborating on Rheme information, as for example in "Look out for *the famous black ravens* in the grounds of the Tower. *These magnificent birds* have been kept here since the 1600s". New Themes, instead, like "you", "legend", "tickets" or the different Adjuncts and preposed attributives mentioned above, are also frequently present. They introduce new topics and draw them to the attention of the user, without making the text incohesive. Scarcely used, the multiple Theme pattern organizes the information and presents various parts of the same idea, as in "The Tower of London has a *colourful history*. *Romans* once occupied it, *it*'s the site of Europe's first fortress, *it* has been a royal palace, a prison, an execution site, an arsenal, a mint, a keep for wild animals and jewel house".

The lexico-grammatical features of the text introducing the Tower of London are included in Table 7-19.

**Table 7-19 Institutional Tower of London: Lexico-grammatical summary**

| Clause complex | Transitivity | Mood | Theme |
|---|---|---|---|
| + long<br>+ complex (2 cl.)<br>only expansion<br>+ parataxis<br>+ extension,<br>addition<br>almost = non-<br>defining &<br>defining relatives<br>clauses<br>+ apposition | + material<br>causative constr.<br>almost = attributive<br>& identifying<br>+ intensive<br>verbal & behavioural<br>only mental percep.<br>+ realized particip.<br>+ landmark<br>+ land. (realized)<br>= landmark & visitor<br>(implied)<br>+ Goal & Carrier<br>(landmark)<br>expressed Senser,<br>implied Actor<br>(visitor)<br>- promoter<br>various Circ,<br>+ location, + time | + residue<br>+ complex<br>residue<br>+ landmark<br>(visitor close) as<br>Subject<br>+ fused Finite<br>+ present<br>+ Circ. Adjuncts<br>+ modalization<br>polarity<br>+ declarative<br>+ statements | + unmarked<br>+ simple<br>+ participants as<br>Theme<br>almost =<br>continuous &<br>linear patterns<br>& new Themes |

### 7.3.2.2. Visual analysis

The webpage has two images, one depicting the Tower of London and the other presenting a scene from the Ceremony of the Keys. The analysis focuses on the picture of the Tower of London for the reasons mentioned in Chapter six. The Tourist Board presents the tower in a small, faded and distant scene. Unlike the image of Canterbury Cathedral, this is not one of the Tower's most representative pictures. It seems difficult to identify the exact topic, as it depicts several buildings enclosed by walls, without a clear vision of how these could merge into an ensemble of buildings. There is no sign or symbol to indicate that this is the Tower of London; it could be any castle in the world. Small like the one depicting Canterbury Cathedral, the picture uses conceptual structures to present the Tower and the landscape as Carriers. The different buildings (towers and wall) and surroundings (sky and trees) are represented as Possessive Attributes, without indicating the way they fit together. The picture is complex, with the Tower as primary process and the landscape as secondary, since it has only the role of background.

Presented to the viewer as an offer, the picture is to be contemplated and observed. The shot is medium; the Tower is neither close nor far away in the distance. The perspective is subjective, as in almost any picture, since the viewer is offered what the image producer wants to offer. The horizontal angle is oblique; the photo is not taken from the front. The lack of details makes it difficult to establish what part of the Tower the picture shows exactly. The vertical angle is eye level, maybe towards low; the buildings just stand there to be admired without necessarily representing a majestic landmark. This can mean that the Tower per se has a meaning; its depiction from a certain significant position makes no difference. The relation created by the interactive metafunction is equal and detached, within reach, but not actually touched. This may be a technique to stir the curiosity of the viewer. S/he can go closer and become involved, by visiting the Tower and finding out the missing details from the picture. Regarding modality, the picture contains more markers of medium modality than other types. The exceptions are colour modulation and contextualization, which are low in modality; the colours are unmodulated, while the details are absent. The picture seems real, as if taken by somebody from a medium distance, probably at sunset, considering the colour of the sky. It is very different from more professional pictures depicting panoramic views found on postcards and leaflets promoting the Tower of London.

The composition of the picture is based on a centre-margin structure. The buildings are placed centred, surrounded by the sky, the branches and the wall. This placement makes them salient. Their colour also contributes to this; sepia stands out from the grey of the wall and the faded blue of the sky.

**Table 7-20 Institutional Tower of London: Visual summary**

| Representational | Interactive | Compositional |
|---|---|---|
| complex<br>conceptual structure<br>unstructured analytical<br>tower & landscape (Carrier)<br>tower + walls, sky + trees<br>(Possessive Attributes) | offer<br>medium shot<br>subjective<br>oblique horizontal angle<br>eye level vertical angle<br>+ medium modality mark. | centre-margin<br>tower (salient)<br>tower (framed) |

### 7.3.2.3. Multimodal act

The picture provides a general view of the landmark. It focuses on the Tower from a long distance and invites users to go closer. The written text seems to draw users into the picture. It is general, like the image, as it does not contain many details apart from several well-known attractions like the Crown Jewels and the Beefeaters. Even if there are no spatial and architectural details, the text seems more focused on the visit than on the landmark, as it explicitly presents what users can do during a visit to the Tower. The Ceremony appears to be the focus of the text and, as such, it is presented in more detail than the Tower. Its depiction is aimed to stir interest and help interpret the experience (McKercher and du Cros 2002, 131). History comes alive through the Ceremony; users are recommended to participate in a part of it. The description is further fictionalised by the link between past and present introduced by the story regarding the only time when the Ceremony did not take place. The story adds dynamism and suspense. All these details can make users speculate how it was to live back then (McKercher and du Cros 2002, 133) and arouse their desire to experience the ceremony portrayed (Yui Ling Ip 2008, 6). Apart from history, the Tourist Board uses also the element of fantasy, usually associated to castles (McKercher and du Cros 2002, 133), in the legend of the ravens. A historical-fantastic picture is constructed around the Tower, aimed to seduce. By visiting the Tower and participating to the Ceremony, users can consume the asset in a spectacle and have a special and extraordinary experience (McKercher and du Cros 2002, 131). It seems that cognitive and emotional manipulation is used in order to cause action (Mocini 2009). This builds a more manipulative message than the one dedicated to Canterbury Cathedral. Subjectivity is also indicated by the connotative language, the appeal to senses or the closeness of the promoter. The Tourist Board comes closer to users than in the text on Canterbury Cathedral, in this way closeness permits manipulation and makes the message more persuasive. The distance is reduced by the use of personal pronouns and imperatives. "You" establishes a dialogue with users and gets them involved in the message (Garcia Álvarez 2006, 83), whereas the few instances of imperatives differentiate them from the mass (Mongkholjuck 2008, 27) and exhort them to do something (Calvi 2011, 83). Giving more space to the human component (Mapelli and Santos López 2010, 102), they project users into the scenery as if they were travelling through it (Garcia Álvarez 2006, 83). The colloquial and oral language is carried on by contractions, deictics, absence of technical words and exaggerations.

The message informs from a communicative immediacy that favours persuasion. Description characterizes the landmark and introduces its attractions, whereas imperatives guide the users' steps and set a path to follow. The Ceremony establishes a priori what it has to offer. The promotional message is culminated by the suggestion to apply for tickets. The possibility to see and experience all the things described is directly offered to users as a call for action. Both image and text instigate users to act. The text seems to fill in the missing details in the picture and bring the Tower closer, as it has done with the relation between promoter and users.

### 7.3.3. Edinburgh in the institutional corpus

The webpage introducing the city of Edinburgh follows the same layout as the other webpages analysed: header and footer; vertical two columns layout with information about the landmark, on the left column, and practical information, on the right column; and horizontal layout for the messages composed by image and text. There are however certain significant differences. One difference is the webpage's length. This seems to be announced from the beginning by the title: "Edinburgh travel guide". As the webpage is not about a particular monument, but about the city, it is expected to be longer than a webpage describing one monument. The title also indicates that the purpose of the message is to guide and, thus, inform users. This can imply the need for a detailed and informative webpage. Another difference is the multimodal arrangement of the information promoted, which follows the top-bottom structure typical of advertising. A huge visual is the promise of the reality presented afterwards in text. Attention is drawn by the various salient elements, like the title, bold subtitles, italic testimony of the visitor, hyperlinks to other information and coloured pictures.

The webpage is more multimodal than the others, since it contains several pictures and two videos. One of the videos has more impact as it occupies the entire screen and is the first thing the user sees when accessing the webpage. It is presented as a photo and can become a video if clicked on the play button. Its composition is based on the same principle as the rotating pictures of the home page: the picture is accompanied by a title, a short description, links to different activities and a map of the country placing the city, as indicated by Fig. 7-9. The other video comes shortly after the main one and, situated on the left, composes a sort of presentation card for the user. It is accompanied by a caption describing Edinburgh and a list of practical details about the city, like its population or closest airport. The idea of the presentation card to be remembered, a sort of memo, is suggested also by the accompanying paper clip. The video presents a quite young Sean Connery talking about his home town. The celebrity technique from the home page is repeated here, adding thus reliability and fame to the message.

Fig. 7-9 Edinburgh institutional webpage[7]

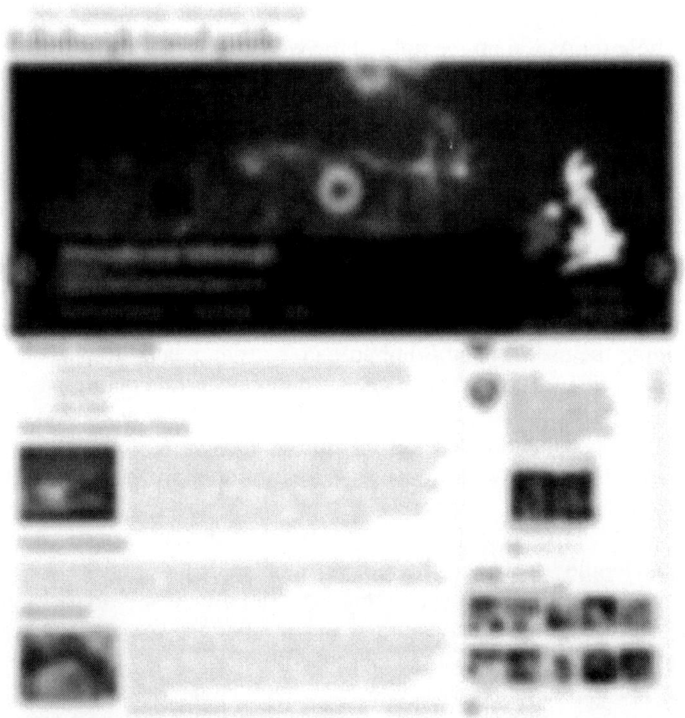

*Source*: VisitBritain (2011)

The last important difference is the high interactivity of the page. Apart from the videos, a tourist's testimony is provided, probably to confer veracity, confidence and a more personal touch to the travel guide to be presented. It can also imply, considering it follows the Sean Connery video, that Edinburgh is an experience for everybody, not only for the famous. The personal touch is increased also by a screenshot from a forum or a socialization network talking about UK. The users are further involved, as they are required for feedback by rating attractions and restaurants following a model provided by TripAdvisor. The model shows, once again, the testimony of others, which is further backed up by a well-known and international travel website. The Tourist Board's presentation

[7] This Figure presents only the first part of the webpage, as the entire one is quite long.

becomes, thus, more trustworthy. In addition, this requirement can make users feel important as if their opinions and tastes matter. The exchange of information probably tries to represent real conversation and get closer to users. The information on the right of the webpage is more interactive than practical, which is different from the other webpages; the discount and deals section has been replaced by links that take to other pages and sites, the offer being no longer direct and at hand.

#### 7.3.3.1. Linguistic analysis

*Overview.* The text can be said to follow the structure of a travel guide as it is divided in short sections, each dedicated to a particular topic. Longer, more detailed and more fragmented than the previous ones, the text guiding the user around Edinburgh goes from general to particular. It starts with a title, followed by a caption announcing the main attractions: Edinburgh Castle, the Royal Mill and the blend of traditional and modern. The actual presentation develops in the following topics: "Old Town meets New Town", where the Tourist Board announces the intention to guide the user through Edinburgh; "Culture & history", which highlights the city's UNESCO World Heritage status; "Attractions", from which an Edinburgh audio guide can be downloaded; a list of top "must-do's" during daytime and night-time; "Shopping"; "Sport"; and "Buy before you fly". The last section seems commercial, as it advertises tickets, facilities and accommodation that can be checked, booked and bought on the Tourist Board's shop webpage. The text introducing Edinburgh is, then, quite complete and organized, reminding users of a paper tourist brochure, with concise sections, bold titles and accompanying small pictures. It can be, however, too long and complicated to follow; the part with rated attractions and restaurants and the top "must-do's" list seem to disrupt the natural and vertical flow of information.

*Logical.* The text describing the city of Edinburgh is very long and contains many subsections as already indicated. It is syntactically developed, but not very complex. The clauses are usually simplex, like "discover Scotland's graceful capital" or "Edinburgh's beautiful Old and New Towns have been awarded UNESCO World Heritage Status twice over", probably due to the division into short sections of the text. Information is not elaborated, but just briefly presented with the aim of including many general ideas and provide, thus, a complete guide of the city. It is further compacted by appositions with additional specifications, as for example in "Let us guide you through Edinburgh-*Scotland's capital city, and one of Britain's most exciting tourist destinations*" (VisitBritain

2011). The few clause complexes are equally divided in parataxis and hypotaxis. The logico-semantic system is varied. Enhancement, the most frequently used, relates clauses mainly by causal-conditional relations, providing reasons for enjoying Edinburgh ("And golf fanatics will love Edinburgh too–*some of the world's best courses can be found in and around the city, including Gullane, the Open Championship course at Muirfield and the Open Qualifying course at Dunbar*") or for visiting the Tourist's Board website ("Don't forget to take a look at VisitBritain's massive selection of accommodation in Edinburgh–*you can book your choice of hotel, B&B or self catering cottage through our website*"). Temporal relations are created to guide the possible visitor's steps through the city ("Stay on the Royal Mile for The Scotch Whisky Experience and Ghost Tours, *then head to the beautiful Royal Botanic Garden for 70 acres of tranquillity*") or to indicate the things to buy before the flight to Britain ("Buy *before you fly*"). There is slightly less extension, bringing new information on Edinburgh and its streets into the text, e.g. "Princes Street, [...], is lined with great department stores; George Street is full of boutiques and bars; St Andrew's Square and Multrees Walk are designer heaven; *and* of course, there's the Royal Mile for some great Scottish souvenirs". Similarly, elaboration adds details about the city, Edinburgh Castle and other attractions, by non-defining relative clauses, as for example in "Edinburgh's Old Town is dominated by Edinburgh Castle, *which rests on a hilltop at the end of the Royal Mile*"; they act as descriptive glosses for the primary clauses. Apart from expansion, the analysis of the logical metafunction indicates also an instance of projection-idea, by means of which the user is suggested not to forget to visit a section on the website ("Don't forget *to take a look at VisitBritain's massive selection of accommodation in Edinburgh*").

*Experiential.* The text presents reality mainly by material processes, with a clear focus on objectivity and facticity (Barker and Galasinki 2001, 71). Some of them, like "create", refer to Edinburgh and its attractions, presented as capturing and dominating. Others, more numerous, indicate possible actions for the visitor, such as "visit" and "discover". It seems that the visitor is guided and shown the city by a tour full of action and dynamism. There is also a high number of relational processes. Mainly attributive, they describe the city as the "home of 4,500 listed buildings" or "a modern, dynamic city of art and culture", its streets as "full of boutiques and bars" or its stadiums as "home to the city's main football clubs". Identifying relational processes are infrequent and identify Edinburgh's unique character ("The combination of these 2 parts of the city, along with its vibrant events and celebrations such as Hogmanay and the Festival Fringe *is* what gives Edinburgh its unique character"), define the Edinburgh Pass as "the best way to explore the Scottish capital" and locate different attractions in space, like "the Witchery" ("*situated* in the shadow of Edinburgh Castle") or "Princess Street" ("*is lined* with great department stores"). Mental processes are also used, quite a lot compared to the other texts in the set. All the three types appear, but cognition is the most frequent. It addresses the possible visitors and encourages them to visit cognitively by learning "everything about Edinburgh's attractions" and discovering "the history behind Edinburgh Castle". The list of processes is completed by behavioural, which suggest the visitors to "stay" or "to take a look", and existential, which introduce different attractions like the Royal Mile ("there*'s* the Royal Mile for some great Scottish souvenirs"). These instances can remind users of a real tour in which the guide introduces attractions and asks tourists to admire them.

Circumstances come to complete the picture mainly by situating the action in space. As expected from the title, the text guides the visitors' steps through the city. This is done mainly by means of locative information, as for example in "Stay *on the Royal Mile* for The Scotch Whisky Experience and Ghost Tours", "Sample a dram *at The Scotch Whisky Experience*" and "Catch a classic theatre production *at the Royal Lyceum Theatre*". An important role is played also by cause circumstances. Significantly present, these indicate the purpose of visiting certain attractions, like the Royal Botanic Garden for "70 acres of tranquillity", as if pointing their benefits. The other circumstances present are few and varied, like manner, "you can book your choice of hotel, B&B or self catering cottage *through our website*", accompaniment, "See Edinburgh from your very own chauffer-driven trike *with Trike Tours Scotland*", or extent in time, "Edinburgh's beautiful Old and New Towns have been awarded UNESCO World Heritage Status *twice over*". There are no time circumstances, the visit being not confined by time and schedule.

The participants observed are very frequent in the text. They are mainly realized, but the implied number is also quite high. The landmark is frequently the participant, as expected. Usually realized, Edinburgh and its attractions mostly have the role of Goal, of the entity on which somebody performs an action, e.g. "Do *the Edinburgh Literary Pub Tour* and discover *Scotland's literary heroes*". Considering the number of material processes and their reference to the visitor, that "somebody" can be the visitor. The landmark appears in other various roles, the Carrier being the most numerous, as in "*The city* is home to 4,500 listed buildings". There are, however, a lot fewer of these than Goal, as predicted by the processes' analysis. The visitor, also frequent, is much more implied than realized, possibly because it is suggested that s/he does things, but never appears as having done them, as indicated by the imperative examples presented above. S/he becomes an expressed or visible Actor at the moment of the real visit, when s/he can act on the landmark. The visitor is sometimes implied also as Senser, as the one who "discovers" and becomes more knowledgeable. For the first time in the set, the promoter is overtly expressed in the text. The Tourist Board appears twice, always realized. It is named directly by the first person imperative "let us" and acts as an Actor who guides the visitor from a subjective perspective, "*Let us* guide you through Edinburgh …". The construction reminds users of the discourse tools real guides use to make people pay attention to them. When indirectly referred to by its shop, it plays the role of Goal, as it is visited by the user ("Visit *our shop* for more exciting offers …").

*Interpersonal.* The mood structure adapts to the different information presented by the long text. It combines in almost an equal proportion the declarative and imperative moods. The declarative is more frequent and presents information about Edinburgh and its attractions as facts and assertive data. The imperative, however, first captures the users' attention, and then suggests to them a list of "must-do's". In the end, users are offered the possibility to transform the suggestions into reality by visiting the Tourist Board's shop for "exciting offers" and "massive selection of accommodation". Statements are, then, associated to the landmark and used to describe, e.g. "Edinburgh is full of fabulous places to shop", whereas suggestions and recommendations address the users directly and guide their steps through the city, e.g. "Eat at The Witchery", as if taking them by hand in a world to discover (Mocini 2009, 12).

The Mood element is mainly composed by Subject and Finite. The Subject position is almost always occupied by Edinburgh, "*Edinburgh* is a haven for sports fans", and its attractions, "*George Street* is full of boutiques and bars", as the most important element. The visitor appears only once as Subject, in the final clause where s/he is presented with the possibility to book accommodation directly through the offered link ("*you* can book your choice of hotel, B&B or self catering cottage through our website"). The direct approach helps to transmit a more persuasive advertising message. Considering this, it can be said that, excepting the imperative constructions, the users are not addressed directly. This also indicates a more general approach. There is, however, another instance of "you", when the users are advised what to do by means of the categorical and authoritative clause "you definitely shouldn't". The construction of the sentence, though, mitigates the force of the advice; it is placed in an embedded clause, the focus being shifted from the users to the Edinburgh pass ("One thing [[*you definitely shouldn't* travel to Edinburgh without]] is an Edinburgh Pass"). This indicates a rather indirect way of addressing the visitor, which is present throughout the text; the Board mostly appears as an invisible guide. In this way, the directness of the high number of directives seems to be reduced. Most of the directives are grouped in the part of the "top must-do's", the rest of the text being constructed around this invisible, knowledgeable guide. The invisibility of the promoter is achieved also by its absence in the text; it appears only once, at the beginning. Referred by the imperative "let us", it asks permission from users to guide them "through Edinburgh …". This can imply that the Board exists only to guide users and for nothing else. The other component of the Mood element, the Finite assigns to the message generic and universal characteristics, as it is mostly fused and in the present tense, like "is" and "are". There is no instance of past; the description of the landmark is framed in the present. The majority of the expressed Finites are modals, which are slightly more frequent than in the other texts in the British set. The modal "can" refers to different possibilities like finding some of the best golf courses in and around the city or booking online, while "will" seems to predict that "golf fanatics" also love Edinburgh. Negation appears only once at the end of the text. Combined with an imperative and addressed directly to users ("Don't' forget"), it emphasises the importance of visiting the website's accommodation section. The reduced use of modals and negative forms make the information presented more evident (Mocini 2009, 160).

The Residue component of the mood structure is much more numerous than the Mood component, as expected due to the high number of imperatives. Usually complex, it always has in its composition at least two elements. The Adjuncts are numerous and mainly circumstantial, adding experiential meaning to the text, as indicated by the examples of circumstances provided earlier. Several conjunctives, not part of the mood structure, give textual cohesion to the message, like "also" and "too". There is also an instance of Mood Adjunct related to polarity, "of course", which adds interpersonal meaning. The copywriter points to the obviousness of the fact that the Royal Mile is a great place to buy "Scottish souvenirs" ("and *of course*, there's the Royal Mile for some great Scottish souvenirs").

*Textual.* The Themes in the text presenting the city of Edinburgh are usually unmarked and simple. Even if unmarked, some of them are more different than the regular unmarked Themes. Heavy Subjects ("One thing you definitely shouldn't travel to Edinburgh without"), non-finite clauses as Subjects ("To find places like the Water of Leith, Holyrood Park and Corstorphine and Blackford Hill in the middle of a city"), interpolation in Theme ("Princes Street, *which separates the Old and New Towns,* is lined with great department stores"), or existential constructions ("there are"), draw users' attention to those particular elements. Their length can, however, make the flow of information difficult and users can find this confusing. Nominalizations, though, confer objectivity to the message (Gotti 2008, 79). Apart from this, processes are more frequently placed in Theme position than participants, since there are numerous imperatives. Instructional Themes imitate real tours' interaction, like "do", "eat" or "go". The short clauses focusing on processes can indicate a succession of happenings both physical and mental, which, in turn, gives dynamism to the message and instigates to action. The visitors' movement through Edinburgh seems, thus, to be set out subjectively (Matthiessen 2007, 56). The few marked Themes are expressed by Adjuncts; the circumstance of accompaniment presents the way the Old and New Edinburgh combine, i.e. "together", while the circumstance of cause provides the reasons for buying an Edinburgh Pass, i.e. "With free entry to over 30 of the city's top attractions, free return airport and city centre bus transport, a free guidebook and lots of exclusive offers". The combination of the two parts of Edinburgh is also persuasively emphasised by the marked Thematic equative structure "The combination of these 2 parts of the city, along with its vibrant events and celebrations such as Hogmanay and the Festival Fringe is what gives Edinburgh its unique character". Regarding multiple Themes, textual Themes, like "and" and "then", are used several times to make the message more cohesive. Interpersonal Themes, like "of course" and "don't", in turn, highlight the obviousness of a piece of information, i.e. there is the Royal Mile for souvenirs, and point out what the users should not forget, i.e. look at the site section on accommodation.

As the entire text is organized and presented differently from the others analysed, its Thematic development is more disrupted. However, it is possible to observe a certain pattern. The message introducing the city of Edinburgh develops predominantly by continuous Themes, which imply a focused and successive flow. The Theme usually focuses on Edinburgh's attractions and the combination of old and new. This could create a repetitive or boring message, but this is not the case, as there is a rich interplay of synonyms, like "combination" or "together". The processes directed to users are also presented by a continuous pattern in order to give importance to guidance and succession. The new Themes are quite numerous and bring new information to the attention of users, like "let us", "there are" or information related to the things to buy before the trip. Also frequent, the linear Thematic pattern cumulatively builds the message introduced in Rheme ("There are *2 sides to Edinburgh*–the historic Old Town with the medieval Edinburgh Castle and cobblestone alleys, and the elegant but classic Georgian New Town. The *combination of these 2 parts of the city*, along with its vibrant events and celebrations such as Hogmanay and the Festival Fringe is what gives Edinburgh its unique character"), whereas the multiple pattern organises information in various steps, setting a balance between repetition and change ("Edinburgh is full of fabulous *places to shop*. *Princes Street* is lined with great department stores, *George Street* is full of boutiques and bars, *St Andrew's Square and Multrees Walk* are designer heaven").

The main characteristics of the text are included in Table 7-21.

**Table 7-21 Institutional Edinburgh: Lexico-grammatical summary**

| Clause complex | Transitivity | Mood | Theme |
|---|---|---|---|
| very long<br>+ simplexes (2 cl.)<br>+ expansion<br>= hypotaxis & parataxis<br>almost = enhancement, extension & elaboration<br>+ non-def. relatives<br>+ apposition | + material<br>+ attributive<br>+ intensive<br>behavioural & existential<br>+ mental cognition<br>+ realized particip.<br>+ landmark<br>+ land. (realized)<br>+ visitor (implied)<br>+ Goal (landmark) Actor (visitor)<br>= Actor & Goal (only realized) (promoter)<br>various Circ,<br>+ location, only place | + residue<br>+ complex residue<br>+ landmark as Subject<br>+ fused Finite<br>+ present<br>+ Circ. Adjuncts<br>+ modalization polarity<br>almost = declarative & imperative<br>almost = statements & commands | + unmarked<br>+ simple<br>+ processes as Theme<br>+ continuous Thematic pattern |

### 7.3.3.2. Visual analysis

The webpage presenting Edinburgh contains many images, as can be seen in Fig. 7-9. The aim is probably to inform by illustration and identification of the particular monuments or places discussed, like Edinburgh Castle or the Royal Botanic Garden, as if showing what tourists can see once they reach the place (Matthiessen 2007, 56). By this, users can be tempted. These pictures resemble the small images from the other webpages. A "luring" role is assigned to the big picture from the beginning, which is totally different from the images in the other webpages. Occupying the entire screen, it offers several rotating alternatives: Fireworks over Edinburgh, Edinburgh Art Festival Installation, Edinburgh Fringe Festival, Greyfriars Kirkyard, the Balmoral Hotel and Calton Hill, all of them emblematic for the city. The images of different attractions are said to reinforce each other and produce a sense of excitement (Yui Ling Ip 2008, 7). The one analysed below is the first of them.

The picture is the shot from a video from the Hogmanay celebration, which indicates the idea of spectacle and experiential discovery. From a panoramic view, it presents the city dominated by the Edinburgh Castle, from the hill at the back, as indicated by the text. The daytime counterpart of the picture is frequently associated with the city and encountered on postcards or leaflets; Edinburgh has long been symbolised by its castle and the rock on which it stands (Hemelryk Donald and Gammack 2007, 46). This one, instead, taken at night, is quite rare and can show how the photographer can provide viewers with images of reality that carry different meanings by simple changes (Yui Ling Ip 2008, 7), like the absence of light. Darkness can add a sense of mystery and romanticism to the city, but it can also confuse the user who can fail to identify the monuments in the picture. This identification may not be, however, the purpose of the picture, as the title is “Fireworks over Edinburgh” and this is what it depicts, the Castle is just secondary information. These fireworks are more connotative than others as they symbolize the New Year and other meanings associated to Hogmanay (“New Year’s Eve” in Scottish). Also built on a conceptual structure, the unstructured analytical process depicts the sky, the fireworks and several monuments, among which the only clearly recognisable one is the Castle, as Possessive Attributes. Their combination into a meaningful whole, the Carrier–the city, is not visibly presented. The picture is simple and contains no other process or circumstance. The placement and the colour of the Castle can, though, indicate a symbolic attributive process; the Castle can be a Symbolic Attribute and stand for the city of Edinburgh.

Presented for contemplation, for watching, actually, since it is a video, the image is an offer. The perspective is, as in the majority of cases, subjective; the viewer being presented only what the image/video producer wants to present. As it is panoramic, it includes many elements, which can be represented from different social distances and angles. The shot is long; the Castle lies in the distance. The horizontal angle may be frontal, if looking at the Castle, or oblique, if looking at something else in the frame.

The same is true for the vertical angle; this may be high or eye level. Even if panoramic, it seems that the picture has as a focus the Castle, probably as a symbol of the city, as already mentioned. Out of reach and in the distance, the powerful and magnificent Castle looks down on the viewers. The frontal angle situates them inside the frame. This can indicate that they have the possibility to engage and get closer. The modality markers build a picture of medium towards low modality. The low modality markers can be present because the picture is taken during night-time; illumination, brightness, colour saturation, differentiation and modulation are absent. The picture should be real as it is part of a video that is actually recorded. It may be that the choice of low modality, absence of details and of almost unrecognisable elements to depict Edinburgh is made with the purpose of stirring the viewers' curiosity to decipher the picture by themselves. The first step is to see the video and, then, the real Edinburgh.

Compositionally, the picture is part of a visual, which again reminds users of advertisements. It occupies the upper part of the frame, whereas, at the bottom, there is a black strip containing the title and some links to more information. This can mean that, by reading the indicated links of real information, users can get to the ideal, i.e. the castle depicted and the city. Importance is given to the green "play" sign, title and UK's map showing where Edinburgh is, depicted as salient elements. Within the actual picture, the Castle is situated in the middle as important information, confirming, once again, that it is the focus of information. The focus on the Castle is also highlighted by its saliency; the lights and the fireworks make it stand out. The fireworks are, in their turn, salient, contributing to the romanticism and spectacle of the city. The Castle seems also framed by darkness.

The visual characteristics of the Edinburgh image are summarised in Table 7-22.

**Table 7-22 Institutional Edinburgh: Visual summary**

| Representational | Interactive | Compositional |
|---|---|---|
| simple<br>conceptual structure<br>unstructured analytical<br>city (Carrier)<br>castle & surroundings (Possessive Attributes) | offer<br>long shot<br>subjective<br>frontal & oblique<br>horizontal angle<br>high & eye level vert. angle<br>almost = low & medium modality markers | top-bottom & centre-margin<br>castle, fireworks (salient)<br>castle (framed) |

### 7.3.3.3. Multimodal act

The communicative act in this webpage is complex and multimodal. The picture is more persuasive than the others in the set, as it plays with the senses. It proposes to users to consume the city of Edinburgh by participating in a symbolical and famous ceremony. The emotional promise is pointed also by the page alignment. Excitement is emphasised by the high moment of any ceremony, the fireworks. The discovery of the city by means of senses is not so obvious in the text, except for the "Attractions" and "Must-do's" sections. The last one seems different from the rest of the text due to its layout, short sentences and imperatives. Action-oriented, the verbal dynamism can lead to mobility (Calvi 2006, 42) and encourage users to react. The possible impoliteness is disregarded; the specification of the action to be performed and its potential beneficial effect on the visitor are more important (Murcia and O'Donnell 2003, 4). The dynamism can also add enthusiasm about visiting the landmark, which provides many attractions apart from monuments, such as shopping, sport, restaurants and pubs, theatres and spooky tours, even after dark. The concentration of various attractions offers users "clustered opportunities" (Jansen-Verbeke and Lievois 2002, 94), apparently preferred by tourists. All these contribute to "its unique blend of traditional and modern Scottish culture", an idea frequently repeated. The Scottish icons, such as golf, landscapes, festivals or whisky, make Scotland an authentic experience, difficult to be manufactured (Yeoman *et al.* 2005, 140-141; Moilanen and Rainisto 2009, 45). The tone is persuasive, as the Tourist Board introduces attractions by their entire name and specifies the uniqueness of each. The imperatives project the users into Edinburgh (Mocini 2008, 12) and guide their steps around its attractions. The direct and colloquial language is counterbalanced by the indirectness of the rest of the message. This focuses on descriptions and goes from general to particular. The presentation of the city concludes with a practical suggestion; the Tourist Board shop offers the possibility to see all the attractions described by "exciting offers". This advertising part, in contrast to the rest of the text, is addressed directly to users by the personal pronoun, as if establishing major trust by contact. The authoritative and knowledgeable voice of the Board is mitigated by the indirect advertising; the shop is the one with the offers, not the Tourist Board.

The message, thus, combines informative passages with commercial ones. The desire to persuade is always present, even if frequently hidden by the indirect and objective voice of the promoter. The picture is blind, whereas the text guides. They are probably aimed to complete each other, the text may guide towards the Castle represented in the picture.

### 7.3.4. Discussion of the British set of institutional webpages

The home page of the British Tourist Board's website is attractive, diversified, but rather long. It communicates clearly the contents of the website, which provide general, practical, transactional and navigational type of information. Its purpose is stated from the beginning: if users are planning holidays, looking for accommodation or tourist information on Great Britain, the site has all they need. The owner's identity is referred to just by its logo, no other specification being included. The webpages analysed follow the same macrostructure: header with navigational menu, main body and footer, indicating a consistent and coherent website. Their layout generally follows that required by website writing, the organization of information in columns (Garzone 2009, 38). Nevertheless, the self-contained blocks of the home page and the page-like flow of text in the webpages remind users of more traditional layouts. The blocks lead to an unclear reading path, and together with the length of the home page, can confuse users. The webpages are clearer than the home page, as they are shorter and arranged like a "typical printed page of text" (Lemke 2002), i.e. title, text and photo, all in usual colours–black text and not very coloured picture. The paragraphs are short and easy to read, as typical for web writing (Garzone 2009, 42). The webpage dedicated to Edinburgh is, however, slightly different from the others due to its more numerous separate blocks of meaning that present a broader topic with a different aim.

The webpages take full advantage of the possibilities provided by "the hypermedia environment" (Garzone 2009, 41) and transmit information in innovative and interesting ways (OMT 1999, 133; 2001, 113) by pictures, videos and interactive links. Their aim is to make experience more real and, ultimately convince users to become tourists. They offer even the possibility to book tours and accommodation and buy tickets by accessing the Tourist Board's shop or exterior travel agencies. This practical possibility is very convenient for users, who can get information and book on the same website and at the same time. It also provides a more reliable and trustworthy character to the whole operation of online booking and paying, as it is guaranteed by the official British Tourist Board. These transactional details on tours or tickets are usually clearly separated as they are not included in the message analysed dedicated to provide general information about the landmark.

All the webpages seem to apply the AIDA model. Attention is drawn by the title, subtitle, and images. Interest is maintained by the caption, which points out the uniqueness of the landmark. Desire is raised by the presentation of the landmark and its attractions, whereas Action can be induced by the must-see section or the commercial part regarding tickets and booking. All the messages follow the same structure: identify the name of the tourist attraction, provide its background and describe it. Additionally, they also provide instructions for tourists, suggesting possible things to see or do. The only page to specify practical information about how to get to the attraction or its services is the one on Edinburgh. The right column on tours can, though, be checked, if needed. As expected, the messages are mixed since their purposes are to inform, persuade and induce to action. The last two are sometimes hidden in the informative function that portrays a true, objective and timeless reality. Users are both informed and directed, with a preference for the first one. The instructional aspect is reduced to the parts dedicated to must-see attractions, which are fully exploited to guide and instigate users. Persuasion seems, thus, to be based more on descriptions. These are general and without many details. They are presented with a visitor in mind, as if preparing her/him for the visit by anticipation. They tend to combine several attractions in the same message, probably to sound more interesting and attractive. Another technique used for the same purpose is the inclusion of stories and legends, which add fantasy to the landmark promoted and make users do more than just see and visit, i.e. experience a spectacle.

The language reflects the purposes of the message, as indicated by the results of the metafunctions' analyses summarized in Table 7-23. The texts are rather long and general, as they try to say something about all the attractions included. They are medium elaborated and syntactically developed. Their message is built on expansion, combining both parataxis and hypotaxis. The logico-semantic relations are not similar among the texts, but the preferred ones seem to be elaboration by non-finite clauses and extension. This can indicate that the texts develop by adding pieces of information and details and not by presenting the relation between them; the landmark is not presented in relation to anything else. The processes used are material and relational, with a preference for the former due to the desire to guide the visitor and get her/him involved. Mental processes are rarely used, which can imply that the discovery of the attraction relies more on description and action than on cognition and perception. The background information is provided mainly by locative circumstances, which situate the attraction in time and space.

The message is centred on the landmark depicted as Goal and Carrier, as expected from a description. The landmark is also frequent in Subject/Theme position, composing a focused message. The visitor is not very frequent, compared to the landmark, and its usual role is that of Actor, the one in power. Direct appellation by second personal pronoun is quite rare; it usually appears at the beginning of the message to draw users' attention and make them feel important as individuals. The Tourist Board is almost absent, except for several implied cases. This may aim to give the impression of informing in an objective and unmanipulated way as a professional expert at the service of users. Even though its voice is not colloquial as in the home page, it still sounds friendly enough to guarantee persuasion. The participants' roles indicate a described landmark, acted upon by the visitor, without the interference of the promoter. The message is assertive, true, generic, timeless and evident, as indicated by the mood analysis. However, there are few exceptions of modalization by "can" and "will", which present users to various possibilities and anticipate the visit. This is also anticipated by imperatives as they project the users in the scenery and guide their steps. The Thematic development is usually mixed in all the texts, with a slight preference for the continuous one. This implies a focused message, usually on information, represented by the landmark, and rarely on instructions, expressed by imperatives. The Theme is unmarked, with the exception of few isolated cases when Adjuncts or relative clauses draw users' attention on their content. The discourse seems, thus, objective, impersonal, indirect and informative, as if the landmark should attract by itself and by what it stands for. This is periodically counterbalanced by a persuasive tone implied by the subjective guidance of the imperative, the direct involvement of the visitor or the connotative and commercial details.

**Table 7-23 British set of institutional websites: Lexico-grammatical summary**

| System | Canterbury Cathedral | Tower of London | Edinburgh |
|---|---|---|---|
| Clause complex | medium long<br>almost = complexes & simplexes (2 cl.)<br>only expansion<br>almost = hypotaxis & parataxis<br>+ elaboration<br>+ non-def. relatives<br>+ defining clauses | + long<br>+ complexes (2 cl.)<br>only expansion<br>+ parataxis<br>+ extension, addition<br>almost = non-defining & defining relatives clauses<br>+ apposition | very long<br>+ simplexes (2 cl.)<br>+ expansion<br>= hypotaxis & parat.<br>almost=enhancement extension & elaboration<br>+ non-def. relatives<br>+ apposition |

| System | Canterbury Cathedral | Tower of London | Edinburgh |
|---|---|---|---|
| Transitivity | + relational<br>+ identifying<br>+ intensive<br>many material<br>only mental percep.<br>+ realized participants<br>+ landmark<br>+ landmark (realized)<br>almost = landmark & visitor (implied)<br>+ Goal, then Carrier & Identified (landmark)<br>Actor (visitor)<br>- promoter<br>+ location, + place | + material<br>causative constr.<br>almost = attributive & identifying<br>+ intensive<br>verbal & behavioural<br>only mental percep.<br>+ realized particip.<br>+ landmark<br>+ landmark (realized)<br>= landmark & visitor (implied)<br>+ Goal & Carrier (landmark)<br>expressed Senser, implied Actor (visit.)<br>- promoter<br>various Circ,<br>+ location, + time | + material<br>+ attributive<br>+ intensive<br>behavioural & existential<br>+ mental cognition<br>+ realized participants<br>+ landmark<br>+ landmark (realized)<br>+ visitor (implied)<br>+ Goal (landmark)<br>Actor (visitor)<br>= Actor & Goal (only realized) (promoter)<br>various Circ,<br>+ location, only place |
| Mood | + residue<br>only complex residue<br>+ landmark as Subject<br>+ fused Finite<br>+ present<br>only Circ. Adjuncts<br>only modalization<br>- polarity<br>+ declarative<br>+ statements | + residue<br>+ complex residue<br>+ landmark (visitor close) as Subject<br>+ fused Finite<br>+ present<br>+ Circ. Adjuncts<br>+ modalization<br>polarity<br>+ declarative<br>+ statements | + residue<br>+ complex residue<br>+ landmark as Subj.<br>+ fused Finite<br>+ present<br>+ Circ. Adjuncts<br>+ modalization<br>polarity<br>almost = declarative & imperative<br>almost = statements & commands |
| Theme | + unmarked<br>+ simple<br>+ participants as Theme<br>almost = new Themes & linear & continuous patterns | + unmarked<br>+ simple<br>+ participants as Th.<br>almost = continuous & linear patterns & new Themes | + unmarked<br>+ simple<br>+ processes as Theme<br>+ continuous Thematic pattern |

The images in the webpages analysed present a rather different message. They are not very informative, as they are slightly unclear and unrepresentative of the depicted landmark. As indicated in Table 7-24, their structure is conceptual. The pictures do not present the entire landmark, but only the parts chosen subjectively by the image producer. They are complex, as they depict also the surrounding of the landmark. They are offered as objects of contemplation in order to draw users' attention and instigate their desire to see the depicted scene in reality. The landmarks are placed in salient positions so that they cannot pass unobserved. These are usually depicted from an oblique and low angle, as standing majestic outside the viewers' world. No matter the distance of the shot, the images always lack details, probably to stir curiosity. Despite the interplay of modality markers depicting realistic pictures, features, like the absence of details, can indicate their digitization in order to present a more focused landmark. The visual message seems, then, persuasive and continues the visual symbolism introduced in the introductory message of the home page.

**Table 7-24 British set of institutional websites: Visual summary**

| System | Canterbury Cathedral | Tower of London | Edinburgh |
|---|---|---|---|
| Representational | complex<br>conceptual structure<br>unstructured<br>analytical<br>cathedral & landscape (Carrier)<br>tower, sky + branches (Possessive Attributes) | complex<br>conceptual structure<br>unstructured<br>analytical<br>tower & landscape (Carrier)<br>tower + walls, sky + trees (Possessive Attributes) | simple<br>conceptual structure<br>unstructured<br>analytical<br>city (Carrier)<br>castle & surroundings (Possessive Attributes) |
| Interactive | offer<br>close shot<br>subjective<br>oblique horizontal angle<br>low vertical angle<br>+ low modality markers | offer<br>medium shot<br>subjective<br>oblique horizontal angle<br>eye level vert. angle<br>+ medium modality markers | offer<br>long shot<br>subjective<br>frontal & oblique horizontal angle<br>high & eye level vertical angle<br>almost = low & medium mod. mark. |
| Compositional | - information structure<br>cathedral (salient)<br>- framing | centre-margin<br>tower (salient)<br>tower (framed) | top-bottom & centre-margin<br>castle, fireworks (salient)<br>castle (framed) |

To summarise, the verbal and visual discourse combine into a sole communicative act, meant to inform and persuade users to visit Britain.

They seem to complement and extend each other (Anthonissen 2003, 302). The overall message is patriotic and focuses on various unique characteristics of the landmarks: antiquity, religion, history or the combination of traditional and modern. These are the main attributes aimed to convince that Britain is worth visiting. They are testified not only by the professional and objective Tourist Board, but also by a number of British celebrities, past international tourists or the famous TripAdvisor.

# CHAPTER EIGHT

# COMMERCIAL CORPUS: RESULTS AND DISCUSSION

This chapter presents the same countries and landmarks as Chapter seven, but from a commercial perspective. The websites chosen belong to tour operators. They are: for Great Britain, Evan Evans Tours; for Spain, Spain Day Tours; and for Romania, Ciao Romania, as mentioned in the Methodology chapter.

## 8.1. Romanian set of commercial webpages

The Romanian commercial website, found at http://www.ciaoromania.co.uk/, is arranged vertically on a light blue background. Blue is considered the most universally favoured colour and, therefore, the safest to use in business. It helps building customer loyalty, as it relates to trust, honesty and dependability. On this page, it may remind users of the blue of the Romanian flag, even if the shade is very different. The home page is short and can be divided in two main areas: the header and the body. The header contains a collage of similar pictures framed by a blue line in the form of a wave. Together, they depict a natural landscape composed by mountain cliffs and forests and inhabited by shepherds, peasants or hikers. Romania is usually depicted in relation to its pastoral and rural features (Light *et al.* 2009). The picture contains also the logo of the tour operator: its name, "Ciao Romania", is written in yellow and can symbolise an encounter and a discovery. It is accompanied by a sun, called the "Sun of East", which probably symbolises Romania and defines it as the sun of Eastern Europe, the most important star or country in the region.

The body of the page can be further divided in two columns. The first one is placed in the left margin and presents the contents of the website. They are numerous because they are not gathered under broad particular topics. This can show a clear and intuitive content, but, at the same time, can make the website less organised and hierarchical. Each link is accompanied by a small symbol that represents the words visually. For example, "Rent a car" has a car next to it or "Sites UNESCO" has the UNESCO logo. This can break the monotony of the page, make the links salient and transmit meaning multimodally. The information proposed by lateral navigational menu is mainly general and related to the tours offered, like "Bucharest Trip" and "Rural Romania Tour". The tours are also illustrated by clients' photos in "PHOTO souvenir", which, apart from presenting different landmarks, depict happy people. This situates the tours in real life and persuades users by depicting attractive surroundings and satisfied people. The links also present general information about Romania, its UNESCO sites and the tour operator. The practical information is limited to guides, transport and links in tourism. The only navigational information is the link to "Home". Interactivity is reduced to the links provided.

The second column presents the main message of the home page. Its layout and its letter font and size remind users of traditional print pages (Lemke 2002). The first word, "Ciao", addresses users and invites them to travel to Romania with the tour operator. The colloquial and direct tone is maintained throughout the message. The message is very persuasive, reminding users of advertising discourse due to its connotations and play on words: "It's time for a new vacation! For a new destination, full of mystery and sensations. It's time to say Ciao Romania!" (Ciao Romania 2012). A picture of one of the tours, "Traditional Romania tour", is placed immediately afterwards to give proof of the previous words. This depicts a picturesque scene with a steam train surrounded by sheep and nature. The message is built on the idea of the existence of a new country to discover in the tourism field. The characteristics of this new country are listed and exemplified by different tours, which now group the tours from the lateral menu bar. This can make the website contents more obvious and clearer, but also repetitive and redundant. The final promise continues to address the senses, "A vacation that will spoil all your senses!". Suggestive words are useful tools in tourism promotion as the product is intangible (Bosch Abarca 2001, 328). After promoting Romania and raising the interest of the users, the tour operator is introduced as the one to make possible the holiday that spoils the senses. The uniqueness of the operator is reflected in its tailor-made tours further listed.

The home page seems to follow the AIDA model (OMT 2005b, 8) in certain ways. Users' Attention is aimed at by the most salient components: the links to tours, the logo and the attractive photos. Interest may be aroused by the persuasive message about Romania and the tour operator and the links to transport and accommodation. Desire is further stimulated by the links to vacations associated to the main characteristics of the country. The call to Action is limited; despite the page encourages users to travel and to read more, it does not offer any immediate possibility to book or interact.

### 8.1.1. The Monastery of Horezu in the commercial corpus

The tour operator does not offer a tour only to the Monastery of Horezu; the landmark is included in the "Grand tour Romania-Unesco tour", which takes visitors across the country and introduces them to the Romanian landmarks that bear the UNESCO designation. The webpage describing this tour follows the same layout as the home page: header, marginal left column and main body. It is very long and contains various types of information.

The webpage starts by a presentation card that contains: title, picture, itinerary, duration and distance. Each day is presented in different sections composed by a title with the day number, the landmarks visited and kilometres done; two pictures of different landmarks and a short presentation of that day. The pictures are salient and framed and seem to be presented as the promised product, whereas the text introduces information about it, as suggested by the top-bottom layout. The description gives details of the landmark, the information on the tour being limited to food and accommodation. It seems persuasion is aimed at by focusing on the landmark's characteristics and not on those of the tour. At the end of the presentation, the tour is situated on a map, which locates users geographically. The map is interactive and can be seen also as a satellite image; the tour operator's proposal looks more real. The description of the tour is followed by more practical and transactional details, like prices, services included and not included. These are listed for a clearer and direct transmission. The conditions, payment and cancelation information are further described briefly. The transparent communication of transactional details puts the tour operator in a professional light. The final message calls to action and instigates users, in a direct and persuasive tone, to "RESERVE NOW" their "place in this GRAND ROMANIA TOUR", so that they can explore the World Heritage of the beautiful Latin country situated among Slavic neighbours.

The Monastery of Horezu is presented in the description dedicated to the second day of the tour and is offered as an alternative to another landmark, the Church of Saint Nicholas.

Fig. 8-1 The Monastery of Horezu commercial webpage

*Source*: Ciao Romania (2012)

### 8.1.1.1. Linguistic analysis

*Overview*[1]. The Monastery of Horezu is described briefly by several of its characteristics. These are aimed to impress and convince users that the landmark is worth visiting, even if it is provided as an alternative which appears in brackets.

*Logical*. The text is very short, but rather complex and syntactically developed. It contains only one clause complex, built by reduced non-defining relative clauses linked by extension ("Alternatively you can visit the Horezu Monastery–UNESCO monument *founded in 1690 by the Prince Constantin Brancoveanu, considered one of the best examples of "Brancovean" style, known for the purity of architectural details and richness of details, for its religious composition, ex–voto portraits and ornamental painting*") (Ciao Romania 2012). The clauses develop on the landmark promoted with the aim of presenting information. The details are packed inside one clause complex. The actual information, which might draw clients' attention, is presented as secondary, since the focus is on the main clause, which states the possibility of visiting "the Horezu Monastery–Unesco monument". The description of the Monastery seems dependent on the information about the tour.

*Experiential*. This duality of information can be further found, as the text seems to have two sections: one directed to users and the other describing the Monastery. The message dedicated to users addresses them directly by the personal pronoun "you" and the material process "visit" ("Alternatively *you* can *visit* the Horezu Monastery"); the communicative immediacy and the persuasive message are more than obvious. The message regarding the Monastery, instead, combines processes, such as material "found", relational causative "consider" and mental cognition "know". It summarizes some of the most important pieces of information about the Monastery, like its foundation and its fame. These are backed up by circumstantial details, e.g. "in 1690".

As for participants, the landmark and the client appear equally expressed in the text. However, the landmark is also implied to a greater extent than expressed. It seems that the client is intended to be the main participant, but the text focuses more on the landmark as its topic. It usually has the role of Goal ("Alternatively you can visit *the Horezu Monastery*"), of something on which action has and can still be done. The

---

[1] The same subheadings (Overview, Logical, Experiential, Interpersonal and Textual) from Chapter seven are used here to guide readers through the linguistic analyses of the webpages.

client is presented as Actor, as the one "visit[ing]" the Monastery. There is no mention of the tour operator; the text, thus, comes across impersonal.

*Interpersonal.* The statement "Alternatively you can visit the Horezu Monastery" presents users with the possibility to visit the Horezu Monastery. This alternative offer to another landmark in the itinerary proposed for the UNESCO tour is indicated by the modal "can" and the Conjunctive Adjunct "alternatively". The expressed Finite is in the present, as if the message is universal (Banks 2002, 6). The Subject position is occupied by the pronoun "you", indicating once again the importance of the users in the message. The communicative directness seems mitigated by modalization.

**Table 8-1 Commercial Monastery of Horezu: Lexico-grammatical summary**

| Clause complex | Transitivity | Mood | Theme |
|---|---|---|---|
| short<br>only complexes (4 clauses)<br>only expansion<br>+ parataxis<br>+ extension, addition<br>+ non-defining relative clause<br>+ non-finite clauses | + material<br>only causative constr<br>- identifying/ attributive<br>only mental cognit.<br>= realized & implied participants<br>+ landmark<br>+ landmark (realized)<br>+ landmark (implied)<br>+ Goal (landmark)<br>+ Actor (client)<br>- operator<br>= location & cause, only time | = mood & residue<br>complex residue<br>only client as Subject<br>only expressed Finite<br>only present<br>only Conjunctive Adjunct<br>only modalization<br>- polarity<br>only declarative<br>only statement | only unmarked<br>only multiple (textual)<br>only participant as Theme<br>- Thematic progression |

*Textual.* The only Theme of the text is unmarked and multiple, "Alternatively you". The placement of the Conjunctive Adjunct "alternatively" in Thematic position highlights the fact that the Horezu Monastery is an option. This can make the tour more interesting as it gathers several important attractions. Nevertheless, it can also reduce the importance of the Monastery as it is placed secondary to other landmark(s). There is no Thematic progression, as there is only one conjoinable clause unit. Information does not flow, but is rather added as notes or observations. Users can be confused by the entangled description of the Monastery. At the same time, this can move users' attention towards the beginning of the message, where the visit is proposed. It seems that attention is focalized on the users' action and not on the description of the Monastery. This is expected in a message supposed not only to describe, but to instigate users to act.

#### 8.1.1.2. Visual analysis

One of the two pictures chosen to represent the landmarks proposed for the second day of the tour depicts the Monastery of Horezu. This is unexpected as the Monastery is presented as an alternative and not as the main option. The picture is easily recognisable because it is frequently associated with the Monastery. The conceptual structure presents the Monastery as Carrier and its church as Possessive Attribute by an unstructured analytical process. At the same time, the process can be understood as symbolical, if the church stands for the complex of the Monastery. The background is also represented by an unstructured analytical process, placing the trees and sky as Possessive Attributes.

The picture is offered, as always, for contemplation. The church of the Monastery is presented entirely from a medium shot. The angles are oblique and low. The building, thus, stands there impressive in its grandeur outside the viewers' world, but still in their reach. This can act as an indirect invitation to go closer and visit the church. The modality markers compose a realistic image. In spite of this, the surrounding colours, especially the green and the blue in the background seem retouched to appear stronger as if to contrast with the white of the building.

The informational structure of the picture is organised on the centre-margin value zones. The church is the centre as the dominant element, as the most important. Its position and colour make it salient and framed.

Table 8-2 contains the visual features of the image depicting the Monastery.

**Table 8-2 Commercial Monastery of Horezu: Visual summary**

| Representational | Interactive | Compositional |
|---|---|---|
| complex<br>conceptual structure<br>unstructured analytical<br>monastery & background (Carrier)<br>church & trees, sky (Possessive Attributes) | offer<br>medium shot<br>subjective<br>oblique horizontal angle<br>low vertical angle<br>+ medium modality markers | centre-margin<br>church (salient)<br>church (framed) |

### 8.1.1.3. Multimodal act

To sum up the analysis, the Monastery is represented by its church as central and dominant. The picture is representative and aims to involve users so that they discover the real version. The text, on the other hand, reduces the importance of the landmark as it presents it as secondary information. The brackets and the Adjunct "alternatively" announce something totally different from the message of the image. The focus is on the users and their possibility to choose from several variants. The communicative immediacy hides the impersonal and objective description of the antiquity and fame of the Monastery. It seems the tour operator wants to impress by the picture, so that afterwards the characteristics speak for themselves. This strategy can be risky; the placement of the text as secondary and the presentation of information by using a text with a rather complex syntax may make users skip the lines and not discover the reasons to visit the Monastery.

## 8.1.2. The Dacian Fortresses of the Orastie Mountains in the commercial corpus

The Dacian Fortresses of the Orastie Mountains are proposed for the third day of the Tour. The text follows the structure of the Monastery's page closely and presents the fortresses as an alternative to the Castle of Hunedoara. The difference is that the landmark is not illustrated by a picture.

Fig. 8-2 The Dacian Fortresses of the Orastie Mountains commercial webpage[2]

> ( Alternatively you can visit the six Dacian fortresses from the Orastie Mountains, built in the style of murus dacicus, in the period from the first century BC to the first century AD as protection from the conquering Romans . The six fortresses form the defensive system of Decebalus and were declared World Heritage by ' UNESCO .)

*Source*: Ciao Romania (2012)

### 8.1.2.1. Linguistic analysis

*Overview*. Presented as an alternative to the main landmarks, the text focuses on the fortresses' past and their UNESCO recognition.

---

[2] This Figure presents only the description of the Dacian Fortresses. The other landmarks' descriptions are not included for reasons of space.

*Logical.* The text is short, but syntactically developed and complex. It is built by two clause complexes, one in a relation of hypotaxis-elaboration ("Alternatively you can visit the six Dacian fortresses from the Orastie Mountains, *built in the style of murus dacicus, in the period from the first century BC to the first century AD as protection from the conquering Romans*") and the other in parataxis-extension-addition ("The six fortresses form the defensive system of Decebalus *and* were declared World Heritage by UNESCO") (Ciao Romania 2012). The Dacian fortresses are introduced to users in the first complex, which elaborates on the details of their foundation. The second complex adds more information about the landmark presented. Information is, thus, provided as additional and not as packed, as in the Monastery text. The lack of embedded clauses supports this claim.

*Experiential.* The transitivity system is represented equally by material and relational processes. Only one of the processes refers to users, offering them the possibility to "visit" the fortresses, including them in the text in the pronoun "you". The other processes refer to the fortresses and identify them as Decebalus' defensive systems and as UNESCO monuments. These features are expected to raise users' interest; the name of the Dacian King can arouse curiosity regarding the type of construction, not frequent in Europe, whereas the UNESCO qualification certifies the fortresses' value as Heritage Site alongside other more famous landmarks. Even though the text is short, there are several circumstances providing background information related to the type, "in the style of murus dacicus", period, "in the period from the first century BC to the first century AD" and role of the Dacian fortresses, "as protection from the conquering Romans".

Regarding the participants, the most frequent one is the landmark, which is both expressed and implied as Goal ("you can visit *the six Dacian fortresses from the Orastie Mountains*") and Identified ("*The six fortresses* form the defensive system of Decebalus"). The client is presented as Actor; not any Actor, but the individual who visits the Dacian fortresses of Orastie Mountains. The tour operator is also absent in this text, the message appearing as impersonal.

*Interpersonal.* The mood is again declarative, the information being presented as fact. Both Mood and Residue are expressed in the text, Mood, mainly in the form of Subject and Finite, and Residue, as complex structures. The expressed Subject position is occupied in an equal proportion by both client and fortresses (see the last two examples above), indicating once again the focus on these participants. The Finites are more expressed than fused, due to passive, "was designated", and modal forms, "can". The present dominates over the past, as if the message is timeless (Banks 2002, 6). The modal "can" mitigates the assertiveness of the message and the directness of the appeal; clients are offered the alternative to leave the main route and visit the Dacian landmark. The Conjunctive Adjunct "alternatively" marks the offer.

*Textual*. The Theme is unmarked and mainly expressed by participants. Two of the three clauses include textual Themes, e.g. "and", and assure the link to the previous messages. The Thematic development makes the message flow in a linear pattern and continuous progression; the Dacian fortresses are picked up from the Rheme and carried continuously as Theme (you can visit *the six Dacian fortresses* […]. *The six fortresses* form …").

The results of the linguistic analysis are summarised in Table 8-3.

**Table 8-3 Commercial Dacian Fortresses of the Orastie Mountains: Lexico-grammatical summary**

| Clause complex | Transitivity | Mood | Theme |
|---|---|---|---|
| short<br>only complexes<br>only expansion<br>= parataxis & hypotaxis<br>= elaboration & extension, addition<br>1 non-defining relative clause<br>1 non-finite clause | = material & relational<br>= causative construc. & identifying<br>only intensive<br>- mental<br>+ realized particip.<br>+ landmark<br>+ land. (realized)<br>only landmark (implied)<br>=Goal & Identified (landmark)<br>+ Actor (client)<br>- operator<br>= extent, manner & role | = mood & residue<br>complex residue<br>= client & landmark as Subj.<br>+ expressed Finites<br>+ present<br>= Conjunctive & Circumstantial Adjunct<br>only modalization<br>- polarity<br>only declarative<br>only statements | only unmarked<br>+ multiple (textual)<br>+ participant as Theme<br>= continuous & linear Thematic progression |

The communicative act, thus, relies only on the verbal mode to transmit information. This can be expected since the landmark is offered as an alternative and not as the focus of the visit. The lack of a visual also reduces the importance of the landmark. The text contributes to enhance the interest in the unknown, by words like "murus dacicus" and "Decebalus". The uniqueness and quality of the place are guaranteed by UNESCO. The message, then, informs briefly about the fortresses and, simultaneously, persuades by the sonority of the words and the quality of the landmark.

## 8.1.3. Sighisoara in the commercial corpus

Sighisoara is proposed for the seventh day of the tour. Differently from the other landmarks analysed, the city is not an alternative, but is part of the basic tour.

Fig. 8-3 Sighisoara commercial webpage

Day 7: Gura Humorului - Bicaz – Sighisoara ( 250 km )

In the morning departure to Bicaz with **Bicaz Canyon**, unique in Romania. Here we stop to buy souvenirs, see the Red Lake and have a walk in the Bicaz Canyon.

We continue to **Sighisoara, the "fortified city"** among the very few in Europe, which retains its medieval centre on the top of the hill. Here was also born Vlad the Impaler, better known as Count Dracula. There are several defensive towers that surround the city, named after the trades of their builders: the Tailors' Tower, the Shoemakers' Tower, the Rope Makers' Tower, the Clock Tower etc **Dinner in the house where Count Vlad was born/or an intimate restaurant medieval style and accommodation** in Sighisoara in the citadel.

*Source*: Ciao Romania (2012)

### 8.1.3.1. Linguistic analysis

*Overview*. The city of Sighisoara is introduced by several of its attractions, such as Count Dracula and the defensive towers. Practical information, such as dinner and accommodation in the city, is also added to stimulate interest and make the place more attractive.

*Logical*. The text is short, but syntactically developed and complex. It favours clause complexes and develops the message by hypotaxis-elaboration, as for example in "We continue to Sighisoara, the "fortified city" among the very few in Europe, *which retains its medieval centre on the top of the hill*" (Ciao Romania 2012). The non-defining relative clauses seem to pack information making the text compact.

*Experiential.* The preferred type of process is relational; it is used to describe the centre of Sighisoara and identify its defensive towers and famous character. There are also instances of other types of processes. The material processes refer to the tour itinerary and to Vlad the Impaler, while the existential one introduces the towers of the city. The background information is detailed and focuses on spatial location, such as "here".

The city, including its attractions, is the most frequent participant as expected from the topic of the text. It appears in different roles, such as Carrier, "*which* retains its medieval centre on the top of the hill", Goal, "Here was also born *Vlad the Impaler*", Attribute, "which retains *its medieval centre* on the top of the hill", and Existent, "There are *several defensive towers …*", none of them being especially prominent. In contrast to the other texts in the set, the tour operator appears, but together with the client. The pronoun "we" is used inclusively; the tour operator and the client form a team and act as Actors as they continue their visit to Sighisoara ("*We* continue to Sighisoara"). This linguistic device signals the inclusion of users into the "virtual tour" (Yui Ling Ip 2008, 8). The message presents also practical details about the tour, like dinner and accommodation, which are expressed in the role of Identifiers ("*Dinner in the house where Count Vlad was born/or an intimate restaurant medieval style and accommodation in Sighisoara in the citadel*").

*Interpersonal.* All the clauses in the text are full declaratives and function as statements. There is an exception represented by the last elliptical clause just mentioned above which introduces the practical information as a telegraphic detail. This can aim to present it as information separated from the main text. The bold letters serve that purpose, apart from indicating the information as salient. The elliptical clause makes the text have more Mood than Residue. The Subject position does not prefer a particular participant; it is occupied by the inclusive "we" and the long noun phases on practical details. Neither the city nor its attractions are ever expressed as Subject in main clauses, as if they were not the topic of the text. The type of Finites is usually present and fused, e.g. "are"; the message they build is general and timeless (Banks 2002, 6). The lack of modality and negation present the information also as evident (Mocini 2009, 160). The Residue element is complex since the clauses are long and contain both Complements and Adjuncts.

*Textual.* The Theme position is usually occupied by participants, so the Themes are mainly unmarked. The sole marked Theme is the Adjunct "here", referring to Sighisoara, which locates the place where Vlad the

Impaler was born ("*Here* was also born Vlad the Impaler"). There are, however, instances of Themes that draw users' attention even if they are unmarked. The enhanced Theme ("there are"), for example, points forward to the content of the Rheme (Thompson 2004, 161), signalling the topic of the clause, i.e. the existence of several defensive towers surrounding the city. The heavy Subject from the elliptical clause, in turn, indicates the possibility to do more than just visit Sighisoara, i.e. have dinner and accommodation and, thus, experience a part of its medieval history. There seems to be no Thematic pattern of progression in the flow of the message. At the beginning, the message is built on the city as a location, but, later, several new Themes, like "there are", are introduced. They can attract due to their position, but they can also confuse the users of the site. The absence of Thematic progression and the development by hypotaxis can lead to an unclear message.

Table 8-4 shows the results of the analysis.

**Table 8-4 Commercial Sighisoara: Lexico-grammatical summary**

| Clause complex | Transitivity | Mood | Theme |
|---|---|---|---|
| short<br>+ complexes<br>only expansion<br>only hypotaxis<br>only elaboration<br>+ non-defining relative clause<br>+ finite clauses | + relational<br>causative construction<br>only attributive<br>only intensive<br>- mental<br>+ existential<br>+ realized participants<br>+ landmark<br>+ land. (realized)<br>only landmark (implied)<br>= Goal, Carrier, Attribute, Existent, implied Identified (landmark)<br>- client<br>+ Actor & Identifier (operator + client)<br>+ location, only place | + mood<br>complex residue<br>=operator & team (we) as Subject<br>+ fused Finite<br>+ present<br>+ Circ. Adjunct<br>-modalization<br>- polarity<br>only declarative,<br>+ full decl.<br>only statements | + unmarked<br>only simple<br>+ participant as Theme<br>- Thematic progression<br>+ new Themes |

### 8.1.3.2. Visual analysis

The image chosen to depict Sighisoara is representative as it presents one of its symbols, the Clock Tower. The conceptual structure refers to the city as Carrier and to the Tower, gate, covered terrace and sky as Possessive Attributes, by means of an unstructured analytical process. The process can also be understood as symbolic, as if the Clock Tower stands for the city of Sighisoara.

The picture is offered for contemplation, but at the same time, seems to invite the viewers to enter the gate under the Tower. It is presented subjectively from a close shot; the angles are rather frontal and low. The viewers are situated in the middle of everything, just standing there, engaged in the observation and impressed by the imposing Tower. The picture seems real, as if taken by somebody going up to the medieval centre. Nevertheless, the modality markers related to colour look modified in order to project the Tower on the blue of the sky. The lack of details also contributes to its saliency.

The Tower is made conspicuous also by the informational structure of the picture. It is presented in the centre, as the most important element or the star. Its colour and size emphasise its saliency and show it as framed, as separated from the other elements in the picture.

The visual features of the picture of Sighisoara are included in Table 8-5.

**Table 8-5 Commercial Sighisoara: Visual summary**

| Representational | Interactive | Compositional |
|---|---|---|
| simple<br>conceptual structure<br>unstructured analytical<br>city (Carrier)<br>Clock Tower, gate, terrace,<br>sky (Possessive Attributes) | offer<br>close shot<br>subjective<br>frontal horizontal angle<br>low vertical angle<br>+ medium modality markers | centre-margin<br>tower (salient)<br>tower (framed) |

### 8.1.3.3. Multimodal act

The picture of the city focuses on one of its attractions and places the users on the scene of a visit. The visual clues and techniques work together to make it real and appealing. The text, however, focuses on the tour and guides the users through the city, pointing out its various towers, one of them represented in the picture. A different experience is promised by medieval restaurants and hostels; the city can be discovered by other senses than sight. The attractiveness of the place is increased by its association to Count Dracula. This seems to be a “parallelism technique”, encountered frequently in advertisements (Myers 1994, 140), which links a product to a famous person or character; it is as if the city borrows all the connotations the character bears, in this case mystery or immortality. The message seems, then, to guide, inform and persuade, at the same time.

### 8.1.4. Discussion of the Romanian set of commercial webpages

The Romanian commercial website combines colours, pictures and short blocks of texts. Its design is simple and clear with a few exceptions, such as the absence of navigational details and more grouped information. The lateral navigational menu can also make readability difficult, especially because there is no horizontal menu. The type of information transmitted is mainly general, related to different tours and details about Romania. The tour operator states its identity and purpose from the beginning in an elaborated and highly connotative message. The blue colour of the website seems to add honesty and credibility to the operator's words and offers. The lack of contact details, however, does not allow a direct and quick contact with the tour operator and questions its availability. Interactive possibilities do not receive any attention from the website, which does not take full advantage of the opportunities offered by the "hypermedia environment" (Garzone 2009, 41).

The home page appears attractive and short, guiding users' attention to its pictures and links. It seems to be developed on both levels: logical, providing informative links to content, and connotative, building a persuasive message (Garzone 2009, 36). The webpage presenting the tour of the World Heritage Sites in Romania follows the same structure as the home page, maintaining the header and lateral menu. It is, however, much longer and its message is more informative than connotative and persuasive. It transmits more general information on the landmarks to be visited and illustrates them by a number of pictures. The Sites are usually identified, related to their background and described by their attractions. These details are expected to draw users' attention and interest in the landmarks. The practical and transactional information on the tour is provided separately at the end. These types are not present in the home page, probably because they are specific to each tour. This indicates a website with a general introductory home page and with specific detailed webpages. The "Reserve" link opens an email window for users to send an email instead of offering a reservation form, obstructing again direct communication. The call to action is rather indirect as indicated by the functionality of the Reserve link and the mitigated "visit" from the actual description of the tour.

The messages considered develop multimodally following a top-bottom organization structure; the section of the Dacian fortresses is an exception because it has no picture to illustrate its ancient ruins. The texts combine information on the tour with relevant details on the landmark promoted in short succinct paragraphs. Despite being the most focused, the information on the landmark is presented as secondary to the tour. The tour, in turn, is referred to only by what it visits, practical details about dinner and accommodation being absent, except for the section dedicated to the city of Sighisoara. This may be explained by the different approach to the landmarks: the Monastery of Horezu and the Dacian fortresses of Orastie Mountains are alternatives, whereas Sighisoara is the main option.

The language of the texts, summarised in Table 8-6, reflects the communicative preferences of the messages. Certain similarities between the texts can be observed. The short texts are complex and syntactically developed. They are built mainly by clause complexes, which develop by both parataxis and hypotaxis. The relations between clauses are elaboration by non-defining relative clauses and extension by addition. Details seem added to previous information, which leads to a compact and cumulative message. Since the texts are short, it is difficult to have a pattern of development; the instances encountered can be rather considered isolated preferences. The tour is introduced by the material process "visit" in order to signal the succession of landmarks. The landmark, in turn, is described by relational processes that highlight its relevant attributes and attractions. Causative constructions point how these are considered and known by the world, e.g. "one of the best examples of 'Brancovean' style". Background information is usually locative, placing the tour in space and the landmark in time. The texts contain more realized participants, the landmark being the most frequent. Despite this, it is not the participant preferred in Subject position, where the client is favoured. This may be due to the fact that the landmark is presented in dependent clauses as secondary information. Its usual role is that of Goal, the entity visited. The client is also present and addressed directly by the personal pronoun "you", communication being immediate and personal. In the text on Sighisoara, "you" is replaced by the inclusive "we". This is the only instance when the tour operator appears in the set analysed. Its absence may be due to a desire to appear impersonal and professional. It also may be explained by the focus on the landmark and not on the tour. The message appears impersonal, objective and timeless also because of the dominance of declarative mood and the preference for present tense and unmarked Themes. This is mitigated by the modals of possibility and Conjunctive Adjuncts. The split focus of the message, already mentioned, is reflected by the different participants in Subject position and the lack of any Thematic progression, except for the message presenting the Dacian fortresses.

**Table 8-6 Romanian set of commercial websites: Lexico-grammatical summary**

| System | The Monastery of Horezu | Dacian Fortresses of the Orastie Mountains | Sighisoara |
|---|---|---|---|
| Clause complex | short<br>only complexes (4cl.)<br>only expansion<br>+ parataxis<br>+ extension, addition<br>+ non-defining relative clause<br>+ non-finite clauses | short<br>only complexes<br>only expansion<br>= parataxis & hypotaxis<br>= elaboration & extension, addition<br>1 non-defining relative clause<br>1 non-finite clause | short<br>+ complexes<br>only expansion<br>only hypotaxis<br>only elaboration<br>+ non-defining relative clause<br>+ finite clauses |
| Transit-ivity | + material<br>only causative constr.<br>- identifying/ attributive<br>only mental cognit.<br>= realized & implied participants<br>+ landmark<br>+ landmark (realized)<br>+ landmark (implied)<br>+ Goal (landmark)<br>+ Actor (client)<br>- operator<br>= location & cause, only time | = material & relational<br>= causative constr. & identifying<br>only intensive<br>- mental<br>+ realized particip.<br>+ landmark<br>+ landmark (realized)<br>only land. (implied)<br>=Goal & Identified (landmark)<br>+ Actor (client)<br>- operator<br>= extent, manner & role | + relational<br>causative constr.<br>only attributive<br>only intensive<br>- mental<br>+ existential<br>+ realized particip.<br>+ landmark<br>+ landmark (realized)<br>only land. (implied)<br>= Goal, Carrier, Attribute, Existent, implied Identified (landmark)<br>- client<br>+ Actor & Identifier (operator + client)<br>+ location, only place |
| Mood | = mood & residue<br>complex residue<br>only client as Subject<br>only expressed Finite<br>only present<br>only Conjunctive Adjunct<br>only modalization | = mood & residue<br>complex residue<br>= client & landmark as Subject<br>+ expressed Finites<br>+ present<br>= Conjunctive & Circumstantial Adj. | + mood<br>complex residue<br>=operator & team (we) as Subject<br>+ fused Finite<br>+ present<br>+ Circumstantial Adj.<br>-modalization |

| System | The Monastery of Horezu | Dacian Fortresses of the Orastie Mountains | Sighisoara |
|---|---|---|---|
| | - polarity<br>only declarative<br>only statement | only modalization<br>- polarity<br>only declarative<br>only statements | - polarity<br>only declarative,<br>+ full decl.<br>only statements |
| Theme | only unmarked<br>only multiple (textual)<br>only participant as Theme<br>- Thematic progression | only unmarked<br>+ multiple (textual)<br>+ participant as Theme<br>= continuous & linear Thematic progression | + unmarked<br>only simple<br>+ participant as Theme<br>- Thematic progression<br>+ new Themes |

The images, whose characteristics are summarised in Table 8-7, are clear and representative for the landmarks depicted.

**Table 8-7 Romanian set of commercial websites: Visual summary**

| System | The Monastery of Horezu | Dacian Fortresses of the Orastie Mountains | Sighisoara |
|---|---|---|---|
| Represent-ational | complex<br>conceptual structure<br>unstructured<br>analytical<br>monastery & background (Carrier)<br>church & trees, sky (Poss. Attributes) | - | simple<br>conceptual structure<br>unstructured<br>analytical<br>city (Carrier)<br>Clock Tower, gate, terrace, sky (Possessive Attributes) |
| Interactive | offer<br>medium shot<br>subjective<br>oblique horiz. angle<br>low vertical angle<br>+ medium modality markers | - | offer<br>close shot<br>subjective<br>frontal horiz. angle<br>low vertical angle<br>+ medium modality markers |
| Composit-ional | centre-margin<br>church (salient)<br>church (framed) | - | centre-margin<br>tower (salient)<br>tower (framed) |

They are built by conceptual structures, which simply illustrate the landmarks, without containing any narrative. The unstructured analytical processes present the landmarks as Carriers and several of their components as Possessive Attributes. These can also be interpreted as symbolic; the church can stand for the Monastery of Horezu and the Clock Tower for the city of Sighisoara. The buildings are offered for contemplation from relatively close shots, engaging users in the contemplation. Either oblique or frontal, they are presented just standing there majestic. The modality markers make the pictures look real. Nevertheless, their placement in the centre, the lack of details, their size and colours show a special focus on the visibility and attractiveness of the landmarks.

To summarise, the two modes used by the Romanian tour operator do not seem to work on the same level. The visual illustrates the landmark by one of its representative buildings as real and majestic. It is situated within the reach of the client, who is invited to enter the frame and go closer. The verbal, on the other hand, does not focus on any component in particular, but provides a more general presentation of the landmark, including several relevant facts. The impersonal description of the landmark is counterbalanced by the information regarding the tour directly related to the client. The client is made to feel special, addressed individually and with the power to choose, while the tour operator appears as professional and friendly, not very intrusive in the tour. The message, then, seems to present the landmark as subordinated to the tour, when in fact the landmark is what is focused on. Persuasion is hidden in the presentation of relevant facts about the landmark, which are left to speak by themselves. UNESCO designation, antiquity, special architectural styles, religious art, Dracula, dinner and accommodation in a medieval house are the facts chosen and highlighted by the texts. They are the ones meant to make the “Grand tour Romania” worth buying and the beautiful Latin country worth visiting. The Latin origin and spirit are frequently present in the tour operator’s message, right from the initial “Ciao”. Latinity is habitually used to promote the Romanian brand (Light 2006). The presence of Latinity and, its simultaneous isolation in a Slavic territory, contribute to the individuality of Romania presented by the landmarks.

## 8.2. Spanish set of commercial webpages

The Spanish commercial website does not use the typical white background, as can be seen at http://www.spaindaytours.com/. Different shades go from dark grey to light grey; the colour, considered neutral and conservative, implies security and reliability. It seems a good background for other colours since it does not attract attention, leaving other elements, like pictures and writing, to stand out. The home page is quite short and organized vertically in three main areas. The header is divided in two sections and contains several pictures. The first section has a picture of a group of people next to a bright red minivan and accompanied by the appraisal "Top Day Tours". This seems to stand for the tour operator as a logo, as if illustrating it by its vehicle, members and service. The other section is composed as a triptych by pictures of some monuments and squares in Spain, taken from a close shot.

The main body is divided in three visual columns, probably for better readability. The first column is narrow and contains the menu of the website. This provides links to general information on the tours offered ("Our day tours", "Our shore excursions") and the tour operator ("About us"), practical details on how to plan a trip with the operator's help ("Flamenco and dinner", "Trip planner", "Useful links") and several possibilities to interact with the operator ("Contact us", "Send quick email"). The tour operator situates itself quite close to the users by the constant use of the first person, such as "our" and "us". The second column appears as the most important one, as it is wider than the others and contains the main message of the website. The tour operator presents itself to the users, in the same informal tone already mentioned, as a "team of friendly and passionate driving-guides and expert guides with a common mission-to make your holiday in Spain memorable and enjoyable!" (Spain Day Tours 2011). It recommends itself as backed up by TripAdvisor to certify its quality. The tour operator also presents what it offers, "top-quality private and semi-private tours with a personal pick-up and drop-off service". The offers, emphasised by their yellow letters, are further developed by various links to different tours, other persons' opinions and other contact possibility. These links are preceded by two photos, which represent the links visually: a car showing movement and trip and several persons laughing and toasting, implying team, friends, good mood and happiness. The uniqueness of the tour operator is reiterated in the closing part of the message signed with its full name "top day tours", probably to show officialism and professionalism. The website interchanges continuously the name of the tour operator between "Spain day tour" and "top day tours", which may be confusing for users. The last column is further separated in two. The top section is framed and made salient by the interplay of colours. It summarises, as if it were an identity card or a slide in a presentation, the main features of the tours offered, such as "Personal & quality tours", "Completely flexible" and "English speaking guides". The other section of the column presents various opinions and "thank-you" messages from former tourists. The testimony of the former tourist comes to certify the professionalism of the tour operator with the aim of convincing users. If these are not enough, a link to more comments is provided.

The footer is composed by two horizontally laid sections that provide other menu options. The first one contains general information on particular types of tours presented in three columns, such as "Madrid Tours" or "South Spain Tours". They are made up of a representative picture, a short caption and a "Read More" link. Much shorter, the second part lists horizontally several navigational options, such as "Home" and "Sitemap"; transactional information on "Privacy" and "Terms & Conditions"; and another interactive link to "Contact us".

The page can be interpreted from the AIDA model's perspective (OMT 2005b, 8). Attention is attracted from the beginning by the general impression of the site, the pictures and the ways to communicate with the tour operator. Interest is maintained by the attractive description of the operator, its aim and offer, and by practical information on how to plan a trip. Desire is aimed at by various links and the summary box. Action is instigated by the continuously repeated possibilities of contacting the operator.

## 8.2.1. The Monastery of El Escorial in the commercial corpus

The webpage dedicated to the Monastery of El Escorial has the same layout as the home page, i.e. header, main body and footer, as can be observed in Fig. 8-4. The header has the same pictures, except for the one illustrating the tour operator. This is used to situate users in the topic of Madrid tours. The main body follows the same layout of three columns. The first one contains a horizontal menu, longer than in the home page, probably at a deeper hierarchical level. The wider column invites users to "discover two important places in the heart of Spain": El Escorial and the Valley of the Fallen. The text begins with a title, a caption, followed by a short description of the tour. Then, a number of pictures alternate to depict the landmarks promoted. They are placed in the middle of the text as part of the same message. However, they come before the actual description of the landmarks, which can remind users of the frequent advertising technique of ideal-real. Each landmark is introduced by a separate paragraph. The message ends with details about the return trip and provides a form for contacting the tour operator. This form can be very useful as it offers a direct and quick way to find out more about availability of a tour at a particular time. It can also indicate a strategy of immediate persuasion; in other words, the users are encouraged to find out more right after the promotional message so that they do not have the opportunity to change their mind after seeing a number of landmarks. The information that checking availability does not commit clients to any payment can contribute to persuasion as it leaves freedom to users and does not commit them to any booking.

The last column presents the main features of the tour in a framed box, similar to the home page. The comments of former tourists have been replaced by more transactional links related to the price of the tour or to the possibility to take the tour by bus and not by minivan. The footer presents more pictures of the two landmarks and repeats the menu bar from the home page.

Fig. 8-4 The Monastery of El Escorial commercial webpage[3]

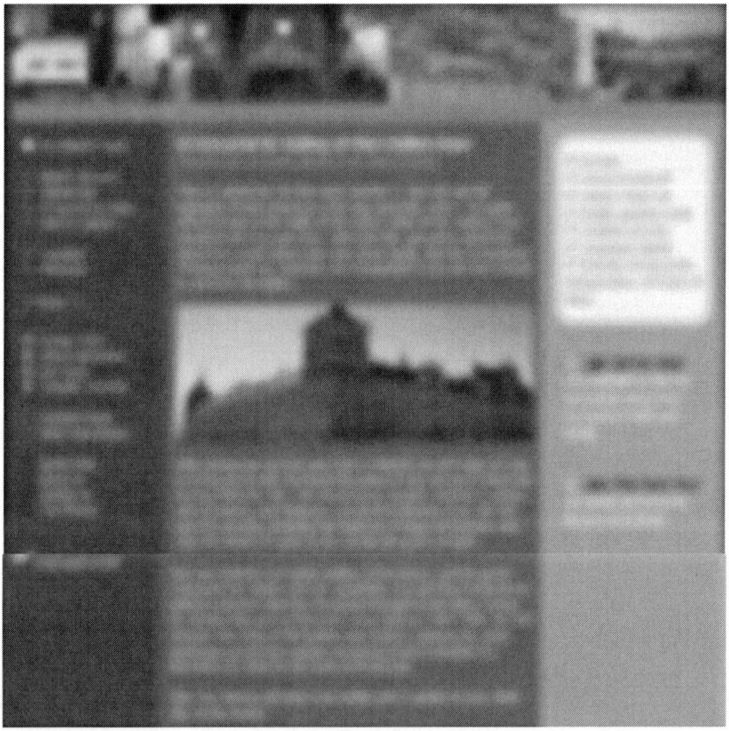

[3] As mentioned in Chapter six, when copyright was not granted, an impression of the structure of the webpage has been included so that the reader can follow the analyses.

*Source:* Spain Day Tours (2011)

#### 8.2.1.1. Linguistic analysis

*Overview*. The linguistic analysis focuses on the paragraph presenting the Royal Monastery of San Lorenzo El Real. The text describes the tour and provides a number of characteristics of the Monastery.

*Logical*. It is rather short, but elaborated and complex, as it contains long and developed clause complexes. The main relation between clauses is hypotaxis, usually enhancement; they are related by temporal and causal-conditional dependency. Temporality may be used to give a sequence to the tour and make it more organised, e.g. "*after picking you up* […], we will make our way to […]" or "we will hear […] *as we wander* […]" (Spain Day Tours 2011). It also establishes a connexion with the actuality of the trip (Calvi 2011, 79), making the tour more tangible by projecting the users in the destination (Mapelli and Piccioni 2011). The other enhancement relations show the purpose of going to "El Escorial", i.e. to "visit the Monastery". There is also an instance of elaboration; the copywriter develops the description of the Monastery by providing further details on its founder ("we will make our way to El Escorial to visit The Royal Monastery of San Lorenzo El Real *built by King Philip the 2nd*"). Apart from hypotaxis, the clauses are linked twice by parataxis, used to add more information and give continuity to the text, as for instance in "The Renaissance complex combines a palace and monastery, *and* features a wonderful collection of art". The text develops, then, by logico-semantic relations of enhancement and extension. Information seems to be transmitted directly as there are no instances of embedding. A reason for this can be the fact that the text focuses more on the description of the tour than on the monument, so that there may be no need to pack information related to the foundation, composition or other details of the monument. This seems also to be announced by the almost absent relation of elaboration.

*Experiential.* The text favours material processes heavily. The majority of them refer to the tour and present its itinerary, such as "visit" or "tour". The "successive movements […] give dynamism" (Calvi 2006, 36) to the message. This can be a strategy to instigate users to action as "verbal dynamism leads to mobility" (Calvi 2006, 42); they are projected at the scene of the tour and their steps are guided through the Monastery. The few instances of relational processes are attributive possessive and refer to the Monastery. They describe what this contains, like "a palace and a monastery" and "a wonderful collection of art". The objectivity of the material processes (Barker and Galasinki 2001, 71) seems to be continued also by the relational ones, which only indicate the components of the landmark, making no direct reference to their features. The list of processes is completed by an instance of mental process, "hear", which implies another type of discovery, one based on perception. The landmark is accessible to users, not only by actions, but also by senses. These involve not only the Monastery, but also the history of Spain since "[we will] hear the history of Spain as we wander this great complex". The relation of the landmark to history and the influences of history on it assign to it more value. There is little background information provided by the text; few circumstances locate the actions in space, e.g. "from your hotel in Madrid". This is quite unexpected, considering the high number of material processes. Circumstantial meaning seems to be conveyed at the logical level and not at the experiential one, as indicated by the dominance of enhancement relations.

All the observed participants, i.e. landmark, client and tour operator, appear in the text; they are more often expressed than implied. The landmark, including its attractions, is the most frequent and has usually the role of Goal, the object of future actions of the tour operator and the client ("We will tour *the complex* …"). The usual role of the frequently present tour operator, i.e. Actor, comes to support this ("*we* will make our way to El Escorial"). The client is expressed only once and acts as Goal, as the person on whom the operator exercises the action of "picking up". This can imply that the tour operator has power over the client. The client can have power and be presented as Actor only if s/he joins the tour and becomes one with the operator, as member of the team suggested by the personal pronoun "we".

*Interpersonal.* The message is presented mainly by full declaratives that express statements and facts. The assertiveness of the message seems to be mitigated by frequent modalization. High modality "will" is used when indicating the actions of the tour operator, possibly accompanied by the client, "make our way" or "tour". This emphasizes the idea of schedule and depicts the tour operator as professional and efficient following a plan. The Mood component contains, besides modalization, a balanced number of instances of expressed and fused Finites, such as "will" and "combines". The types of Finites situate the action in the future, when referring to the tour, and in the present, when presenting the landmark. In this way, the tour is given more credibility (Calvi 2011, 82), whereas the landmark becomes timeless (Banks 2002, 6). The Subject position is occupied by the tour operator and the inclusive "we". The tour operator, and possibly the client, gain, thus, importance over the landmark. The distance between them is shortened by the use of "we", which makes the tour operator human and brings it closer to the client as if they form a team, ready to go on tour. The combination of the personal pronoun and the modal "will" aims to project users in the scenery of the tour as if performing and sensing all the things mentioned. The Residue element, slightly more numerous than the Mood due to ellipsis ("and *[ø]* hear the history of Spain"), is complex. However, there are few Adjuncts, all circumstantial, for instance "to El Escorial".

*Textual.* The Theme is usually unmarked and expressed equally by Subjects and Predicators, due to Subject ellipsis (McCabe 1999). In case of ellipsis, the flow of information is carried on by textual Themes, the message being presented as compact, like "We will tour the complex, including the Pantheon of Kings and basilica, *and [ø] hear* the history of Spain". The only exception to the pattern of unmarkedness is found at the beginning of the text, i.e. "After picking you up from your hotel in Madrid"; the dependent circumstantial temporal clause in Theme position indicates the beginning of the text promoting the Monastery of El Escorial. It also frames the tour in time as all the events specified in the text happen after the client is picked up from the hotel. The Thematic progression is organised into a multiple Theme pattern ("After picking you up from your hotel in Madrid, *we* will make our way to *El Escorial* […]. *The Renaissance complex* […]. *We* …"), which introduces the most important elements of the text, "we" and "Escorial", in Rheme position. Each of them is then carried on by continuous Themes.

The results of the analyses are indicated in Table 8-8.

**Table 8-8 Commercial Monastery of El Escorial: Lexico-grammatical summary**

| Clause complex | Transitivity | Mood | Theme |
|---|---|---|---|
| short<br>only complexes (3 & 4 clauses)<br>only expansion<br>+ hypotaxis<br>+ enhancement<br>1 non-defining relative clause<br>+ non-finite cl.<br>+ apposition | + material<br>only attributive<br>only possessive<br>only mental percep.<br>+ realized particip.<br>+ landmark<br>+ landmark (realized)<br>+ tour operator (implied)<br>+ Goal (landmark)<br>only Goal (client)<br>+ Actor (operator)<br>only location, only place | + residue<br>only complex residue<br>+ operator & client as Subject<br>= expressed & fused Finites<br>= present & future<br>only Circ. Adj.<br>only modalization<br>- polarity<br>only declarative,<br>+ full decl.<br>only statements | + unmarked (dependent cl.-Theme)<br>+ simple<br>= participant & process as Th.<br>= multiple & continuous progression |

### 8.2.1.2. Visual analysis

The webpage uses various images to illustrate the Monastery, as already mentioned. The picture analysed is usually associated with the Monastery. It presents, by means of conceptual structures, a building and the sky as Possessive Attributes. The way they compose their Carriers, i.e. the Monastery and the landscape, is not expressed visually as the processes are unstructured analytical.

The Monastery is presented from a medium shot as an object of contemplation. The angles are slightly oblique and eye level. Only the towers appear, situated at a low level, implying the Monastery's grandeur. The relation established is not clear cut, as if the image were combining various perspectives; the Monastery is both within the users' world and out of reach, as if close enough to be contemplated, but not enough to have contact with it. The users seem to have the freedom to go closer or remain at a distance. The modality markers present a realistic representation of the Monastery. However, some seem to add a sensory touch to the picture, such as contextualization, representation or illumination. In this way, the

Monastery is not fully contextualised or represented and the light appears to focus on the Monastery, probably with the aim of awakening the clients' curiosity.

There is no recognizable information structure in the picture. It simply presents a part of the Monastery that occupies the entire frame. The part is made salient by its size and colour. It is also framed by the blue sky in the background.

**Table 8-9 Commercial Monastery of El Escorial: Visual summary**

| Representational | Interactive | Compositional |
|---|---|---|
| complex<br>conceptual structure<br>unstructured analytical<br>monastery & landscape (Carrier)<br>building & sky (Possessive Attributes) | offer<br>medium shot<br>subjective<br>oblique horizontal angle<br>eye level vertical angle<br>+ medium modality markers | - information structure<br>building (salient)<br>building (framed) |

### 8.2.1.3. Multimodal act

To sum up, the multimodal presentation of the visit to the Monastery of El Escorial starts with a picture that depicts a part of the landmark standing in the middle distance. Its aim may be to attract users and then invite them to visit. The text takes them into the picture; its dynamism and modalization place the users inside the scenery, visiting the landmark. It guides them from the hotel to the Monastery and points out parts to be visited like the palace, the monastery and the collection of arts. The following of a plan as a team presents the tour operator as professional and friendly, at the same time. The focus of the visual message is the Monastery, whereas that of the linguistic one is the operator joined by the client. It appears, then, that the picture informs about the Monastery, while the text describes the tour, both with the aim of convincing.

## 8.2.2. The Alhambra in the commercial corpus

The webpage presenting the Alhambra is laid out in the same way as the pages discussed previously. The main body follows a similar pattern to the one from the Monastery of El Escorial. The Alhambra is part of the "Granada Tour", which invites users to "explore magnificent Granada and Alhambra Palaces". The region of Granada is considered a well-known cultural tourist destination (Precedo Ledo *et al.* 2007).

Fig. 8-5 The Alhambra commercial webpage[4]

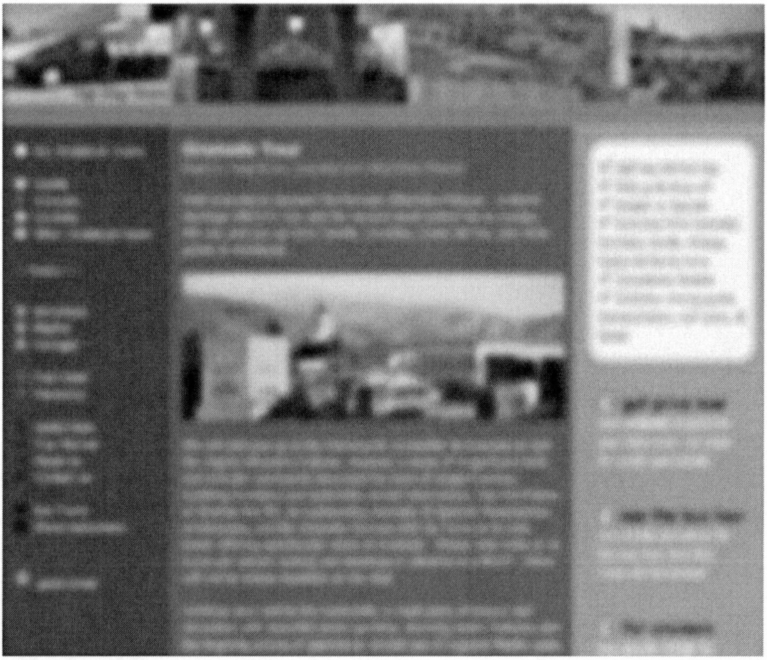

*Source:* Spain Day Tours (2011)

### 8.2.2.1. Linguistic analysis

*Overview*. The text that describes the tour of the Alhambra is composed by two paragraphs, one about the Alhambra palaces and the other about its gardens.

*Logical*. It is longer than the text on the Monastery of El Escorial, syntactically elaborated and medium complex. Its clauses are usually organized in complexes and linked mainly by hypotaxis. The logico-semantic relations preferred are elaboration and enhancement. Elaboration expands on the Alhambra and its attractions ("Discover a maze of magnificent halls and intimate courtyards *decorated by rows of elegant arches, bubbling fountains and splendidly carved decorations*"), whereas enhancement creates a causal-conditional frame for the action, related in

[4] This Figure presents only the description of the Alhambra. The other landmarks' descriptions, the practical information and the form to submit are not included for reasons of space.

particular to the purpose of the tour and the reason for booking ("We will pick you up in the morning for a transfer to Granada *to visit the mighty Alhambra Palaces*") (Spain Day Tours 2011). Apart from expansion, there is also the projection of an idea, by which attention is drawn politely to the necessity to book in advance a ticket for the Alhambra ("Please note *entry is 18 Euros per person (extra) and bookings in advance is a MUST–there will not be tickets available on the day!*"). This is aimed to warn users so that they know what to do, making them assume responsibility. At the same time, it can be a strategy to show the fame of the landmark; this is highly visited and "there will not be tickets available on the day". The exclamation mark accompanying the information emphasises its importance. The message as a whole is compact due to the frequent reduced relative clauses, e.g. "offering spectacular views of Granada", and appositions, e.g. "an outstanding example of Spanish Renaissance architecture".

*Experiential.* The Transitivity system is composed mainly by material processes. They name various activities that the visitor and/or tour operator can do, such as "visit", "continue" or "discover". This verbal dynamism may lead to mobility (Calvi 2006, 42) and encourage users to do as suggested. The relational processes refer mainly to administrative details, identifying and describing the process of booking a ticket ("bookings in advance *is* a MUST"). The existential process emphasises the necessity of booking, by pointing out the absence of available tickets on the same day of the tour ("*there will not be* tickets available on the day!"). There are a few mental processes, like "see" or "note", which address users. Circumstances are not frequent in the text, considering the preference for material processes. The most frequently used are location, which set the action in time, "in the morning", and in place, "to the Generalife", and create, thus, a scenario for the visit.

The processes appear to refer to the tour and not to the landmark. Its description is not done by processes, but by elaborated noun phrases. This can be the reason why the landmark, more expressed than implied, usually has the role of Goal ("Discover *a maze of magnificent halls and intimate courtyards*"). The Actor performing an action on it is the client. However, s/he is implied by imperative forms and never expressed ("*[you]* See the Palace of Charles the 5th …"), as if s/he has to follow the suggestions in order to become a real Actor. The client is expressed only once, when s/he is identified as Goal, "We will pick *you* up in the morning for a transfer to Granada". This relation is not with the landmark, but with the tour operator, expressed this time by the exclusive "we", which is the one that carries out the action of "pick[ing]". The operator, the tour and its offers are always overtly expressed and clear, with no dominating role, but appearing equally as Actor–"*We* will pick you up in the morning for a transfer to Granada", Goal–"Continue *your visit* to the Generalife ...", Carrier–"*bookings in advance* is a MUST", Identified–"*entry* is 18 Euros per person (extra)" and Existent–"there will not be *tickets* available on the day". The participants in the text are, thus, more expressed than implied; the landmark is more frequent, whereas the client and the tour operator also have a prominent role. The use of personal pronouns reduces the distance between producer and addressee.

*Interpersonal.* Unlike the previous text on the Monastery of El Escorial, the mood preferred is the imperative, which "creates a communicative immediacy, imitating interpersonal communication" (Janoschka 2004, 121). The possible clients are told to "discover", "see", "note" and "continue", as if guided during the tour and through the Alhambra. In this way, important attractions are pointed out, such as "the Palace of Charles the 5th" or "Generalife", as components of a pre-established itinerary. The aesthetic judgments on them are presented in an assertive manner (Calvi 2006, 35; Mapelli and Piccioni 2011, 64; Pérez Vázquez 2011, 307), for instance "Continue your visit to the Generalife*, a royal place of leisure and recreation with beautiful exotic gardens, stunning water features and the lingering aroma of jasmine to remind you of a grand Muslim past*". The tour operator seems, thus, in power as it plays the role of the guide and expert. This authoritarian tone is once softened by the Comment Adjunct "please", e.g. "*Please* note". The operator refers to itself by the personal pronoun "we", instead of the name, probably to sound more personal and reduce distance. Its importance is suggested by placing it in Subject position in the only declarative of the text, "*We* will pick you up in the morning for a transfer to Granada". As an expert, the tour operator presents a plan, by using modalization. The only statement contains the modal "will", which, apart from expressing the Finite and conveying a future time to the action, can imply high certainty and prediction. The mood is structured mainly by the Residue, due to the frequent imperatives. The Residue elements are usually complex, containing Complements and few Circumstantial Adjuncts.

*Textual.* The text develops by unmarked and simple Themes. The processes in imperative mood are the ones that occupy the Theme position and make the text resemble an instruction list with steps for the client to follow. This procedural organization provides dynamism to the message, as if an actual tour were taking place; "the description unfolds as if the reader were travelling through it" (Mocini 2009, 55). The clients are introduced in Rheme and then carried on until the end of the text, creating a continuous Thematic pattern ("We will pick *you* up in the morning for a transfer to Granada […] *Discover* a maze of magnificent halls and intimate courtyards …"). The instances of entire Rhemes constituted by dependent clauses, e.g. "entry is 18 Euros per person (extra), and bookings in advance is a MUST–there will not be tickets available on the day", and the long postmodification, e.g. "a royal place *of leisure and recreation with beautiful exotic gardens, stunning water features and the lingering aroma of jasmine to remind you of a grand Muslim past*", can make sometimes the message difficult to follow or unclear.

The lexico-grammatical summary of the text on the Alhambra is presented in Table 8-10.

**Table 8-10 Commercial Alhambra: Lexico-grammatical summary**

| Clause complex | Transitivity | Mood | Theme |
|---|---|---|---|
| medium long<br>+ complexes (4 cl.)<br>+ expansion<br>+ hypotaxis<br>= elaboration & enhancement<br>+ non-defining relative clause<br>+ non-finite cl. | + material<br>+ identifying<br>+ intensive<br>only mental percep.<br>+ existential<br>+ realized particip.<br>+ landmark<br>= landmark & operator (realized)<br>+ client (implied)<br>+ Goal (landmark) expressed as Goal, implied as Actor (client)<br>= Actor, Goal, Carrier, Identified, Existent (operator)<br>+ location, + time | + residue<br>+ complex residue<br>only operator as Subject<br>only expressed Finites<br>only future<br>+ Circ. Adjuncts<br>only modalization<br>- polarity<br>+ imperative<br>+ commands | only unmarked (many dep. cl. – Rheme)<br>+ simple<br>+ process as Theme<br>+ continuous progression |

### 8.2.2.2. Visual analysis

The image analysed illustrates a panoramic view of the Alhambra, which is usually associated with the landmark. The conceptual structure depicts it partially by an unstructured analytical process. Various buildings represent the Possessive Attributes of the Alhambra as a Carrier. The landscape is composed by vegetation, mountains and sky by the same type of process.

The landmark is presented as an offer; it stands majestic on the mountains in the medium distance only to be admired. The horizontal angle oscillates between frontal and oblique, depending on the building focused. The vertical angle is eye level, as if the Alhambra is perceived from a high place. The purpose may be to capture as much as possible of the complex. The relation suggested by the interactive elements seems to be placed secondary to the presentation of the landmark as it is, like in a postcard, i.e. majestic. The users are free, once again, to go closer and visit the place or just admire it from the distance. The interplay of modality markers illustrates the picture as real. Nevertheless, the colours of the bricks, illumination and brightness seem to make the buildings more salient, warmer and attractive.

The visual information does not follow any particular organizational structure. However, the landmark looks central, surrounded by a natural landscape. This centrality is sustained by its colour and size, which make it salient and framed.

Table 8-11 present the summary of the picture depicting the Alhambra.

**Table 8-11 Commercial Alhambra: Visual summary**

| Representational | Interactive | Compositional |
|---|---|---|
| complex<br>conceptual structure<br>unstructured analytical<br>landmark & landscape (Carrier)<br>buildings & vegetation, mountains, sky (Possessive Attributes) | offer<br>medium shot<br>subjective<br>frontal & oblique horizontal angle<br>eye level vertical angle<br>+ medium modality markers | - information structure<br>landmark (salient)<br>landmark (framed) |

### 8.2.2.3 Multimodal act

The communicative act plays with the two modes; the picture illustrates, while the text guides. The picture depicts the landmark in the distance in an objective and realistic way. The text brings the distant landmark closer without focusing on it or providing any facts or historical background. It centres rather on clients and their experience while visiting it. It takes them by hand to discover the Alhambra's halls and courtyards, to see several of its attractions, such as the Vela tower, and to continue to the Generalife. The tour operator is the expert offering a planned tour and various indications from a friendly position. The high number of connotative words and the appeal to senses by words like "recreation" or "jasmine" create a special atmosphere, as if taken from palace stories that remind visitors of a "grand Muslim past". They also describe the visit as a pleasant and all-senses experience. The message tends to be as suggestive as possible, having in mind the intangibility of the tourist product (Bosch Abarca 2001, 328).

### 8.2.3. Santiago de Compostela in the commercial corpus

Fig. 8-6 Santiago de Compostela commercial webpage[5]

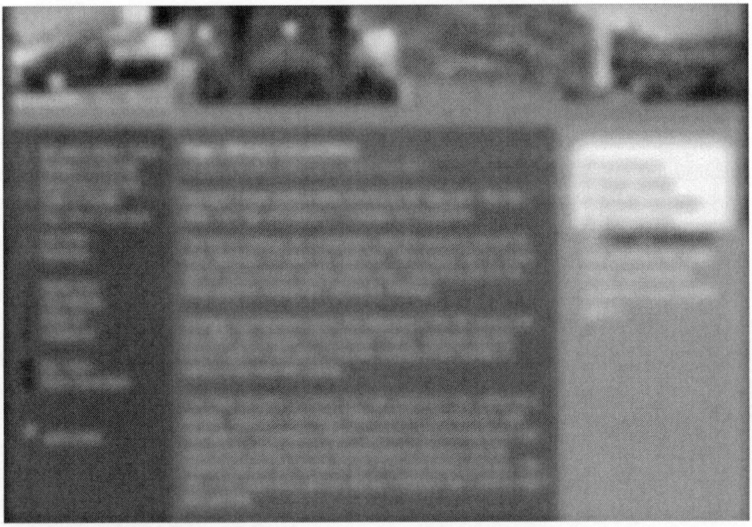

*Source:* Spain Day Tours (2011)

The webpage introducing Santiago de Compostela proposes a "Shore excursion to Vigo" in order to "discover the beautiful Galicia". The region of Galicia is important as it acts as a "second-level brand" for the "supra-brand" Spain (Morgan and Pritchard 2000, 289). The page does not use the attractions of Santiago de Compostela as the only selling point, but offers them as an alternative to the cities of Vigo and Baiona. It follows the same layout as the other pages of the company. Nevertheless, there are certain differences. The main body does not provide a photo to illustrate any of the possible landmarks offered. The footer, not shown here,

[5] This Figure presents only the description of Santiago de Composela. The other landmarks' descriptions, the practical information, the form and the footer are not included for reasons of space.

contains, however, some pictures dedicated only to the Cathedral of Santiago. The preference for blocks of texts can be rather unattractive and difficult to read (OMT 2001, 113). At the same time, they may indicate the adaptation of printed material for the computer screen (Garzone 2009, 50).

### 8.2.3.1. Linguistic analysis

*Overview.* The section about Santiago de Compostela, composed by three paragraphs, relates the city to pilgrimage and presents briefly some of its main attractions.

*Logical.* The text is medium long, elaborated and complex. Even if it contains a higher number of clause simplexes, e.g. "The trip to Santiago de Compostela visits the beautiful city and its main attraction the towering cathedral", the difference is compensated by embedding, e.g. "This magical city is a must see for many tourists *visiting Galicia*", and developed clause complexes, e.g. "This city is very impressive and can also be combined with a visit to Vigo if time permits" (Spain Day Tours 2011). The logico-semantic system favours both parataxis and hypotaxis. In the first case, which is slightly more frequent, information on the city is extended by commas and addition conjunctions, as indicated in the previous example by "and can also be combined with a visit to Vigo". In the other case, the clauses provide details about the Raxoi Palace and present the condition for a combined tour to the city of Vigo, encountered in the same example, "if time permits".

*Experiential.* The transitivity system provides information on the landmark and favours relational processes. The text focuses on description and identification rather than on action, in contrast with the other texts in the Spanish commercial set. It mainly describes the city, associating it with strongly connotative words, such as "must see", "famous" or "very impressive". The text also names a number of places in Santiago, such as Plaza Obradoiro and Raxoi Palace, and situates them in space as in a guided tour ("*The Plaza Obradoiro* is where the main entrance to the cathedral is situated, opposite is *the Raxoi Palace*"). A few material processes refer to the attractions the trip visits, such as the Cathedral, and to the foundation date of the city. Background information is scarce, probably due to the few material processes used. Circumstances mainly locate the action in time, referring to the dates when Santiago was founded and became famous, like "around the beginning of the 5th century not long after the collapse of the Roman Empire" and "in the early 9th century".

The landmark is the most frequently realized participant. It is usually expressed and has the role of Carrier ("*This magical city* is a must see for many tourists …"). The client is only mentioned once, in the role of Attributor. The reference is general, "a must see for *many tourists*", and implies the lack of personal or direct contact. This is also supported by the way the tour operator is referred to. There is neither a personal pronoun nor a name for the tour operator, but only general words related to it like "trip" or "visit". Even in this formula, the operator is rarely present, occasions in which it is assigned the roles of Actor and Identifier. It is presented impersonally; "the trip to Santiago de Compostela" visits the city and can be combined with a visit to another city, not the tour operator and/or the visitor.

*Interpersonal*. All the clauses are declaratives and present information as fact. The Subject position gives importance to the landmark as it is occupied frequently by Santiago or its different monuments. The Finites are mainly fused, such as "is", due to the few instances of passives or modals. The tense is present, e.g. "visits"; the focus is more on present descriptions than on past ones. These features of the Finite make the message general and timeless (Banks 2002, 6). There is an instance of modalization expressed by "can", which indicates low modality. It presents the client with the possibility or opportunity to combine two cities in one trip and can be seen as an offer from the tour operator. Its form is rather indirect and leaves more freedom to the client (Ares Ares 2011, 148) because it is related to a third person pronoun ("*it* can"). The little use of modalization and the lack of negation confer to the message the power of "straightforward evidence" (Mocini 2009, 160).

**Table 8-12 Commercial Santiago de Compostela: Lexico-grammatical summary**

| Clause complex | Transitivity | Mood | Theme |
|---|---|---|---|
| medium long<br>+ simplexes (3 cl. complex)<br>only expansion<br>+ parataxis<br>+ extension<br>+ defining relative clause<br>+ non-finite clauses | + relational<br>+ attributive<br>+ intensive<br>- mental<br>+ realized particip.<br>+ landmark<br>+ land. (realized)<br>only land. (implied)<br>+ Carrier (landmark)<br>only Attributor (client)<br>Actor & Identifier (operator)<br>+ location, only time | = mood & resid.<br>only complex residue<br>+ landmark as Subject<br>+ fused Finites<br>+ present<br>+ Circ. Adjuncts<br>only modalization<br>- polarity<br>only declarative<br>only statements | only unmarked<br>+ simple<br>+ participant as Theme<br>+ continuous progression (little difference) |

The Residue element is complex, containing usually both Complements and Adjuncts. The Adjuncts are frequently circumstantial, e.g. "with the discovery of the remains of the Apostle St. James", and contribute to the experiential meaning of the text.

*Textual*. The Themes are unmarked and simple; usually the participant Santiago or its attractions are in Theme position, as the topic of the text. The Thematic progression combines different patterns. The message develops mainly continuously the Theme "Santiago" and "city", which sometimes can sound too repetitive. The monotony is broken by few new Themes introducing Santiago's attractions, such as Plaza Obradoiro or its historic quarter. These emphasize the attractions and make the message direct and practical as in a real visit.

The webpage relies, then, only on the written mode to present Santiago de Compostela and persuade users to visit it. This may be the reason why the text focuses on the landmark; as there is no picture to illustrate it, the text attempts to be informative, detailed and impressive. This focus makes it different from the other texts analysed since the tour operator and the client are not central anymore. The city and its attractions are presented from an objective, general and impersonal perspective. Facts, like the city's religious fame, antiquity, historic quarters or diverse architecture, are expected to impress by themselves. The frequent repetition of the adjective "impressive" seems also to indicate this. The interest in Santiago is increased by the possibility to visit the city of Vigo "if time permits", users being offered a "clustered opportunity" (Jansen-Verbeke and Lievois 2002, 94). The mainly informative message aims to show why Santiago is worth visiting and to persuade that "this magical city is a must see for many tourists", among which the users can be numbered. The lack of a picture can indicate the city has many landmarks to offer so that it is impossible to select only one. It can also provoke users' curiosity about how it looks.

### 8.2.4. Discussion of the Spanish set of commercial webpages

The website of the Spanish tour operator impacts firstly by its colour implying neutrality and reliability. This leads attention to fall on its other elements. The contents are listed in a lateral navigational menu that can affect readability. This presents only the main topics of the website and points out practical and contact details, instead of general information on the tours. The menu appears as concise, but not as very intuitive. The main body and the footer, however, shed more light on the menu and present links on each topic. The message of the tour operator is clear and persuasive; it states its identity, aim and offers. The characteristics of the offers are further emphasized by their layout as a framed list. The human component is frequently repeated, indicating a close and friendly tour operator, whose professionalism is guaranteed by TripAdvisor and former clients.

The home page is attractive, short and simply designed. The accent seems to fall, however, more on the verbal message than on the visual one, its reading being more traditional or page-like. The message develops more on a connotative level than on a logical one (Garzone 2009, 36), persuasive descriptions being preferred over the site's general content. The webpages analysed follow the same model, regarding layout, structure and colloquial tone, suggesting a cohesive website. Nevertheless, their visual elements are more frequent and conspicuous, except the page on Santiago, which has no picture in the main body. The inclusion of several rotating pictures of the different landmarks promoted by the tour may raise curiosity, as they "reinforce each other and produce a sense of excitement" (Yui Ling Ip 2008, 7). The webpages' message is rather general; it identifies the landmark and describes its background and attractions. These sections aim to draw attention and arouse interest. Desire seems to be evoked by linguistic devices, such as future and imperative forms that project users into the tour and connotative words that impress. The interactional information is placed at the end of the message and provides a further contact form with the purpose of calling to action. The action is, however, indirect, as users are encouraged not to book, but to contact. The multimodal and interactive possibilities offered by hypermedia do not seem to be fully exploited.

The webpages analysed provide slightly different messages and this can be observed in the characteristics of their texts. The one dedicated to the Monastery of El Escorial oscillates between personal and impersonal tone and presents the landmark more related to the tour than by itself. The webpage on the Alhambra, in turn, is personal and didactic, guiding the users' steps through sights and sensations. Unlike these, the text on Santiago de Compostela is impersonal while it describes, identifies and situates locatively the attractions of the city. This can be due to the absence of a picture to illustrate visually the city; the text aims to do both.

Even if the texts are different, a certain common pattern can be observed, as indicated by Table 8-13. The texts are medium long, syntactically elaborated and complex, as the clause complexes are very long. These are preferred over clause simplexes and are developed mainly by expansion hypotaxis-enhancement. The causal-conditional and temporal relations refer to the tour, not to the landmark. They aim to provide a logic and reasoned presentation of the tour, instead of just adding or elaborating on ideas. This is also the reason for the few relative clauses. The non-finite dependent clauses add dynamism to the description. The information on the landmark, however, is constructed usually by extension-addition, which lists details successively. The most frequent processes are material; they present the tour and guide the users' steps. The type of relational processes usually encountered is attributive intensive, used to describe the landmark and its attractions. The mental processes contribute to the presentation of the tour, which includes reference to the senses, not only to actions. The background information situates the actions in time and place. The landmark, the most frequent participant, appears as Goal, as the entity visited by the client. The client, in turn, has the role of Goal, being affected by the tour operator's actions, when alone, and of Actor, acting on the landmark, when forming a team with the operator. The text presenting Santiago is different, as already mentioned. Its focus on the landmark is reflected by the preference for relational processes, the presentation of the landmark as Carrier/Subject/Theme, the scarce appearance of the client and the absence of the tour operator. This may reflect a simple adaptation from paper to web, and not an adaptation to the new medium (Lemke 2002). The preferred mood is declarative, except for the text on the Alhambra, which is mainly imperative. The differences between the texts are even more visible in the interpersonal metafunction, as far as the types of participant in Subject position, Finites, tense and modals are concerned. Thematic organization is, however, rather similar; unmarked and simple Themes–some participants, some processes–succeed each other in a continuous pattern in order to develop the message.

**Table 8-13 Spanish set of commercial websites: Lexico-grammatical summary**

| System | The Monastery of El Escorial | The Alhambra | Santiago de Compostela |
|---|---|---|---|
| Clause complex | short<br>only complexes (3 & 4 clauses)<br>only expansion<br>+ hypotaxis<br>+ enhancement<br>1 non-defining relative clause<br>+ non-finite clauses<br>+ apposition | medium long<br>+ complexes (4 cl.)<br>+ expansion<br>+ hypotaxis<br>= elaboration & enhancement<br>+ non-defining relative clause<br>+ non-finite clauses | medium long<br>+ simplexes (3 cls. complex)<br>only expansion<br>+ parataxis<br>+ extension<br>+ defining relative clause<br>+ non-finite clauses |

| System | The Monastery of El Escorial | The Alhambra | Santiago de Compostela |
|---|---|---|---|
| Transitivity | + material<br>only attributive<br>only possessive<br>only mental perception<br>+ realized participants<br>+ landmark<br>+ landmark (realized)<br>+ tour operator (implied)<br>+ Goal (landmark)<br>only Goal (client)<br>+ Actor (operator)<br>only location, only place | + material<br>+ identifying<br>+ intensive<br>only mental percep.<br>+ existential<br>+ realized particip.<br>+ landmark<br>= landmark & operator (realized)<br>+ client (implied)<br>+ Goal (landmark)<br>expressed as Goal, implied as Actor (client)<br>= Actor, Goal, Carrier, Identified, Existent (operator)<br>+ location, + time | + relational<br>+ attributive<br>+ intensive<br>- mental<br>+ realized particip.<br>+ landmark<br>+ land.(realized)<br>only landmark (implied)<br>+ Carrier (landmark)<br>only Attributor (client)<br>Actor & Identifier (operator)<br>+ location, only time |
| Mood | + residue<br>only complex residue<br>+ operator & client as Subject<br>= expressed & fused Finites<br>= present & future<br>only Circ. Adjuncts<br>only modalization<br>- polarity<br>only declarative,<br>+ full decl.<br>only statements | + residue<br>+ complex residue<br>only operator as Subject<br>only expressed Finites<br>only future<br>+ Circ. Adjuncts<br>only modalization<br>- polarity<br>+ imperative<br>+ commands | = mood & residue<br>only complex residue<br>+ landmark as Subject<br>+ fused Finites<br>+ present<br>+ Circ. Adjuncts<br>only modalization<br>- polarity<br>only declarative<br>only statements |
| Theme | + unmarked (dependent cl. –Th.)<br>+ simple<br>= participant & process as Theme<br>= multiple & continuous progr. | only unmarked (many dep. cl. – Rheme)<br>+ simple<br>+ process as Theme<br>+ continuous progression | only unmarked<br>+ simple<br>+ participant as Theme<br>+ continuous progression (little difference) |

The images analysed, unlike the texts, are very similar, as reflected in Table 8-14. They illustrate the Monastery of El Escorial and the Alhambra from representative perspectives. They are built by complex conceptual structures, which present the landmark and its surrounding landscape by unstructured analytical processes. The landmark appears as a complex of buildings offered for contemplation. The oblique and eye level angles emphasise the idea of contemplation and lack of involvement. Nevertheless, the medium shot depicts the landmark within viewers' reach, but not actually in front of their eyes. Viewers have the freedom to just look or go closer. The pictures are presented as real, as "postcards", without any informational organization. The saliency and framing of the landmark, provided by the interplay of the modality markers, can, however, indicate a desire to increase the attractiveness or importance of the buildings in the picture.

**Table 8-14 Spanish set of commercial websites: Visual summary**

| System | The Monastery of El Escorial | The Alhambra | Santiago de Compostela |
|---|---|---|---|
| Represent-ational | complex<br>conceptual structure<br>unstructured analytical<br>monastery & landscape (Carrier)<br>building & sky (Possessive Attributes) | complex<br>conceptual structure<br>unstructured analytical<br>landmark & landscape (Carrier)<br>buildings & vegetation, mountains, sky (Possessive Attributes) | - |
| Interactive | offer<br>medium shot<br>subjective<br>oblique horizontal angle<br>eye level vertical angle<br>+ medium modality markers | offer<br>medium shot<br>subjective<br>frontal & oblique horizontal angle<br>eye level vertical angle<br>+ medium modality markers | - |
| Composit-ional | - information structure<br>building (salient)<br>building (framed) | - information structure<br>landmark (salient)<br>landmark (framed) | - |

The communicative acts are, thus, rather different. The tour operator does not seem consistent in the composition of the verbal message. The visual one, instead, is similar and included in the webpage before the actual description of the landmark, as if illustrating the promised product. The modes complement each other since the visual illustrates and the verbal foresees and guides, bringing the landmark closer. When the visual is absent, the verbal mainly describes and hardly guides at all. Each message points a different reason for buying the tour, indicating a varied offer. Whether users search for history and art; Renaissance architecture, Muslim influences, gardens and sensations; or pilgrimage route, antiquity, Romanesque, Baroque and Neo Classical architecture and art, the tour operator has them all.

## 8.3. British set of commercial webpages

The home page of the British commercial website (www.evanevans tours.co.uk) is medium long and vertically organized. It can be divided into various easily distinguishable sections. The short header presents the name of the tour operator, on the left, and its phone number, on the right. The name, highlighted visually by colour, font size and type, is defined overtly persuasively as “Britain’s Finest Sightseeing by Coach and Rail” (Evan Evans Tours 2014). The header includes a menu bar with links to general information on the agency and its privacy policy (“About Us”, “Privacy”), practical information related to travel (“Pick up Service”, “Group Travel”, “FAQ”), interactive details for users (“Get Social”, “Contact Us”) and specialised area for agents (“Agent Login”). There is no link to navigational details.

The main section of the home page can be divided in two parts. The first one contains two columns. The left one is marginal and includes a navigational lateral menu; the lateral layout seems to affect readability (Rodríguez Abella 2011, 161). This shows links to commercial activities (“Shopping Cart”), navigational instructions (“Home”) and many names of tours and attractions presenting the offers of the agency (“London Tours”, “Stonehenge” or “River Cruises”). More interactive elements are included, like the possibility to find a particular tour and join the agency communities on social networks. Finally, the column draws attention to a certificate of excellence from TripAdvisor, which guarantees the tour operator’s professionalism and trustworthiness, and to a special service accompanying the tours called “Vox radioguide”. The right column is more important, occupying almost the entire screen. It can be further divided in two sections. The first one has the heading “Best selling tours & attractions”. This name seems an indirect technique to attract attention to these particular items; their popularity among previous users seems to certify their quality. The section repeats some of the offers from the navigational lateral menu. They are presented as a sort of triptych composed by several small pictures accompanying the attractions, as if illustrating them in order to obtain a higher impact. The second section of the column presents a long list with attractions and tickets; each item contains a small representative picture, the type of tour, its name and a short description. The links and details on the tours seem, thus, quite exhaustive and sometimes repetitive.

The second part of the main section contains a text that gives a brief presentation of the tour operator, its long existence, tours and attractions. It highlights its collaboration with the London Tourist Board, probably to persuade users about its reliability and value. The operator provides information on its services, like pick up, secure online payment and free Wi-Fi. The last message points out, again, its professionalism as recommended by VisitBritain and the United States Tour Operators Association. The address and telephone are then provided for further contact. The footer is short and refers to copyright and to other associations having the tour operator as a member.

The home page follows the principles of the AIDA model, frequently used in marketing to focus on the way the product is related to Attention, Interest, Desire and Action, as explained previously (OMT 2005b, 8). Attention is drawn by the attractive pictures, tours and attractions, logo, the presentation of the tour operator and the possibility to communicate with it. Interest is captured by the persuasive descriptions and pictures accompanying the list of items presented. These can also stimulate Desire. Action is induced by the "Shopping Cart" and the different possibilities of interaction.

### 8.3.1. Canterbury Cathedral in the commercial corpus

There is no webpage dedicated entirely to Canterbury Cathedral; the landmark is part of a tour, together with other landmarks in the region of Kent. The tour operator seems to follow the principle of "clustered opportunities" (Jansen-Verbeke and Lievois 2002, 94) to increase the interest in a tour. In this case, the offer tours Leeds Castle, Canterbury Cathedral and Dover. The webpage presenting the tour follows the same layout as the home page: header, left marginal column, wide main body and footer. The main message has a vertical organization and can be divided in two main sections, reminding users of the typical advertising layout. The visual section stands for the promised product and includes the pictures of the promoted landmark, as if it were a postcard. It is displayed like a mosaic of pictures: three small pictures laid vertically on the right, whereas, on the left, one of them can be enlarged, depending on the users' choice. They are accompanied by a short catchy phrase describing the tour ("Select Sightseeing–A full day to discover the treasures of Kent–Leeds Castle, Canterbury Cathedral and the White Cliffs of Dover"). The verbal section follows the promised product in order to describe it and offer the possibility to get to it. This can be further divided in three parts. The first one lists and highlights the contents of the tour, the second describes each landmark briefly, whereas the last one presents practical information on the radio guide mentioned in the home page, the prices and programme of the tour, including the possibility to book.

Fig. 8-7 Canterbury Cathedral commercial webpage

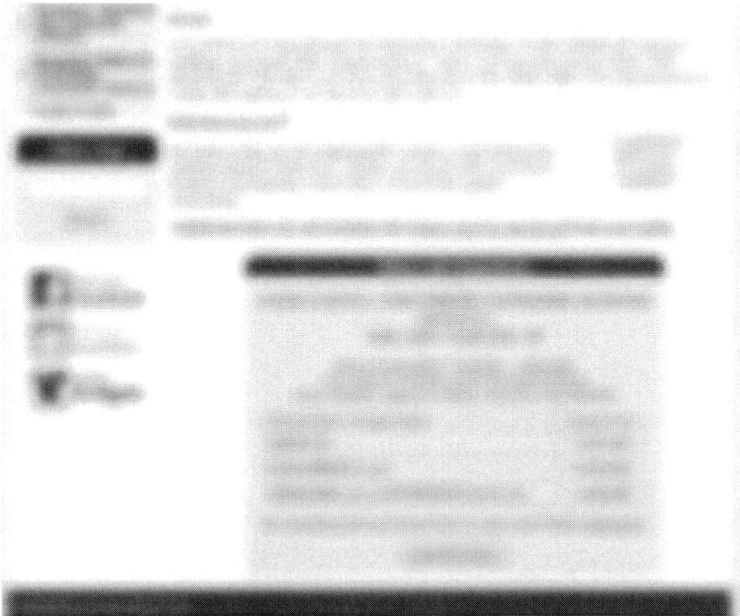

*Source:* Evan Evans Tours (2014)[6]

It seems, then, that the pictures and the tour "highlights" attract users, the description informs them about the landmarks, whereas the "book" button offers them the opportunity to buy immediately. The webpage can be recommended or shared on social networks, users becoming in their turn promoters. The reading of the top-bottom layout seems guided by salient elements, since attention is drawn to the title, pictures, subtitles and prices box.

### 8.3.1.1. Linguistic analysis

*Overview*. The text presenting Canterbury Cathedral emphasises its importance for the Anglican faith. Several attractions are named, like the central "Bell Harry Tower" or the crypt where Archbishop Thomas Beckett was murdered. The opportunities "to explore the narrow streets of Canterbury" and have lunch are presented as a bonus to the visit of the Cathedral.

---

[6] As mentioned in Chapter six, when copyright was not granted, an impression of the structure of the webpage has been included so that the reader can follow the analyses.

*Logical*. The text, developed in one paragraph, is short, medium syntactically elaborated and complex. It slightly favours clause complexes for its clauses' organization. The types of relations between clauses are equally distributed between parataxis and hypotaxis. Parataxis extends information by adding details, either about the Cathedral, "The central 'Bell Harry Tower' dates back to 1498, *and* the crypt to the 11th Century", or about the tour, "It is here where your guide will tell the story of the shocking murder of Archbishop Thomas Beckett in 1170 *and* there will also be time to explore the narrow streets of Canterbury" (Evan Evans Tours 2014). The constructions seem similar to oral language, where the conjunction "and" is frequently used to give continuity and fluidity to the speech (Halliday 1989). The simulation of spoken language is a technique used by advertising discourse to minimise the distance from its audience and persuade (van Leeuwen 2005, 155). The text also uses non-finite clauses, either embedded, "known as the 'Garden of England'", or dependent, "to visit the Cathedral", to make information more compact. The hypotactic relations enhance and fix a referential frame for the events; they present the way to get to Canterbury with the purpose of visiting its Cathedral ("*Traveling through Kent, the county known as the 'Garden of England'*, we make our way to Canterbury *to visit the Cathedral*").

*Experiential*. The text is built using a balance of material and relational processes. The material processes, like "travel" and "visit", start the message and refer to the tour and the activities included. The relational processes, mainly identifying, present the Cathedral as "the most important church within the worldwide Anglican faith". They also link it to the past and the story of "the shocking murder of Archbishop Thomas Becket". Attributive processes are used to describe the Cathedral's central tower and crypt, as for example in "The central 'Bell Harry Tower' *dates back* to 1498". The main aim of the relational processes is to set the location, both spatial and temporal, of the attractions. There are also a few instances of existential processes towards the end, which again refer to the tour and highlight the existence of time to explore the city of Canterbury and to have lunch. The text seems, then, to present both organizational details and landmark descriptions. Circumstances are rarely used and, when there, provide a spatial location for the action, e.g. "to Canterbury".

The participants considered are more often expressed than implied, the most frequently expressed being the landmark and the most implied the tour operator. The landmark is presented mainly in the role of Carrier as the entity whose features are described, e.g. "*The central 'Bell Harry Tower'* dates back to 1498". The tour operator is presented as close to the visitor, as it is referred to by the personal pronoun "we", which plays around the idea of team or togetherness. "We" is most often used by speakers to group themselves with one or more participants (Halliday and Hassan 1976 in Fontaine 2006). As such, it can be interpreted inclusively, with the visitor part of the tour operator's plans. The pronoun is overtly expressed only once, in the beginning of the text, signalling the "inclusion of the users into the virtual tour" (Yui Ling Ip 2008, 8); in the other instances, it is implied. Its role is always that of Actor, the person who travels and visits ("*we* make our way to Canterbury").

*Interpersonal*. The chosen mood is declarative and information is presented as fact by means of statements. The text does not focus on the landmark or the visitor exclusively since they are not placed in Subject position frequently. However, the Cathedral and its attractions appear more often as Subjects than the visitor. The Finites are frequently fused ("is"), except for several cases of modalization. The tense is present ("dates back"), except, again, for the future expressed by modality. The information presented seems to be general and timeless (Banks 2002, 6). The modal "will" adds certainty to the tour, acting as a predictor. The text presents the tour as organised, as if following a plan. This can denote professionalism, which is further emphasised by the impersonal tone suggested by the existential constructions ("there will be"). The plan is general, not focused on the agency or the client, and can be considered a fact. All the clauses are positive. There are equal percentages of Mood and Residue. The Residue element is usually complex, except for an instance of Predicator ellipsis, e.g. "and the crypt *[dates back]* to the 11th Century", which makes the message more compact.

*Textual*. The Thematic structure is mainly unmarked and simple ("*This magnificent Cathedral* is the most important church within the worldwide Anglican faith"), though there are some exceptions. The marked instance places a dependent clause as Theme, e.g. "Traveling through Kent", focusing on the way to get to Canterbury. There are a number of enhanced Themes, predicated and existential, which balance the objectivity of the unmarked Themes. They also postpone the activation of the Subject in discourse (Moya Guijarro 2006, 20). Since the predicated Theme may be used to structure the clause in two components (Halliday 1994, 59) and focus on one of them, in this case, the focus is on "here", as the place where the guide will tell the story of the Archbishop's murder, and not somewhere else ("*It is here* where your guide will tell the story of the shocking murder of Archbishop Thomas Beckett in 1170"). The existential instances, "there will be", instead, draw attention to spare time to explore something else than the Cathedral and to the opportunity to have lunch in the city. These Themes make the visit more interesting as they emphasise other possibilities apart from visiting a religious landmark. There are some cases of multiple Themes, all expressed by the textual conjunction "and".

As for Thematic development, there is no clear pattern. The majority are new Themes, e.g. "this magnificent cathedral" and "there will be", which can confuse readers. Nevertheless, some of them can be retrieved from dependent clauses, by synecdoche, like "the tower", or pronouns without a clear referent, like "it" and "here". Information, thus, does not flow, but seems to stop at almost every sentence. This can be a technique to draw users' attention to the particular item placed in Theme position. It can be, however, ineffective, confusing users.

The linguistic analysis is presented in Table 8-15.

**Table 8-15 Commercial Canterbury Cathedral: Lexico-grammatical summary**

| Clause complex | Transitivity | Mood | Theme |
|---|---|---|---|
| short<br>almost =<br>complexes &<br>simplexes<br>only expansion<br>= parataxis &<br>hypotaxis<br>= extension &<br>enhancement<br>- non-def. relatives<br>+ non-finite<br>clauses | = material &<br>relational<br>+ identifying<br>+ circumstantial<br>+ existential<br>+ realized particip.<br>+ landmark<br>+ landmark (realized)<br>only tour operator<br>+ client (implied)<br>+ Carrier (landmark)<br>- client alone<br>Actor (operator +<br>visitor)<br>only location, only<br>place | = mood &<br>residue<br>+ complex<br>residue<br>+ landmark as<br>Subject<br>+ fused Finite<br>+ present<br>+ Circ. Adjuncts<br>only<br>modalization<br>- polarity<br>only declarative<br>only statements | + unmarked<br>+ enhanced<br>+ simple<br>+ participants<br>as Theme<br>- Thematic<br>progression |

### 8.3.1.2. Visual analysis

The image chosen as representation of Canterbury Cathedral, very similar to the institutional variant already analysed, is usually associated with the landmark. The conceptual structure presents the Cathedral and the landscape as Carriers, by means of unstructured analytical processes. The towers and other parts of the Cathedral represent the Possessive Attributes of the Cathedral, whereas the sky and branches belong to the landscape. The eye is directed more to the Cathedral than to the landscape.

As regards the type of interaction, the Cathedral is offered for contemplation. The perspective is subjective and presents it from close, low and oblique angles; users see its lateral upper part. These angles engage users, but also place them outside the surroundings of the Cathedral, which stands there dominant. The lack of details can emphasise the unknown and arouse interest; users can go inside the world of the Cathedral and investigate it. The picture looks realistic, as if taken by somebody there. However, the size and colours seem to have been modified with the aim of persuasion, as if to present the Cathedral as more dominant.

Analysing the image for its composition, the viewer finds it hard to see evidence of information structure, as it focuses only on the Cathedral. The colour and size, as mentioned already, make it salient and even framed, contributing to its importance.

The results of the visual analysis are summarised in Table 8-16.

**Table 8-16 Commercial Canterbury Cathedral: Visual summary**

| Representational | Interactive | Compositional |
|---|---|---|
| complex<br>conceptual structure<br>unstructured analytical<br>cathedral & landscape (Carrier)<br>tower, other components, sky + branches (Poss. Attributes) | offer<br>close shot<br>subjective<br>oblique horiz. angle<br>low vertical angle<br>+ medium modality markers | - information structure<br>cathedral (salient)<br>cathedral (framed) |

### 8.3.1.3. Multimodal act

To sum up, the multimodal webpage presents Canterbury Cathedral to users. The picture represents the monument, whereas the text describes it. The picture focuses only on a part of the Cathedral, as if inviting users to find out more by themselves. The text guides the users' steps, accompanied by the tour operator, through Kent, the "Garden of England", to visit the Cathedral. The landmark is described briefly, attention being drawn to its importance for religion, its antiquity and tumultuous past. The possibility to do other things than visit the Cathedral contributes to the attractiveness of the landmark and raises users' curiosity. The message appears objective, transparent and impersonal. Nevertheless, the voice of the tour operator is noticeable in the first person pronoun and modalization. The ideas of team and predictability seem to confer a persuasive tone to the message and give it more power. The message, then, includes both practical and general information. The practical details situate the tour and indicate possible things to do. The general facts, instead, present various attractions of the landmark, as if to emphasise its importance and confirm it as a must-see.

### 8.3.2. The Tower of London in the commercial corpus

The webpage analysed for the Tower of London follows the same layout as the previous ones. Information is displayed similarly: visual message as promise and verbal message as description. The presentation card with practical details such as price and timetable is also kept. This tour is called "Majestic London" and includes Westminster Abbey, Buckingham Palace, St Paul's Cathedral and the Tower of London.

Fig. 8-8 The Tower of London commercial webpage[7]

*Source:* Evan Evans Tours (2014)

---

[7] This Figure presents only the description of the Tower of London. The included highlights, the other landmarks' descriptions and the practical information are not included for reasons of space.

#### 8.3.2.1. Linguistic analysis

*Overview*. The text presents the Tower of London and situates it in its historical background. It also mentions several attractions: the Beefeaters and the Crown Jewels.

*Logica*l. The text is short, syntactically developed and complex. Clause simplexes and complexes are used in almost equal proportions. The clause complexes develop only by expansion and the usual relation is that of hypotaxis-elaboration, as for example in "The Beefeaters *who guard the Tower* will regale you with stories of its past" (Evan Evans Tours 2014). The dependent clauses are non-defining relative clauses that elaborate on the noun phrases and make the message more compact, as frequently encountered in promotional discourse (Gotti 2008, 94). Some of them are even non-finite, e.g. "founded by William the Conqueror in 1066-7", which further contribute to the compactness of the text and density of information already announced by the syntactical elaboration of the text mentioned above (Gotti 2008, 94).

*Experiential*. The Tower is presented mainly by material processes, which are considered markers of "objectivity and facticity" (Barker and Galasinki 2001, 71). They refer to its construction ("enlarge") and to one of its attractions, the Beefeaters ("guard"). They also name what the visitor can "visit". The few instances of relational processes both identify the Tower as "one of the world's most famous and spectacular fortresses" and classify it according to its past functions as "Royal Palace", "armoury" and "place of imprisonment and execution". The circumstances place the action into a temporal background, pointing out the site's antiquity, e.g. "in 1066-7".

The focused participants, i.e. the landmark, the client and the tour operator, are more often overtly expressed than implied. The landmark is the most frequently realized participant. It mainly performs the role of Goal, the entity on which action was, is and will be performed, as for example in "We will visit *the Crown Jewels* ...". The client is expressed only once, as Beneficiary. This role is quite persuasive; the possible visitor is presented as benefiting from the tour, particularly from the stories that the Beefeaters will "regale" her/him with. The relation is direct as the second person pronoun "you" is used, making the experience more personal and individual. The tour operator seems to pass the responsibility for the users' pleasure on to the Beefeaters; they are the ones to perform an action in favour of the users, not the operator. The aim may be to sound more objective, impersonal and professional. The tour operator, as frequently represented as the visitor, is referred to by the personal pronoun "we" at the end of the text. The pronoun also includes the visitor and plays the role of Actor, indicating the attractions to be visited ("*We* will visit the Crown Jewels …"). The idea of togetherness implied can make users feel safer, belonging to a group. The interplay of the pronouns in the text builds up a persuasive message.

*Interpersonal.* The number of conjoinable clause units analysed for mood and theme is not high, considering the dominance of hypotactic clause complexes. The mood of the text is declarative, information being presented assertively as statement. The Subject position is always occupied by important participants, either the Tower or the tour operator, the former being the most predominant. The Finites are mainly expressed by modals. They refer in equal proportions to present, when dealing with the Tower ("the Tower of London *is* one of the world's …"), and to future, when describing the tour ("We *will* visit …"). The modalization of the section dedicated to the tour places it in a professional light. The high modality expressed by the modal "will" presents the visit as happening according to a plan. The tour operator's professionalism is made more human by its reference to the inclusive "we". The Residue element has a complex structure, even though it lacks Adjuncts. There is only one instance of Circumstantial Adjunct, "over the past 1000 years", which can indicate that background information is placed secondary to the description of the landmark and the tour.

*Textual.* The Themes appear in equal proportions as marked and unmarked. The marked ones show a focus on the construction of the Tower and its antiquity, as indicated by the preposed attributives, "Founded by William the Conqueror in 1066-7 and enlarged by successive sovereigns", and the extent circumstance, "Over the past 1000 years", placed in Theme position. There is even an interpolation in Theme, which draws the attention of the reader to the Beefeaters' identity, e.g. "The Beefeaters *who guard the Tower* will regale …". The unmarked Themes are expressed by participants and add an objective tone to the message, as for instance in "*We* will visit the Crown Jewels …". All the Themes are simple; the copywriter seems to be more concerned with the focalization of information than with the flow of the message. This is also shown by the lack of any Thematic progression; the Themes are all new, none derives from any other. The lack of continuity produces a text that seems to be made up of a series of unconnected sentences. Its coherence has to be created by the reader.

The result of the linguistic analysis is summarised in Table 8-17.

**Table 8-17 Commercial Tower of London: Lexico-grammatical summary**

| Clause complex | Transitivity | Mood | Theme |
|---|---|---|---|
| short<br>= complexes & simplexes<br>only expansion<br>+ hypotaxis<br>+ elaboration<br>+ non-defining relatives<br>+ non-finite cls.<br>- post-modification | + material<br>= identifying & attributive<br>only intensive<br>- other processes<br>+ realized particip.<br>+ landmark<br>+ land. (realized)<br>only land. (implied)<br>+ Goal (landmark)<br>only Beneficiary (client)<br>Actor (operator + visitor)<br>= location & extent, time | = mood & residue<br>only complex residue<br>+ landmark as Subject<br>+ expressed Finite<br>= present & future<br>1 Circ. Adjunct only<br>modalization<br>- polarity<br>only declarative<br>only statements | = unmarked & marked<br>enhanced<br>only simple<br>+ participants as Theme<br>- Thematic progression<br>all new Themes |

### 8.3.2.2. Visual analysis

The picture representing the tour of the Tower of London does not depict only the Tower; it is panoramic and presents one of the banks of the River Thames. It seems to be taken from the deck of a boat. The aim may be to impress by showing a panoramic view of London, but the lack of focus on the Tower may also confuse users. They may be impressed by the conglomerate of buildings and possible attractions, but never by the Tower. Its size, colour and position on the bottom right corner of the riverbank seem to contribute to this. The attention falls on other elements in the picture.

The structure of the picture is conceptual and is built on unstructured analytical processes. The riverbank and the landscape are depicted as Carriers for the Possessive Attributes represented by the numerous buildings, the Thames with its boats and the sky. The depiction of the landscape looks secondary to that of the riverbank. The inclusion of the Tower as one among many other buildings in the picture indicates the lack of focalization mentioned earlier.

The riverbank is shot from a long, oblique angle; the buildings are presented standing in the distance. This emphasises the fact that the picture is presented for contemplation as its components are placed outside the viewers' world, as if out of their reach. The vertical angle is eye level towards high; viewers seem to be given the power to contemplate and look down on the elements depicted indirectly. The interplay of the modality markers presents a realistic scene.

The picture does not follow any informational structure as it just depicts a conglomerate of buildings. The salient elements appear to be the tall buildings at the back and the boat. As already mentioned, there is no detail to indicate that the picture is about the Tower of London. The image seems rather to aim to impress by the "clustered opportunities" (Jansen-Verbeke and Lievois 2002, 94) to visit offered by the monuments on the riverbank and a possible river cruise than by a detailed representation of the Tower.

The visual summary of the picture is presented in Table 8-18.

**Table 8-18 Commercial Tower of London: Visual summary**

| Representational | Interactive | Compositional |
|---|---|---|
| complex<br>conceptual structure<br>unstructured analytical<br>riverbank & landscape (Carrier)<br>buildings & Thames & sky (Possessive Attributes) | offer<br>long shot<br>subjective<br>oblique horizontal angle<br>eye level towards high<br>vertical angle<br>+ medium mod. markers | - information structure<br>tall buildings & boat (salient)<br>-framing |

### 8.3.2.3. Multimodal act

The different modes of communication contribute to the meaning of the message transmitted by the webpage analysed. The picture presents a distant and insignificant Tower of London, as if inviting users either to contemplate from the distance or to find out more by going closer. The text completes the picture and identifies the Tower among the conglomerate of buildings. The landmark is linked to its past and present by an apparent objective and impersonal description. Nevertheless, the connotative language, the marked Themes and the personal pronouns confer subjectivity to the message. The text seems informative, as it highlights the construction and age of the Tower, its importance for Britain and the world, and its attractions, such as the Beefeaters or the Crown Jewels. Persuasion seems concealed in the language; the planned tour is carried on together with the sole aim of benefiting the visitor.

### 8.3.3. Edinburgh in the commercial corpus

Fig. 8-9 Edinburgh commercial webpage[8]

*Source:* Evan Evans Tours (2014)

The webpage dedicated to "the Royal city" has the same layout as the others discussed so far. The difference is that the page presents only Edinburgh; there are no other specific landmarks included in the tour. The

[8] The practical information related to prices and timetable is similar to the others. For reason of space, it has not been included in this Figure.

tour per se is unescorted and provides the optional service of staying overnight.

#### 8.3.3.1. Linguistic analysis

*Overview*. The text takes users by train to Edinburgh, where they can board the open-top sightseeing bus and see different attractions, such as the Old Town quarter, the Scott Monument or Edinburgh Castle.

*Logical*. This text is medium long, elaborated and complex. There are slightly more clause simplexes than complexes, for instance "The train from London's King Cross Station arrives at the Royal City of Edinburgh at around 11.30am" (Evan Evans Tours 2014). In the case of clause complexes, the pattern of development is mainly elaboration. There is, however, an instance of projection, a type encountered only in this text from the British commercial set. It projects an idea by proposing different actions visitors may do in Edinburgh, such as "wander through the cobbled streets" or "stroll along Princess Street checking out the tartan, whisky and shortbreads that have made Scotland so famous". These proposals are further emphasised by the exclamation mark accompanying them. The tactic relation between clauses is usually of hypotaxis-extension; the main clauses extend by further details, expressed by non-finite clauses, e.g. "The train back to London leaves Edinburgh in the late afternoon *returning to London's King's Cross at around 10:30pm*". The high number of non-finite clauses makes the message more compact (Gotti 2008, 94).

*Experiential*. The text develops mainly by material processes, which provide objective information about the train to and from Edinburgh ("arrive"), the sightseeing bus ("allow"), and the activities visitors can perform ("wander" and "stroll"). Mental processes are also present and refer to what visitors may "want" and "see". These also indicate some of the most important places in the city; their close succession conveys a sense of motion and "dynamic excitement" (Yui Ling Ip 2008, 7). Mental processes of affection appear for the first time in this set and can help the copywriter reduce the distance and make users feel special, whereas perception ones present the experience as real and produce a better communicative efficiency (Pérez Vázquez 2011, 310). The appeal to senses, perceptions and wishes, frequently encountered in promotional genres, is used to achieve persuasion easier (Mapelli and Piccioni 2011, 68; Mariottini 2012, 106). There is only one instance of relational process, which identifies what the tour includes, i.e. tickets to Edinburgh Castle. There are quite a lot of background details locating the actions. Spatial location, such as "London's King Cross Station" or "centre streets", is more frequent than the temporal one, such as "11.30am". The high number of details may be due to the fact that the tour operator wants to give a precise description of the tour, as it is unescorted. The details may make the tourists feel safer.

The presentation of the participants is different from the other texts, as the landmark is no more the most realized participant, its place being taken by the client. This can have the same reason as the high number of details, i.e. guide users. Apart from providing detailed background information, the tour operator wants to convince users by paying them more attention. They are addressed directly by the second person pronoun "you", which establishes a communicative immediacy (Janoschka 2004, 121). The client is expressed overtly as Senser, as the one who sees and wants ("*You* might want"). At the same time, s/he is the only participant implied, in which case s/he is understood as Actor ("*[you]* to wander through the cobbled city centre streets"). The interplay of roles can be symbolic; users become expressed Actors only after going on the visit. Regarding the landmark promoted, the city of Edinburgh and its attractions are rarely represented. They appear mainly as Phenomenon, as the entity the visitor can see, "You will see *the Old Town quarter ...*". They are also frequently found as circumstances of spatial location ("at the Royal City of Edinburgh"), i.e. as optional information. The tour operator, in turn, is as infrequent as the landmark. It does not have a preferred role, but is expressed equally as Actor ("*The hop-on hop-off ticket* allows you the freedom …"), Identified and Identifier ("*Your tour* includes *tickets to Edinburgh Castle*"). The operator is neither mentioned by name nor referred to, but can be inferred from the practical details such as "tickets" and "tour". This can be due to the unescorted type of tour.

*Interpersonal*. The declarative mood states information as fact, as in the other texts analysed so far. The Subject usually refers either to the client or to information related to the tour, the client being more frequent. The "train" to and from Edinburgh seems to play an important part in the message since it is the other participant occupying the Subject position; it specifies spatial and temporal details about a predetermined schedule. Edinburgh never appears in Subject position. The message, then, seems focused on the client, who is guided to the discovery of the meaningful aspects of the city. The other element in the Mood component, the Finite, is usually fused and present, like "allows"; the tour appears as notional and timeless (Banks 2002, 6). The assertiveness of the clauses is slightly mitigated by modalization. The modal "will" announces several attractions to be seen, e.g. "You *will* see the Old Town quarter …", while "might" refers to the visitors' possible wishes, e.g. "You *might* want to wander through the cobbled city centre streets …". This way different alternatives and possibilities are proposed. The low modality can also be used to make visitors feel free, with the power to choose what to do on the tour, as they are neither guided nor imposed by the guide. As for the Residue element, this is almost always complex, except for the proposal instance, and contains a high number of Circumstantial Adjuncts, for instance "right by the station" and "in the late afternoon".

*Textual*. The Thematic structure of the text relies mainly on unmarked and simple Themes, expressed by participants like "the train", "the hop-on hop-off ticket" or "you". The only marked Theme emphasizes a spatial location, particularly the place where the visitors can take the open-top sightseeing bus, i.e. "right by the station", after they arrive. There is no preference for any Thematic pattern; the text combines in equal proportions various patterns. The message develops cumulatively and presents information related to the bus ("Right by the station, you board the open-top sightseeing *bus* […]. *The hop-on hop-off ticket* allows you the freedom …"), whereas it keeps a continuous focus on the visitor and the train ("*You* will see […]. *You* might want …"). The new Themes draw attention to vital information like the place to take the bus or the tickets included by the tour.

The main characteristics of the text on Edinburgh are presented in Table 8-19.

**Table 8-19 Commercial Edinburgh: Lexico-grammatical summary**

| **Clause complex** | **Transitivity** | **Mood** | **Theme** |
|---|---|---|---|
| medium long<br>+ simplexes<br>+ expansion<br>+ parataxis<br>+ extension, addition<br>1 defining relative clause<br>+ non-finite clauses | + material<br>only identifying<br>only possessive<br>+ mental perception<br>+ realized particip.<br>+ client<br>+ client (realized)<br>only client (implied)<br>+ Phenomenon (landmark) expressed as Senser, implied as Actor (client)<br>= Actor, Identified & Identifier (operator)<br>only location, + place | = mood & residue<br>+ complex residue<br>+ client as Subject<br>+ fused Finite<br>+ present<br>only Circ. Adj.<br>only modalization<br>- polarity<br>only declarative<br>only statements | + unmarked<br>only simple<br>+ participants as Theme<br>= continuous, linear & new Themes |

### 8.3.3.2. Visual analysis

The three pictures of the webpage are dedicated to Edinburgh, as it is the only landmark promoted. The first presents a panoramic view of various monuments, the second focuses on St. Giles Cathedral, while the third one advertises the open bus touring the capital. The first picture has been chosen for this analysis for reasons indicated in Chapter six, on Methodology. This is not representative for the city, as it contains many constructions, but none close enough to be more distinguishable and stand for Edinburgh. The conceptual structure uses unstructured analytical processes to represent the city. Several buildings, such as the Scott Monument, Dugald Steward Monument or the ones on Calton Hill, appear as Possessive Attributes of the Carrier, i.e. Edinburgh. Secondary, the sky and the firth represent the landscape.

The picture is panoramic and offers a general view on the city for users' contemplation. Contemplation is further suggested by the long shot and the oblique and high angles. The city is out of reach, standing there for the users to look at it; the only power they have is that of observation. The modality markers present a realistic picture. The colours are, however, quite faded and the depth is not very clear. This may be due to the long shot, which seem to project the buildings on the background, as if part of the landscape.

Again, the image reveals no clear informational structure. The conglomerate of buildings just appears in the picture as it is, without a particular arrangement. As suggested before, this may aim to impress by the numerous attractions. The visual focus falls on the different towers, due to their size and colour. The emergence of the sky with the firth on the horizon line seems to give a romantic feel to the picture.

The visual characteristics of the picture of Edinburgh are included in Table 8-20.

**Table 8-20 Commercial Edinburgh: Visual summary**

| Representational | Interactive | Compositional |
|---|---|---|
| complex<br>conceptual structure<br>unstructured analytical<br>city & landscape (Carrier)<br>several buildings & sky +<br>firth (Possessive Attributes) | offer<br>long shot<br>subjective<br>oblique horiz. angle<br>high vertical angle<br>+ medium modality<br>markers | - information structure<br>towers (salient)<br>-framing |

#### 8.3.3.3. Multimodal act

To summarize, the webpage offers the picture of Edinburgh for contemplation. Its postcard-like appearance can raise the users' interest in discovering the buildings depicted. The text, however, is more focused on users than on the landmark. As the tour is unescorted, users are guided and oriented to the open bus and to various attractions. The message presents information in a detailed, objective and impersonal way. In spite of this, the users are addressed continuously. The communicative immediacy aims to persuade by connotative words and perceptions. Users are left the freedom to experience and investigate in different ways the items that made Edinburgh and Scotland famous. Authentic Scottish icons are named, like tartan, whisky, shortbreads (Morgan and Pritchard 2000; Yeoman *et al.* 2005, 140-141; Moilanen and Rainisto 2009, 45), guaranteeing a special experience. The communicative act seems to be divided according to the mode of transmission; the picture presents Edinburgh in the distance, whereas the text brings the city closer, identifies certain monuments from the picture and guides the users through the sights and tastes of the city, situating them spatially and temporally. The picture, then, represents, whereas the text persuades.

### 8.3.4. Discussion of the British set of commercial webpages

The home page of the British tour operator has a simple and clear design. The contents are listed both horizontally and vertically; the horizontal referring more to the tour operator, its services and interactive possibilities, whereas the vertical presenting mainly the tours and attractions offered. The separation of the offers from the other pieces of information seems to make them more conspicuous while providing an intuitive navigation. Their lateral vertical arrangement is considered, however, to affect readability (Rodríguez Abella 2011, 161). Reading is guided by colours and links; attractive pictures draw attention to a number of links to best-selling offers and tours. The links are, however, limited to the information on tours. The information related to the tour operator's identity and purpose is presented by long blocks of texts. These are stated clearly and, together with the connotative slogan, create the first image users have of the tour operator. The large amount of information, however, the long list of tours or the details related to the operator's services can make the home page too long and its message unclear and complicated. These pieces of information could have been placed on another webpage in order not to shift the focus from the main message. The home page, then, appears to be divided in two: a visual and telegraphic section that captures users' attention and a verbal and detailed section intended to maintain their interest and arouse their curiosity. It seems a rather rational home page, which presents the general contents of the website and pays little or no attention to emotions.

The webpages analysed follow the structure of the home page and maintain the initial layout, indicating a consistent and intuitive website (OMT 2001, 94; 2005b, 9). The interactive possibilities like search base and shopping cart, are also maintained. The webpages are medium long and arranged along a vertical axis like in magazine advertisements and marketing oriented websites (Myers 1994); the picture illustrates the promised product, whereas the text describes the facts and provides details about prices and schedules. They also appear to be divided in two like the home page. The picture, its caption, the "tour highlights" and the practical information from the end are easy to read and favour users that only scan information. The text, nonetheless, looks like traditional printed pages; the long blocks of text, even if divided in paragraphs and separated by subtitles, still require a lot of mental effort (OMT 2001, 113).

The message aims to inform by identifying the attraction, providing its background and describing it. The title, pictures and short introduction activate users' attention, whereas the background and description raise their interest in the landmark. The tour's highlights and services are provided to maintain users' desire. The message also intends to persuade and encourages users to act, especially by means of the form with practical information about the tour, which offers the possibility to book, included at the end.

The lexico-grammatical features of the texts, summarised in Table 8-21, indicate the informative aim of the messages. A common pattern is clear, no matter the individual differences that sometimes exist. The texts are rather short, made up of medium syntactically elaborated and complex clauses; neither type is too long and elaborated. The lack of complexity and elaboration is also reflected by the preference for clause simplexes. The instances of clause complexes are usually built by expansion on both parataxis and hypotaxis and developed by extension-addition. Information is just added to previous details so that the message flows cumulatively. It is not, however, compacted, because elaboration, relative clauses and postmodification are not very frequent. This can indicate that information is successive, with facts just coming one after the other. The transitivity system is composed mainly by material processes, which depict the visit and its schedule. The circumstantial background offers the spatial location of the tour. The landmark is mainly identified; its attractions are named without being described. It is the most frequent and realized participant as if it were the topic of the text rather than the tour itself. This is also indicated by its placement in Subject/Theme position. The landmark does not have the same role in the texts, but alternates between Carrier, Goal and Phenomenon. The text on Edinburgh is an exception; the client replaces the landmark and acts as Senser. S/he needs guidance because the tour is different from the others since it is unescorted. The absence of the tour operator is shown also in the text, where the inclusive first person pronoun is substituted by the second person pronoun. The client is also present in the other texts. Here, s/he is placed in the same team with the tour operator by the inclusive form indicated. In this formula, the role is that of Actor, the one that travels and visits. Even if the idea of team brings the tour operator closer to the users, they are never addressed directly, except for the unescorted tour of Edinburgh. The message appears factual, general, timeless, impersonal and objective due to the dominance of statements; the preference for fused Finites, present tense and unmarked Themes; and the lack of negation. The presence of modalization, however, slightly mitigates this and presents the tour as progressing according to a plan established by the professional operator. The presence of a subjective voice is shown also by the frequency of enhanced and new Themes, which draw attention to particular attractions. There is no clear Thematic progression in the texts, except for the one on Edinburgh, which is continuously centred on the client. The flow of the message is, thus, disrupted by different pieces of information, which, despite being conspicuous, can make it incohesive and difficult to follow.

**Table 8-21 British set of commercial websites: Lexico-grammatical summary**

| System | Canterbury Cathedral | Tower of London | Edinburgh |
|---|---|---|---|
| Clause complex | short<br>almost = complexes & simplexes<br>only expansion<br>= parataxis & hypotaxis<br>= extension & enhancement<br>- non-def. relatives<br>+ non-finite clauses | short<br>= complexes & simplexes<br>only expansion<br>+ hypotaxis<br>+ elaboration<br>+ non-defining relatives<br>+ non-finite clauses<br>- post-modification | medium long<br>+ simplexes<br>+ expansion<br>+ parataxis<br>+ extension, addition<br>1 defining relative clause<br>+ non-finite clauses |

| System | Canterbury Cathedral | Tower of London | Edinburgh |
|---|---|---|---|
| Transitivity | = material & relational<br>+ identifying<br>+ circumstantial<br>+ existential<br>+ realized participants<br>+ landmark<br>+ landmark (realized)<br>only tour operator<br>+ client (implied)<br>+ Carrier (landmark)<br>- client alone<br>Actor (operator + visitor)<br>only location, only place | + material<br>= identifying & attributive<br>only intensive<br>- other processes<br>+ realized participants<br>+ landmark<br>+ land. (realized)<br>only landmark (implied)<br>+ Goal (landmark)<br>only Beneficiary (client)<br>Actor (operator + visitor)<br>= location & extent, time | + material<br>only identifying<br>only possessive<br>+ mental perception<br>+ realized particip.<br>+ client<br>+ client (realized)<br>only client (implied)<br>+ Phenomenon (landmark)<br>expressed as Senser, implied as Actor (client)<br>= Actor, Identified & Identifier (operator)<br>only location, + place |
| Mood | = mood & residue<br>+ complex residue<br>+ landmark as Subject<br>+ fused Finite<br>+ present<br>+ Circ. Adjuncts<br>only modalization<br>- polarity<br>only declarative<br>only statements | = mood & residue<br>only complex residue<br>+ landmark as Subj.<br>+ expressed Finite<br>= present & future<br>1 Circ. Adjunct<br>only modalization<br>- polarity<br>only declarative<br>only statements | = mood & residue<br>+ complex residue<br>+ client as Subject<br>+ fused Finite<br>+ present<br>only Circ. Adjuncts<br>only modalization<br>- polarity<br>only declarative<br>only statements |
| Theme | + unmarked<br>+ enhanced<br>+ simple<br>+ participants as Theme<br>- Thematic progression | = unmarked & marked<br>enhanced<br>only simple<br>+ participants as Th.<br>- Thematic progress.<br>all new Themes | + unmarked<br>only simple<br>+ participants as Theme<br>= continuous, linear & new Themes |

The images depicting the World Heritage Sites promoted are not representative, except for the one of Canterbury Cathedral. They present a conglomerate of several monuments that do not stand for or symbolize the landmarks. The structures are conceptual and the processes unstructured analytical, as indicated by Table 8-22. They show the buildings for users' contemplation from a long shot, except for the Cathedral. This places them in the distance and the oblique horizontal angle situates them outside the users' world, as if out of reach. In this way, the contemplative and informative functions are further emphasised. This may be intended to produce an effect of objectivity; the focus is apparently not on the landmarks, but on their spatial arrangement, which is further observed from the distance. Power seems to receive no importance since each picture has a different vertical angle. The pictures are presented as they are in reality, as indicated by the modality markers and the lack of any information structure or particular saliency.

**Table 8-22 British set of commercial websites: Visual summary**

| System | Canterbury Cathedral | Tower of London | Edinburgh |
|---|---|---|---|
| Represent ational | complex<br>conceptual structure<br>unstructured<br>analytical<br>cathedral & landscape (Carrier)<br>tower, other components, sky + branches (Possessive Attributes) | complex<br>conceptual structure<br>unstructured<br>analytical<br>riverbank & landscape (Carrier)<br>buildings & Thames & sky (Possessive Attributes) | complex<br>conceptual structure<br>unstructured<br>analytical<br>city & landscape (Carrier)<br>several buildings & sky + firth (Possessive Attrib.) |
| Interactive | offer<br>close shot<br>subjective<br>oblique horizontal angle<br>low vertical angle<br>+ medium modality markers | offer<br>long shot<br>subjective<br>oblique horiz. angle<br>eye level towards<br>high vertical angle<br>+ medium modality markers | offer<br>long shot<br>subjective<br>oblique horizontal angle<br>high vertical angle<br>+ medium modality markers |
| Compositi onal | - information structure<br>cathedral (salient)<br>cathedral (framed) | - information str.<br>tall buildings & boat (salient)<br>-framing | - information structure<br>towers (salient)<br>-framing |

The multimodal communicative act, then, presents the picture as the promised product and the text as the information required to get to it. The modes seem to complement and extend each other (Anthonissen 2003, 302). The relation between them is, however, different in the three messages. In the one dedicated to Canterbury Cathedral, the text describes the Cathedral illustrated in the picture; in the one on the Tower of London, the text identifies the Tower from the buildings on the riverbank depicted, whereas, in the one presenting the city of Edinburgh, the text only names some buildings from the picture without giving any other details as it focuses on the users, their senses and wishes. No matter their relation, the verbal seems to bring the picture closer. The messages appear mainly informative. There is not much information and orientation; the senses are not appealed to. The landmark is not described; it is just identified as part of the tour, represented by what it stands for and exemplified by several attractions. Persuasion is masked in the amount of information on the importance of the landmarks for religion and history, their fame in the world, their antiquity, opulence and the stories of the past accompanying them. These details are sometimes exaggerated as usually encountered in advertising discourse. The call to action is also disguised in the future forms and addressee inclusion that indicate the things to see and situate the users already in the scenario of the tour.

# CHAPTER NINE

# COMPARISON AND INTERPRETATION OF RESULTS

In this chapter, the results of the analyses presented in Chapters seven and eight are compared in order to answer the Research Questions set by the study. The basis for comparison is set by: a) the organization of the websites and their webpages and b) the lexico-grammatical and visual features of the promotional messages observed from a Systemic Functional perspective. The comparison looks first at the different types of websites and aims to answer Research Question 1 regarding the similarities and differences between the institutional and commercial websites promoting the same landmarks. The promotional strategies are, then, interpreted with respect to the online promotional tourism framework considered for this study.

Section 9.2 focuses on the different countries of the websites and tries to show the similarities and differences between the multimodal promotional messages of the Romanian, Spanish and British sets, as postulated by Research Question 2. The findings indicated by the comparisons are accounted for from the point of view of the context dimension of cultural variability.

## 9.1. Comparison of promotional strategies by tourist boards and tour operators

This section first summarises the results of the analyses presented in the previous chapters, indicating the similarities and differences found in the two sets. Then, it considers them together and looks at the ways the institutional and commercial sites promote their World Heritage Sites. The variables compared are: organization and layout; contents and message; linguistic message; visual message; multimodal and communicative act; and promotion. Research Question 1 is repeated below:

- *What similarities and differences can be found between the institutional and the commercial promotion of the same landmarks?*

### 9.1.1. Characteristics of institutional websites

The institutional set, as already indicated, includes the websites produced by national Tourist Boards. Despite their obvious differences, they still share certain similarities, common patterns being observable in at least two of them. The institutional home pages are rather short, attractive and vertically organised as typical for websites. Their organization into columns makes for easier reading; general information on the country is included in the left column and practical information on the ways to get to the country in the right one. Their white background guides the eyes to pictures and texts, the verbal message being slightly more used than the visual one. All the websites have two menus: one more practical, interactive and navigational and the other more general and related to the contents included. Even if more salient, the contents menu is situated after the general one. The contents are further repeated and detailed throughout the page so that the message is clear and transparent. This makes the pages more rational than connotative, since attention is paid to providing information (Garzone 2009, 36).

The Tourist Boards are represented from the very beginning by their logos and slogans. The logos contain the colours of each national flag and the slogans address the audience directly, inviting it to come and explore the countries. The Boards indicate their identity and mission in few words. This information does not have a particular place in the layout of the home page. In the case of Spain or Great Britain, the promotion of the country is backed up by famous people, such as sportsmen, artists or chefs, who build on the reasons for the country's greatness. In this way, promotion speaks through celebrities known worldwide. In all cases, the message can be visualised in various languages.

The websites transmit information in the innovative and interesting ways provided by the hypermedia environment (OMT 1999, 133; 2001, 113; Garzone 2009, 41). Both multimodality and interactivity are present frequently. Pictures, videos, blocks of text and interactive links interplay in order to be as informative as possible, make experience more real and, ultimately, convince users to become tourists. Interactivity includes, apart from content links, also the possibility to search in databases; participate in forums and social networks; and book transport, accommodation and, in some cases, entry tickets to landmarks and events. All the websites, thus, link to other websites, mainly social and service-related. The sites themselves have no direct commercial aims and so do not promote any tickets or trips.

The webpages analysed on each site follow the same organization regarding length, layout and structure. This indicates a cohesive website. Nevertheless, they are not as modern as their home pages; looking more like traditional print pages (Lemke 2002) and favouring the verbal mode of communication. Each World Heritage Site has its own page and is depicted multimodally. Even if there is no particular preference for the order of the images, these are subsidiary to the text, as if part of it. The messages of the webpages are mainly informative: they identify the name of the tourist attraction, provide its background and describe it. Persuasion is concealed most of the time in an informative, objective and timeless presentation. Thus, information is usually general. It serves to draw attention, by titles and images, and maintain interest, by the presentation of the landmark and its attractions. The presentation can also make users want or desire to see the attractions. The instructional and practical details, such as must-see specifications and service information, are fewer and placed separately from the main message. They contribute to users' desire, but also induce to action. The call is, however, mainly indirect and secondary to the information on the landmarks. The webpages on the Heritage cities constitute an exception, being more direct, exhortatory and personal. The sender of the message is present in an obvious way to give more force to the message.

The analysis shows many similarities in the lexico-grammatical characteristics of the texts on the three pages, as summarised in Table 9-1. They reflect an informative message focused on identifying the World Heritage Sites. The texts are medium long, medium elaborated and complex. They are built by clause complexes, which develop by expansion-hypotaxis, information being presented cumulatively. The dependent clauses are mainly connected by elaboration through non-defining relative clauses, which add details on particular noun phrases, usually the attractions. Enhancement is hardly ever present, indicating the lack of attention to circumstantial relations that set a frame for information. The type of process preferred is identifying relational, which establishes the purpose of the text. Attributive relational processes are also quite frequent and describe the landmark. The most frequently present type is intensive, with little or no attention paid to possessive and circumstantial relations. Material processes are also frequent and usually refer to the construction of the landmarks. Mental processes, in turn, appear rarely. This may indicate that objectivity is chosen over sensations.

Background information is mainly provided by location circumstance, facts and attractions being situated spatially and temporally.

As for participants, these are more often expressed than implied. The favoured one is the landmark, as expected since it is the topic of the text. Its placement as Subject and Theme also reflects its importance. Its role is usually that of Goal, Carrier and Identified. This indicates that its presentation is less important than its identification, the landmark appearing as the entity built, visited and described. The possible visitor is not very frequent in the texts. When present, s/he is addressed directly and individually, by personal pronouns or imperatives, or included in a group of visitors, by general terms. Her/his roles are of Senser, the one that sees and discovers, when expressed, and of Actor, the one that visits, when implied. It seems the text tries to persuade by visual identification and description. The way the visitor is frequently inferable, rather than present, in the role of Actor can suggest that s/he can act on the landmark only in the actual and real moment of the visit. The Tourist Board is almost absent, producing an impersonal and objective message, typical for a national promoter. In the few instances it appears, it maintains the impersonal tone as it is referred to by its possessions. Its shop or website is presented as Goal, acted upon by the visitor.

Regarding the interpersonal metafunction, the clauses are declarative and express statements about the landmarks. The Mood element contains fused and present Finites, conferring to the message a universal and timeless feature. The few instances of modalization mitigate the power of the assertive message by presenting different possibilities and offers to users. Negation is almost absent from the texts, contributing to the factuality of information. The Residue element, in turn, is more numerous than the Mood one due to ellipsis and imperatives. It is complex, constituted by mainly Circumstantial Adjuncts, which add experiential meaning to the propositions. Finally, the Themes of the texts are unmarked and simple and are usually expressed by participants. The Thematic patterns are combined, containing a high frequency of continuous progression. This indicates, once again, the continuous focus on the landmark promoted and its attractions. Thematic focus is sometimes shifted by new Themes, which draw attention to the new pieces of information introduced.

The visual characteristics, presented in Table 9-2, also indicate a similar pattern in the three official sites. The pictures are built on conceptual structures composed by unstructured analytical processes. The Possessive Attributes, represented by different components of the landmark, are depicted without showing the entire Carrier, the landmark.

The act is an offer; the landmark is presented as informative for the viewers' contemplation. The perspective is always subjective since the photograph is taken from a particular angle. The oblique horizontal angle shows the landmark as standing outside the viewers' world, majestic and detached. Nonetheless, the type of shot, which varies between close and medium, engages viewers and places the landmark within their reach (Kress and van Leeuwen 2006, 128). It seems, then, the angle presents and informs, whereas the shot attracts attention and engages. There is no favoured vertical angle in the whole institutional set, as if particular power relations are not important; the image is there to represent the landmark and be contemplated by the users. The pictures appear as realistic, although some modality markers, such as contextualization, representation, colour saturation or illumination, can indicate digitization. They seem sometimes modified in order to present the landmark as prominent or as fragmented, all with the aim of stirring curiosity and attract. The picture's compositional structure sustains this duality: the occasional lack of organisational information structure indicates spontaneous photographs, whereas the centre-margin structure, the saliency and framing of the landmark or its components can imply a planned image aimed to confer sensory impressions.

Apart from these similarities, certain differences have been observed among the three websites of the institutional set. The Romanian website is more traditional and less multimodal and interactive. Its logo is not related to the national flag, but to the theme of the slogan, i.e. nature. Its initial message is longer and more formal; the Tourist Board presents itself as very professional. In fact, the voice of the objective professional seems important on this site; the promotional message as a whole is not supported by famous people, but by travel guides. The website's contents are more general; there is little practical information and none related to transactions and actions. The website appears only in one language, suggesting it is specialised in an English-speaking audience. The information regarding the World Heritage Sites in Romania is centralized; all the Sites are presented together in a webpage dedicated specially to the topic. The linguistic messages in the set are more similar in their lexico-grammatical features than those in the other two institutional sets. The text is more syntactically elaborated and complex. The Thematic progression is constant, but frequently marked. More attention is paid to the landmark's spatial and temporal location by both processes and circumstances. The circumstantial information is, however, kept in the background. The framed visual message is presented as more real than in the other two sites. The inclusion of people, the frontal angle and the lack of a clear pattern of information structure contributes to this. The people depicted can appeal easily to viewers and invite the users of the page to identify with them. It seems that in the Romanian website, the visual is used to highlight important information, but the site is dominated by the written message (Anthonissen 2003, 302).

The Spanish institutional website is more connotative and less informative. It is also more highly coloured and modern. It includes more pictures and less text than the other two sites. These are placed on a black background and arranged according to the connotative top-bottom layout. The map of the country situates the users visually. The slogan, the menu and the absence of the Tourist Board emphasize an indirect transmission of information. The call for action is also indirect, concealed in the practical information expressed by the telegraphic service details and travel links, resembling paper travel brochures. The message is not backed up by any official tourist authority. The text is mainly short and with many clause simplexes. The only logical relations are hypotaxis-elaboration, indicating a cumulative message. The landmark and its attractions are more identified than described. There are no new Themes; the Themes are introduced by Thematic patterns, but none is dominant. The message can sometimes appear as unelaborated, but complicated. The lack of a recognizable pattern can also make it less intuitive and indicate a random use of the choices available in structuring the text, in other words, a "lack of intentional structure" (Fontaine and Kodratoff 2002, 6). The visual message is more consistent and is built by large, impressive and connotative pictures. They are simply structured, symbolic, centrally focused and shot from the interior. The multimodal message of the Spanish webpages is articulated mainly visually (Anthonissen 2003, 302).

Finally, the British site focuses more on the transmission of information, regardless of the possibility of redundancy. Because of this, its pages are longer and highly multimodal. The website's content is transparent and clear from the beginning, placing its complex menu first on the page. The menu pays more attention to other types of information than to contact and navigational details, which are left for the footer. This can, however, obstruct navigation and contact. This website is the only one of the three that does include a commercial aim and offers the possibility to buy tickets or other services, either from its online shop or from tour operators recommended. The message transmitted is more oriented to the visitors and the visit than in the other two sites, as it addresses and guides users directly by instructions, must-see attractions and high modality. Both the home page and the heritage site webpages have longer texts than found in the other sites. Information is not only expanded, but also projected as ideas. The clause complexes are less structured due to parataxis and extension. The transitivity system is more varied; behavioural, verbal and existential processes interplay to create a complex text. Material and attributive relations are frequent and contribute to a more objective and descriptive message, apart from guiding users physically and aesthetically. The visitors are more frequently addressed directly and individually; this attracts them and creates a communicative immediacy. Information is sometimes negotiated by negation and highlighted by new Themes. The pictures, in turn, are small and not representative for the landmarks. Their structures are more complex, as they depict not only the landmark, but also its surroundings. Their centre-margin organization makes them more focused. The verbal and visual messages of the British webpages seem to complement and extend each other (Anthonissen 2003, 302).

To summarise, the way the visual and verbal modes combine to transmit information is different from website to website, as mentioned before. What is clear is that they serve to create an image around the landmarks promoted, which ultimately transfers to the country. The uniqueness mentioned by each Tourist Board from a perspective, often indirect and objective and sometimes connotative, is similar up to a certain point. The World Heritage Sites are constructed around the ideas of antiquity, history, religious importance or the UNESCO award. Nonetheless, each Tourist Board expresses a particularity that cannot be duplicated; the Romanian fascinates by unique art and buildings, medieval towns and natural parks; the Spanish impresses by an imperial past with Muslim influences, whereas the British proposes a combination of tradition and modernity. Myth, legends and stories are suggested and depicted in order to add fantasy and make users do more than just see and visit. They are invited to experience mysterious atmospheres inhabited by Dracula's shadow, mesmerising surroundings taken from the 1001 nights or locking ceremonies of Towers' gates. These characteristics make the World Heritage Sites and their countries worth seeing. Tourist Boards, famous people, TripAdvisor, travel guides, former tourists, all certify their existence and fascination.

### 9.1.2. Characteristics of commercial websites

The commercial set compares the websites belonging to the tour operators discussed in Chapter eight. Similarities have been found also here. The websites provide a simple and clear design with a header, a lateral menu and a main body, placed on coloured backgrounds. The navigational menus are placed vertically on the left lateral and provide links to the tours offered by the operator. General information seems to be chosen over other types. The tour operator's identity and purpose are stated from the beginning by a clear and connotative message presented in a close and friendly tone, reminding users of advertising discourse. In all cases, the operator's professionalism is guaranteed by TripAdvisor. The websites appear usually only in English.

The home pages are short and their information flows in a rather traditional way, by verbal messages arranged in a print-page layout. The visual clues guide the reading path. Their presence is not, however, indispensable, since not all the landmarks are illustrated visually. The webpages analysed follow the same layout and structure as the home page, except that they are longer. There is no page dedicated entirely to a particular World Heritage Site, but they are grouped in tours with other landmarks according to their spatial proximity. The informative aim of the message is predominant and obvious; it identifies the attraction by pictures and text, provides its background and describes it. These pieces of information are meant to draw users' attention and arouse their interest. The top-bottom connotative arrangement of the multimodal act stimulates desire and the presence of numerous pictures contributes to attraction. The presentation of the landmark follows the structure of a tour, during which the client is guided or directed through the landmark and its attractions, which are further described. The persuasive and instigative functions are expressed secondarily and minimally by practical and interactional details. They are, however, highlighted by boxes and other visual clues. Their separation from the rest of the text transmits a clearer message. The call to action is expressed directly. This succinct presentation of important information can also contribute to the transparency of the message and can be useful for those users that only scan the webpage.

The lexico-grammatical features of the texts from the three commercial websites have the following similarities, summarised in Table 9-3. The texts dedicated to the World Heritage Sites analysed are short, but syntactically elaborated and complex. The predominant clause complexes only expand; they do so by both hypotaxis and parataxis, the former being slightly more frequent. There is no preference for any logico-semantic relation; extension, elaboration and enhancement interplay. The message is made compact by the use of non-finite clauses. Material processes dominate and refer mainly to the tour and the visitor and/or operator's actions. The landmarks are described by relational processes, which are also numerous; these identify and describe the attractions. There are instances of existential and mental processes, which indicate the items to be seen, as in a real tour. The circumstances situate the information in time and place. Regarding the participants, the landmark is the most frequent, even if the topic is the tour and its development. Its centrality is supported also by its placement in Subject/Theme position. The landmark usually has the role of Goal, the entity visited. Clients are usually expressed and addressed directly, but have no particular dominant role. The client alone, unaccompanied by the tour operator, is little represented, but does appear in the company of the tour operator. In these cases, their role is of Actor visiting the landmark, as if projected in the tour scenario. The tour operator also appears alone, rather more frequently than together with the client. Its usual role is that of Actor picking up the client. It also has the roles of Identified and Identifier, when expressed by items related to the tour, visits and tickets it provides. The commercial message presents factual, timeless and objective information, as indicated by the dominance of the declarative mood; the preference for present tense and unmarked Themes; and the lack of negation. This is counterbalanced by high modalization and expressed Finites. The Themes are simple and often not organized in any clear Thematic pattern. In some cases, continuous progression was found, indicating a focused message.

In the commercial sites, the visual message, when present, offers a clear illustration of the World Heritage Site (see summary of features in Table 9-4). The pictures are complex, representing both the landmark and the surroundings by conceptual structures. The participants have the roles of Carrier in unstructured analytical processes. They are offered for contemplation from a subjective perspective. There is no dominant choice of shot, but the medium is slightly more used. The landmark is presented in a medium distance from an oblique angle, as if situated outside the viewers' world, but still in their reach. Clients can choose whether to contemplate or to act and go closer. Also the vertical angle has no particular option, as if power relations are secondary to information and contemplation. No consistent pattern for the interactive function was found in the set. The majority of the modality markers and the absence of any compositional informational structure present the pictures as realistic. Nonetheless, illumination and other markers, together with saliency and framing, make the landmark or its representative in the picture look retouched for more appeal.

A number of differences were also found between the websites of the commercial set. The Romanian tour operator is the only to have a logo, paying, thus, attention to the importance of the image of a brand. However, though it may be easy to remember the company, it is difficult to contact it. The absence of clear contact details in the home page and of direct contact opportunities in the navigational menu can block communication with the operator, which may make users give up and leave the site. The World Heritage Sites in Romania are all grouped together in the same trip, which sometimes offers the possibility of choosing among several landmarks. Practical information is much more detailed; the site contains a map that situates the tour in the country. The operator has no tourist authority to guarantee its professionalism.

The linguistic message is divided clearly between tour and landmark, each being presented separately; the client does not discover the landmark during the visit, but is told about it as secondary information. The description of the landmark is subordinated to that of the tour, since it is almost always placed in dependent clauses. Despite this, the landmark is much more evident than any other participant. The Romanian texts are more descriptive than those in the other sets. The clauses are usually complexes, presenting information by mainly non-defining relative clauses. The material and relational processes are combined to present the tour and the landmark. The frequent causative constructions shift the focus from the Attributor to the Attribute, making the process more universal and assertive. Mental processes are almost absent, as if the discovery of the landmark is not done by senses. This supports the division between landmark and tour already mentioned. The background is more varied, but related to the landmark and not to the tour. It is developed in the subordinate clauses as secondary information. This is reflected in the small number of Circumstantial Adjuncts. The landmark has no particular role assigned to it, while the client is the Actor, the one visiting. This time, s/he is alone, not accompanied by the tour operator which is almost absent from the message. S/he is always realized and addressed directly. This happens in the alternative World Heritage Sites. In contrast, when the Site is a main one, the client is not alone anymore, but in the company of the operator. All the participants are placed in Subject position, none being chosen in particular as the topic of the message. The lack of a focus on the landmark is the result of the analysis since it is frequently placed in subordinate clauses, which are not included here. The Finites are more expressed because of modalization. The low modal introduces the tour not as a plan, but as an alternative. The alternative is also supported by Conjunctive Adjuncts/textual Themes. These Themes connect the text to the previous one(s). The message has usually no Thematic progression, which is not unexpected considering the small number of conjoinable clause units. As for the pictures, these are simpler than those in the other sets, focusing on the landmark by closer, frontal and low angles. Their central organization also contributes to the focalization of information.

The two modes used by the Romanian tour operator do not seem to work on the same level; the visual focalises, whereas the verbal generalises.

Turning now to the Spanish commercial website, this does not provide an exhaustive lateral navigational menu, but a rather concise and less intuitive one. Its focus is more on practical and contact details than on general information regarding the tours offered. It brings, however, more details on the tours by a navigational menu placed in the footer. The call for action is rather indirect in the Spanish webpages since the contact form offers the opportunity to contact the operator for availability, not for booking. The texts are not very similar, making this set the most inconsistent. The Spanish commercial texts are longer than those in the other sets, with many clauses in each clause complex. The logical relations favoured are hypotaxis-enhancement; the message is developed by circumstantial details, which frame the tour. The background information provides mainly temporal location for the tour and situates the landmark's construction in time. The landmark is presented more connotatively by attributes meant to impress and reach the senses. The client appears as the Goal of the tour operator's actions. The landmark is almost always placed in Subject position, while the client is never Subject. The team constituted by the tour operator and the client is rarely used; the preference seems to be for individual entities. The frequent future tense presents the tour as a plan and situates the client inside the scene. The Residue element is more frequent than the Mood due to imperatives and ellipsis. These are reflected in the high number of implied participants, which shift the focus to processes. This is also shown in the frequent presence of processes in Thematic position. All the Spanish texts have a recognizable Thematic progression; the favourite is the continuous one, indicating a focused message. The visual message is involved as it depicts the landmark from fontal and eye level angles. The modes seem to complement each other: one illustrates, while the other guides.

The British commercial website is more complex, at least as indicated by the navigational menu. It has a second menu providing information on the tour operator, its services and interactive possibilities. This means its content is more detailed and clearly transmitted. Interactions and transactions are continuously encouraged by the search box and the shopping cart. The home page is longer, more visual and highly coloured. The tour operator's introduction is shorter, more related to the tours and less persuasive. The offers appear to be more important than the operator: the text focuses on them, not on the introduction to the company. The message of the webpages seems more separated: the basic data names the attraction, illustrates and highlights the contents, while a fairly long text describes it in detail. The pages seem to try to be clear, concise and web-like, and, at the same time, descriptive and text-like. The text oscillates between clause complex and simplex, details being often just enumerated as different pieces of information. It identifies more than describes, presenting the landmark by what it stands for and not by its attributes. The facts are mainly located spatially and refer to the tour itself. Neither the landmark nor the client has a particular role assigned. The tour operator appears more alone than accompanied by the client. The message is more universal due to the fused Finites. There is no Thematic progression in the texts; information is focalized by enhanced and new Themes, which make it more conspicuous. All the landmarks are illustrated by pictures. These are, however, not very representative as they present a conglomerate of buildings, without focusing on any in particular, from a long shot and high angle. The verbal and visual modes seem to complement and extend each other.

The commercial set of websites, then, contains a varied array of communicative acts. The two modalities studied combine in different ways, and so produce different messages. Nevertheless, either complementary or opposed, their aim is to inform and, ultimately, persuade users by visual illustration and verbal presentation and guiding, each in their own degree. The landmark, either presented simultaneously with the tour or described impersonally, is what is used to impress. The tours are not in themselves special, except for few exceptions; the landmarks are. The attractions in the offers are similar: history, art, antiquity and religion. However, each country's tour operator offers a different focus.

### 9.1.3. Comparison of institutional and commercial websites

Common features have been encountered in both institutional and commercial sets, the former set being more consistent. Regardless of their differences, a pattern can be distinguished for each set. The comparison is presented in sections to provide a clearer and more concise picture.

*Organization and layout.* All the websites are attractive, colourful and short. They have a simple and clear design with a header, main body and sometimes a footer, all arranged vertically as typical for screen layouts. Information is organised in columns for easier reading, but somewhat differently. In both sets, one of the columns introduces the main body of the page, but the other has different content and function in the two sets. In the institutional set, it is placed on the right, after the main body, and provides practical ideas or advertises tickets and tours. In the commercial set, the narrow column comes first and contains the menu of the websites.

The official pages seem to enclose more numerous and diverse pieces of information, whereas the commercial ones limit themselves to the tours. Colours, pictures and links guide reading. The home pages of the institutional set are predominantly visual, whereas the commercial ones develop more by text. The background colour plays an important role in the way information is presented; the institutional prefers the usual and traditional white, while the commercial goes for more connotative colours that convey reliability and trustworthiness and differentiate the company from its competitors. The webpages follow the same length, layout and structure as their home pages, indicating organized, cohesive and intuitive websites. The multimodal arrangement is different in the two sets: the institutional set prefers a horizontal brochure-like layout with the picture embedded or secondary to the text, while the commercial set adopts the vertical layout of advertisements, which proposes the picture as the promised product and the text as the practical description. It seems the institutional set pays more attention to visual representation and the commercial to visual persuasion.

*Contents and message*. The contents are varied and usually laid out in two menus: one related to the general content of the website and the other to other details, such as practical, navigational and interactive information. The institutional set focuses more on information about the country, whereas the commercial set provides an extensive list of tours. The content of the commercial set is more obvious and intuitive as it specifies the information offered clearly. The distribution of information is also different: the institutional set places both menus horizontally at the top of the page, usually one after the other, to help users capture the content of the website rapidly (OMT 2001, 94; 2005b, 9). The commercial set, however, places one horizontally and the other vertically on the lateral, a position that can affect readability.

The transmission of information relies on different modes, as already mentioned. The institutional set is more multimodal than the commercial one, especially in its home pages. Both sets are modern and include images, texts, videos and interactive links. The webpages, on the other hand, appear more traditional due to more use of written text. The institutional set is also more interactive, offering much more than just links to information, but search bases, forums and social networks. This set seems to take more advantage of the hypermedia environment; it uses different strategies to provide a complete message, convince and reach a wide audience.

Each of the landmarks analysed has a page dedicated entirely to it in the institutional set, whereas, in the commercial set, the landmarks are combined with other landmarks depending on spatial proximity. The webpages of both sets transmit a mainly informative overall message; they identify, illustrate, provide a background and describe the landmarks and their attractions. Persuasive elements are there, but usually concealed by an apparently impersonal and objective message. Orientation also appears in both sets, but is more frequent and visible in the commercial one, as here visitors are guided through a virtual tour. Instructional and practical details are secondary to the description of the landmark and, as such, are presented separately from the main information for a clearer message. The call to action is, however, different: more indirect in the institutional set and more direct and exhortative in the commercial one.

*Linguistic message*. The institutional set presents the World Heritage Sites in longer texts than the commercial one, as indicated by Tables 9-1 and 9-3. This may be because the institutional dedicates a whole page to the landmarks, while the commercial combines several attractions in a page. Both texts are complex, but the institutional is less syntactically developed. Even if longer, its clauses are shorter and its message less syntactically elaborated. In both sets, clause complexes composed by expansion are the type most frequently used. Hypotaxis is the most frequent tactic relation in the sets, but the commercial one also uses a high number of parataxis, which indicates a less compact message. The institutional message expands mainly by elaboration; the use of non-defining relative clauses makes it more compact. The commercial one, however, does not prefer a particular logico-semantic relation and uses elaboration, extension and enhancement. Enhancement is almost absent in the institutional set, whereas, in the commercial one, it is used frequently to set the framework of the tour. It seems the institutional set presents its message by providing details cumulatively, whereas the commercial set both offers details and sets a framework, given its more dynamic approach, showing the visitor around the tourist site.

The most frequent types of processes are different in the two sets: the institutional identifies the tour by relational processes, while the commercial presents the tour by material ones. Relational processes are, however, also used in the commercial set to describe the landmark. This set gives more attention to mental and existential processes that can serve to guide the tourists' gaze and make them discover. The background information is similar in both sets; spatial and temporal circumstances locate the tour and/or landmark. The most frequent participant is the landmark, which is unexpected in the commercial set since it is more centred on tours and clients. The focus on the landmark is shown also by its placement in Subject/Theme position. The landmark's role is that of

Goal, the entity built and visited, in both sets. The institutional set presents the landmark frequently also as Carrier and Identified, since it is the entity described. The visitor is not very frequent in either of the sets though it appears more in the commercial set; the commercial websites address users directly and do not refer to them by general terms as the institutional set sometimes does. The entity emitting the message is present differently in the two sets: the Tourist Board is almost absent, whereas the tour operator is very frequently present. The operator is presented as Actor and its tours and offers as Identified and Identifier. The commercial set contains a further participant not found in the institutional set: the team formed by the tour operator and the client and indicated by the inclusive "we". The role of this team is of Actor; when accompanied by the tour operator, the client is undoubtedly an Actor. The message seems clear: the user is an Actor only in the landmark, as a visitor. If not there, s/he remains a Senser in the institutional set and has no definite role in the commercial one.

Regarding the interpersonal metafunction, both sets choose declaratives, present Finites, absence of negation, complex Residues and frequent Circumstantial Adjuncts, thus, building up an assertive, universal and complex message. The focus is on experiential meaning, interpersonal and textual Adjuncts being almost absent. In the case of the institutional set, the message is more universal due to the frequent fused Finites. The Finites in the commercial set are more often expressed by passive and modal forms. In both sets, modalization is rare, but is slightly more frequent in the commercial one. The sets highlight different degrees of modality: the institutional set expresses low modality, providing users with a number of possible things to do and see in their visit, while the commercial set indicates mainly high modality, anticipating the things to do and see and projecting visitors already in the tour. The institutional message seems to emphasise freedom, possibility of choice and variety of attractions, whereas the commercial one transmits certainty, planning and professionalism.

Finally, the Themes of both sets are unmarked and simple. A combination of patterns of Thematic development is found, although there is still a clear focus dominating the message as indicated by the frequent continuous progression. Nonetheless, the institutional set sometimes shifts the topic by introducing new Themes, drawing readers' attention to specific pieces of information. Texts in the commercial set often seem to have no Thematic pattern at all, so there is no flow of information, but just an enumeration of ideas. Both techniques may confuse readers.

*Visual message*. The visual characteristics, summarised in Tables 9-2 and 9-4, are more similar in the two sets than the linguistic ones. Visual similarity exists also within each set, with some exceptions. Both the institutional and commercial sets present photos usually associated visually with the landmarks promoted. However, the commercial set does not seem to consider illustration crucial since not all the landmarks are represented visually. The images use conceptual structures composed by unstructured analytical processes. These depict Possessive Attributes, such as different components and surrounding elements, of the Carriers, i.e. the landmark and the landscape. The most frequent interactive tools are: subjective perspective, medium shot, oblique horizontal angle and realistic modality markers. The modality in the images seems sometimes modified to highlight the landmark or to hide parts of it, perhaps in order to arouse interest. Attention is also drawn by saliency and framing. No vertical angle is favoured by either of the sets. The landmark is placed there for contemplation, outside the viewers' world, but within their reach. They can either approach or leave. In both sets, the pictures are usually not composed according to any information value structure, as if they were spontaneous. The institutional set, however, has frequent instances of centre-margin organization, which present the landmark as connotatively more conspicuous.

*Multimodal and communicative act*. The linguistic and visual messages combine differently in the two sets. The institutional set has no preference for its multimodal act, while the commercial one presents the modes as complementary. No matter the relation between modes, the communicative act is meant to inform, illustrating visually and presenting verbally. The verbal message in the commercial set guides more overtly than in the institutional counterpart. With respect to content, the unique characteristics of the site presented by the Tourist Board and the tour operator are similar; they are related to antiquity, history, religious importance or UNESCO recognition. While both sets use similar features of the sites to attract the client, the promise of a special experience is more present in the institutional set. Its commercial counterpart just mentions the existence of stories and myths, building its message connotatively around them in order to create a suggestive atmosphere.

*Promotion*. The sender of the message is indicated clearly in both sets, along with its purpose; both the Tourist Board and the tour operator present themselves as there to help users. Their messages address users directly and invite them to visit the country or to take a tour. The operator's message is, however, longer, clearer and more persuasive and is presented from the position of a close and friendly expert. The Tourist

Board pays more attention to its image on the market by having an iconic logo and a catchy slogan to identify with and be recognised for. It promotes by national icons, celebrities and sportsmen and addresses an international audience, as indicated by the possibility to see the website in more languages than English. The boards also involve the users and their former clients in their promotion. Both sets use TripAdvisor to certify the tourist entities' existence, reliability and professionalism.

To summarise, the institutional and commercial sets of websites share a number of similarities and differ in particular ways, as expected considering their types. They are organized, cohesive and intuitive, providing attractive, coloured and short webpages. Their simple and clear design organizes and presents their multimodal and informative message in similar ways. The linguistic message is complex, structured, assertive, universal, objective, focused and little modalized. The focus is on the landmark promoted. The same is true for the image: the landmark, or parts of it, is presented for contemplation outside the viewers' world, but in their reach. The users are shown, informed and invited to visit the World Heritage Sites.

The differences between the institutional and commercial sets can be summarised as follows. The institutional set prefers a more visual representation, modern in its multimodality, but traditional in its layout. It takes full advantage of the hypermedia environment since its multimodality and interactivity are high. Its content is presented from the beginning and focuses more on the country it represents. The call to action is less direct. Every landmark has its own page. The linguistic message is longer, less developed and mainly elaborated by adding adjacent details. The processes identify and describe the landmark. The message is more universal and the Tourist Board is almost absent. Modalization centres on possible attractions so that more things to see and do accumulate and raise interest in the landmark. The attractions are presented as conspicuous both by the new Themes in the text and the central organization in the image. The commercial set, in turn, presents its unstructured and less focused message more persuasively by connotative layouts and colours and extensive information on tours. It addresses the client, who, either alone or in the company of the tour operator, is guided through the landmark according to a plan, by movement, sight and circumstantial relations, so that, in the end, s/he is instigated overtly to act. The modes complement each other in the description of the landmark, but the verbal one is favoured.

To conclude this comparison, the institutional website seems to transmit a more objective and impersonal message. The numerous modes and links; the different types of information; the long and descriptive text; and the representative visuals aim to transmit detailed and complete information in order to inform users about the landmark and persuade them to visit it by themselves. The landmark is the participant focused both linguistically and visually. The photos seem more professional since they are very suggestive. As for the commercial set, this relies on both modes to illustrate, but more on the verbal one to persuade. Its message is personal, involved and centred on the client. The description of the tour guides the client and informs her/him briefly about a number of attractions found along the way. The landmark is secondary to the tour, but provides its attraction, so that the tour operator promotes its tours through the landmark, which should persuade, attract and make the users book the tour. Therefore, similarities between the two sets appear to be related to web organization and layout, tourist promotion and topic, whereas the differences reflect the websites' types and functions. The institutional set is as informative and suggestive as possible, while remaining impersonal and objective. The commercial set, in its turn, is less detailed, more succinct, dynamic and centred on the client's orientation through the landmark. In the institutional set, persuasion is hidden in the transmission of information, and in the commercial set, in the projection of the tourist in the tour scenario. Both sets rely on a similar individuality of their landmarks; the way they promote it makes the difference.

### 9.1.4. Interpretation of promotional strategies

The comparison between institutional and commercial websites has indicated a pattern for the resemblances and divergences found. These findings show the influence of a number of factors in the final product presented by the websites. Ranging from informative to persuasive and from direct to indirect, the promotional nature of the websites exists; their purpose being that of encouraging (international) tourists to visit. The analysis has also shown that the Tourist Boards pay more attention to the message constructed than do the tour operators, as they are probably more aware of the importance of branding and marketing. They also have more financial resources to invest in professionals and develop promotion strategies. They build the destination as a brand and transform the landmarks into attractions, by linking them to sensations, stories, spectacles and legends (McKercher and du Cros 2002, 127-134) for a maximum suggestive force, as required by the intangibility of the tourist product (Bosch Abarca 2001, 328). For the same reasons, their images are more professional and impressive, special attention being paid to the "*visual*[1] brand" (Hiippala 2007, 25). Regarding the commercial set, this adopts strategies of advertising discourse, like tourists' implication and inclusion or direct address to the client. It also projects tourists directly into the destination, by a virtual tour.

---

[1] The author's italics.

**Table 9-1 Institutional set of websites: Lexico-grammatical summary**

| Sys | ROMANIAN | | | SPANISH | | | BRITISH | | |
|---|---|---|---|---|---|---|---|---|---|
| | **Monastery of Horezu** | **Dacian Fortresses** | **Sighisoara** | **Monastery El Escorial** | **Alhambra** | **Santiago de Compostela** | **Canterbury Cathedral** | **Tower of London** | **Edinburgh** |
| CLAUSE COMPLEX | short | medium long | medium long | medium long | short | very short | medium long | + long | very long |
| | + complex (2 clauses) | + complexes (2 & 3 cl.) | + complexes (3 cl.) | + complexes (3 clauses) | + simplex | + simplexes | almost= complex & simpl. (2 cl) | + complexes (2 cl.) | + simplexes (2 cl.) |
| | only expansion | only expansion | only expansion | only expansion | only expansion | only expansion | only expansion | only expansion | + expansion |
| | only hypotaxis | almost = hypotaxis & parataxis | + hypotaxis | almost = parataxis & hypotaxis | only hypotaxis | only hypotaxis | almost = hypotaxis & parataxis | + parataxis | = hypotaxis & parataxis |
| | only elaboration | almost = elaboration & extension | + elabora-tion | + extension | only elaboration | only elaboration | + elabora-tion | + extension, addition | almost = enhanc., ext. & elab. |
| | + non-def. relative cls. | + non-def. relative cl. | + non-def. relative cl. | + non-def. relative cl.<br>+ non-finite clauses | + non-def. relative cl.<br>1 non-finite clause | 1 non-def. relative cl.<br>+ non-finite clause | + non-def. relative cl.<br>+ defining clauses | almost=non-def. & def.<br>+ apposition | + non-def. relative cl.<br>+ apposition |
| | | + apposition | + apposition | + apposition | | | | | |
| TRAN | + relational | + relational | + relational causative construction | + relational | + relational causative construction | + material | + relational | + material causative construction | + material |
| | + attributive | = identif. & attributive | = identif. & attributive | + identi-fying | only identifying | + identi-fying | + identi-fying | almost=atrib & identif. | + attributive |
| | = intensive & circumst. & possess. | + circumst. | + intensive | + circumst. | only intensive | + intensive | + intensive | + intensive | + intensive |

| Sys | ROMANIAN | | | SPANISH | | | BRITISH | | |
|---|---|---|---|---|---|---|---|---|---|
| | Monastery of Horezu | Dacian Fortresses | Sighisoara | Monastery El Escorial | Alhambra | Santiago de Compostela | Canterbury Cathedral | Tower of London | Edinburgh |
| TRANSITIVITY | | ment, percep & affection | many material only mental perception | existential only mental perception | - mental | only mental perception | many material only mental perception | verbal & behavioural only mental perception | behave. & existential + mental cognition |
| | realized (little dif.) | + realized participants | + realized participants | + realized participants | only realiz. participants | + realized | + realized participants | + realized | + realized |
| | only landmark | + landmark | + landmark | + landmark | only landmark | + landmark | + landmark | + landmark | + landmark |
| | only landmark | + landmark (realized) | only landmark | only landmark | only landmark | + landmark (realized) | + landmark (realized) | + landmark (realized) | + landmark |
| | only landmark | + landmark (implied) | + landmark (implied) | + landmark (implied) | - implied participants | only visitor (implied) | almost=land & visitor (implied) | = landmark & visitor (implied) | + visitor (implied) |
| | + Carrier (landmark) | + Carrier (landmark) | almost=Goal Carrier & Identifier | + Identified (landmark) | + Identified | + Goal (landmark) | + Goal, then Carrier & Identified | + Goal & Carrier (landmark) | + Goal (landmark) |
| | - visitor | expressed Senser, impl. Actor (visitor) | only Senser (only implied) | only implied as Senser (visitor) | - visitor | = Actor & Senser (visitor) | Actor (visitor) | expressed Senser implied Actor | Actor (visitor) |
| | - promoter | - promoter | - promoter | - promoter | - promoter | only Goal (promoter) | - promoter | - promoter | = Actor & Goal (only realized) (promoter) |
| | various Circ + location = time & pl. | various Circ + location = time & pl. | various Circ + location + time | + location + time | - circums-tances | only location + place | + location + place | various Circ + location + time | various Circ + location only place |
| | = mood & residue | = mood & residue | = mood & residue | + residue | = mood & residue | + residue | + residue | + residue | + residue |

| Sys | ROMANIAN | | | SPANISH | | | BRITISH | | |
|---|---|---|---|---|---|---|---|---|---|
| | **Monastery of Horezu** | **Dacian Fortresses** | **Sighisoara** | **Monastery El Escorial** | **Alhambra** | **Santiago de Compostela** | **Canterbury Cathedral** | **Tower of London** | **Edinburgh** |
| MOOD | + complex residue<br>+ landmark as Subject<br>only fused Finites | only complex res.<br>+ landmark as Subject<br>almost = fused & expres. Fin. | only complex res.<br>+ landmark as Subject<br>+ fused Finites | only complex res.<br>only land. as Subject<br>+ fused Finites | only complex res.<br>only landmark<br>+ fused Finites | only complex res.<br>+ visitor as Subject<br>+ expressed Finites | only complex res.<br>+ landmark as Subject<br>+ fused Finites | + complex residue<br>+ land. (visitor close)<br>+ fused | + complex residue<br>+ landmark as Subject<br>+ fused Finites |
| | + present | + present | almost = pres. & past | + present | + present | + present | + present | + present | + present |
| | only Circ. Adjuncts<br>- modality | + Circumst. Adjuncts<br>only modalization | + Circumst. Adjuncts<br>only modalization | + Circumst. Adjuncts<br>only modalization | - Adjunct<br>- modality | + Circumst. Adjuncts<br>only modalization | only Circ. Adjuncts<br>only modalization | + Circumst. Adjuncts<br>+ modalization | + Circumst. Adjuncts<br>+ modalization |
| | - polarity<br>only declarative, + full<br>only statements | - polarity<br>only declarative<br>only statements | - polarity<br>only declarative<br>only statements | - polarity<br>only declarative<br>+ full decl.<br>only statements | - polarity<br>only declarative<br>only statements | polarity<br>+ declarative<br>+ statements | - polarity<br>+ declarative<br>+ statements | polarity<br>+ declarative<br>+ statements | polarity<br>almost = decl. & imperative<br>almost=stat. &command |
| THEME | almost = unmarked & marked | almost = unmarked & marked | + unmarked | + unmarked | only unmarked | + unmarked | + unmarked | + unmarked | + unmarked |
| | only simple<br>only particip as Theme<br>almost = mult. & cont & new Th. | + simple<br>+ participant as Theme<br>+continuous progression | + simple<br>+ participant as Theme<br>=continuous & linear patterns | + simple<br>+ participant as Theme<br>+continuous progression | only simple<br>+ participant as Themes<br>+ multiple progression | only simple<br>+ participant (little dif.)<br>+ linear progression | + simple<br>+ participant as Theme<br>almost = new Th. & lin. & cont. | + simple<br>+ participant<br>almost = cont. & lin. & new The. | + simple<br>+ processes as Theme<br>+continuous Thematic pattern |

**Table 9-2 Institutional set of websites: Visual summary**

| Sys | ROMANIAN | | | SPANISH | | | BRITISH | | |
|---|---|---|---|---|---|---|---|---|---|
| | **Monastery of Horezu** | **Dacian Fortresses** | **Sighisoara** | **Monastery El Escorial** | **Alhambra** | **Santiago de Compostela** | **Canterbury Cathedral** | **Tower of London** | **Edinburgh** |
| REPRESENTATIONAL | simple<br>conceptual<br>structure<br>un-<br>structured<br>analytical<br>monastery<br>& back-<br>ground (Ca)<br>components<br>& sur-<br>roundings<br>(Pos.Attrib)<br>+ humans | complex<br>conceptual<br>structure<br>symbolic<br>attributive<br>fortresses<br>(Carrier)<br>ruins of<br>amphithea-<br>tre (Symb.<br>Attributes)<br>nar. vector:<br>ruins<br>(Actor) | simple<br>conceptual<br>structure<br>un-<br>structured<br>analytical<br>city<br>(Carrier)<br>Clock<br>Tower,<br>Dracula's<br>house &<br>visitor<br>(Pos.Attrib)<br>+ humans | simple<br>conceptual<br>structure<br>un-<br>structured<br>analytical<br>monastery<br>(Carrier)<br>component<br>& garden<br>(Possessive<br>Attributes) | complex<br>conceptual<br>structure<br>un-<br>structured<br>analytical<br>courtyard &<br>landscape<br>(Carrier)<br>columns,<br>fountain,<br>statues,<br>pavement &<br>sky<br>(Pos.Attrib) | simple<br>conceptual<br>structure<br>unstructured<br>analytical<br>city<br>(Carrier)<br>cathedral,<br>buildings &<br>sky (Pos.<br>Attributes) | complex<br>conceptual<br>structure<br>unstructured<br>analytical<br>cathedral &<br>landscape<br>(Carrier)<br>tower<br>sky +<br>branches<br>(Possessive<br>Attributes) | complex<br>concept.<br>structure<br>un-<br>structured<br>analytical<br>tower &<br>landscape<br>(Carrier)<br>tower +<br>walls<br>sky+trees | simple<br>conceptual<br>structure<br>un-<br>structured<br>analytical<br>city<br>(Carrier)<br>castle &<br>surrounding<br>(Possessive<br>Attributes) |
| INTERACT | offer<br>close &<br>medium sh.<br>subjective<br>oblique<br>horiz. angle<br>eye level<br>vertical ang | offer<br>close shot<br>subjective<br>frontal<br>horiz. angle<br>panoramic<br>high | offer<br>close &<br>med. shot<br>subjective<br>frontal &<br>oblique<br>low vertical<br>angle | offer<br>close shot<br>subjective<br>oblique<br>horiz. angle<br>high vert.<br>angle | offer<br>close &<br>medium<br>subjective<br>frontal<br>horizontal<br>eye level<br>vertical | offer<br>medium<br>shot<br>subjective<br>oblique<br>horiz. angle<br>low vertical<br>angle | offer<br>close shot<br>subjective<br>oblique<br>horiz. angle<br>low vertical<br>angle | offer<br>medium<br>shot<br>subjective<br>oblique<br>horizontal<br>eye level<br>vertical | offer<br>long shot<br>subjective<br>frontal &<br>oblique<br>high & eye<br>level |

| Sys | ROMANIAN | | | SPANISH | | | BRITISH | | |
|---|---|---|---|---|---|---|---|---|---|
| | Monastery of Horezu | Dacian Fortresses | Sighisoara | Monastery El Escorial | Alhambra | Santiago de Compostela | Canterbury Cathedral | Tower of London | Edinburgh |
| IVE | + medium modality markers | + low | + medium modality markers | = low & medium modality | + medium modality markers | + medium modality markers | + low modality markers | + medium modality markers | almost = low & medium |
| COMPOSITIONAL | - informa-tion struct. | centre-margin | - informa-tion struct. | - informa-tion struct. | centre-margin | centre-margin | -information structure | centre-margin | top-bottom & centre-margin |
| | monastery & nun (sal.) | ruins (salient) | tower & house | monastery (salient) | fountain | cathedral | cathedral (salient) | tower (salient) | castle, fireworks (s) |
| | buildings of monastery (framed) | ruins (framed) | tower | - framing | - framing | - framing | - framing | tower (framed) | castle (framed) |

## Table 9-3 Commercial set of websites: Lexico-grammatical summary

| Sys | ROMANIAN | | | SPANISH | | | BRITISH | | |
|---|---|---|---|---|---|---|---|---|---|
| | Monastery of Horezu | Dacian Fortresses | Sighisoara | Monastery El Escorial | Alhambra | Santiago de Compostela | Canterbury Cathedral | Tower of London | Edinburgh |
| CLAUSE | short | short | short | short | medium long | medium long | short | short | med. long |
| | onlycomplex (4 cls.) | only complexes | + complexes | only complexes (3 & 4 cl.) | + complexes (4 cls.) | + simplexes (3 cls.compl) | almost = complexes & simplexes | = complexes & simplexes | + simplexes |
| | only expansion | only expansion | only expansion | only expansion | + expansion | only expansion | only expansion | only expansion | + expansion |
| | + parataxis | = parataxis & hypotaxis | only hypotaxis | + hypotaxis | + hypotaxis | + parataxis | = parataxis & hypotaxis | + hypotaxis | + parataxis |
| | + extension, | = elaboration | only | + enhance- | = elaboration | + extension | = extension | + elaboration | + extension, |

| S | ROMANIAN | | | SPANISH | | | BRITISH | | |
|---|---|---|---|---|---|---|---|---|---|
| Sys | Monastery of Horezu | Dacian Fortresses | Sighisoara | Monastery El Escorial | Alhambra | Santiago de Compostela | Canterbury Cathedral | Tower of London | Edinburgh |
| C O | addition | & extension, addition | elaboration | ment | & enhance-ment | | & enhance-ment | | addition |
| M P L E X | + non-def. relative cls.<br>+ non-finite clauses | 1 non-def. relative cls.<br>1 non-finite clause | + non-def. relative cls.<br>+ finite clauses | 1 non-def. relative cls.<br>+ non-finite clauses<br>+ apposition | + non-def. relative cls.<br>+ non-finite clauses | + defining relative cl.<br>+ non-finite clauses | - non-def. relative cls.<br>+ non-finite clauses | + non-def. relative cls.<br>+ non-finite clauses<br>- post-modification | 1 defining relative cl.<br>+ non-finite clauses |
| | + material | = material & relational | + relational | + material | + material | + relational | = material & relational | + material | + material |
| | only causati-ve constr. | = causative construction | + causative construction | | | | | | |
| | - identifying/ attributive | & identif. | only attributive | only attributive | + identifying | + attributive | + identifying | = identifying & attributive | only identifying |
| T | - | only intensive | only intensive | only possessive | + intensive | + intensive | + circum-stantial | only intensive | only possessive |
| R A | only mental cognition | - mental | – mental | only mental perception | only mental perception | – mental | + existential | - other processes | + mental perception |
| N | | | + existential | | + existential | | | | |
| S I | = realized & implied part. | + realized participants | + realized participants | + realized participants | + realized participants | + realized participants | + realized participants | + realized participants | + realized participants |
| T | + landmark | + landmark | + landmark | + landmark | + landmark | + landmark | + landmark | + landmark | + client |
| I V | + landmark (realized) | + landmark (realized) | + landmark (realized) | + landmark (realized) | = landmark & operator | + landmark (realized) | + landmark (realized) | + landmark (realized) | + client (realized) |
| I T Y | + landmark (implied) | only landmark (implied) | only landmark (implied) | + operator (implied) | + client (implied) | only landmark (implied) | only tour operator + client (impl.) | only landmark (implied) | + only client (implied) |
| | + Goal (landmark) | =Goal & Identified | = Goal, Car., Attribute, | + Goal (landmark) | + Goal (landmark) | + Carrier (landmark) | + Carrier (landmark) | + Goal (landmark) | + Phenome-non (land.) |

| Sys | ROMANIAN | | | SPANISH | | | BRITISH | | |
|---|---|---|---|---|---|---|---|---|---|
| | **Monastery of Horezu** | **Dacian Fortresses** | **Sighisoara** | **Monastery El Escorial** | **Alhambra** | **Santiago de Compostela** | **Canterbury Cathedral** | **Tower of London** | **Edinburgh** |
| | | (landmark) | Existent, implied Identified (landmark) | | | | | | |
| | + Actor (client) | + Actor (client) | - client | only Goal (client) | expressed as Goal, implied as Actor (cl.) | only Attributor (client) | - client alone | only Beneficiary (client) | expressed as Senser, implied as Actor (cl.) |
| | - operator | - operator | + Actor & Identifier (operator + client) | + Actor (operator) | = Actor, Goal, Car., Identified, Existent | Actor & Identifier (operator) | Actor (operator + client) | Actor (operator + visitor) | = Actor, Identified & Identifier (operator) |
| | = location & cause only time | = extent, manner & role | + location only place | only location only place | + location + time | + location only time | only location place | = location & extent, time | only location + place |
| MOOD | = mood & residue | = mood & residue | + mood | + residue | + residue | = mood & residue | = mood & residue | = mood & residue | = mood & residue |
| | complex residue | complex residue | complex residue | only complex res. | + complex residue | only complex res. | +complex residue | only complex res. | + complex residue |
| | + only client as Subject | = client & landmark as expres. Sub. | = operator & team (we) as Subject | + operator & client as Subject | only operator as Subject | + landmark as Subject | + landmark as Subject | + landmark as Subject | + client as Subject |
| | only expres. Finites | + expressed Finites | + fused Finites | = expressed & fused Fin. | only expressed | + fused Finites | + fused Finites | + expressed Finites | + fused Finites |
| | only present | + present | + present | = present & future | only future Finites | + present Finites | + present | = present & future | + present |
| | only Conj. Adjuncts | = Conj. & Circ. Adj. | + Circumst. Adjuncts | only Circumst. | + Circumst. Adjuncts | + Circumst. Adjuncts | + Circumst. Adjuncts | 1 Circumst. Adjunct | only Circumst. |

| Sys | ROMANIAN | | | SPANISH | | | BRITISH | | |
|---|---|---|---|---|---|---|---|---|---|
| | Monastery of Horezu | Dacian Fortresses | Sighisoara | Monastery El Escorial | Alhambra | Santiago de Compostela | Canterbury Cathedral | Tower of London | Edinburgh |
| | only modali-zation<br>- polarity<br>only declarative<br>only statement | only modali-zation<br>- polarity<br>only declarative<br>only statements | - modaliza-tion<br>- polarity<br>only declara-tive<br>+ full decl.<br>only statements | Adjuncts<br>only modali-zation<br>- polarity<br>only declara-tive<br>+ full decl.<br>only statements | only modali-zation<br>- polarity<br>+ imperative<br>+ commands | only modali-zation<br>- polarity<br>only declarative<br>only statements | only modali-zation<br>- polarity<br>only declarative<br>only statements | only modali-zation<br>-polarity<br>only declarative<br>only statements | Adjuncts<br>only mod-alization<br>-polarity<br>only declarative<br>only statements |
| THEME | only unmarked<br>onlymultiple (textual)<br>onlypartic ip. as Theme<br>- Thematic progression | only unmarked<br>+ multiple (textual)<br>+ participant as Theme<br>= continuous & linear Th. progression | + unmarked<br>only simple<br>+ participant as Theme<br>- Thematic progression<br>+ new Themes | + unmarked (dependent clause–Th.)<br>+ simple<br>= participant & process as Theme<br>= multiple & continuous progression | only unmarked (many dep. cl.-Rheme)<br>+ simple<br>+ process as Theme<br>+ continuous progression | only unmarked<br>+ simple<br>+ participant as Theme<br>+ continuous progression (little dif.) | + unmarked<br>+ enhanced<br>+ simple<br>+ participant as Theme<br>- Thematic progression | = unmarked & marked<br>enhanced<br>only simple<br>+ participant as Theme<br>- Thematic progression<br>all new Themes | + unmarked<br>only simple<br>+ particip. as Theme<br>= continu-ous, linear & new Themes |

**Table 9-4 Commercial set of websites: Visual summary**

| Sys | ROMANIAN | | | SPANISH | | | BRITISH | | |
|---|---|---|---|---|---|---|---|---|---|
| | **Monastery of Horezu** | **Dacian Fortresses** | **Sighisoara** | **Monastery El Escorial** | **Alhambra** | **Santiago de Compostela** | **Canterbury Cathedral** | **Tower of London** | **Edinburgh** |
| REPRESENTATIONAL | complex conceptual structure<br>unstructured analytical<br>monastery & background (Carrier)<br>church & trees, sky (Possessive Attributes) | -<br>-<br>-<br>-<br>- | simple conceptual structure<br>unstructured analytical<br>city (Carrier)<br>Clock Tower, gate, terrace, sky (Pos. Attrib) | complex conceptual structure<br>unstructured analytical<br>monastery & landscape (Carrier)<br>building & sky (Possessive Attributes) | complex conceptual structure<br>unstructured analytical<br>landmark & landscape (Carrier)<br>buildings & vegetation, mountains, sky (Pos. Attrib.) | -<br>-<br>-<br>-<br>- | complex conceptual structure<br>unstructured analytical<br>cathedral & landscape (Carrier)<br>tower, other components sky + branches (Pos. Attrib) | complex conceptual structure<br>unstructured analytical<br>riverbank & landscape (Carrier)<br>buildings & Thames sky (Possessive Attributes) | complex conceptual structure<br>unstructured analytical<br>city & landscape (Carrier)<br>several buildings & sky + firth (Possessive Attributes) |
| INTERACTIVE | offer<br>medium shot<br>subjective oblique<br>horizontal angle<br>low vertical angle<br>+ medium modality markers | -<br>-<br>-<br>-<br>-<br>- | offer<br>close shot<br>subjective frontal<br>horizontal angle<br>low vertical angle<br>+ medium modality markers | offer<br>medium shot<br>subjective oblique<br>horizontal angle<br>eye level vertical angle<br>+ medium modality markers | offer<br>medium shot<br>subjective frontal &<br>oblique hor. angle<br>eye level vertical angle<br>+ medium modality markers | -<br>-<br>-<br>-<br>-<br>- | offer<br>close shot<br>subjective oblique<br>horizontal angle<br>low vertical angle<br>+ medium modality markers | offer<br>long shot<br>subjective oblique<br>horizontal angle<br>eye level tow. high vertical an.<br>+ medium modality markers | offer<br>long shot<br>subjective oblique<br>horizontal angle<br>high vertical angle<br>+ medium modality markers |

| Sys | ROMANIAN | | | SPANISH | | | BRITISH | | |
|---|---|---|---|---|---|---|---|---|---|
| | **Monastery of Horezu** | **Dacian Fortresses** | **Sighisoara** | **Monastery El Escorial** | **Alhambra** | **Santiago de Compostela** | **Canterbury Cathedral** | **Tower of London** | **Edinburgh** |
| CO<br>MP<br>OS<br>IT<br>IO<br>NA<br>L | centre-<br>margin<br>church<br>(salient)<br>church<br>(framed) | -<br><br>-<br><br>- | centre-<br>margin<br>tower<br>(salient)<br>tower<br>(framed) | - informa-<br>tion struct.<br>building<br>(salient)<br>building<br>(framed) | - informa-<br>tion struct.<br>landmark<br>(salient)<br>landmark<br>(framed) | -<br><br>-<br><br>- | - informa-<br>tion struct.<br>cathedral<br>(salient)<br>cathedral<br>(framed) | - informa-<br>tion struct.<br>tall build-<br>ings & boat<br>-framing | -information<br>value<br>towers<br>(salient)<br>-framing |

## 9.2. Comparison between the national characteristics of web promotion

The discussion moves from the comparison of different types of websites to that of different countries. The section observes the way each website behaves according to its country: Romania, Spain and Great Britain, and tries to answer Research Question 2, presented below.

- *Do the three countries–Romania, Spain and Great Britain–use similar and/or different multimodal communication strategies to promote their national landmarks in an online environment?*

For this, it first indicates the similarities and differences between the websites belonging to the same country. Then, in the next section, it compares the patterns between the three countries. As indicated in the previous section, similarities and differences exist between the two types of sets as well as among the websites composing each set[1]. Some characteristics seem to be specific to a particular country.

### 9.2.1. Romanian sets of websites

The Romanian websites seem more consistent in their presentation. Their contents are mentioned in the menu and reiterated in the home page, a technique that can provide a redundant, but clear message. The websites focus on general information, regarding the country and the tours, the navigational, contact and interactive details being left aside. Their home pages are attractive, short and transparent; they operate at a logical level introducing users to the contents of the websites. Both sets dedicate a page to the World Heritage Sites in Romania, instead of presenting them separately. This webpage follows the same structure as the home page, indicating a consistent website. It is long and composed by different sections, each presenting a site or a day of the tour. The sections seem arranged to fit the computer screen. The little multimodality and interactivity, the long text and the lateral menu can appear unattractive and difficult to read. The message of the emitter is clear and stated from the beginning. It addresses users and is presented as important since it occupies almost the whole body of the home page. The entities seem to aim at an impression of professionalism, supported also by the presence of logos and slogans.

---

[1] The features of the messages are indicated in Tables 9-1, 9-2, 9-3 and 9-4.

As for the linguistic message presenting the World Heritage Sites, this is mainly informative and provides cultural, historical and artistic details about the landmarks. The text is elaborate and complex, built mainly by clause complexes. It expands by hypotaxis-elaboration; adding details to different attractions in a compact message, indicated by the high number of reduced non-defining relative clauses. Enhancement does not exist at all; the framing of the text and its succession of information are not given any attention. The landmarks' attractions are both identified and described in order to offer a complete presentation. The landmarks are the most frequent participant in the text; the visitor appears very little, while the promoter is totally absent. The varied and numerous circumstances set the landmark, not the visit, in a background, providing mainly spatial and temporal details. The message is complex, timeless and factual as shown by the complex mood structure, present Finites, lack of negations and dominance of statements. This is rarely mitigated by low modality, which, when used, indicates various things to see and presents users with different possibilities.

The visual message is simpler, presenting the landmarks as Carriers in an unstructured analytical process. It is also more connotative and directly addressed to viewers, as reflected by the close and medium shots, frontal angle, subjective perspective and salient and framed elements. The images of the landmarks are offered for contemplation, but the visual features and modality markers place viewers in the middle of things, standing close to the landmark in their admiration. They appear real and illustrative, but slightly modified in their colours, illumination, brightness and modalization in order to present the landmarks as more impressive and salient.

The multimodal message of the two sets is similar only in the verbal dominance; the particular function of each mode and the way the modes combine into a meaningful whole differ. Regardless of the differences, their communicative act seems to emphasise the diverse and unknown character of Romania. The individuality of the landmarks is identified by the UNESCO recognition, special architectural styles, medieval atmosphere or the legend of Dracula. To summarise, the Romanian websites seem quite similar. Their messages are consistent, organised and clear. Nonetheless, they are sometimes incomplete, not very attractive and unclear. The information on the Romanian World Heritage Sites is presented in a focused way. The linguistic presentation is informative and detailed, whereas the visual depiction is connotative and direct.

## 9.2.2. Spanish sets of websites

The Spanish sets contain the most varied and different messages. However, the analysis shows areas of similarity. Both the institutional and commercial websites transmit meaning through colours. Their home pages are attractive, short and simply designed. The menu is concise, but not very intuitive, a characteristic of the Spanish set of websites. It does not provide general information on the contents, but refers to practical, interactive and navigational details. Special attention is paid to the human component, by indicating links to information on the owner of the website and its contact data. The home pages seem more emotional than rational, persuasion by images and/or texts being used instead of presentation of general content. The structure of the webpages and their multimodal persuasive top-bottom layout are the most consistent features in the Spanish websites. The webpage on the city of Santiago de Compostela is the most different from the common pattern in both sets. Apart from informing and persuading, the content of the webpages also induces to action. The call is, nonetheless, indirect; the direct call to booking and/or buying does not appear at all in the Spanish sets.

The linguistic message develops by expansion-hypotaxis, packing information. It is general and mainly identifies a number of attractions of the landmark. These are described briefly by a particular characteristic related to year of foundation, founder, components and/or appearance. Mental processes of perception are used to present the landmark. The most frequently realized participant is the landmark, with the client and the tour operator being distributed differently. Information is not framed circumstantially as the number of circumstances is very small. The overall message is complex, universal, timeless, factual and objective, as indicated by the numerous Residue components, the fused and present Finites, the lack of negation, the preference for declaratives and the unmarked Themes. Mitigation is absent since modalization is almost inexistent. Information flows according to a Thematic pattern.

As for the visual message, this is more consistent and similar than the linguistic one. The websites illustrate their promoted landmarks by representative photos. The pictures are different, but their structure is almost the same. They are built by unstructured analytical processes that indicate the landmark as Carrier. This is focused since it is presented as salient and framed. The images offer a part of the landmark in a medium distance from an oblique angle; the viewer can go closer and visit or stay more distant and contemplate. They look real and spontaneous, as indicated by the interplay of the modality markers and the lack of a pre-established compositional structure. However, the saturated colours, illumination, brightness, representation and contextualisation appeal to senses and show how images of reality can carry different meanings.

There is no clear similarity between the ways the two Spanish websites use multimodality to present the landmarks, except for their connotative top-bottom layout and the special attention paid to the visual mode. The topic of promotion is, however, the same: history, exotic gardens, sensations and pilgrimage. The Spanish sets, then, seem to construct their communicative and multimodal acts on visual and connotative structures and layouts. Their messages are general, indirect and suggestive, with the informative function left in the background.

### 9.2.3. British sets of websites

The British Tourist Board and the British tour operator are similar in certain aspects. The two entities collaborate to promote Great Britain; the operator is recommended and its tours are advertised by the official board. Their identity and purpose are presented rather succinctly, the emphasis being on their complete offer. Their image is well established by their logo and slogan.

The British websites are long and so are their webpages. They are attractive, colourful and varied; the visual and verbal modes interplay continuously to provide a complete and informative message, especially in their home pages. Apart from highly multimodal, the home pages are also interactive, providing the opportunity to search in their database and participate to social networks. The modernity of the home pages is counterbalanced by more traditional webpages. These are similar to print pages since they rely on verbal message and reduce the colours to minimum by white backgrounds and faded images. Both websites use different layouts, structures and strategies to present the city of Edinburgh compared to the other landmarks. The webpages on the city are longer, detailed and addressed directly to the users. They contain more than one picture to illustrate the attractions of the city and remind users of paper guides and brochures. They also provide practical information on transport and attractions. The varied and complete contents of the British websites refer to general, practical, interactive and transactional types of information. Their clear purposes are stated directly: inform, persuade and induce to action. The call to action is placed separately from the main body and indicated visually and overtly. The commercial feature is also indicated clearly by prices or shopping carts. The transmission of complete and clear information is primordial; the other types of data, although important, subordinate to this purpose.

The linguistic message of the two sets is general; the numerous attractions are described concisely by representative data. The texts are medium syntactically elaborated and complex, developing by both clause complexes and simplexes. They usually expand by parataxis-extension and hypotaxis-elaboration. Relations of enhancement also exist to set the framework for the visit of the landmark and of the website. The relative and/or non-finite clauses are not numerous. The British message, then, does not seem very packed, but rather varied and easy to follow. The transitivity system uses material processes predominantly; they refer to the tourists' visit. This places the focus on the guidance of tourists and not on the landmark. The landmark is not only presented, but also discovered through the tourists' movement, acting as both Carrier and Goal. The background information is mainly locative, providing a spatial framework for the action. Even if dependent on the visit, the landmark is the most represented and expressed participant, usually occupying the Subject/Theme position. The visitor is frequently implied, while the tourist entity is almost absent, indicating an apparent impersonal and objective message. The linguistic message is also factual, complete, universal and timeless, as shown by the declarative mood, the complex Residue, the number of Circumstantial Adjuncts and the fused and present Finites. The message is sometimes mitigated by modalization, which refers to different possible attractions and anticipates them to users. The unmarked and simple Themes do not follow a similar pattern in the two websites. The marked Themes and/or new Themes appear in important numbers in both sets, indicating focalized information.

The images selected to depict the landmarks maintain the objective and impersonal tone of the message. They might aim to be informative by presenting the landmark and its surroundings in the background using conceptual structures composed by unstructured analytical processes. Nonetheless, the distance from which they are shot can make the visual message too general. The choice of pictures not iconic for the landmarks can also indicate a less direct and clear message. The pictures of Canterbury Cathedral are an exception. They are almost the same image and present the Cathedral partly and from a close shot. The visual message is more similar than the linguistic one; both websites present the images as offers from a subjective perspective and an oblique angle. The landmarks' components have the role of Possessive Attributes and are presented as salient. The faded colours and the lack of framing contribute to the images' impersonal and objective message. The pictures look naturalistic, depicting reality as it really is, without a pre-established order.

Nonetheless, the size, the faded colours or the lack of contextualization and representation can indicate modifications intended to impress.

The British sets are different in the layout of their multimodal acts, but the verbal and visual modes function similarly. They complement and extend each other in order to provide complete and elaborate information. The promotional message in both sets is similar and indicates the British individuality, which relies on religious importance, history and antiquity. In sum, it seems the similarities between the two British sets are related to the transmission of information. They mainly provide complete, clear and direct messages. Their images, however, may lack the directness and clarity of the verbal message, as they are usually vague and general.

## 9.3. Cultural differences revealed by the multimodal analysis of web promotion

The findings discussed in the previous section can indicate the existence of cultural patterns. As discussed in Chapter five, culture influences discourse and, at the same time, is influenced by discourse (Şerbănescu 2007, 255). More specifically, the analysis of the metafunctions can show cultural characteristics, while cultural characteristics can predict patterns in communication (Şerbănescu 2007; Martin and Rose 2008). Among the dimensions of cultural variability existing in intercultural communication, that of context (Hall 1976; 2000; Hall and Hall 1990) has been chosen for this study since it appeared more relevant to the type of message studied and its function. Context is a complex concept, as explained in the chapter dedicated to culture. In brief, context is the information that surrounds an event, inextricably bound up with the meaning of that event (Hall and Hall 1990, 6). Considering this, the overall organization of discourse and its logical composition, the reality presented and the relation between its producers and receptors can indicate the preference for a certain context of communication.

The national characteristics of web promotion indicated by the three sets of websites (Romanian, Spanish and British) can be compared from the cultural perspective of context. This comparison attempts to answer Research Question 3, below:

- *Can the results of the analysis of online national promotional messages, including their language and image, be accounted for from the point of view of the cultural dimension of context?*

The three countries under discussion here and their cultures have been classified by specialised intercultural studies (Neuliep 2006, 60, 78; Şerbănescu 2007, 143) according to their communication styles. Romanian and Spanish cultures are seen as high-context, i.e. much of the information is contained in the nonverbal part of the message, with communication based on restricted code systems. British culture is, instead, considered low-context, i.e. convey explicit and clear messages, relying on elaborated code systems. As was pointed out, it should be remembered that cultural dimensions are situated on a continuum (Hofstede *et al.* 2002, 40; Şerbănescu 2007, 153); no culture is considered to be at either one extreme or the other.

### 9.3.1. Comparison between the Romanian, Spanish and British sets of websites

The same variables used in section 9.1 above are considered also in this comparison, i.e. organization and layout; contents and message; linguistic message; visual message; multimodal and communicative act; and promotion, for the purpose of a clearer and more concise presentation.

*Organization and layout.* The websites are attractive and colourful, the Spanish ones making the most out of these features. The webpages are usually short, except for the British, which takes more space for its message. The Romanian webpages are also long, but the sections presenting the monuments promoted are arranged to fit the computer screen. In all cases, the home pages are more modern than the webpages, combining different modes and types of information in a fragmented message. The webpages, on the other hand, maintain the format of traditional print pages. The exception is found in the Spanish sets, which are more visual and connotative. This means that their home pages are more emotional than rational. The webpages follow the structure of the home pages, indicating intuitive and cohesive websites. The webpages with a city as a topic are the most different from the pattern of the set in the cases analysed. This, however, is not observable in the Romanian webpages, which adopt a different strategy to present their landmarks; they bring together all the World Heritage Sites in Romania on the same page. This may indicate a more focused message. It can also suggest the importance Romanian tourist entities pay to this recognition.

All the three sets are multimodal and interactive, but the degree of use is different. The Romanian set is mostly verbal; the Spanish is highly visual, whereas the British set is the most multimodal. The same hierarchy can be applied in the case of interactivity. These features, together with the long page and the lateral menu can make the Romanian set look less attractive. The multimodal message of the webpages is not laid out similarly in any set. The Spanish set is, however, more similar, as both websites favour the top-bottom layout of the promised product vs. the real one.

The cultural patterns established by the organization and layout of the websites are different. The Romanian and British sets have more features of low-context cultures, as indicated by their elaborated and clear presentation, webpages dominated by the verbal mode and highly organised websites (Şerbănescu 2007, 141). The Romanian sets have also a clear topic due to their focused content, but, at the same time, the lack of attention to attractiveness and readability may make the page less clear. The Romanian and British modern home pages can, however, indicate a fragmented and visual message as typical of high-context communication (Şerbănescu 2007, 142); this is especially true in the case of the British sets. On the other hand, the Spanish sets do not present information overtly, but rely on restricted code systems. They convey meaning by highly visual, connotative and fragmented messages and layouts, indicating, thus, a high-context pattern. At the same time, they are concise and cohesive websites, as typical of low-context cultures. It seems the Romanian and British sets have more low-context characteristics, whereas the Spanish are particularly high-context, as far as their organization and layout are concerned.

*Contents and message*. The menu is usually concise and intuitive, except for the Spanish set, which has a more connotative and less informative menu. In the Romanian and British sets, parts of it are repeated in the main body of the home page, for a clearer, though redundant, overview of the website. The placement of the menu follows no pattern in the sets, but the Romanian use more the lateral layout, while the British favour the horizontal one. As for the Spanish set, its institutional and commercial websites are totally different in this aspect. The contents of the websites are mainly centred on general information on the country and on the tours promoted, except for the Spanish sets. Other types of information are encountered, but in different amounts. The Romanian sets reduce all types of information to a minimum, whereas the Spanish sets, combine practical, interactive and navigational information, paying special attention to the contact with the tourist entity. The British sets are the most diversified; they contain practical, interactive and even transactional types, but lack navigational details. The methods used by the sets to instigate to action are also different. The Romanian sets, even if they do not have a common pattern, show they are not concerned with instigating users to action. As for the Spanish, these are indirect, but continuously suggestive, whereas the British are direct and provide possibilities to book and buy there and then. These types of information are usually separated from the main message and signalled visually.

Thus, from a contextual perspective, the Romanian and British sets continue to have clear and, in general, succinct messages, as usual in low-context communication. In the same style, the British sets offer varied and complete information in a direct way. Contrary to this, the Romanian sets do not provide complete information on the ways to visit the landmarks and country; incomplete messages are preferred as in high-context cultures (Hall 2000). As for the Spanish sets, these are more suggestive, connotative and indirect than informative, as typical for high-context cultures.

*Linguistic message*. The Romanian sets are more descriptive and give a number of features. The Spanish and British sets, on the other hand, have a general message that mainly identifies different attractions and describes them briefly via a particular characteristic. The texts in the sets have different lengths, amount of elaboration, complexity and structures; thus, no clear pattern can be established. The British sets, though, are more consistent. They are medium syntactically elaborated and complex, combining clause complexes with clause simplexes. Their symmetry is reflected also in the logico-semantic relations. In contrast, the Romanian and Spanish sets present a more packed message due to hypotaxis-elaboration. The frameworks of the texts are established by enhancement relations in the British sets, whereas these are totally absent in the Romanian ones.

Regarding the transitivity system, this is different in the three sets. The Romanian sets are centred on the landmark, identifying and describing it, while the British focus on guiding the visitors and rely on material processes to do so. The Spanish sets add sight perception in the discovery of the landmark. The background information is varied and detailed in the Romanian and British sets, which favour locative circumstances, whereas this is almost inexistent in the Spanish sets. The difference in the circumstantial frameworks is that the Romanian sets use it for the landmark itself, while the British use it for the visit to the landmark. The landmark is the most represented participant in all the sets and occupies the Subject/Theme position frequently. The visitor appears rarely in all the sets, while the tourist entity is almost absent, except for the Spanish commercial set. In the Romanian sets, it is totally absent. No particular role is established for any of the participants in any of the texts, except for the British sets, which present the landmark as Goal and Carrier.

The Mood choices indicate a complex, timeless, factual and objective message in all the three sets. A few instances of modalization mitigate the assertive tone of the messages in the Romanian and British sets. In the Romanian sets, the visitors are presented with several alternatives, whereas in the British, modalization is more varied and is mainly used to point out different attractions and anticipate them to the visitors. In the Spanish sets, modalization is almost absent, negotiation of meaning being totally excluded. The Themes are usually unmarked and simple and develop in different ways; no national pattern is evident from the texts' Thematic development.

The contextual pattern indicated by the linguistic text is, again, that of low-context cultures for the Romanian and British sets. These have organised, structured, elaborated and consistent messages. They are also detailed, factual and objective. The linguistic message is focalised by topic, continuous progression or new Themes. The presence of modalization, however, can indicate negotiation of meaning, as found in high-context communication. The Spanish sets, however, are less detailed and focalised, but more personal and related to perception, as it is characteristic of high-context cultures ("Cross Cultural Business Management" 2014, 49). Unexpectedly though, in the Spanish set, information is not negotiated, but presented as fact. This is a technique more common in low-context cultures.

*Visual message*. The landmarks are usually illustrated by one of the most representative images, except for the case of the British sets. Here, even if the photos are sometimes modern or curious, they do not depict the landmark clearly, but make it hard to recognize. The features of the visual message are more consistent in all the sets. They are also quite similar in the different national sets. Almost all of them use conceptual structures composed by unstructured analytical processes to depict elements of the landmarks as Possessive Attributes of the Carrier.

The interactive metafunction is the one that makes the images more different, especially the shots, angles and colours. The Romanian sets are very different from the others; the close and medium shots and the frontal angle situate the viewers inside the scene, looking at the monument captured in the photograph. In the Spanish and British sets, in turn, the oblique angle presents the landmark as outside the viewers' world. In the former case, the medium shot brings it closer to the viewers encouraging them to visit. The British sets, though, have no favoured shot. Nevertheless, the landmark is usually placed in the distance, for contemplation. It seems the websites want to offer a general perspective in an informative visual message. This can, however, interfere with the directness of the message and the clear identity of the landmark represented. Other characteristics, such as subjective perspective, type of image act and realistic modality are similar in the three sets. The degree of modality is, nevertheless, different; the Romanian pictures place viewers inside the scene of the images by direct experience; the Spanish are colourful and appealing to senses, while the British ones are faded and distant.

The composition of the photos is built around the landmarks, which are usually salient and framed. There seems to be no pattern of the structure of the image, as encountered also in the composition of the linguistic message. The photos have either a centre-margin structure or no structure at all.

The visual message changes the cultural patterns indicated so far slightly. The most clear low-context feature, encountered in almost all the images, is the focalisation of information by composition aimed to transmit clearer, more informative messages. The Romanian sets are explicit in their visual message, as in low-context cultures, but use images that suggest further possible meanings and evoke sensations (Şerbănescu 2007, 142). The Spanish sets also change their style in the visual mode. Now, they are more low-context, as they are visually descriptive, informative and explicit. Nonetheless, they still maintain their strong colours that appeal to senses. Besides the focalization of information, the British sets are no longer clear and explicit as the layout and linguistic message indicated. They inform by general and distant pictures, but appear quite indirect, and even vague, as in high-context cultures. In their visual communication, then, the national strategies behave differently. The Romanian set combines features of both types of context dependency, the Spanish images are more coherent with low-context cultures, while the British with high-context cultures.

*Multimodal and communicative act.* The sets analysed have different multimodal acts; the interplay of visual and verbal modes do not coincide in the way they create their message. The British sets are the exception, since their modes complement and extend each other's message in their aims of informing, persuading and inducing to action. The webpages of the three countries, then, present a cline in the coherence between the modes. While in the Romanian sets, the commercial pages do not even seem to be organized as a sole act of communication, the Spanish commercial set does not maintain the predominant visuality of the official one and the British sets offer an informative and organised message. It seems, then, that in multimodal composition, this new communicative possibility breaks the typical patterns to a certain extent in the case of the

Romanian and Spanish sets. The Romanian sets are sometimes more disorganised in their multimodal message and less low-context, while the Spanish sets are not always dominantly visual, connotative and high-context, indicating deviations from a strict pattern. As for the British sets, they are consistent in their pattern typical of low-context.

*Promotion*. The tourist entities identify themselves from the beginning and present their purposes by their logos, slogans and introductory messages. The Spanish Tourist Board is an exception since it is almost absent from the website. The clearly stated messages are presented succinctly in the British sets, in contrast to the long texts in the Romanian sets. The tone is different in all the texts, each creating a particular message from a specific position. The Romanian sets coincide, however, in the impression of professionalism given by the tourist entities. The presence of the emitters is different in the actual messages analysed; the Romanian emitters are impersonal, but guiding indirectly. The Spanish are more impersonal, while the British are more direct and instigative.

The overall message of the websites promotes a particular identity in the case of the three countries. The sets propose the following characteristics to the visitor: the Romanian, UNESCO recognition, special architectural styles, medieval atmosphere and Dracula's legend; the Spanish, history, exotic gardens and sensations, and pilgrimage; and the British, religious importance, history and antiquity. As can be observed, all the countries boast about their history. Nonetheless, its influence is different and this is what confers them individuality. The Romanian sets intrigue by their diversity and the unknown; the uniqueness of the architectural styles of past rulers is confirmed by UNESCO, while the medieval buildings and atmospheres are inhabited by legends. The Spanish sets present emblematic landmarks of the country's once imperial status, in particular the Muslim influence, exotic gardens and key pilgrimage routes for the Christians all over the world. The British sets promote historic sites, influenced by a tumultuous past or by their importance on the Anglican religious stage.

Regarding the promotional message, a number of cultural features can be identified. The introductory presentation of all the tourist entities is clear and precise, as in low-context cultures. However, in the Romanian sets, the connotative and suggestive features make it more persuasive and high-context. The absence of the identification of the Spanish Board is surprising and can only be explained by the supposition of shared knowledge, typical of high-context cultures ("Cross Cultural Business Management" 2014, 49); the copywriter supposes users will recognize the logo and slogan and so identify the site. The directness in the British sets is indicative of low-context communication, whereas the Romanian and Spanish sets are more indirect, and thus, more high-context. The overall messages of the websites analysed contain, in all cases, characteristics of high-context communication since they all rely on experience and senses to promote. Either overtly or indirectly, the legend of Dracula, in the case Romania; the captivating scented gardens, in Spain; and the stories of the Beefeaters and the spectacle of the Ceremony of the Keys, in Great Britain, are meant to appeal and suggest.

### 9.3.2. Interpretations of cultural findings

As the previous section showed, the national strategies used to promote the World Heritage Sites online can indicate patterns related to the context dimension of cultural variability. The interpretation that follows presents the results of the analyses within the framework of national cultural communication styles. Rather than reinforcing stereotypes, it evaluates the effect of the features of multimodality found.

The differences between the three sets of websites are rarely total, but rather a matter of degree. The Romanian sets are informative and more verbal. They seem to develop in an elaborated code system, based on the direct and clear expression of information, typical of low-context cultures. Thus, their message is organised and their information focalised, as indicated by the special sections dedicated to the World Heritage Sites in the country. Nevertheless, the websites are on occasions unclear, less informative and over general, as frequent in high-context cultures. This movement between different cultural patterns is indicated also by the multimodal acts; the linguistic text is detailed and informative, as in low-context cultures, whereas the visual is suggestive and connotative, as in high-context cultures. The images involve the viewers and make them identify with them, as in a context in which expectations and knowledge is shared. However, the visual message is direct and clear, indicating a feature of low-context culture. The cultural contextual patterns of the Romanian sets seem, then, to be more mixed than in the cases of Spain and Britain. On the one hand, they are informative, descriptive and focused, as in low-context cultures, and, on the other hand, they are less informative and clear, appealing to shared experiences and expectation, as in high-context cultures. The fact that users probably know very little about the country makes it possible to exploit a suggestive message. Nonetheless, the high-context characteristics appear as secondary to low-context, as if concealed or embedded in it.

Turning to the Spanish sets, these are more visual, connotative and suggestive, placing the verbal message in a subsidiary position. The restricted code system which constructs the message and its implied shared knowledge indicates a high-context culture. The linguistic message is built in the same way, as it is subjective and suggestive rather than informative. The Spanish sets are also indirect and impersonal, as typical of high-context cultures. Some pieces of information are either never, or only indirectly, expressed, as if relying on inferences and contextual predictions (Würtz 2005). The visual message is also connotative and less informative, more centred on the recognition and identification of the landmark than on its representation. However, the images present information in a more direct and clear way than the linguistic mode, a feature encountered in low-context cultures. Even if it is more informative in the visual message, in general, the Spanish websites remain consistent in the main appeal to feelings and shared knowledge, as usual in high-context cultures. The Spanish promotional message relies on glorious history and religious importance from a suggestive and connotative position.

Finally, the British sets are more informative, direct, instigative, clear, objective and practical. Their linguistic messages are general, consistent, intuitive and clear, as far as their elaboration, complexity and structure are concerned. The visual messages are also general and informative, but, at the same time, impersonal, indirect and sometimes unclear. Consistence is also respected in the composition of the multimodal message presenting the landmarks. The British tourist entities address users directly and guide them by visitor-oriented messages. These features seem typical of low-context cultures because they rely on an elaborated code system and indicate a clear, explicit, detailed and focalised message (Şerbănescu 2007, 141). This is not the case, however, in the images chosen, which appear to be based on the situational information regarding the landmarks and not on their actual description. Also, the British sets promote their landmarks in relation to a glorious and tumultuous past and to religious fame, as if this were well-know. Their position is, though, less connotative than the one in the Spanish sets.

To conclude, the Romanian, Spanish and British websites seem similar in the arrangement and structure of the information of their webpages; the types of linguistic message, its interpersonal and textual elements; and the representation and composition of their visual messages. On the other hand, they appear different in the transmission of information and their preferred mode; in the structure of the linguistic message, its logical and representational functions; and in the interactive characteristics of the images. The Romanian sets combine informative and objective aspects with subjective and connotative ones. In the case of the Spanish sets, they favour visual elements, connotation and indirectness, whereas the British sets are more informative, direct and clear. The composition of the multimodal act of the text and the image does not set a conclusive pattern in any of the sets from the three countries.

**Table 9-5 Cultural summary**

| CONTEXT | ROMANIAN | SPANISH | BRITISH |
|---|---|---|---|
| LOW-CONTEXT | + verbal website<br>+ focalised webpage<br>+ organised & informative message<br>+ informative & detailed linguistic message<br>+ direct & clear visual message<br>+ elaborated code system | + direct & clear visual information | + informative & clear website<br>+ practical & objective website<br>+ direct & instigative message<br>+ general, consistent & clear linguistic message<br>+ general & informative visual message<br>+ elaborated code system |
| HIGH-CONTEXT | + unclear & general website<br>- informative website<br>+ suggestive & connotative visual message<br>+ visual appeal to senses<br>+ shared experience | + visual, - verbal website<br>+ connotative & suggestive website<br>+ indirect & impersonal message<br>+ subjective & suggestive linguistic message<br>+ connotative & - informative visual message<br>+ restricted code system<br>+ shared knowledge<br>+ appeal to feelings | + impersonal, indirect & unclear visual message<br>+ situational visual information |
| PATTERN | COMBINED PATTERN | HIGH-CONTEXT | LOW-CONTEXT |

These similarities and differences can be explained by cultural variability. The context dimension chosen shows this, as reflected in Table

9-5. The Spanish and British sets, with few exceptions, behave as predicted by the literature consulted (Hall 2000; Würtz 2005; Neuliep 2006, 58-60, 320; Şerbănescu 2007, 141-142; Peace Corps 2011, 78; "Cross Cultural Business Management" 2014, 49), i.e. as belonging to high-context (the Spanish set) and low-context (the British set) types of cultures. The Romanian sets are not entirely high-context as expected, but combine features of both types of cultures. Deviations from the cultural classification do also exist in the other sets, supporting the claim that cultures are "dynamic, continuously developing, and evolving" (Barker and Galasinki 2001, 124; Besnier 2004, 95; Neuliep 2006, 45) and may be influenced by different factors (Şerbănescu 2007, 155). These are mostly present in the visual mode, as if indicating a visual inconsistency with the theory consulted.

The cultural interpretation of the different national strategies used by the websites has shown the Spanish and British sets to be more consistent with the literature on intercultural communication consulted than the Romanian set. This can position their cultures as more stable and dominant. Their strong cultures, which do not easily accept influences on their communicative styles from outside, may be partly due to the glorious past the websites refer to so much. The analysis of the Romanian set does not indicate a consistent contextual culture, but one that gives evidence of combining features of both types. This may mean that Romanian culture is more adaptable and/or in the course of change. However, even if not as obvious as in the Romanian sets, the Spanish and British sets sometimes deviate from the patterns, especially in their visual messages.

The deviations from the typical cultural patterns found may indicate cultural changes, as already mentioned (Barker and Galasinki 2001, 124; Besnier 2004, 95; Neuliep 2006, 45). Romanian recent history has undergone dramatic changes, both political and economic, influencing the culture, which is changing continuously and visibly. Similarly, Spanish communication styles, though basically having features of a high-context culture, might be influenced, internally, by changes in terms of politics, economy and society over the last decades and/or, externally, by globalisation and the expansion of Anglo-American culture. It cannot be forgotten, either, that the Spanish language and the websites in Spanish are part of a large linguistic community, that of Latin and Central America, with a very strong influence from North America. In the case of the British set, culture is probably influenced by the internationalisation of the English language. British culture may also be losing ground to the powerful American language and culture. The departures from the expected cultural context features seem to have occurred in relation to the characteristics and strategies of the medium and context of communication. Online promotion, a new way of communication, is only one of the many recent changes in the use of technology for transmitting messages. The Internet, as medium of communication, is considered low-context (Würtz 2005), whereas promotion, as context of communication, is classified as high-context (Cook 1992, 176). These factors are among those that influence culture, as claimed by intercultural communication (de Cillia *et al.* 1999, 154; Lehtonen 2000, 12; Şerbănescu 2007, 155; Dumitrescu 2009, 123). The findings of a detailed, multimodal analysis show the complex interrelation of these different influences in the corpus of websites analysed.

# PART IV:

# CONCLUSIONS

# CHAPTER TEN

# CONCLUSIONS

This chapter concludes the study of the online promotion of UNESCO World Heritage Sites in different countries (Romania, Spain and Great Britain) and presents a summary of the findings. It also indicates some of their practical implication in the field of online tourism promotion.

## 10.1. Summary of results

In order to answer the three Research Questions in the study, the following aspects have been compared: the organization, layout, contents and message of the home page, on one hand, and the linguistic and visual messages and the multimodal act of the webpages dedicated to the World Heritage Sites chosen in each website, on the other. The Questions focus on the similarities and differences between the institutional and commercial websites, the countries' communicative strategies and their possible cultural interpretation.

The comparison of the two types of websites indicates that they share a number of similarities and differ in particular ways. The institutional message is informative, impersonal and objective, aiming to give users information about the landmark and so encourage them to visit it. In the official sites, the landmark is the participant focused on both linguistically and visually; the images appear more professional and suggestive than those on the commercial sites. The commercial message is less detailed, more succinct and dynamic. This message depends more on the verbal than the visual; the language seems to guide the tourist during a visit to the landmark, informing her/him briefly about a number of attractions found there. Thus, the commercial websites use the landmark's attractions to persuade users to book the tour by projecting the tourist into the actual scene of the visit. In the institutional set, the persuasive intent is not visible, but rather concealed in the transmission of information. While the same characteristics of their landmarks are the focus, the method of promotion leads to differences in the use of language and image.

In general, the institutional and commercial websites share characteristics typical of web organization and layout, tourist promotion and topic. Apart from this, the product is further shaped by its sub-field, i.e. tourism promotion of World Heritage Sites. While mode and field bring the sets together, the differences found between them reflect their specific functions. Features of the sets revealed by the analysis have confirmed their belonging to different types of websites–institutional/promotional or commercial–up to a certain point. While their purpose is basically the same, informative-persuasive, the specific function of the website moves it towards one or other end of the continuum. Either overtly or indirectly, both websites have the purpose of advertising a particular destination. The analyses have shown a number of strategies to present the identity of the sender of the message, the owner of the websites, and the effects they produce on the user. The sites may give information or act on the users, placing them on the scene of the landmark and guiding them around. In the same way, the findings have revealed the construction of the user as the client to be informed or persuaded by experiencing the possible visit. The analysis has also indicated that the Tourist Boards seem to invest more in producing a successful message than do the tour operators. As national institutions, they probably work with professionals and are very aware of the importance of branding and marketing. For these professionals, this study of the use of multimedia has revealed an interesting area, that of the different possible ways language and image may combine and their effects. Three possibilities have been identified: either of the modes may support and extend the other; each may produce a different message, but take the addressee in the same direction; or they may produce messages so different as to be not totally compatible.

Regarding the analysis of the sets in relation to their source country, a number of similarities and differences in the national characteristics of web promotion have been observed. The Romanian, Spanish and British sets are similar in the arrangement and structure of their webpages; the types of linguistic message, its interpersonal and textual elements; and the representation and composition of their visual messages. At the same time, they differ in the transmission of information and their preferred mode; in the structure of the linguistic message and its logical and representational functions; as well as in the interactive characteristics of the images. The Romanian sets combine informative and objective features with subjective and connotative ones. The Spanish sets favour visual elements, connotation and indirectness, whereas the British sets are more informative, direct and clear. Here, the study of the composition of the multimodal act, of the role of image and text, while producing interesting results, does not set a conclusive pattern in any of the sets from the three countries.

The resemblances and differences between the national characteristics just mentioned can be accounted for from a cultural point of view. The context dimension of cultural variability shows the communication differences between the cultures under discussion. The Spanish and British sets, with few exceptions, behave as predicted by the literature consulted (Hall 2000; Würtz 2005; Neuliep 2006; Şerbănescu 2007), i.e. the Spanish webs having many features of high-context cultures, like the preference for visual and suggestive communication, the British as belonging to low-context cultures with features of elaborated code systems. The Romanian sets, however, combine features of both types of cultures and do not follow Romania's usual cultural classification as high-context. Besides the features expected for the cultures studied, in all the sets of websites, especially in the visual mode, departures from the usual cultural patterns were found. There are no pure cultures, but only "culturally hybrid" (Hall 1994, 207) and "multidimensional" (Hofstede *et al.* 2002, 126) nations.

The consistency of the Spanish and British cultures with their cultural classification (Neuliep 2006; Şerbănescu 2007) can be seen as indicating stable and dominant communicational styles. The Romanian culture, on the other hand, appears more permeable to change. The cultural deviations present in all the three sources, found to a greater or lesser extent in each, may be due to cultural and communicational changes produced by globalisation, the expansion of Anglo-American culture, internal changes in terms of politics, economy, society, and/or the emergence of new ways of communication and new technologies. The study, then, of the linguistic and visual features of the websites in the framework of the context dimension of cultural variability has shown ways in which the cultures, with varying positions internationally, react in the new online marketing world. Even cultures with global dominance allow permeation of cultural styles from the opposite end of the contextual cline to combine with their traditional preferences when using novel ways of communication.

To conclude, especially interesting is the way the theoretical framework used is able to move from the macro-level to the specific features of language and image to explain the different effects of the choices and their combinations in the messages analysed. These can be revealing for a wide array of fields, from online communication, to strategies of building a country's brand and promoting it internationally, to studies of national and cultural communication patterns. Specifically, the study supports previous findings claiming that promotional websites can be effectively analysed multimodally and culturally (Stoian 2013a; 2015).

A better understanding of the power of language and image to interact with others, to represent and compose meaning, as well as of the different cultural and contextual communication styles, can make the online promotion of tourism more successful. They all contribute to the construction and promotion of the brand of a country.

## 10.2. Practical implications for the field of online tourism

A more secondary, but practical objective of the study has been to provide evidence for the importance of factors such as multimodal composition and intercultural communication for successful worldwide promotion of a country and its landmarks. The multimodal analysis and cultural interpretation have shown a multitude of possible messages encoded in language and image. These emphasise, if emphasis is still needed, the complexity of communication; slight changes in one or more features of a multimodal text can produce a totally different message. Communication is about choice; the sum of choices composes the final message, but only one uninspired choice can affect the whole message. The communicative choices will be felicitous only if the right choices are made at the extralinguistic, cultural level (Arús *et al.* forthcoming). Language, image and the way they combine into a multimodal act to communicate meaning in intercultural contexts are vitally important for a website's success.

The study, then, has aimed to provide a more complete picture of the complexity of online tourism promotion. As shown, its success depends on many factors. Sub-section 2.3.1 in the Theoretical Background (Chapter two) presented a number of characteristics required by a tourism website in order to be successful. They have been collected from different sources (OMT 1999; 2001; 2005b; Morgan and Pritchard 2000; Majó and Galí 2002; Crystal 2004; Djonov 2005; Miller 2011), in different domains (tourist information, websites, hypermedia discourse analysis, commerce, marketing, advertising and language). Not all the websites have observed them and this has affected the final message. For example, it is recommended that a website should establish its identity and mission (OMT 2001, 113; Djonov 2005, 113; Miller 2011, 229), but this was not found in the Spanish institutional website. The effect of this absence has already been discussed in the relevant sections of this study. This is only one example of failing to follow recommendations for communication in a specialized field. An understanding of the role of the presence of the institution for the user of the page would make clear the need for this apparent detail. Information provided by principled research can clearly play a part in the work of professionals behind the promotion of tourism.

Considering discursive and cultural diversity, together with the growing tendency of online tourism, particular attention should be paid to this type of communication. Website owners and promoters need to understand that the composition and production of appealing and efficient websites is not an easy task. A very diverse team is needed to cooperate in the online promotion of tourism, made up of professionals in the domains of graphics, computer communication, English language, public orientation or marketing. Some tourist entities have understood the importance of this, like the British Tourist Board, which has also joined forces with the private domain for the promotion of the country (Morgan and Pritchard 2000, 282). The majority, though, have no grounded knowledge of how to improve their websites to attract potential consumers (Morgan and Pritchard 2000, 274).

It is hoped that this study will be a useful tool not only in theoretical fields like Systemic Functional Linguistics, but also in areas like composition of promotional messages, online promotion, tourism discourse and its strategies, or intercultural communication, both theoretically and practically. An important finding, on the practical side, is the way the present study has been able to make explicit the complexity of website communication and provide tools to help users take better advantage of its possibilities. These can be applied to the field studied and to others. Training providing basic knowledge about meaning-making in image and text for the area of online promotion using the model applied here and explaining the types of cultural differences identified would be useful in many areas.

# APPENDIX A

# LINGUISTIC ANALYSES

This part contains the linguistic analyses of the entire corpus discussed in this study. As mentioned in the Methodology section, for reasons of space, the whole collected data and obtained results cannot be included in the Appendix. Following the same structure of Chapters seven and eight, the Appendix presents first the institutional corpus and, then, the commercial one, in the same order, i.e. Romanian, Spanish and British sets. The analyses are divided in (1) logical and (2) experiential, interpersonal and textual, for each text.

## 1. Institutional websites

### 1.1. Romanian set of institutional webpages

#### 1.1.1. The Monastery of Horezu in the institutional corpus

*Logical analysis*

| | |
|---|---|
| =β | (1i) Founded in 1690 by Prince Constantine Brancoveanu, |
| α | (1ii) the monastery of Horezu is a masterpiece of the 'Brancovenesti' style. |
| =β | (2i) Renown for the richness of its sculptural detail, the treatment of its religious compositions and its painted decorative works, |
| α | (2ii) the monastery houses precious collections of frescos and icons [[dating from the end of the 17th century and beginning of the 18th century]]. |
| α | (3i) The Hurezi School of mural and icon painting |
| <=β> | (3ii) established at the monastery in the 18th century |
| α | (3i) had a profound influence on religious art and architecture in the Balkan region. |
| α | (4i) The monastery museum, |
| <=β> | (4ii) housed in the princely residence, |
| α | (4i) features masterpieces of Brancovenesti art: icons, books, embroideries, silver collections and an interesting library of old books |
| =γ | (4iii) containing approximately 4,000 volumes. |
| CL. SIMPLEX | (5) Overnight accommodation available. |

## *Experiential, interpersonal and textual analyses*

(1i) Founded in 1690 by Prince Constantine Brancoveanu, (1ii) the monastery of Horezu is a masterpiece of the 'Brancovenesti' style.

<table>
<tr><td rowspan="3">Founded in 1690 by Prince Constantine Brancoveanu</td><td>the monastery of Horezu</td><td colspan="2">is</td><td>a masterpiece of the 'Brancovenesti' style</td></tr>
<tr><td>Subject</td><td>Finite '(present)</td><td>Predicator be'</td><td>Complement</td></tr>
<tr><td colspan="2">MOOD</td><td colspan="2">RESIDUE</td></tr>
<tr><td>-</td><td>Carrier</td><td colspan="2">Pr: Relational (attributive - intensive)</td><td>Attribute</td></tr>
<tr><td colspan="2">experiential</td><td colspan="3" rowspan="2">RHEME</td></tr>
<tr><td colspan="2">THEME</td></tr>
</table>

(1i) Founded in 1690 by Prince Constantine Brancoveanu - dependent clause, not part of Interpersonal and Textual analyses.

| *[which]* | *[was]* Founded | in 1690 | by Prince Constantine Brancoveanu |
|---|---|---|---|
| *[Goal]* | Pr: Material | Circ: Location (time) | Actor |

(2i) Renown for the richness of its sculptural detail, the treatment of its religious compositions and its painted decorative works, (2ii) the monastery houses precious collections of frescos and icons [[dating from the end of the 17th century and beginning of the 18th century]].

<table>
<tr><td rowspan="3">Renown for the richness of its sculptural detail, the treatment of its religious compositions and its painted decorative works</td><td>the monastery</td><td colspan="2">houses</td><td>precious collections of frescos and icons [[dating from the end of the 17th century and beginning of the 18th century]]</td></tr>
<tr><td>Subject</td><td>Finite '(present)</td><td>Predicator house'</td><td>Complement</td></tr>
<tr><td></td><td>MOOD</td><td colspan="2">RESIDUE</td></tr>
<tr><td>-</td><td>Carrier</td><td colspan="2">Pr: Relational (attributive-circumstantial)</td><td>Attribute</td></tr>
<tr><td colspan="2">experiential</td><td colspan="3" rowspan="2">RHEME</td></tr>
<tr><td colspan="2">THEME</td></tr>
</table>

(2i) Renown for the richness of its sculptural detail, the treatment of its religious compositions and its painted decorative works - dependent clause, not part of Interpersonal and Textual analyses.

| *[which]* | *[is]* | Renowned | for the richness of its sculptural detail, the treatment of its religious compositions and its painted decorative works, |
|---|---|---|---|

<table>
<tr><td>[Carrier]</td><td>[Pr: Relational (attributive - intensive)]</td><td>Attribute</td><td>Circ: Cause (reason)</td></tr>
</table>

$_{(3i)}$ The Hurezi School of mural and icon painting $_{(3ii)}$ established at the monastery in the 18th century $_{(3i)}$ had a profound influence on religious art and architecture in the Balkan region.

<table>
<tr><td>The Hurezi School of mural and icon painting <<//established at the monastery in the 18th century//>></td><td colspan="2">had a profound influence on/ meaning influenced</td><td>profoundly</td><td>religious art and architecture</td><td>in the Balkan region</td></tr>
<tr><td>Subject</td><td>Finite '(past)</td><td>Predicator have influence'</td><td>Adjunct: circ</td><td>Complement</td><td>Adjunct: circ</td></tr>
<tr><td colspan="2">MOOD</td><td colspan="4">RESIDUE</td></tr>
<tr><td>Identified/ Token</td><td colspan="2">Pr: Relational (identifyingintensive)</td><td>Circ: Manner (quality)</td><td>Identifier/ Value</td><td>Circ: Location (place)</td></tr>
<tr><td>experiential</td><td colspan="5"></td></tr>
<tr><td>THEME</td><td colspan="5">RHEME</td></tr>
</table>

$_{(3ii)}$ established at the monastery in the 18th century - dependent clause, not part of Interpersonal and Textual analyses.

| *[which]* | *[was]* established | at the monastery | in the 18th century |
|---|---|---|---|
| *[Goal]* | Pr: Material | Circ: Location (place) | Circ: Location (time) |

$_{(4i)}$ The monastery museum, $_{(4ii)}$ housed in the princely residence, $_{(4i)}$ features masterpieces of Brancovenesti art: icons, books, embroideries, silver collections and an interesting library of old books $_{(4iii)}$ containing approximately 4,000 volumes.

<table>
<tr><td>The monastery museum, <<//housed in the princely residence//>>,</td><td colspan="2">features</td><td>masterpieces of Brancovenesti art: icons, books, embroideries, silver collections and an interesting library of old books</td></tr>
<tr><td>Subject</td><td>Finite '(present)</td><td>Predicator feature'</td><td>Complement</td></tr>
<tr><td colspan="2">MOOD</td><td colspan="2">RESIDUE</td></tr>
<tr><td>Carrier: possessor</td><td colspan="2">Pr: Relational (attributivepossessive)</td><td>Attribute: possessed</td></tr>
<tr><td>experiential</td><td colspan="2" rowspan="2"></td><td rowspan="2">RHEME</td></tr>
<tr><td>THEME</td></tr>
</table>

(4ii) housed in the princely residence

| *[which]* | *[is]* housed | in the princely residence |
|---|---|---|
| *[Carrier]* | Pr: Relational (attributive-circumstantial) | Attribute |

(4iii) *containing approximately 4,000 volumes* - dependent clauses, not part of Interpersonal and Textual analyses.

| *[which]* | *[is]* containing | approximately 4,000 volumes |
|---|---|---|
| *[Identified/ Token: possessor]* | Pr: Relational (identifying-possessive) | Identifier/ Value: possessed |

(5) Overnight accommodation available.

| Overnight accommodation | *[is]* | | available |
|---|---|---|---|
| Subject | *[Finite '(present)* | *be' Predicator]* | Complement |
| MOOD | | RESIDUE | |
| Carrier | *[Pr: Relational (attributive - intensive)]* | | Attribute |
| experiential | RHEME | | |
| THEME | | | |

## 1.1.2. The Dacian Fortresses of Orastie Mountains in the institutional corpus

### *Logical analysis*

=β 1 (1i) Dating from the 1st centuries B.C. and A.D.
+2 (1ii) and strewn from Orastie to Retezat Mountains,
α (1iii) the Dacian and Roman fortresses
<=γ> (1iv) recognized by UNESCO as World Heritage Sites
α (1iii) are an archeologist's delight.
=β (2i) Built as a defense ring around the capital of the Dacian kingdom, Sarmizegetusa,
α (2ii) they include the ruins of the fortresses at **Banita, Capalna, Costesti - Blidaru, Costesti – Cetatuie, Luncani - Piatra Rosie,** as well as pre-Roman Dacian capital (**Sarmisegetuza**).
CL. SIMPLEX (3) The fortresses show an unusual fusion of military and religious architectural techniques and concepts from the classical world and the late European Iron Age.
1 (4i) The six defensive sites, the nucleus of the Dacian Kingdom, were conquered by the Romans at the beginning of the 2nd century A.D.;
+2 (4ii) their extensive and well-preserved remains stand in spectacular natural surroundings
+3 (4iii) and give a dramatic picture of a vigorous and innovative civilization.
CL. SIMPLEX (5) At Sarmisegetuza you can still see the remains of the forum and the elliptical brick and stone amphitheatre [[where gladiator shows were held]].

α (6i) Hiking enthusiasts can enjoy the trails in the nearby Retezat National Park, the oldest in Romania
=β (6ii) (established 1935).
=β (7i) Covering 95,000 acres of pristine forests, alpine meadows, peaks, and some 80 glacial lakes,
1 α (7ii) the area was designated as a UNESCO Biosphere Reservation
+2 (7iii) and provides unforgettable hiking experiences among its peaks, valleys, rivers and gorges.
CL. SIMPLEX (8) The area is best explored during the summer season with proper hiking equipment and directions.

## *Experiential, interpersonal and textual analyses*

(1i) Dating from the 1st centuries B.C. and A.D. (1ii) and strewn from Orastie to Retezat Mountains, (1iii) the Dacian and Roman fortresses (1iv) recognized by UNESCO as World Heritage Sites (1iii) are an archeologist's delight.

<table>
<tr><td rowspan="3">Dating from the 1st centuries B.C. and A.D. and strewn from Orastie to Retezat Mountains</td><td>the Dacian and Roman fortresses <<//recognized by UNESCO as World Heritage Sites//>></td><td colspan="2">are</td><td>an archeologist's delight</td></tr>
<tr><td>Subject</td><td>Finite '(present)</td><td>be' Predicator</td><td>Complement</td></tr>
<tr><td colspan="2">MOOD</td><td colspan="2">RESIDUE</td></tr>
<tr><td>-</td><td>Carrier</td><td colspan="2">Pr: Relational (attributive - intensive)</td><td>Attribute</td></tr>
<tr><td colspan="2">experiential</td><td colspan="3" rowspan="2">RHEME</td></tr>
<tr><td colspan="2">THEME</td></tr>
</table>

(1i) Dating from the 1st centuries B.C. and A.D. - dependent clause, not part of Interpersonal and Textual analyses.

| *[which]* | *[are]* Dating from | the 1st centuries B.C. and A.D. |
|---|---|---|
| *[Carrier]* | Pr: Relational (attributive-circumstantial) | Attribute |

(1ii) and strewn from Orastie to Retezat Mountains,

| and | *[which]* | *[are]* strewn | from Orastie to Retezat Mountains |
|---|---|---|---|
| - | *[Carrier]* | Pr: Relational (attributive-circumstantial) | Attribute |

(1iv) recognized by UNESCO as World Heritage Sites

| *[which]* | *[are]* recognized | by UNESCO | as World Heritage Sites |
|---|---|---|---|
| *[Carrier]* | Pr: Causative | Attributor | Attribute |

(2i) Built as a defense ring around the capital of the Dacian kingdom, Sarmizegetusa, (2ii) they include the ruins of the fortresses at Banita, Capalna, Costesti - Blidaru, Costesti – Cetatuie, Luncani - Piatra Rosie, as well as pre-Roman Dacian capital (Sarmisegetuza).

<table>
<tr><td rowspan="3">Built as a defense ring around the capital of the Dacian kingdom, Sarmizegetusa</td><td>they</td><td colspan="2">include</td><td>the ruins of the fortresses at Banita, Capalna, Costesti - Blidaru, Costesti – Cetatuie, Luncani - Piatra Rosie, as well as pre-Roman Dacian capital (Sarmisegetuza)</td></tr>
<tr><td>Subject</td><td>Finite '(present)</td><td>Predicator include'</td><td>Complement</td></tr>
<tr><td colspan="2">MOOD</td><td colspan="2">RESIDUE</td></tr>
<tr><td>-</td><td>Identified / Token: possessor</td><td colspan="2">Pr: Relational (identifying - possessive)</td><td>Identifier/ Value: possessed</td></tr>
<tr><td colspan="2">experiential</td><td colspan="3" rowspan="2">RHEME</td></tr>
<tr><td colspan="2">THEME</td></tr>
</table>

(2i) Built as a defense ring around the capital of the Dacian kingdom, Sarmizegetusa - dependent clause, not part of Interpersonal and Textual analyses.

| *[which]* | *[are]* Built | as a defense ring around the capital of the Dacian kingdom, Sarmizegetusa, |
|---|---|---|
| *[Goal]* | Pr: Material | Circ: Role (guise) |

(3) The fortresses show an unusual fusion of military and religious architectural techniques and concepts from the classical world and the late European Iron Age.

<table>
<tr><td>The fortresses</td><td colspan="2">show</td><td>an unusual fusion of military and religious architectural techniques and concepts from the classical world and the late European Iron Age</td></tr>
<tr><td>Subject</td><td>Finite '(present)</td><td>show'Predicator</td><td>Complement</td></tr>
<tr><td colspan="2">MOOD</td><td colspan="2">RESIDUE</td></tr>
<tr><td>Identified / Token</td><td colspan="2">Pr: Relational (identifying - intensive)</td><td>Identifier / Value</td></tr>
<tr><td>experiential</td><td colspan="2" rowspan="2"></td><td rowspan="2">RHEME</td></tr>
<tr><td>THEME</td></tr>
</table>

(4i) The six defensive sites, the nucleus of the Dacian Kingdom, were conquered by the Romans at the beginning of the 2nd century A.D.; (4ii) their extensive and well-preserved remains stand in spectacular natural surroundings (4iii) and give a dramatic picture of a vigorous and innovative civilization.

| The six defensive sites , the nucleus of the Dacian Kingdom | were | conquered | by the Romans | at the beginning of the 2nd century A.D. |
|---|---|---|---|---|
| Subject | Finite | Predicator | Adjunct: circ | Adjunct: circ |
| MOOD | | RESIDUE | | |
| Goal | - | Pr: Material | Actor | Circ: Location (time) |
| experiential | | | | |
| THEME | RHEME | | | |

| their extensive and wellpreserved remains | stand | | in spectacular natural surroundings |
|---|---|---|---|
| Subject | Finite ‘(*present*) | *stand*’ Predicator | Complement |
| MOOD | | RESIDUE | |
| Carrier | Pr: Relational (attributive–circumstantial) | | Attribute |
| experiential | RHEME | | |
| THEME | | | |

| and | *[their extensive and well-preserved remains]* | give | | a dramatic picture of a vigorous and innovative civilization |
|---|---|---|---|---|
| (Conjunction) | *[Subject]* | Finite ‘(*present*) | *give*’ Predicator | Complement |
| | MOOD | | RESIDUE | |
| - | *[Actor]* | Pr: Material | | Goal |
| textual | experiential | | | RHEME |
| | THEME | | | |

(5) At Sarmisegetuza you can still see the remains of the forum and the elliptical brick and stone amphitheatre [[where gladiator shows were held]].

| At Sarmisegetuza | you | can | still | see | the remains of the forum and the elliptical brick and stone amphitheatre [[where gladiator shows were held]] |
|---|---|---|---|---|---|
| Adjunct: circ | Subject | Finite | Adjunct: mood | Predicator | Complement |
| RESIDUE | MOOD | | | | |
| Circ: Location (place) | Senser | - | - | Pr: Mental (perception) | Phenomenon |
| experiential | RHEME | | | | |
| THEME | | | | | |

(6i) Hiking enthusiasts can enjoy the trails in the nearby Retezat National Park, the oldest in Romania (6ii) (established 1935).

| Hiking enthusiasts | can | enjoy | the trails | in the nearby Retezat National Park, the oldest in Romania |
|---|---|---|---|---|
| Subject | Finite | Predicator | Complement | Adjunct: circ |
| MOOD | | RESIDUE | | |
| Senser | - | Pr: Mental (affection) | Phenomenon | Circ: Location (place) |
| experiential | RHEME | | | |
| THEME | | | | |

(6ii) *(established 1935)* - dependent clause, not part of Interpersonal and Textual analyses.

| *[which]* | *[was/were]* established (ambiguous goal) | *[in]* 1935 |
|---|---|---|
| *[Goal]* | Pr: Material | Circ: Location (time) |

(7i) Covering 95,000 acres of pristine forests, alpine meadows, peaks, and some 80 glacial lakes, (7ii) the area was designated as a UNESCO Biosphere Reservation (7iii) and provides unforgettable hiking experiences among its peaks, valleys, rivers and gorges.

| Covering 95,000 acres of pristine forests, alpine meadows, peaks, and some 80 glacial lakes | the area | was | designated | as a UNESCO Biosphere Reservation |
|---|---|---|---|---|
| | Subject | Finite | Predicator | Complement |
| | MOOD | | RESIDUE | |
| - | Carrier | - | Pr: Causative | Attribute |
| experiential | | RHEME | | |
| THEME | | | | |

| and | *[the area]* | provides | | unforgettable hiking experiences | among its peaks, valleys, rivers and gorges |
|---|---|---|---|---|---|
| (Conjunction) | *[Subject]* | Finite '(*present*) | Predicator *provide*' | Complement | Adjunct: circ |
| | MOOD | | RESIDUE | | |
| - | *[Identified/ Token: possessor]* | Pr: Relational (identifying - possessive) | | Identifier/ Value: possessed | Circ: Location (place) |
| textual | experiential | | | RHEME | |
| | THEME | | | | |

(7i) Covering 95,000 acres of pristine forests, alpine meadows, peaks, and some 80 glacial lakes - dependent clause, not part of Interpersonal and Textual analyses.

| *[which]* | *[is]* Covering | 95,000 acres of pristine forests, alpine meadows, peaks, and some 80 glacial lakes |
|---|---|---|
| *[Identified/ Token]* | Pr: Relational (identifying-circumstance) | Identifier/ Value |

(8) The area is best explored during the summer season with proper hiking equipment and directions.

| The area | is | best | explored | during the summer season | with proper hiking equipment and directions |
|---|---|---|---|---|---|
| Subject | Finite | Adjunct: circ | Predicator | Adjunct: circ | Adjunct: circ |
| MOOD | | RESIDUE | | | |
| Goal | - | Circ: Manner (quality) | Pr: Material | Circ: Location (time) | Circ: Manner (means) |
| experiential | RHEME | | | | |
| THEME | | | | | |

## 1.1.3. Sighisoara in the institutional corpus

### *Logical analysis*

=β (1i) Founded by German craftsmen and merchants [[known as the Saxons of Transylvania]],

α (1ii) Sighisoara is a fine example of a small, fortified medieval town [[which played an important strategic and commercial role on the fringes of central Europe for several centuries]].

CL. SIMPLEX (2) Sighisoara, one of the most beautiful towns in the heart of Transylvania, looks today [[much as it did 500 years ago]].
α (3i) This medieval town was also the birthplace of Vlad Dracula -
<=β> (3ii) nicknamed Vlad Tepes (Vlad the Impaler) -
α (3i) ruler of Walachia from 1456 to 1462.
CL. SIMPLEX (4) It was he [[who inspired Bram Stoker's fictional creation, Count Dracula]].
CL. SIMPLEX (5) His house is just one of the many attractions here.
α (6i) Others include the Church on the Hill, with its 500–year old frescos; the Church of the Dominican Monastery,
<=β> (6ii) renown for its Renaissance carved altarpiece, baroque painted pulpit, Oriental carpets and 17th-century organ;
α (6i) and the Venetian House,
=γ (6iii) built in the 13th century.
α (7i) Among the most striking attractions is the 210-feet high Clock Tower (Council Tower),
=β (7ii) built in the 14th century,
=γ (7iii) where each day a different wooden figure emerges from the belfry on the stroke of midnight.
α (8i) The tower was raised in the 13th and 14th centuries
=β (8ii) when Sighisoara became a free town controlled by craft guilds,
=γ 1 (8iii) each of which had to finance the construction of a bastion
+2 (8iv) and defend it during wartime.
1 α (9i) The fortification walls,
<=β> (9ii) built in the 14th and 15th centuries,
1 (9i) were up to 50-feet high
+2 (9iii) and featured 14 defense towers.
CL. SIMPLEX (10) Most of the old structure and 9 of the defense towers can still be admired today…

## *Experiential, interpersonal and textual analyses*

(1i) Founded by German craftsmen and merchants [[known as the Saxons of Transylvania]], (1ii) Sighisoara is a fine example of a small, fortified medieval town [[which played an important strategic and commercial role on the fringes of central Europe for several centuries]].

<table>
<tr><td rowspan="3">Founded by German craftsmen and merchants [[known as the Saxons of Transylvania]]</td><td>Sighisoara</td><td colspan="2">is</td><td>a fine example of a small, fortified medieval town [[which played an important strategic and commercial role on the fringes of central Europe for several centuries]]</td></tr>
<tr><td>Subject</td><td>Finite '(present)</td><td>Predicator be'</td><td>Complement</td></tr>
<tr><td colspan="2">MOOD</td><td colspan="2">RESIDUE</td></tr>
<tr><td>-</td><td>Carrier</td><td colspan="2">Pr: Relational (attributive - intensive)</td><td>Attribute</td></tr>
<tr><td colspan="2">experiential</td><td colspan="3" rowspan="2">RHEME</td></tr>
<tr><td colspan="2">THEME</td></tr>
</table>

(1i) Founded by German craftsmen and merchants [[known as the Saxons of Transylvania]] - dependent clause, not part of Interpersonal and Textual analyses.

| *[which]* | *[was]* Founded | by German craftsmen and merchants |
|---|---|---|
| *[Goal]* | Pr: Material | Actor |

(2) Sighisoara, one of the most beautiful towns in the heart of Transylvania, looks today much as it did 500 years ago.

| Sighisoara, one of the most beautiful towns in the heart of Transylvania | looks | | today | [[much as it did 500 years ago]] |
|---|---|---|---|---|
| Subject | Finite '(*present*) | *look*' Predicator | Adjunct: circ | Complement |
| MOOD | | RESIDUE | | |
| Carrier | Pr: Relational (attributive circumstantial) | | Circ: Location (time) | Attribute |
| experiential | | | | |
| THEME | RHEME | | | |

(3i) This medieval town was also the birthplace of Vlad Dracula (3ii) - nicknamed Vlad Tepes (Vlad the Impaler) - (3i) ruler of Walachia from 1456 to 1462.

| This medieval town | was | | also | the birthplace of Vlad Dracula, ruler of Walachia from 1456 to 1462 |
|---|---|---|---|---|
| Subject | Finite '(*past*) | Predicator *be*' | Adjunct: conjunctive | Complement |
| MOOD | | RESI- | | -DUE |
| Identified / Token | Pr: Relational (identifying - intensive) | | - | Identifier / Value |
| experiential | | | | |
| THEME | | | RHEME | |

(3ii) - nicknamed Vlad Tepes (Vlad the Impaler) - dependent clause, not part of Interpersonal and Textual analyses

| *[Vlad Dracula]* | *[was]* nicknamed | Vlad Tepes (Vlad the Impaler) |
|---|---|---|
| Carrier | Pr: Causative | Attribute |

(4) It was he [[who inspired Bram Stoker's fictional creation, Count Dracula]].

| It | was | | he | [[who inspired Bram Stoker's fictional creation, Count Dracula]] |
|---|---|---|---|---|
| Sub- | Finite '*(past)* | *be*' Predicator | Complement | -ject |
| MOOD | | RESIDUE | | |
| Iden- | Pr: Relational (identifying - intensive) | | Identified / Token | -tifier / Value |
| experiential | | | | RHEME |
| THEME | | | | |

(5) His house is just one of the many attractions here.

| His house | is | | just | one of the many attractions | here |
|---|---|---|---|---|---|
| Subject | Finite '*(present)* | Predicator *be*' | Adjunct: mood | Complement | Adjunct: circ |
| MOOD | | RESIDUE | | | |
| Identified/ Token | Pr: Relational (identifying-intensive) | | - | Identifier/ Value | Circ: Location (place) |
| experiential | | | RHEME | | |
| THEME | | | | | |

(6i) Others include the Church on the Hill, with its 500–year old frescos; the Church of the Dominican Monastery, (6ii) renown for its Renaissance carved altarpiece, baroque painted pulpit, Oriental carpets and 17th-century organ; (6i) and the Venetian House, (6iii) built in the 13th century.

| Others | include | | the Church on the Hill, with its 500–year old frescos; the Church of the Dominican Monastery; and the Venetian House |
|---|---|---|---|
| Subject | Finite '*(present)* | *include*' Predicator | Complement |
| MOOD | | RESIDUE | |
| Identified/ Value | Pr: Relational (identifying-intensive) | | Identifier / Token |
| experiential | RHEME | | |
| THEME | | | |

(6ii) renown for its Renaissance carved altarpiece, baroque painted pulpit, Oriental carpets and 17thcentury organ, (6iii) built in the 13th century - - dependent clauses, not part of Interpersonal and Textual analyses.

| *[which]* | *[is]* | renowned | for its Renaissance carved altarpiece, baroque painted pulpit, Oriental carpets and 17th-century organ |
|---|---|---|---|
| *[Carrier]* | *[Pr: Relational (attributive – intensive)]* | Attribute | Circ: Cause (reason) |

| *[which]* | *[was]* built | in the 13th century |
|---|---|---|
| *[Goal]* | Pr: Material | Circ: Location (time) |

(7i) Among the most striking attractions is the 210-feet high Clock Tower (Council Tower), (7ii) built in the 14th century, (7iii) where each day a different wooden figure emerges from the belfry on the stroke of midnight.

| Among the most striking attractions | is | | the 210-feet high Clock Tower (Council Tower) |
|---|---|---|---|
| Subject | Finite '(*present*) | *be*' Predicator | Complement |
| MOOD | | RESIDUE | |
| Identified / Value | Pr: Relational (identifying - intensive) | | Identifier / Token |
| experiential | RHEME | | |
| THEME | | | |

(7ii) built in the 14th century, (7iii) where each day a different wooden figure emerges from the belfry on the stroke of midnight - dependent clauses, not part of Interpersonal and Textual analyses.

| *[which]* | *[was]* built | in the 14th century |
|---|---|---|
| *[Goal]* | Pr: Material | Circ: Location (time) |

| where | each day | a different wooden figure | emerges | from the belfry | on the stroke of midnight |
|---|---|---|---|---|---|
| Circ: Location (place) | Circ: Location (time) | Actor | Pr: Material | Circ: Location (place) | Circ: Location (time) |

(8i) The tower was raised in the 13th and 14th centuries (8ii) when Sighisoara became a free town controlled by craft guilds, (8iii) each of which had to finance the construction of a bastion (8iv) and defend it during wartime.

| The tower | was | raised | in the 13th and 14th centuries |
|---|---|---|---|
| Subject | Finite | Predicator | Adjunct: circ |

| MOOD | | RESIDUE | |
|---|---|---|---|
| Goal | - | Pr: Material | Circ: Location (time) |
| experiential | | | |
| THEME | RHEME | | |

| when | Sighisoara | became | a free town controlled by craft guilds, |
|---|---|---|---|
| Circ: Location (time) | Carrier | Pr: Relational (attributive - intensive) | Attribute |

| each of which | had to finance | the construction of a bastion |
|---|---|---|
| Actor | Pr: Material | Goal |

| and | *[each of which]* | *[had]* defend | it | during wartime |
|---|---|---|---|---|
| - | *[Actor]* | Pr: Material | Goal | Circ: Extent (time) |

(9i) The fortification walls, (9ii) built in the 14th and 15th centuries, (9i) were up to 50-feet high (9iii) and featured 14 defense towers.

| The fortification walls, <<//built in the 14th and 15th centuries//>>, | were | | up to 50-feet high |
|---|---|---|---|
| Subject | Finite '*past* | *be*' Predicator | Complement |
| MOOD | | RESIDUE | |
| Carrier | Pr: Relational (attributive - intensive) | | Attribute |
| experiential | RHEME | | |
| THEME | | | |

| and | *[the fortification walls]* | featured | | 14 defense towers |
|---|---|---|---|---|
| (Conjunction) | *[Subject]* | Finite '(*past)* | *feature*' Predicator | Complement |
| | Mood | | Residue | |
| - | *[Carrier]* | Pr: Relational (attributive-possessive) | | Attribute |
| textual | experiential | | | RHEME |
| | T HEME | | | |

(9ii) built in the 14th and 15th centuries - dependent clause, not part of Interpersonal and Textual analyses.

| *[which]* | *[was]* built | in the 14th and 15th centuries |
|---|---|---|
| *[Goal]* | Pr: Material | Circ: Location (time) |

(10) Most of the old structure and 9 of the defense towers can still be admired today…

<table>
<tr><td>Most of the old structure and 9 of the defense towers</td><td>can</td><td>still</td><td>be admired</td><td>today</td></tr>
<tr><td>Subject</td><td>Finite</td><td>Adjunct: mood</td><td>Predicator</td><td>Adjunct: circ</td></tr>
<tr><td colspan="3">MOOD</td><td colspan="2">RESIDUE</td></tr>
<tr><td>Phenomenon</td><td>-</td><td>-</td><td>Pr: Mental (perception)</td><td>Circ: Location (time)</td></tr>
<tr><td>experiential</td><td colspan="4" rowspan="2">RHEME</td></tr>
<tr><td>THEME</td></tr>
</table>

## 1.2. Spanish set of institutional webpages

### 1.2.1. The Monastery of El Escorial in the institutional corpus

*Logical analysis*

| | |
|---|---|
| CL. SIMPLEX | (1) The Monastery of El Escorial was the first example of the architectural style [[which came to be known as Herrerian after its creator, Juan de Herrera]]. |
| CL. SIMPLEX | (2) It holds the designation of World Heritage site. |
| CL. SIMPLEX | (3) Philip II used this Royal Site for his family pantheon. |
| 1 | (4i) Construction work began in 1563 under Juan de Toledo, |
| +2 α | (4ii) and on his death was continued by Juan de Herrera, |
| =β | (4iii) who completed the building in 1584. |
| 1 | (5i) It is built in granite |
| +2 | (5ii) and divided into three areas. |
| CL. SIMPLEX | (6) The central area is the Kings' Courtyard. |
| α | (7i) There is a tower at each of its four corners |
| =β | (7ii) measuring 55 metres, |
| =γ | (7iii) each crowned by a metal sphere. |
| α | (8i) The building's premises include the Ministries, Casa de los Oficios (Artisans' Houses), Compaña (Company Quarters), Infantes and Reina rooms, |
| =β | (8ii) all connected via arches. |
| 1 | (9i) The church is laid out in the shape of a Greek cross |
| +2 | (9ii) and the funerary monuments to Charles V and Philip II can be seen in the main chapel. |
| CL. SIMPLEX | (10) The library is also of particular interest. |
| 1 | (11i) It is on the second floor of the west wing, |
| +2 | (11ii) and contains close to 45,000 documents from the 15th and 16th centuries. |

1 (12i) It was designated a Historic-Artistic site in 1971
+2 (12ii) and received the World Heritage designation in 1984.
1 (13i) The building was designed by Juan de Herrera
+2 (13ii) and gave rise to an architectural style [[known as Herrerian]].
α (14i) It is a large construction,
xβ (14ii) as can be seen from its 15 cloisters, 13 oratories, 86 staircases, 88 fountains, more than 1,600 paintings, 9 towers and 73 sculptures.

## *Experiential, interpersonal and textual analyses*

(1) The Monastery of El Escorial was the first example of the architectural style [[which came to be known as Herrerian after its creator, Juan de Herrera]].

| The Monastery of El Escorial | was | | the first example of the architectural style [[which came to be known as Herrerian after its creator, Juan de Herrera]] |
|---|---|---|---|
| Subject | Finite '(*past*) | *be'* Predicator | Complement |
| MOOD | | RESIDUE | |
| Identified / Token | Pr: Relational (identifying - intensive) | | Identifier / Value |
| experiential | RHEME | | |
| THEME | | | |

(2) It holds the designation of World Heritage site.

| It | holds | | the designation of World Heritage site |
|---|---|---|---|
| Subject | Finite '(*present*) | *hold*' Predicator | Complement |
| MOOD | | RESIDUE | |
| Identified/ Token: possessor | Pr: Relational (identifying-possessive) | | Identifier/ Value: possessed |
| experiential | RHEME | | |
| THEME | | | |

(3) Philip II used this Royal Site for his family pantheon.

| Philip II | used | | this Royal Site | for his family pantheon. |
|---|---|---|---|---|
| Subject | Finite '(*past*) | *use*' Predicator | Complement | Adjunct: circ |
| MOOD | | RESIDUE | | |
| Actor | Pr: Material | | Goal | Circ: Cause (purpose) |
| experiential | RHEME | | | |
| THEME | | | | |

(4i) Construction work began in 1563 under Juan de Toledo, (4ii) and on his death was continued by Juan de Herrera, (4iii) who completed the building in 1584.

| Construction work | began | | in 1563 | under Juan de Toledo |
|---|---|---|---|---|
| Subject | Finite'(*past*) | *began*' Predicator | Adjunct: circ | Adjunct: circ |
| MOOD | | RESIDUE | | |
| Goal | - | Pr: Material | Circ: Location (time) | Actor |
| experiential | RHEME | | | |
| THEME | | | | |

| and | on his death | *[construction work]* | was | continued | by Juan de Herrera |
|---|---|---|---|---|---|
| (Conjunction) | Adjunct: circ | *[Subject]* | Finite | Predicator | Adjunct: circ |
| | RESIDUE | MOOD | | | |
| - | Circ: Location (time) | *[Goal]* | - | Pr: Material | Actor |
| textual | experiential | RHEME | | | |
| THEME | | | | | |

(4iii) who completed the building in 1584 - dependent clause, not part of Interpersonal and Textual analyses.

| who | completed | the building | in 1584 |
|---|---|---|---|
| Actor | Pr: Material | Goal | Circ: Location (time) |

(5i) It is built in granite (5ii) and divided into three areas.

| It | is | built | in granite |
|---|---|---|---|
| Subject | Finite | Predicator | Adjunct: circ |
| MOOD | | RESIDUE | |
| Goal | | Pr: Material | Circ: Manner (means) |
| experiential | RHEME | | |
| THEME | | | |

<table>
<tr><td>and</td><td>[it]</td><td>[is]</td><td>Divided</td><td>into three areas</td></tr>
<tr><td rowspan="2">(Conjunction)</td><td>[Subject]</td><td>[Finite]</td><td>Predicator</td><td>Adjunct: circ</td></tr>
<tr><td colspan="2">[MOOD]</td><td colspan="2">RESIDUE</td></tr>
<tr><td>-</td><td>[Goal]</td><td>-</td><td>Pr: Material</td><td>Circ: Manner (quality)</td></tr>
<tr><td>textual</td><td colspan="3">experiential</td><td rowspan="2">RHEME</td></tr>
<tr><td colspan="4">THEME</td></tr>
</table>

(6) The central area is the Kings' Courtyard.

<table>
<tr><td>The central area</td><td colspan="2">is</td><td>the Kings' Courtyard</td></tr>
<tr><td>Subject</td><td>Finite '(present)</td><td>be' Predicator</td><td>Complement</td></tr>
<tr><td colspan="2">MOOD</td><td colspan="2">RESIDUE</td></tr>
<tr><td>Identified / Value</td><td colspan="2">Pr: Relational (identifying - intensive)</td><td>Identifier / Token</td></tr>
<tr><td>experiential</td><td colspan="2" rowspan="2">RHEME</td><td rowspan="2"></td></tr>
<tr><td>THEME</td></tr>
</table>

(7i) There is a tower at each of its four corners (7ii) measuring 55 metres, (7iii) each crowned by a metal sphere.

<table>
<tr><td>There</td><td colspan="2">is</td><td>a tower</td><td>at each of its four corners</td></tr>
<tr><td>Subject</td><td>Finite '(present)</td><td>be' Predicator</td><td>Complement</td><td>Adjunct: circ</td></tr>
<tr><td colspan="2">MOOD</td><td colspan="3">RESIDUE</td></tr>
<tr><td>-</td><td colspan="2">Pr: Existential</td><td>Existent</td><td>Circ: Location (space)</td></tr>
<tr><td colspan="3">experiential</td><td colspan="2" rowspan="2">RHEME</td></tr>
<tr><td colspan="3">THEME</td></tr>
</table>

(7ii) measuring 55 metres, (7iii) each crowned by a metal sphere - dependent clause, not part of Interpersonal and Textual analyses.

| **elided which* | **elided is* measuring | 55 metres |
|---|---|---|
| *Carrier* | Pr: Relational (attributive-circumstantial) | Attribute |

| each | **elided is* crowned | by a metal sphere |
|---|---|---|
| Identified/ Value | Pr: Relational (identifying-circumstantial) | Identifier/ Token |

(8i) The building's premises include the Ministries, Casa de los Oficios (Artisans' Houses), Compaña (Company Quarters), Infantes and Reina rooms, (8ii) all connected via arches.

| The building's premises | include | | the Ministries, Casa de los Oficios (Artisans' Houses), Compaña (Company Quarters), Infantes and Reina rooms, |
|---|---|---|---|
| Subject | '(*present*) Finite | *include*' Predicator | Complement |
| MOOD | | RESIDUE | |
| Identified/ Token: possessor | Pr: Relational Identifier/ Value: possessed | | (identifying-possessive) |
| experiential | RHEME | | |
| THEME | | | |

(8ii) all connected via arches - dependent clause, not part of Interpersonal and Textual analyses.

| all | **elided are* connected | via arches |
|---|---|---|
| Identified / Value | Pr: Relational (identifying-circumstantial | Identifier / Token |

(9i) The church is laid out in the shape of a Greek cross (9ii) and the funerary monuments to Charles V and Philip II can be seen in the main chapel.

| The church | is | laid out | in the shape of a Greek cross |
|---|---|---|---|
| Subject | Finite | Predicator | Adjunct: circ |
| MOOD | | RESIDUE | |
| Identified / Value | - | Pr: Relational (identifying-circumstantial) | Identifier / Token |
| experiential | RHEME | | |
| THEME | | | |

| and | the funerary monuments to Charles V and Philip II | can | be seen | in the main chapel |
|---|---|---|---|---|
| (Conjunction) | Subject | Finite | Predicator | Adjunct: circ |
| | MOOD | | RESIDUE | |
| - | Phenomenon | - | Pr: Mental (perception) | Circ: Location (place) |
| textual | experiential | RHEME | | |
| THEME | | | | |

(10) The library is also of particular interest.

| The library | is | | also | of particular interest |
|---|---|---|---|---|
| Subject | Finite '(*present*) | *be*' Predicator | Adjunct: conjunctive | Complement |
| MOOD | | RESIDUE | | |
| Carrier | Pr: Relational (attributive - intensive) | | - | Attribute |
| experiential | | | | |
| THEME | | | RHEME | |

(11i) It is on the second floor of the west wing, (11ii) and contains close to 45,000 documents from the 15th and 16th centuries.

| It | is | | on the second floor of the west wing |
|---|---|---|---|
| Subject | Finite '(*present*) | *be*' Predicator | Adjunct: circ |
| MOOD | | RESIDUE | |
| Identified/ Value | Pr: Relational (identifying - circumstantial) | | Identifier/ Token |
| experiential | RHEME | | |
| THEME | | | |

| and | *[it]* | Contains | | close to 45,000 documents from the 15th and 16th centuries |
|---|---|---|---|---|
| (Conjunction) | *[Subject]* | Finite '(*present*) | Predicator *contain*' | Complement |
| | MOOD | | RESIDUE | |
| - | *[Identified/ Token: possessor]* | Pr: Relational (identifying - possessive) | | Identifier/ Value: possessed |
| textual | experiential | | | RHEME |
| THEME | | | | |

(12i) It was designated a Historic-Artistic site in 1971 (12ii) and received the World Heritage designation in 1984.

| It | was | designated | a Historic-Artistic site | in 1971 |
|---|---|---|---|---|
| Subject | Finite | Predicator | Complement | Adjunct: circ |
| MOOD | | RESIDUE | | |
| Carrier | - | Pr: Causative | Attribute | Circ: Location (time) |
| experiential | RHEME | | | |
| THEME | | | | |

| and | *[it]* | received | | the World Heritage designation | in 1984 |
|---|---|---|---|---|---|
| (Conjunction) | *[Subject]* | '(*past*) Finite | *receive*' Predicator | Complement | Adjunct: circ |
| | MOOD | | RESIDUE | | |
| - | *[Beneficiary]* | Pr: Material | | Goal | Circ: Location (time) |
| textual | experiential | | | RHEME | |
| THEME | | | | | |

(13i) The building was designed by Juan de Herrera (13ii) and gave rise to an architectural style known as Herrerian.

| The building | was | designed | by Juan de Herrera |
|---|---|---|---|
| Subject | Finite | Predicator | Adjunct: circ |
| MOOD | | RESIDUE | |
| Goal | - | Pr: Material | Actor |
| experiential | RHEME | | |
| THEME | | | |

| and | *[the building]* | gave rise to | | an architectural style known as Herrerian |
|---|---|---|---|---|
| (Conjunction) | *[Subject]* | Finite '(*past*) | *give rise to*' Predicator | Complement |
| | MOOD | | RESIDUE | |
| - | *[Actor]* | Pr: Material | | Goal |
| textual | experiential | | | RHEME |
| THEME | | | | |

(14i) It is a large construction, (14ii) as can be seen from its 15 cloisters, 13 oratories, 86 staircases, 88 fountains, more than 1,600 paintings, 9 towers and 73 sculptures.

| It | is | | a large construction, |
|---|---|---|---|
| Subject | Finite '(*present*) | *be*' Predicator | Complement |
| MOOD | | RESIDUE | |
| Carrier | Pr: Relational (attributive - intensive) | | Attribute |
| experiential | | | |
| THEME | RHEME | | |

(14ii) as can be seen from its 15 cloisters, 13 oratories, 86 staircases, 88 fountains, more than 1,600 paintings, 9 towers and 73 sculptures - dependent clause, not part of Interpersonal and Textual analyses.

| as | can be seen | from its 15 cloisters, 13 oratories, 86 staircases, 88 fountains, more than 1,600 paintings, 9 towers and 73 sculptures |
|---|---|---|
| - | Pr: Mental (perception) | Phenomenon |

## 1.2.2. The Alhambra in the institutional corpus

### *Logical analysis*

CL. SIMPLEX (1) The Alhambra is a beautiful complex of buildings and gardens.
α (2i) Its leafy tree-lined walkways provide pleasant shade and coolness,
=β (2ii) enhanced by the abundance of water [[that flows in its streams]].
CL. SIMPLEX (3) It was the largest political and aristocratic centre of the Moslem West.
α (4i) The Palace premises are made up of beautiful rectangular courtyards and numerous fountains, as well as the Nasrid buildings
=β (4ii) that served as living quarters for the monarchs and their servants.
CL. SIMPLEX (5) The oldest building is the Alcazaba (citadel).
α (6i) One of the most important structures is the La Vela tower,
=β (6ii) which offers one of the loveliest views of the Alhambra.
CL. SIMPLEX (7) The courtyard of the Lions with its fountains is one of the most beautiful in the compound.

## *Experiential, interpersonal and textual analyses*

(1) The Alhambra is a beautiful complex of buildings and gardens.

| The Alhambra | is | | a beautiful complex of buildings and gardens |
|---|---|---|---|
| Subject | Finite '(*present*) | *be*' Predicator | Complement |
| MOOD | | RESIDUE | |
| Carrier | Pr: Relational ibutive - (attr intensive) | | Attribute |
| experiential | RHEME | | |
| THEME | | | |

(2i) Its leafy tree-lined walkways provide pleasant shade and coolness, (2ii) enhanced by the abundance of water [[that flows in its streams]].

| Its leafy tree-lined walkways | provide | | pleasant shade and coolness |
|---|---|---|---|
| Subject | Finite '(*present*) | *provide*' Predicator | Complement |
| MOOD | | RESIDUE | |
| Identified / Token: possessor | Pr: Relational (identifying - possessive) | | Identifier / Value: possessed |
| experiential | RHEME | | |
| THEME | | | |

(2ii) enhanced by the abundance of water [[that flows in its streams]] - dependent clause, not part of Interpersonal and Textual analyses.

| *[which]* | *[is]* enhanced | by the abundance of water |
|---|---|---|
| *[Goal]* | Pr: Material | Actor |

(3) It was the largest political and aristocratic centre of the Moslem West.

| It | was | | the largest political and aristocratic centre of the Moslem West |
|---|---|---|---|
| Subject | Finite '(*past*) | *be*' Predicator | Complement |
| MOOD | | RESIDUE | |
| Identified / Token | Pr: Relational (identifying - intensive) | | Identifier / Value |
| experiential | RHEME | | |
| THEME | | | |

(4i) The Palace premises are made up of beautiful rectangular courtyards and numerous fountains, as well as the Nasrid buildings (4ii) that served as living quarters for the monarchs and their servants.

| The Palace premises | are | made up | of beautiful rectangular courtyards and numerous fountains, as well as the Nasrid buildings |
|---|---|---|---|
| Subject | Finite | Predicator | Complement |
| MOOD | | RESIDUE | |
| Identified / Value | | Pr: Relational (identifying - possessive) | Identifier / Token |
| experiential | | | |
| THEME | RHEME | | |

(4ii) that served as living quarters for the monarchs and their servants - dependent clause, not part of Interpersonal and Textual analyses.

| that | served as | living quarters | for the monarchs and their servants |
|---|---|---|---|
| Identified/ Token | Pr: Relational (identifying-intensive) | Identifier/ Value | Assigner |

(5) The oldest building is the Alcazaba (citadel).

| The oldest building | is | | the Alcazaba (citadel) |
|---|---|---|---|
| Subject | Finite '(*present*) | *be*' Predicator | Complement |
| MOOD | | RESIDUE | |
| Identified / Value | Pr: Relational (identifying - intensive) | | Identifier / Token |
| experiential | RHEME | | |
| THEME | | | |

(6i) One of the most important structures is the La Vela tower, (6ii) which offers one of the loveliest views of the Alhambra.

| One of the most important structures | is | | the La Vela tower |
|---|---|---|---|
| Subject | Finite '(*present*) | *be*' Predicator | Complement |
| MOOD | | RESIDUE | |
| Identified / Value | Pr: Relational (identifying - intensive) | | Identifier / Token |
| experiential | RHEME | | |
| THEME | | | |

(6ii) which offers one of the loveliest views of the Alhambra - dependent clause, not part of Interpersonal and Textual analyses.

| which | offers | one of the loveliest views of the Alhambra |
|---|---|---|
| Identified/ Token: possessor | Pr: Relational (identifying-possessive) | Identifier/ Value: possessed |

(7) The courtyard of the Lions with its fountains is one of the most beautiful in the compound.

| The courtyard of the Lions with its fountains | is | | one of the most beautiful in the compound |
|---|---|---|---|
| Subject | Finite '(*present*) | *be*' Predicator | Complement |
| MOOD | | RESIDUE | |
| Identified / Token | Pr: Relational (identifying - intensive) | | Identifier / Value |
| experiential | RHEME | | |
| THEME | | | |

## 1.2.3. Santiago de Compostela in the institutional corpus

### *Logical analysis*

CL. SIMPLEX (1) Discover Santiago de Compostela, the capital of the Region of Galicia.
α (2i) Millions of people from all over the world come to this city every year,
=β (2ii) many of them reaching the end of the Way of Saint James pilgrimage route.
CL. SIMPLEX (3) Its historic centre has been designated a World Heritage Site by the UNESCO.
CL. SIMPLEX (4) This is not the only reason [[to come]], however.
CL. SIMPLEX (5) Here you can discover the main reasons [[to visit Santiago]].
CL. SIMPLEX (6) see more

### *Experiential, interpersonal and textual analyses*

(1) Discover Santiago de Compostela, the capital of the Region of Galicia.

| Discover | Santiago de Compostela, the capital of the Region of Galicia |
|---|---|
| Predicator | Complement |
| RESIDUE | |
| Pr: Material | Goal |
| experiential | RHEME |
| THEME | |

(2i) Millions of people from all over the world come to this city every year, (2ii) many of them reaching the end of the Way of Saint James pilgrimage route.

| Millions of people from all over the world | come | | to this city | every year |
|---|---|---|---|---|
| Subject | Finite '(*present*) | Predicator *come*' | Adjunct: circ | Adjunct: circ |
| MOOD | | RESIDUE | | |
| Actor | Pr: Material | | Circ: Location (place) | Circ: Location (time) |
| experiential | RHEME | | | |
| THEME | | | | |

(2ii) many of them reaching the end of the Way of Saint James pilgrimage route - dependent clause, not part of Interpersonal and Textual analyses.

| many of them | **elided are* reaching | the end of the Way of Saint James pilgrimage route |
|---|---|---|
| Actor | Pr: Material | Goal |

(3) Its historic centre has been designated a World Heritage Site by the UNESCO.

| Its historic centre | has | been designated | a World Heritage Site | by the UNESCO |
|---|---|---|---|---|
| Subject | Finite | Predicator | Complement | Adjunct: circ |
| MOOD | | RESIDUE | | |
| Carrier | - | Pr: Causative | Attribute | Attributor |
| experiential | RHEME | | | |
| THEME | | | | |

(4) This is not the only reason [[to come]], however.

| This | is not | | the only reason [[to come]] | however |
|---|---|---|---|---|
| Subject | Finite: neg'(*present*) | Predicator *be*' | Complement | Adjunct: conjunctive |
| MOOD | | RESIDUE | | |
| Identified / Token | Pr: Relational (identifying - intensive) | | Identifier / Value | - |
| experiential | RHEME | | | |
| THEME | | | | |

(5) Here you can discover the main reasons [[to visit Santiago]].

<table>
<tr><td>Here</td><td>you</td><td>can</td><td>discover</td><td>the main reasons [[to visit Santiago]]</td></tr>
<tr><td>Adjunct: circ</td><td>Subject</td><td>Finite</td><td>Predicator</td><td>Complement</td></tr>
<tr><td>RESIDUE</td><td colspan="2">MOOD</td><td colspan="2"></td></tr>
<tr><td>Circ: Location (place)</td><td>Senser</td><td>-</td><td>Pr: Mental (cognition)</td><td>Phenomenon</td></tr>
<tr><td>experiential</td><td colspan="4"></td></tr>
<tr><td>THEME</td><td colspan="2"></td><td colspan="2">RHEME</td></tr>
</table>

(6) see more

<table>
<tr><td>see</td><td>more</td></tr>
<tr><td>Predicator</td><td>Complement</td></tr>
<tr><td colspan="2">RESIDUE</td></tr>
<tr><td>Pr: Mental (perception)</td><td>Phenomenon</td></tr>
<tr><td>experiential</td><td rowspan="2">RHEME</td></tr>
<tr><td>THEME</td></tr>
</table>

## 1.3. British set of institutional webpages

### 1.3.1. Canterbury Cathedral in the institutional corpus

*Logical analysis*

1 (1i) Canterbury has been a key location for the Church of England for nearly five centuries
+2 (1ii) and you'll find many important religious buildings and monuments in the area.
1 (2i) Canterbury Cathedral was founded in AD597
=2 (2ii) (that's over 1,400 years ago!)
+3 (2iii) and is the Mother Church of the Anglican Communion.
α (3i) It has a perpendicular nave, 12th-century Gothic choir, stunning stained glass windows
<=β> (3ii) that fill the church with colour
α (3i) and a Romanesque crypt.
CL. SIMPLEX (4) The Cathedral is the site of the Archbishop Thomas Becket's martyrdom in AD1170.
CL. SIMPLEX (5) His shrine became one of the most visited in the Middle Ages by pilgrims [[travelling the Pilgrims' Way from London and Winchester]].
α (6i) Another important church is the Church of St Martin just outside the city's medieval wall,
=β (6ii) half of which survives today.

=β (7i) Probably built as a Roman church in the 4th century,
α (7ii) St Martin is the oldest church in England [[that's still in use as a parish church]].
CL. SIMPLEX (8) Many visitors miss St Augustine's Abbey because of its location just outside the city centre.
CL. SIMPLEX (9) The ruins of this once great abbey are an impressive sight.
α (10i) Another [[not to miss]] is Christ Church Cathedral, a breathtaking mixture of Romanesque and Perpendicular Gothic,
=β (10ii) where Archbishop Thomas Becket was murdered in 1170.
CL. SIMPLEX (11) step back in time with this audiovisual experience of the sights, sounds and smells of the middle ages in this stunning reconstruction of 14th century England.
α (12i) Canterbury West Gate Towers - One of England's finest medieval gates
=β (12ii) built as part of the city defences in the 1380s.
1 (13i) See the exhibit [[featuring Canterbury's war history]]
+2 (13ii) and visit the prison cells inside the towers.
CL. SIMPLEX (14) Canterbury Roman Museum - Located underground at the levels of Roman Canterbury.
CL. SIMPLEX (15) Features a mix of excavated real objects and buildings and lifelike reconstructions including computer-generated images.

## *Experiential, interpersonal and textual analyses*

(1i) Canterbury has been a key location for the Church of England for nearly five centuries (1ii) and you'll find many important religious buildings and monuments in the area.

| Canterbury | has | been | a key location | for the Church of England | for nearly five centuries |
|---|---|---|---|---|---|
| Subject | Finite | Predicator | Complement | Adjunct: circ | Adjunct: circ |
| MOOD | | RESIDUE | | | |
| Carrier | - | Pr: Relational (attributive - intensive) | Attribute | Attributor | Circ: Extent (time) |
| experiential | RHEME | | | | |
| THEME | | | | | |

| and | you | 'll | find | many important religious buildings and monuments | in the area |
|---|---|---|---|---|---|
| (Conjunction) | Subject | Finite: mod | Predicator | Complement | Adjunct: circ |
| | MOOD | | RESIDUE | | |
| - | Actor | - | Pr: Material | Goal | Circ: Location (place) |
| textual | experiential | RHEME | | | |
| THEME | | | | | |

(2i) Canterbury Cathedral was founded in AD597 (2ii) (that's over 1,400 years ago!) (2iii) and is the Mother Church of the Anglican Communion.

| Canterbury Cathedral | was | founded | in AD597 |
|---|---|---|---|
| Subject | Finite | Predicator | Adjunct: circ |
| MOOD | | RESIDUE | |
| Goal | - | Pr: Material | Circ: Location (time) |
| experiential | RHEME | | |
| THEME | | | |

| that | 's | | over 1,400 years ago |
|---|---|---|---|
| Subject | Finite '(*present*) | *be*' Predicator | Adjunct: circ |
| MOOD | | RESIDUE | |
| Identified / Token | Pr: Relational (identifying – circumstantial) | | Identifier / Value |
| experiential | RHEME | | |
| THEME | | | |

| and | *[Canterbury Cathedral]* | is | | the Mother Church of the Anglican Communion |
|---|---|---|---|---|
| (Conjunction) | *[Subject]* | Finite '(*present*) | *be*' Predicator | Complement |
| | MOOD | | | RESIDUE |
| - | *[Identified / Token]* | Pr: Relational (identifying – intensive) | | Identifier / Value |
| textual | experiential | | | RHEME |
| | THEME | | | |

(3i) It has a perpendicular nave, 12th-century Gothic choir, stunning stained glass windows (3ii) that fill the church with colour (3i) and a Romanesque crypt.

| It | has | | a perpendicular nave, 12th-century Gothic choir, stunning stained glass windows [[that fill the church with colour]] and a Romanesque crypt |
|---|---|---|---|
| Subject | Finite '(*present*) | Predicator *have*' | Complement |
| | MOOD | | RESIDUE |
| Carrier: possessor | Pr: Relational (attributive-possessive) | | Attribute: possessed |
| experiential | | | RHEME |
| THEME | | | |

(3ii) that fill the church with colour – dependent clause, not part of Interpersonal and Textual analyses.

| that | fill | the church | with colour |
|---|---|---|---|
| Actor | Pr: Material | Goal | Circ: Manner (means) |

(4) The Cathedral is the site of the Archbishop Thomas Becket's martyrdom in AD1170.

| The Cathedral | is | | the site of the Archbishop Thomas Becket's martyrdom in AD1170 |
|---|---|---|---|
| Subject | Finite '(*present*) | *be*' Predicator | Complement |
| MOOD | | RESIDUE | |
| Identified / Token | Pr: Relational (identifying - intensive) | | Identifier / Value |
| experiential | RHEME | | |
| THEME | | | |

(5) His shrine became one of the most visited in the Middle Ages by pilgrims [[travelling the Pilgrims' Way from London and Winchester]].

| His shrine | became | | one of the most visited in the Middle Ages by pilgrims [[travelling the Pilgrims' Way from London and Winchester]] |
|---|---|---|---|
| Subject | Finite '(*past*) | Predicator *become*' | Complement |
| MOOD | | RESIDUE | |
| Identified/ Token | Pr: Relational (identifying-intensive) | | Identifier/ Value |
| experiential | RHEME | | |
| THEME | | | |

(6i) Another important church is the Church of St Martin just outside the city's medieval wall, (6ii) half of which survives today.

| Another important church | is | | the Church of St Martin just outside the city's medieval wall |
|---|---|---|---|
| Subject | Finite '(*present*) | *be*' Predicator | Complement |
| MOOD | | RESIDUE | |
| Identified / Value | Pr: Relational (identifying - intensive) | | Identifier / Token |
| experiential | RHEME | | |
| THEME | | | |

(6ii) half of which survives today – dependent clause, not part of Interpersonal and Textual analyses.

| half of which | survives | today |
|---|---|---|
| Carrier | Pr: Relational (attributivecircumstantial) | Attribute |

(7i) Probably built as a Roman church in the 4th century, (7ii) St Martin is the oldest church in England [[that's still in use as a parish church]].

| Probably built as a Roman church in the 4th century, | St Martin | is | | the oldest church [[that's still in use as a parish church]] |
|---|---|---|---|---|
| | Subject | Finite '(*present*) | *be*' Predicator | Complement |
| | MOOD | | RESIDUE | |
| | Identified / Token | Pr: Relational (identifying - intensive) | | Identifier / Value |
| experiential | | RHEME | | |
| THEME | | | | |

(8) Many visitors miss St Augustine's Abbey because of its location just outside the city centre.

| Many visitors | miss | | St Augustine's Abbey | because of its location just outside the city centre |
|---|---|---|---|---|
| Subject | Finite '(*present*) | *miss*' Predicator | Complement | Adjunct: circ |
| MOOD | | RESIDUE | | |
| Actor | Pr: Material | | Goal | Circ: Cause (reason) |
| experiential | RHEME | | | |
| THEME | | | | |

(9) The ruins of this once great abbey are an impressive sight.

| The ruins of this once great abbey | are | | an impressive sight |
|---|---|---|---|
| Subject | Finite '(*present*) | *be*' Predicator | Complement |
| MOOD | | RESIDUE | |
| Carrier | Pr: Relational (attributive - intensive) | | Attribute |
| experiential | RHEME | | |
| THEME | | | |

(10i) Another [[not to miss]] is Christ Church Cathedral, a breathtaking mixture of Romanesque and Perpendicular Gothic, (10ii) where Archbishop Thomas Becket was murdered in 1170.

| Another [[not to miss]] | is | | Christ Church Cathedral, a breathtaking mixture of Romanesque and Perpendicular Gothic |
|---|---|---|---|
| Subject | Finite '(*present*) | *be*' Predicator | Complement |
| MOOD | | RESIDUE | |
| Identified / Value | Pr: Relational (identifying - intensive) | | Identifier / Token |
| experiential | RHEME | | |
| THEME | | | |

(10ii) where Archbishop Thomas Becket was murdered in 1170 – dependent clause, not part of Interpersonal and Textual analyses.

| where | Archbishop Thomas Becket | was murdered | in 1170 |
|---|---|---|---|
| Circ: Location (place) | Goal | Pr: Material | Circ: Location (time) |

(11) step back in time with this audiovisual experience of the sights, sounds and smells of the middle ages in this stunning reconstruction of 14th century England.

| step back | in time | with this audiovisual experience of the sights, sounds and smells of the middle ages | in this stunning reconstruction of 14th century England |
|---|---|---|---|
| Predicator | Adjunct: circ | Adjunct: circ | Adjunct: circ |
| RESIDUE | | | |
| Pr: Material | Circ: Location (place) | Circ: Manner (means) | Circ: Location (place) |
| experiential | RHEME | | |
| THEME | | | |

(12i) Canterbury West Gate Towers - One of England's finest medieval gates (12ii) built as part of the city defences in the 1380s.

| Canterbury West Gate Towers | - [**meaning are*] | | One of England's finest medieval gates |
|---|---|---|---|
| Subject | Finite '(*present*) | *be*' Predicator | Complement |
| MOOD | | RESIDUE | |
| Identified/ Token | *Pr: Relational (identifying-intensive)* | | Identifier/ Value |
| experiential | RHEME | | |
| THEME | | | |

(12ii) built as part of the city defences in the 1380s – dependent clause, not part of Interpersonal and Textual analyses.

| *[which]* | *[is]* built | as part of the city defences in the 1380s |
|---|---|---|
| *[Goal]* | Pr: Material | Circ: Role (guise) |

(13i) See the exhibit [[featuring Canterbury's war history]] (13ii) and visit the prison cells inside the towers.

| See | the exhibit [[featuring Canterbury's war history]] |
|---|---|
| Predicator | Complement |
| RESIDUE | |
| Pr: Mental (perception) | Phenomenon |
| experiential | RHEME |
| THEME | |

| and | visit | the prison cells inside the towers |
|---|---|---|
| (Conjunction) | Predicator | Complement |
| | RESIDUE | |
| - | Pr: Material | Goal |
| textual | experiential | RHEME |
| THEME | | |

(14) Canterbury Roman Museum - Located underground at the levels of Roman Canterbury.

| Canterbury Roman Museum | *[is]* | Located | underground at the levels of Roman Canterbury |
|---|---|---|---|
| Subject | *[Finite]* | Predicator | Complement |
| MOOD | | RESIDUE | |
| Identified/ Value | - | Pr: Relational (identifying-circumstantial) | Identifier/ Token |
| experiential | RHEME | | |
| THEME | | | |

(15) Features a mix of excavated real objects and buildings and lifelike reconstructions including computergenerated images.

<table>
<tr><td>[Canterbury Roman Museum]</td><td colspan="2">Features</td><td>a mix of excavated real objects and buildings and lifelike reconstructions including computer-generated images</td></tr>
<tr><td>[Subject]</td><td>Finite '(present)</td><td>Predicator feature'</td><td>Complement</td></tr>
<tr><td colspan="2">MOOD</td><td colspan="2">RESIDUE</td></tr>
<tr><td>[Carrier: possessor]</td><td colspan="2">Pr: Relational (attributive-possessive)</td><td>Attribute: possessed</td></tr>
<tr><td>experiential</td><td colspan="3" rowspan="2">RHEME</td></tr>
<tr><td>THEME</td></tr>
</table>

## 1.3.2. The Tower of London in the institutional corpus

### *Logical analysis*

=β (1i) Spanning over 900 years of British history,<br>
α α (1ii) the Tower of London was built by William the Conqueror<br>
xβ 1 (1iii) to protect London<br>
+2 (1iv) and assert his power.<br>
=β (2i) Fortress, palace, prison, arsenal and garrison,<br>
α (2ii) it is one of the most famous fortified buidings in the world.<br>
CL. SIMPLEX (3) In houses the Crown Jewels, armouries, Yeoman Warders and ravens.<br>
CL. SIMPLEX (4) The Tower of London has a colourful history [[dating back to the 11th century]].<br>
1 (5i) Romans once occupied it,<br>
+2 (5ii) it's the site of Europe's first fortress,<br>
+3 (5iii) it has been a royal palace, a prison, an execution site, an arsenal, a mint, a keep for wild animals and jewel house -<br>
+4 (5iv) and you can see artefacts from every part of this remarkable history.<br>
1 (6i) During a visit to the Tower you can see Britain's most precious treasure - The Crown Jewels,<br>
+2 (6ii) stand on the execution site of 3 English queens<br>
+3 (6iii) and explore the legends of this world-famous landmark.<br>
CL. SIMPLEX (7) Look out for the famous black ravens in the grounds of the Tower.<br>
1 (8i) These magnificent birds have been kept here since the 1600s,<br>
+2 α (8ii) and legend has it<br>
"β α (8iii) the Tower will fall, along with the Kingdom,<br>
xβ (8iv) if the ravens ever leave the site.<br>
α (9i) You'll also see the Beefeaters (or Yeoman Warders)<br>
=β (9ii) who have been guarding the tower for over 600 years.<br>
CL. SIMPLEX (10) A visit to the Tower of London offers a millennium of British history in one day.<br>
1 (11i) This exceptional heritage site is a great day out<br>
+2 (11ii) and holds daily exhibitions and events throughout the year.<br>
CL. SIMPLEX (12) The Ceremony of the Keys is the traditional locking-up of the Tower of London.<br>
CL. SIMPLEX (13) It's happened every night without fail for at least 700 years.

CL. SIMPLEX (14) Don't miss your chance [[to watch this fascinating tradition]] on your trip to Britain.
1 α (15i) Every night, at exactly 21:53, the Chief Yeoman Warder of the Tower emerges from the Byward Tower
xβ 1 (15ii) wearing his long red coat and Tudor bonnet
+2 (15iii) and carrying a candle lantern and the Queen's Keys.
1 (16i) The Chief Yeoman Warder then meets his military escort (members of the Tower of London Guard),
+2 (16ii) and together they lock the main gates of the Tower.
xβ (17i) As they pass,
α (17ii) all of the Tower's guards salute the Keys.
1 (18i) The Chief Yeoman Warder and his escort then retrace their steps,
+2 (18ii) and lock the great oak gates of the Middle and Byward Towers on the way.
CL. SIMPLEX (19) The only time [[the ceremony has been interrupted in the last 700 years]] was during the Second World War.
α (20i) During an air raid, bombs fell onto the old Victorian guardroom
xβ (20ii) as the Chief Yeoman Warder and his escort were coming through the Bloody Archway.
1 (21i) The shock and the noise of the bombs sent the group flying to the floor,
+2 (21ii) but they stood up,
+3 (21iii) dusted themselves down,
+4 (21iv) and carried on.
1 (22i) Tickets to the Ceremony of the Keys are free,
+2 (22ii) but due the popularity of the ceremony, you must apply in writing at least 2 months in advance.
CL. SIMPLEX (23) For details [[on how to apply for tickets]], visit the Tower of London - Ceremony of the Keys.

## *Experiential, interpersonal and textual analyses*

(1i) Spanning over 900 years of British history, (1ii) the Tower of London was built by William the Conqueror (1iii) to protect London (1iv) and assert his power.

<table>
<tr><td rowspan="4">//Spanning over 900 years of British history//</td><td>the Tower of London</td><td>was</td><td>built</td><td>by William the Conqueror</td></tr>
<tr><td>Subject</td><td>Finite</td><td>Predicator</td><td>Adjunct: circ</td></tr>
<tr><td colspan="2">MOOD</td><td colspan="2">RESIDUE</td></tr>
<tr><td>Goal</td><td>-</td><td>Pr: Material</td><td>Actor</td></tr>
<tr><td colspan="2">experiential</td><td colspan="3" rowspan="2">RHEME</td></tr>
<tr><td colspan="2">THEME</td></tr>
</table>

(1iii) *to protect London,* (1iv) *and assert his power* – dependent clauses, not part of Interpersonal and Textual analyses.

| **implied the tower of London/ William* (ambiguous) | to protect | London |
|---|---|---|
| *Actor* | Pr: Material | Goal |

| and | **implied the tower of London/ William* (ambiguous) | assert | his power |
|---|---|---|---|
| - | *Identified / Token* | Pr: Relational (identifying -intensive) | Identifier / Value |

(2i) Fortress, palace, prison, arsenal and garrison, (2ii) it is one of the most famous fortified buildings in the world.

<table>
<tr><td rowspan="4">Fortress, palace, prison, arsenal and garrison</td><td>it</td><td colspan="2">is</td><td>one of the most famous fortified buildings in the world</td></tr>
<tr><td>Subject</td><td>Finite ‘(present)</td><td>be’ Predicator</td><td>Complement</td></tr>
<tr><td colspan="2">MOOD</td><td colspan="2">RESIDUE</td></tr>
<tr><td>Identified/ Token</td><td colspan="2">Pr: Relational (identifying -intensive)</td><td>Identifier/ Value</td></tr>
<tr><td colspan="2">experiential</td><td colspan="3" rowspan="2">RHEME</td></tr>
<tr><td colspan="2">THEME</td></tr>
</table>

(3) It houses the Crown Jewels, armouries, Yeoman Warders and ravens.

<table>
<tr><td>It</td><td colspan="2">houses</td><td>the Crown Jewels, armouries, Yeoman Warders and ravens</td></tr>
<tr><td>Subject</td><td>Finite ‘(present)</td><td>house’ Predicator</td><td>Complement</td></tr>
<tr><td colspan="2">MOOD</td><td colspan="2">RESIDUE</td></tr>
<tr><td>Carrier</td><td colspan="2">Pr: Relational (attributive-circumstantial)</td><td>Attribute</td></tr>
<tr><td>experiential</td><td colspan="3" rowspan="2">RHEME</td></tr>
<tr><td>THEME</td></tr>
</table>

(4) The Tower of London has a colourful history [[dating back to the 11th century]].

<table>
<tr><td>The Tower of London</td><td colspan="2">has</td><td>a colourful history [[dating back to the 11th century]]</td></tr>
<tr><td>Subject</td><td>Finite ‘(present)</td><td>have’ Predicator</td><td>Complement</td></tr>
<tr><td colspan="2">MOOD</td><td colspan="2">RESIDUE</td></tr>
<tr><td>Carrier: possessor</td><td colspan="2">Pr: Relational (attributive - possessive)</td><td>Attribute: possessed</td></tr>
<tr><td>experiential</td><td colspan="3" rowspan="2">RHEME</td></tr>
<tr><td>THEME</td></tr>
</table>

(5i) Romans once occupied it, (5ii) it's the site of Europe's first fortress, (5iii) it has been a royal palace, a prison, an execution site, an arsenal, a mint, a keep for wild animals and jewel house (5iv) - and you can see artefacts from every part of this remarkable history.

| Romans | once | occupied | | it |
|---|---|---|---|---|
| Subject | Adjunct: circ | Finite '(*past*) | *occupy*' Predicator | Complement |
| MO- | | -OD | | |
| | RE- | | -SIDUE | |
| Actor | Circ: Location (time) | Pr: Material | | Goal |
| experiential | | | | |
| THEME | RHEME | | | |

| it | 's | | the site of Europe's first fortress |
|---|---|---|---|
| Subject | Finite '(*present*) | *be*' Predicator | Complement |
| MOOD | | RESIDUE | |
| Identified / Token | Pr: Relational (identifying - intensive) | | Identifier / Value |
| experiential | RHEME | | |
| THEME | | | |

| it | has | been | a royal palace, a prison, an execution site, an arsenal, a mint, a keep for wild animals and jewel house |
|---|---|---|---|
| Subject | Finite | Predicator | Complement |
| MOOD | RESIDUE | | |
| Carrier | - | Pr: Relational (attributive - intensive) | Attribute |
| experiential | | | |
| THEME | RHEME | | |

| and | you | can | see | artefacts from every part of this remarkable history |
|---|---|---|---|---|
| (Conjunction) | Subject | Finite: mod | Predicator | Complement |
| | MOOD | RESIDUE | | |
| - | Senser | - | Pr: Mental (perception) | Phenomenon |
| textual | experiential | | | |
| THEME | | RHEME | | |

(6i) During a visit to the Tower you can see Britain's most precious treasure - The Crown Jewels, (6ii) stand on the execution site of 3 English queens (6iii) and explore the legends of this world-famous landmark.

<table>
<tr><td>During a visit to the Tower</td><td>you</td><td>can</td><td>see</td><td>Britain's most precious treasure - The Crown Jewels</td></tr>
<tr><td>Adjunct: circ</td><td>Subject</td><td>Finite: mod</td><td>Predicator</td><td>Complement</td></tr>
<tr><td>RESIDUE</td><td colspan="2">MOOD</td><td colspan="2"></td></tr>
<tr><td>Circ: Location (time)</td><td>Senser</td><td>-</td><td>Pr: Mental (perception)</td><td>Phenomenon</td></tr>
<tr><td>experiential</td><td colspan="4" rowspan="2">RHEME</td></tr>
<tr><td>THEME</td></tr>
</table>

<table>
<tr><td>[you]</td><td>[can]</td><td>stand</td><td>on the execution site of 3 English queens</td></tr>
<tr><td>[Subject]</td><td>[Finite: mod]</td><td>Predicator</td><td>Adjunct: circ</td></tr>
<tr><td colspan="2">[MOOD]</td><td colspan="2">RESIDUE</td></tr>
<tr><td>[Behaver]</td><td>-</td><td>Pr: Behavioural</td><td>Circ: Location (place)</td></tr>
<tr><td colspan="3">experiential</td><td rowspan="2">RHEME</td></tr>
<tr><td colspan="3">THEME</td></tr>
</table>

<table>
<tr><td>and</td><td>[you]</td><td>[can]</td><td>explore</td><td>the legends of this world-famous landmark</td></tr>
<tr><td rowspan="2">(Conjunction)</td><td>[Subject]</td><td>[Finite: mod]</td><td>Predicator</td><td>Complement</td></tr>
<tr><td colspan="2">[MOOD]</td><td colspan="2">RESIDUE</td></tr>
<tr><td>-</td><td>[Actor]</td><td>-</td><td>Pr: Material</td><td>Goal</td></tr>
<tr><td>textual</td><td colspan="3">experiential</td><td rowspan="2">RHEME</td></tr>
<tr><td colspan="4">THEME</td></tr>
</table>

(7) Look out for the famous black ravens in the grounds of the Tower.

<table>
<tr><td>Look out for</td><td>the famous black ravens</td><td>in the grounds of the Tower</td></tr>
<tr><td>Predicator</td><td>Complement</td><td>Adjunct: circ</td></tr>
<tr><td colspan="3">RESIDUE</td></tr>
<tr><td>Pr: Material</td><td>Goal</td><td>Circ: Location (place)</td></tr>
<tr><td>experiential</td><td colspan="2" rowspan="2">RHEME</td></tr>
<tr><td>THEME</td></tr>
</table>

(8i) These magnificent birds have been kept here since the 1600s, (8ii) and legend has it (8iii) the Tower will fall, along with the Kingdom, (8iv) if the ravens ever leave the site.

| These magnificent birds | have | been kept | here | since the 1600s |
|---|---|---|---|---|
| Subject | Finite | Predicator | Adjunct: circ | Adjunct: circ |
| MOOD | RESIDUE | | | |
| Goal | - | Pr: Material | Circ: Location (place) | Circ: Extent (time) |
| experiential | RHEME | | | |
| THEME | | | | |

| and | legend | has it | |
|---|---|---|---|
| (Conjunction) | Subject | Finite '(*present*) | *have it*' Predicator |
| | | MOOD | RESIDUE |
| - | Sayer | Pr: Verbal | |
| textual | experiential | RHEME | |
| THEME | | | |

(8iii) the Tower will fall, along with the Kingdom, (8iv) if the ravens ever leave the site – dependent clauses, not part of Interpersonal and Textual analyses.

| the Tower | will fall, | along with the Kingdom, |
|---|---|---|
| Actor | Pr: Material | Circ: Accompaniment (comitation) |

| if | the ravens | ever | leave | the site |
|---|---|---|---|---|
| - | Actor | Circ: Location (time) | Pr: Material | Range |

(9i) You'll also see the Beefeaters (or Yeoman Warders) (9ii) who have been guarding the tower for over 600 years.

| You | 'll | also | see | the Beefeaters (or Yeoman Warders) |
|---|---|---|---|---|
| Subject | Finite: mod | Adjunct: conjunctive | Predicator | Complement |
| MOOD | | | RESIDUE | |
| Senser | - | - | Pr: Mental (perception) | Phenomenon |
| experiential | RHEME | | | |
| THEME | | | | |

(9ii) who have been guarding the tower for over 600 years – dependent clause, not part of Interpersonal and Textual analyses.

| who | have been guarding | the tower | for over 600 years |
|---|---|---|---|
| Actor | Pr: Material | Goal | Circ: Extent (time) |

(10) A visit to the Tower of London offers a millennium of British history in one day.

<table>
<tr><td>A visit to the Tower of London</td><td colspan="2">offers</td><td>a millennium of British history in one day</td></tr>
<tr><td>Subject</td><td>Finite ‘(present)</td><td>offer’ Predicator</td><td>Complement</td></tr>
<tr><td colspan="2">MOOD</td><td colspan="2">RESIDUE</td></tr>
<tr><td>Identified/ Token: possessor</td><td colspan="2">Pr: Relational (identifying-possessive)</td><td>Identifier/ Value: possessed</td></tr>
<tr><td>experiential</td><td colspan="3" rowspan="2">RHEME</td></tr>
<tr><td>THEME</td></tr>
</table>

(11i) This exceptional heritage site is a great day out (11ii) and holds daily exhibitions and events throughout the year.

<table>
<tr><td>This exceptional heritage site</td><td colspan="2">is</td><td>a great day out</td></tr>
<tr><td>Subject</td><td>Finite ‘(present)</td><td>be’ Predicator</td><td>Complement</td></tr>
<tr><td colspan="2">MOOD</td><td colspan="2">RESIDUE</td></tr>
<tr><td>Carrier</td><td colspan="2">Pr: Relational (attributive - intensive)</td><td>Attribute</td></tr>
<tr><td>experiential</td><td colspan="3" rowspan="2">RHEME</td></tr>
<tr><td>THEME</td></tr>
</table>

<table>
<tr><td>and</td><td>[this exceptional heritage site]</td><td colspan="2">holds</td><td>daily exhibitions and events</td><td>throughout the year</td></tr>
<tr><td rowspan="2">(Conjunction)</td><td>[Subject]</td><td>Finite ‘(present)</td><td>Predicator hold’</td><td>Complement</td><td>Adjunct: circ</td></tr>
<tr><td colspan="2">MOOD</td><td colspan="3">RESIDUE</td></tr>
<tr><td>-</td><td>[Carrier]</td><td colspan="2">Pr: Relational (attributive-circumstantial)</td><td>Attribute</td><td>Circ: Location (time)</td></tr>
<tr><td>textual</td><td colspan="5">experiential</td></tr>
<tr><td colspan="4">THEME</td><td colspan="2">RHEME</td></tr>
</table>

(12) The Ceremony of the Keys is the traditional locking-up of the Tower of London.

| The Ceremony of the Keys | is | | the traditional locking-up of the Tower of London |
|---|---|---|---|
| Subject | Finite '(*present*) | *be*' Predicator | Complement |
| MOOD | | RESIDUE | |
| Identified/ Token | Pr: Relational (identifying-intensive) | | Identifier/ Value |
| experiential | RHEME | | |
| THEME | | | |

(13) It's happened every night without fail for at least 700 years.

| It | 's | happened | every night | without fail | for at least 700 years |
|---|---|---|---|---|---|
| Subject | Finite | Predicator | Adjunct: circ | Adjunct: circ | Adjunct: circ |
| MOOD | RESIDUE | | | | |
| Actor | - | Pr: Material | Circ: Location (time) | Circ: Manner (quality) | Circ: Extent (time) |
| experiential | RHEME | | | | |
| THEME | | | | | |

(14) Don't miss your chance [[to watch this fascinating tradition]] on your trip to Britain.

| Don't | miss | your chance [[to watch this fascinating tradition]] | on your trip to Britain |
|---|---|---|---|
| Finite: neg | Predicator | Complement | Adjunct: circ |
| MOOD | RESIDUE | | |
| - | Pr: Material | Goal | Circ: Location (time) |
| interpersonal | experiential | RHEME | |
| THEME | | | |

(15i) Every night, at exactly 21:53, the Chief Yeoman Warder of the Tower emerges from the Byward Tower (15ii) wearing his long red coat and Tudor bonnet (15iii) and carrying a candle lantern and the Queen's Keys.

| Every night, at exactly 21:53, | the Chief Yeoman Warder of the Tower | emerges | | from the Byward Tower |
|---|---|---|---|---|
| Adjunct: circ | Subject | Finite '(*present*) | Predicator *emerge*' | Adjunct: circ |
| RESI- | MOOD | | -DUE | |
| Circ: Location (time) | Actor | Pr: Material | | Circ: Location (place) |

| experiential | RHEME |
|---|---|
| THEME | |

*(15ii)* wearing his long red coat and Tudor bonnet (15iii) and carrying a candle lantern and the Queen's Keys – dependent clauses, not part of Interpersonal and Textual analyses.

| *[he]* | *[is]* wearing | his long red coat and Tudor bonnet |
|---|---|---|
| *[Actor]* | Pr: Material | Goal |

| and | *[he]* | *[is]* carrying | a candle lantern and the Queen's Keys |
|---|---|---|---|
| - | *Actor* | Pr: Material | Goal |

(16i) The Chief Yeoman Warder then meets his military escort (members of the Tower of London Guard), (16ii) and together they lock the main gates of the Tower.

| The Chief Yeoman Warder | then | meets | | his military escort (members of the Tower of London Guard) |
|---|---|---|---|---|
| Subject | (Conjunction) | Finite '(*present*) | Predicator *meet*' | Complement |
| MO- | | -OD | RESIDUE | |
| Actor | - | Pr: Material | | Goal |
| experiential | RHEME | | | |
| THEME | | | | |

| and | together | they | lock | | the main gates of the Tower |
|---|---|---|---|---|---|
| (Conjunction) | Adjunct: circ | Subject | Finite '(*present*) | Predicator *lock*' | Complement |
| | RESIDUE | MOOD | | | |
| - | Circ: Accompaniment (additive) | Actor | Pr: Material | | Goal |
| textual | experiential | RHEME | | | |
| THEME | | | | | |

(17i) As they pass, (17ii) all of the Tower's guards salute the Keys.

| //As they pass// | all of the Tower's guards | salute | | the Keys |
|---|---|---|---|---|
| | Subject | Finite '(*present*) | *salute*' Predicator | Complement |
| | MOOD | | RESIDUE | |
| | Actor | Pr: Material | | Goal |
| experiential | | | | |
| THEME | RHEME | | | |

(18i) The Chief Yeoman Warder and his escort then retrace their steps, (18ii) and lock the great oak gates of the Middle and Byward Towers on the way.

| The Chief Yeoman Warder and his escort | then | retrace their | steps |
|---|---|---|---|
| Subject | (Conjunction) | Finite '(*present*) | Predicator *retrace*' |
| MO- | | -OD | RESIDUE |
| Actor | - | Pr: Material | |
| experiential | | | |
| THEME | RHEME | | |

| and | *[The Chief Yeoman Warder and his escort]* | lock | | the great oak gates of the Middle and Byward Towers | on the way |
|---|---|---|---|---|---|
| (Conjunction) | *[Subject]* | Finite '(*present*) | Predicator *lock*' | Complement | Adjunct: circ |
| | MOOD | | RESIDUE | | |
| - | *[Actor]* | Pr: Material | | Goal | Circ: Location (time) |
| textual | experiential | | RHEME | | |
| THEME | | | | | |

(19) The only time [[the ceremony has been interrupted in the last 700 years]] was during the Second World War.

| The only time [[the ceremony has been interrupted in the last 700 years]] | was | | during the Second World War |
|---|---|---|---|
| Subject | Finite '(*past*) | *be*' Predicator | Complement |
| MOOD | | RESIDUE | |
| Identified/ Token | Pr: Relational (identifying - circumstantial) | | Identifier/ Value |
| experiential | RHEME | | |
| THEME | | | |

(20i) During an air raid, bombs fell onto the old Victorian guardroom (20ii) as the Chief Yeoman Warder and his escort were coming through the Bloody Archway.

| During an air raid, | bombs | fell | | onto the old Victorian guardroom |
|---|---|---|---|---|
| Adjunct: circ | Subject | Finite '(*past*) | Predicator *fall*' | Adjunct: circ |
| RESIDUE | MOOD | | | |
| Circ: Location (time) | Actor | Pr: Material | | Circ: Location (place) |
| experiential | RHEME | | | |
| THEME | | | | |

(20ii) as the Chief Yeoman Warder and his escort were coming through the Bloody Archway – dependent clause, not part of Interpersonal and Textual analyses.

| as | the Chief Yeoman Warder and his escort | were coming | through the Bloody Archway |
|---|---|---|---|
| - | Actor | Pr: Material | Circ: Location (place) |

(21i) The shock and the noise of the bombs sent the group flying to the floor, (21ii) but they stood up, (21iii) dusted themselves down, (21iv) and carried on.

| The shock and the noise of the bombs | sent | | the group | flying | to the floor |
|---|---|---|---|---|---|
| Subject | Finite '(*past* | Pre- *send flying*' | Complement | -dicator | Adjunct: circ |
| MOOD | | RESIDUE | | | |
| Agent | Pr: Causative | | Actor | Pr: Material | Circ: Location (place) |
| experiential | RHEME | | | | |
| THEME | | | | | |

| but | they | stood up | |
|---|---|---|---|
| (Conjunction) | Subject | Finite '(*past*) | *stand up*' Predicator |
| | MOOD | | RESIDUE |
| - | Actor | Pr: Material | |
| textual | experiential | RHEME | |
| THEME | | | |

| *[they]* | dusted | | themselves | down |
|---|---|---|---|---|
| [*Subject]* | Finite '(*past*) | *dust down*' Predi- | Complement | -cator |
| MOOD | | RESIDUE | | |
| *[Actor]* | Pr: Mate- | | Goal | -rial |
| experiential | | | RHEME | |
| THEME | | | | |

| and | *[they]* | carried on | |
|---|---|---|---|
| (Conjunction) | [*Subject]* | Finite '(*past*) | *carry on*' Predicator |
| | MOOD | | RESIDUE |
| - | *[Actor]* | Pr: Material | |
| textual | experiential | | |
| THEME | | RHEME | |

(22i) Tickets to the Ceremony of the Keys are free, (22ii) but due the popularity of the ceremony, you must apply in writing at least 2 months in advance.

| Tickets to the Ceremony of the Keys | are | | free |
|---|---|---|---|
| Subject | Finite '(*present*) | *be*' Predicator | Complement |
| MOOD | | RESIDUE | |
| Carrier | Pr: Relational (attributive-intensive) | | Attribute |
| experiential | RHEME | | |
| THEME | | | |

| but | due the popularity of the ceremony, | you | must apply | | in writing | at least 2 months in advance |
|---|---|---|---|---|---|---|
| (Conjunction) | Adjunct: circ | Subject | Finite: mod | Predicator *apply*' | Adjunct : circ | Adjunct: circ |
| | RESIDUE | MOOD | | | | |
| - | Circ: Cause (reason) | Actor | Pr: Material | | Circ: Manner (means) | Circ: Location (time) |
| textual | experiential | RHEME | | | | |
| THEME | | | | | | |

(23) For details [[on how to apply for tickets]], visit the Tower of London - Ceremony of the Keys.

| For details [[on how to apply for tickets]] | visit | the Tower of London - Ceremony of the Keys |
|---|---|---|
| Adjunct: circ | Predicator | Complement |
| RESIDUE | | |
| Circ: Cause (purpose) | Pr: Material | Goal |
| experiential | RHEME | |
| THEME | | |

## 1.3.3. Edinburgh in the institutional corpus

### *Logical analysis*

CL. SIMPLEX (1) discover Scotland's graceful capital
CL. SIMPLEX (2) Learn everything about Edinburgh's attractions from its historic landmarks like Edinburgh Castle and the Royal Mile to its unique blend of traditional and modern Scottish culture
CL. SIMPLEX (3) "The best things about Edinburgh are the great natural spaces [[that exist within it]].
CL. SIMPLEX (4) [[To find places like the Water of Leith, Holyrood Park and Corstorphine and Blackford Hill in the middle of a city]] is exceptional."
CL. SIMPLEX (5) Old Town meets New Town
CL. SIMPLEX (6) Let us guide you through Edinburgh - Scotland's capital city, and one of Britain's most exciting tourist destinations.
CL. SIMPLEX (7) There are 2 sides to Edinburgh – the historic Old Town with the medieval Edinburgh Castle and cobblestone alleys, and the elegant but classic Georgian New Town.

CL. SIMPLEX (8) The combination of these 2 parts of the city, along with it's vibrant events and celebrations such as Hogmanay and the Festival Fringe is [[what gives Edinburgh its unique character]].

α (9i) Together, they create a dynamic and fascinating city

=β (9ii) which truly captures the magical spirit of Scotland.

CL. SIMPLEX (10) Edinburgh's beautiful Old and New Towns have been awarded UNESCO World Heritage Status twice over.

1 (11i) The city is home to 4,500 listed buildings – the highest concentration in the world –

+2 (11ii) and is also a modern, dynamic city of art and culture with its museums, galleries, universities and festivals.

α (12i) Edinburgh's Old Town is dominated by Edinburgh Castle ,

=β (12ii) which rests on a hilltop at the end of the Royal Mile.

1 (13i) Stay on the Royal Mile for the The Scotch Whisky Experience and Ghost Tours ,

x2 (13ii) then head to the beautiful Royal Botanic Garden for 70 acres of tranquillity.

CL. SIMPLEX (14) And the events for your diary: Burns Night in January, Edinburgh Military Tattoo and Edinburgh Festival Fringe in August, and of course, Hogmanay in December.

CL. SIMPLEX (15) Download a free Edinburgh audio guide from mp3cityguides.com.

xβ (16i) To download more mp3 walking guides

α (16ii) check out www.mp3cityguides.com .

CL. SIMPLEX (17) Discover the history behind Edinburgh Castle .

CL. SIMPLEX (18) Visit Musselburgh Links – the world's oldest golf playing course.

CL. SIMPLEX (19) See Edinburgh from your very own chauffer-driven trike with Trike Tours Scotland.

CL. SIMPLEX (20) Sample a dram at The Scotch Whisky Experience .

α (21i) Take a spooky Ghost Tours –

xβ (21ii) if you dare!

CL. SIMPLEX (22) Go to a Ceilidh (traditional Scottish dance) at The Lot .

1 (23i) Do the Edinburgh Literary Pub Tour

+2 (23ii) and discover Scotland's literary heroes.

α (24i) Eat at The Witchery, a great restaurant

=β (24ii) situated in the shadow of Edinburgh Castle.

CL. SIMPLEX (25) Catch a classic theatre production at the Royal Lyceum Theatre.

CL. SIMPLEX (26) Edinburgh is full of fabulous places to shop.

1 α (27i) Princes Street,

<=β> (27ii) which separates the Old and New Towns,

α (27i) is lined with great department stores;

+2 (27iii) George Street is full of boutiques and bars;

+3 (27iv) St Andrew's Square and Multrees Walk are designer heaven;

+4 (27v) and of course, there's the Royal Mile for some great Scottish souvenirs.

CL. SIMPLEX (28) Edinburgh is a haven for sports fans.

CL. SIMPLEX (29) Easter Road stadium and Tynecastle Stadium are home to the city's main football clubs, Hibernian F.C and Heart of Midlothian (Hearts) F.C.

1 (30i) And golf fanatics will love Edinburgh too –

X2 (30ii) some of the world's best courses can be found in and around the city, including Gullane, the Open Championship course at Muirfield and the Open Qualifying course at Dunbar.

α (31i) Buy

xβ (31ii) before you fly

CL. SIMPLEX (32) One thing [[you definitely shouldn't travel to Edinburgh without]] is an Edinburgh Pass .

CL. SIMPLEX (33) With free entry to over 30 of the city's top attractions, free return airport and city centre bus transport, a free guidebook and lots of exclusive offers, the Edinburgh Pass is the best way [[to explore the Scottish capital]].

CL. SIMPLEX (34) Visit our shop for more exciting offers, including Edinburgh Dungeon Tickets , Haggis Adventures Tours and Royal Edinburgh Tickets - VisitBritain Shop .

1 α (35i) Don't forget

'β (35ii) to take a look at VisitBritain's massive selection of accommodation in Edinburgh –

X2 (35iii) you can book your choice of hotel, B&B or self catering cottage through our website.

## *Experiential, interpersonal and textual analyses*

(1) discover Scotland's graceful capital

| discover | Scotland's graceful capital |
|---|---|
| Predicator | Complement |
| RESIDUE | |
| Pr: Material | Goal |
| experiential | RHEME |
| THEME | |

(2) Learn everything about Edinburgh's attractions from its historic landmarks like Edinburgh Castle and the Royal Mile to its unique blend of traditional and modern Scottish culture.

| Learn | everything about Edinburgh's attractions from its historic landmarks like Edinburgh Castle and the Royal Mile to its unique blend of traditional and |
|---|---|
| | modern Scottish culture |
| Predicator | Complement |
| RESIDUE | |
| Pr: Mental (cognition) | Phenomenon |
| experiential | RHEME |
| THEME | |

(3) "The best things about Edinburgh are the great natural spaces [[that exist within it]].

| The best things about Edinburgh | are | | the great natural spaces [[that exist within it]] |
|---|---|---|---|
| Subject | Finite '(*present*) | *be*' Predicator | Complement |
| MOOD | | RESIDUE | |
| Identified / Value | Pr: Relational (identifying- intensive) | | Identifier / Token |
| experiential | RHEME | | |
| THEME | | | |

(4) [[To find places like the Water of Leith, Holyrood Park and Corstorphine and Blackford Hill in the middle of a city]] is exceptional."

| [[To find places like the Water of Leith, Holyrood Park and Corstorphine and Blackford Hill in the middle of a city]] | is | | exceptional |
|---|---|---|---|
| Subject | '(*present*) Finite | *be*' Predicator | Complement |
| MOOD | | RESIDUE | |
| Carrier | Pr: Relational (attributive - intensive) | | Attribute |
| experiential | RHEME | | |
| THEME | | | |

(5) Old Town meets New Town

| Old Town | meets | | New Town |
|---|---|---|---|
| Subject | Finite '(*present*) | *meet*' Predicator | Complement |
| MOOD | | RESIDUE | |
| Actor | Pr: Material | | Goal |
| experiential | RHEME | | |
| THEME | | | |

(6) Let us guide you through Edinburgh - Scotland's capital city, and one of Britain's most exciting tourist destinations.

| Let us | guide | you | through Edinburgh - Scotland's capital city, and one of Britain's most exciting tourist destinations |
|---|---|---|---|
| Subject | Predicator | Complement | Adjunct: circ |
| MOOD | RESIDUE | | |
| Actor | Pr: Material | Goal | Circ: Location (place) |
| experiential | RHEME | | |
| THEME | | | |

(7) There are 2 sides to Edinburgh – the historic Old Town with the medieval Edinburgh Castle and cobblestone alleys, and the elegant but classic Georgian New Town.

| There | are | | 2 sides to Edinburgh – the historic Old Town with the medieval Edinburgh Castle and cobblestone alleys, and the elegant but classic Georgian New Town |
|---|---|---|---|
| Subject | Finite '(*present*) | Predicator *be*' | Complement |
| MOOD | | RESIDUE | |
| - | Pr: Existential | | Existent |
| experiential | | | RHEME |
| THEME | | | |

(8) The combination of these 2 parts of the city, along with it's vibrant events and celebrations such as Hogmanay and the Festival Fringe is [[what gives Edinburgh its unique character]].

| The combination of these 2 parts of the city, along with it's vibrant events and celebrations such as Hogmanay and the Festival Fringe | is | | [[what gives Edinburgh its unique character]] |
|---|---|---|---|
| Subject | Finite '(*present*) | *be*' Predicator | Complement |
| MOOD | | RESIDUE | |
| Identified / Token | Pr: Relational (identifying - intensive) | | Identifier / Value |
| experiential | RHEME | | |
| THEME | | | |

(9i) Together, they create a dynamic and fascinating city (9ii) which truly captures the magical spirit of Scotland.

| Together, | they | create | | a dynamic and fascinating city |
|---|---|---|---|---|
| Adjunct: circ | Subject | Finite'(*present*) | *create*' Predicator | Complement |
| RESIDUE | MOOD | | | |
| Circ: Accompaniment (comitation) | Actor | Pr: Material | | Goal |
| experiential | RHEME | | | |
| THEME | | | | |

(9ii) which truly captures the magical spirit of Scotland – dependent clause, not part of Interpersonal and Textual analyses.

| which | truly | captures | the magical spirit of Scotland |
|---|---|---|---|
| Actor | Circ: Manner (quality) | Pr: Material | Goal |

(10) Edinburgh's beautiful Old and New Towns have been awarded UNESCO World Heritage Status twice over.

| Edinburgh's beautiful Old and New Towns | have | been awarded | UNESCO World Heritage Status | twice over |
|---|---|---|---|---|
| Subject | Finite | Predicator | Complement | Adjunct: circ |
| MOOD | | RESIDUE | | |
| Beneficiary: Recipient | - | Pr: Material | Goal | Circ: Extent (frequency) |
| experiential | | | | |
| THEME | RHEME | | | |

(11i) The city is home to 4,500 listed buildings – the highest concentration in the world – (11ii) and is also a modern, dynamic city of art and culture with its museums, galleries, universities and festivals.

| The city | is | | home to 4,500 listed buildings – the highest concentration in the world – |
|---|---|---|---|
| Subject | Finite '(*present*) | *be*' Predicator | Complement |
| MOOD | | RESIDUE | |
| Carrier | Pr: Relational (attributive - intensive) | | Attribute |
| experiential | | | |
| THEME | RHEME | | |

| and | *[it]* | is | | also | a modern, dynamic city of art and culture with its museums, galleries, universities and festivals |
|---|---|---|---|---|---|
| (Conjunction) | *[Subject]* | '(*present*) Finite | *be*' Predicator | Adjunct: conjunctive | Complement |
| | MOOD | | RESIDUE | | |
| - | *[Carrier]* | Pr: Relational (attributive-intensive) | | - | Attribute |
| textual | experiential | | | RHEME | |
| | THEME | | | | |

(12i) Edinburgh's Old Town is dominated by Edinburgh Castle , (12ii) which rests on a hilltop at the end of the Royal Mile.

| Edinburgh's Old Town | is | dominated | by Edinburgh Castle |
|---|---|---|---|
| Subject | Finite | Predicator | Complement |
| MOOD | | RESIDUE | |
| Goal | - | Pr: Material | Actor |
| experiential | RHEME | | |
| THEME | | | |

(12ii) which rests on a hilltop at the end of the Royal Mile – dependent clause, not part of Interpersonal and Textual analyses.

| which | rests | on a hilltop at the end of the Royal Mile |
|---|---|---|
| Carrier | Pr: Relational (attributive - circumstantial) | Attribute |

(13i) Stay on the Royal Mile for the The Scotch Whisky Experience and Ghost Tours , (13ii) then head to the beautiful Royal Botanic Garden for 70 acres of tranquillity.

| Stay | on the Royal Mile | for the The Scotch Whisky Experience and Ghost Tours |
|---|---|---|
| Predicator | Adjunct: circ | Adjunct: circ |
| RESIDUE | | |
| Pr: Behavioural | Circ: Location (place) | Circ: Cause (purpose) |
| experiential | RHEME | |
| THEME | | |

| then | head | to the beautiful Royal Botanic Garden | for 70 acres of tranquillity |
|---|---|---|---|
| (Conjunction) | Predicator | Adjunct: circ | Adjunct: circ |
| | RESIDUE | | |
| - | Pr: Material | Circ: Location (place) | Circ: Cause (purpose) |
| textual | experiential | RHEME | |
| THEME | | | |

(14) And the events for your diary: Burns Night in January, Edinburgh Military Tattoo and Edinburgh Festival Fringe in August, and of course, Hogmanay in December.

| And | the events for your diary | : | | Burns Night in January, Edinburgh Military Tattoo and Edinburgh Festival Fringe in August, and of course, Hogmanay in December |
|---|---|---|---|---|
| Adjunct: conjunctive | Subject | *[Finite] '(present)* | *[Predicator] be'* | Complement |
| | MOOD | | RESIDUE | |
| - | Identified / Value | Pr: Relational (identifying-intensive) | | Identifier / Token |
| textual | experiential | RHEME | | |
| THEME | | | | |

(15) Download a free Edinburgh audio guide from mp3cityguides.com.

| Download | a free Edinburgh audio guide | from mp3cityguides.com |
|---|---|---|
| Predicator | Complement | Adjunct: circ |
| RESIDUE | | |
| Pr: Material | Goal | Circ: Location (place) |
| experiential | RHEME | |
| THEME | | |

(16i) To download more mp3 walking guides (16ii) check out www.mp3cityguides.com .

| //To download more mp3 walking guides// | check out | www.mp3cityguides.com |
|---|---|---|
| | | |
| | Predicator | Complement |
| | RESIDUE | |
| - | Pr: Material | Goal |
| experiential | RHEME | |
| THEME | | |

(17) Discover the history behind Edinburgh Castle .

| Discover | the history behind Edinburgh Castle |
|---|---|
| Predicator | Complement |
| RESIDUE | |
| Pr: Mental (cognition) | Phenomenon |
| experiential | RHEME |
| THEME | |

(18) Visit Musselburgh Links – the world's oldest golf playing course.

| Visit | Musselburgh Links – the world's oldest golf playing course |
|---|---|
| Predicator | Complement |
| RESIDUE | |
| Pr: Material | Goal |
| experiential | RHEME |
| THEME | |

(19) See Edinburgh from your very own chauffer-driven trike with Trike Tours Scotland.

| See | Edinburgh | from your very own chauffer-driven trike | with Trike Tours Scotland |
|---|---|---|---|
| Predicator | Complement | Adjunct: circ | Adjunct: circ |
| RESIDUE | | | |
| Pr: Mental (perception) | Phenomenon | Circ: Location (place) | Circ: Accompaniment (comitation) |
| experiential | RHEME | | |
| THEME | | | |

(20) Sample a dram at The Scotch Whisky Experience .

| Sample | a dram | at The Scotch Whisky Experience |
|---|---|---|
| Predicator | Complement | Adjunct: circ |
| RESIDUE | | |
| Pr: Material | Goal | Circ: Location (place) |
| experiential | RHEME | |
| THEME | | |

(21i) Take a spooky Ghost Tours (21ii) – if you dare!

| Take | a spooky Ghost Tours |
|---|---|
| Predicator | Complement |
| RESIDUE | |
| Pr: Material | Goal |
| experiential | RHEME |
| THEME | |

(21ii) – if you dare! - – dependent clause, not part of Interpersonal and Textual analyses.

| if | you | dare |
|---|---|---|
| - | Actor | - |

(22) Go to a Ceilidh (traditional Scottish dance) at The Lot .

| Go | to a Ceilidh (traditional Scottish dance) | at The Lot |
|---|---|---|
| Predicator | Adjunct: circ | Adjunct: circ |
| RESIDUE | | |
| Pr: Material | Circ: Location (place) | Circ: Location (place) |
| experiential | RHEME | |
| THEME | | |

(23i) Do the Edinburgh Literary Pub Tour (23ii) and discover Scotland's literary heroes.

| Do | the Edinburgh Literary Pub Tour |
|---|---|
| Predicator | Complement |
| RESIDUE | |
| Pr: Material | Goal |
| experiential | RHEME |
| THEME | |

| and | discover | Scotland's literary heroes |
|---|---|---|
| (Conjunction) | Predicator | Complement |
| | RESIDUE | |
| - | Pr: Mental (cognition) | Phenomenon |
| textual | experiential | RHEME |
| | THEME | |

(24i) Eat at The Witchery, a great restaurant (24ii) situated in the shadow of Edinburgh Castle.

| Eat | at The Witchery a great restaurant |
|---|---|
| Predicator | Adjunct: circ |
| RESIDUE | |
| Pr: Material | Circ: Location (place) |
| experiential | RHEME |
| THEME | |

(24ii) situated in the shadow of Edinburgh Castle – dependent clause, not part of Interpersonal and Textual analyses.

| *[which]* | *[is]* situated | in the shadow of Edinburgh Castle |
|---|---|---|
| *[Identified/Value]* | Pr: Relational (identifying-circumstantial) | Identifier/ Token |

(25) Catch a classic theatre production at the Royal Lyceum Theatre.

| Catch | a classic theatre production | at the Royal Lyceum Theatre |
|---|---|---|
| Predicator | Complement | Adjunct: circ |
| RESIDUE | | |
| Pr: Material | Goal | Circ: Location (place) |
| experiential | | |
| THEME | RHEME | |

(26) Edinburgh is full of fabulous places to shop.

| Edinburgh | is | | full of fabulous places to shop |
|---|---|---|---|
| Subject | Finite '(*present*) | *be*' Predicator | Complement |
| | MOOD | RESIDUE | |
| Carrier | Pr: Relational (attributive - intensive) | | Attribute |
| experiential | RHEME | | |
| THEME | | | |

(27i) Princes Street, (27ii) which separates the Old and New Towns, (27i) is lined with great department stores; (27iii) George Street is full of boutiques and bars; (27iv) St Andrew's Square and Multrees Walk are designer heaven; (27v) and of course, there's the Royal Mile for some great Scottish souvenirs.

| Princes Street, <<// which separates the Old and New Towns//>>, | is | lined | with great department stores |
|---|---|---|---|
| Subject | Finite | Predicator | Complement |
| MOOD | | RESIDUE | |
| Identified / Value | - | Pr: Relational (identifying-circumstantial) | Identifier / Token |
| experiential | RHEME | | |
| THEME | | | |

| George Street | is | | full of boutiques and bars |
|---|---|---|---|
| Subject | Finite '(*present*) | *be*' Predicator | Complement |

| MOOD | | RESIDUE |
|---|---|---|
| Carrier | Pr: Relational (attributive - intensive) | Attribute |
| experiential | | |
| THEME | RHEME | |

| St Andrew's Square and Multrees Walk | are | | designer heaven |
|---|---|---|---|
| Subject | Finite '(*present*) | *be*' Predicator | Complement |
| MOOD | | RESIDUE | |
| Carrier | Pr: Relational (attributive - intensive) | | Attribute |
| experiential | RHEME | | |
| THEME | | | |

| and | of course, | there | 's | | the Royal Mile | for some great Scottish souvenirs |
|---|---|---|---|---|---|---|
| (Conjunction) | Adjunct: mood | Subject | Finite '(*present*) | Predicator *be*' | Complement | Adjunct: circ |
| | MOOD | | | RESIDUE | | |
| - | - | | Pr: Existential | | Existent | Circ: Cause (purpose) |
| textual | interpersonal | experiential | | | RHEME | |
| | THEME | | | | | |

(28) Edinburgh is a haven for sports fans.

| Edinburgh | is | | a haven for sports fans |
|---|---|---|---|
| Subject | Finite '(*present*) | *be*' Predicator | Complement |
| | MOOD | RESIDUE | |
| Carrier | Pr: Relational (attributive - intensive) | | Attribute |
| experiential | | | |
| THEME | RHEME | | |

(29) Easter Road stadium and Tynecastle Stadium are home to the city's main football clubs, Hibernian F.C and Heart of Midlothian (Hearts) F.C.

| Easter Road stadium and Tynecastle Stadium | are | | home to the city's main football clubs, Hibernian F.C and Heart of Midlothian (Hearts) F.C. |
|---|---|---|---|
| Subject | Finite '(*present*) | Predicator *be*' | Complement |
| MOOD | | RESIDUE | |
| Carrier | Pr: Relational (attributive - intensive) | | Attribute |
| experiential | RHEME | | |
| THEME | | | |

(30i) And golf fanatics will love Edinburgh too (30ii) – some of the world's best courses can be found in and around the city, including Gullane, the Open Championship course at Muirfield and the Open Qualifying course at Dunbar.

| And | golf fanatics | will | love | Edinburgh | too |
|---|---|---|---|---|---|
| Adjunct: conjunctive | Subject | Finite | Predicator | Complement | Adjunct: conjunctive |
| | MOOD | | RESIDUE | | |
| - | Senser | - | Pr: Mental (affection) | Phenomenon | - |
| textual | experiential | RHEME | | | |
| THEME | | | | | |

| some of the world's best courses | can | be found | in and around the city |
|---|---|---|---|
| Subject | Finite: mod | Predicator | Adjunct: circ |
| MOOD | | RESIDUE | |
| Goal | - | Pr: Material | Circ: Location (place) |
| experiential | RHEME | | |
| THEME | | | |

(31i) Buy (31ii) before you fly

| Buy |
|---|
| Predicator |
| RESIDUE |
| Pr: Material |
| experiential |
| THEME |

(31ii) before you fly – dependent clause, not part of Interpersonal and Textual analyses.

| before | you | fly |
|---|---|---|
| - | Actor | Pr: Material |

(32) One thing [[you definitely shouldn't travel to Edinburgh without]] is an Edinburgh Pass .

| One thing [[you definitely shouldn't travel to Edinburgh without]] | is | | an Edinburgh Pass |
|---|---|---|---|
| Subject | Finite '(*present*) | *be*' Predicator | Complement |
| MOOD | | | RESIDUE |
| Carrier | Pr: Relational (attributive - intensive) | | Attribute |
| experiential | | | |
| THEME | RHEME | | |

(33) With free entry to over 30 of the city's top attractions, free return airport and city centre bus transport, a free guidebook and lots of exclusive offers, the Edinburgh Pass is the best way [[to explore the Scottish capital]].

| With free entry to over 30 of the city's top attractions, free return airport and city centre bus transport, a free guidebook and lots of exclusive offers | the Edinburgh Pass | is | the best way [[to explore the Scottish capital]] | |
|---|---|---|---|---|
| Adjunct: circ | Subject | Finite '(*present*) | *be*' Predicator | Complement |
| | MOOD | | | |
| RESIDUE | | | | |
| Circ: Cause (reason) | Identified / Token | Pr: Relational (identifying – intensive) | | Identifier / Value |
| experiential | RHEME | | | |
| THEME | | | | |

(34) Visit our shop for more exciting offers, including Edinburgh Dungeon Tickets , Haggis Adventures Tours and Royal Edinburgh Tickets - VisitBritain Shop .

| Visit | our shop | for more exciting offers, including Edinburgh Dungeon Tickets , Haggis Adventures Tours and Royal Edinburgh Tickets - VisitBritain Shop |
|---|---|---|
| Predicator | Complement | Adjunct: circ |
| RESIDUE | | |

| Pr: Material | Goal | Circ: Cause (purpose) |
|---|---|---|
| experiential | | |
| THEME | RHEME | |

$_{(35i)}$ Don't forget $_{(35ii)}$ to take a look at VisitBritain's massive selection of accommodation in Edinburgh $_{(35ii)}$ – you can book your choice of hotel, B&B or self catering cottage through our website.

| Don't | forget |
|---|---|
| Finite: neg | Predicator |
| MOOD | RESIDUE |
| - | Pr: Mental (cognition) |
| interpersonal | experiential |
| THEME | |

| you | can | book | your choice of hotel, B&B or self catering cottage | through our website |
|---|---|---|---|---|
| Subject | Finite: mod | Predicator | Complement | Adjunct: circ |
| MOOD | | RESIDUE | | |
| Actor | - | Pr: Material | Goal | Circ: Manner (means) |
| experiential | | | | |
| THEME | RHEME | | | |

$_{(35ii)}$ to take a look at VisitBritain's massive selection of accommodation in Edinburgh - – dependent clause, not part of Interpersonal and Textual analyses.

| to take a look | at VisitBritain's massive selection of accommodation in Edinburgh |
|---|---|
| Pr: Behavioural | Circ: Location (place) |

## 2. Commercial websites

### 2.1. Romanian set of commercial webpages

#### 2.1.1. The Monastery of Horezu in the commercial corpus

*Logical analysis*

α $_{(1i)}$ ( Alternatively you can visit the Horezu Monastery – UNESCO monument
=β 1 $_{(1ii)}$ founded in 1690 by the Prince Constantin Brancoveanu,
+2 $_{(1iii)}$ considered one of the best examples of "Brancovean" style,

+3 (1iv) known for the purity of architectural details and richness of details, for its religious composition, ex – voto portraits and ornamental painting.)

## *Experiential, interpersonal and textual analyses*

(1i) Alternatively you can visit the Horezu Monastery – UNESCO monument (1ii) founded in 1690 by the Prince Constantin Brancoveanu, (1iii) considered one of the best examples of "Brancovean" style, (1iv) known for the purity of architectural details and richness of details, for its religious composition, ex – voto portraits and ornamental painting.

<table>
<tr><td>Alternatively</td><td>you</td><td>can</td><td>visit</td><td>the Horezu Monastery – UNESCO monument</td></tr>
<tr><td rowspan="2">Adjunct: conjunctive</td><td>Subject</td><td>Finite</td><td>Predicator</td><td>Complement</td></tr>
<tr><td colspan="2">MOOD</td><td colspan="2">RESIDUE</td></tr>
<tr><td>-</td><td>Actor</td><td>-</td><td>Pr: Material</td><td>Goal</td></tr>
<tr><td>interpersonal</td><td>textual</td><td colspan="3" rowspan="2">RHEME</td></tr>
<tr><td colspan="2">THEME</td></tr>
</table>

(1ii) founded in 1690 by the Prince Constantin Brancoveanu, (1iii) considered one of the best examples of "Brancovean" style, (1iv) known for the purity of architectural details and richness of details, for its religious composition, ex – voto portraits and ornamental painting – dependent clauses, not part of Interpersonal and Textual analyses.

| *[which]* | *[was]* founded | in 1690 | by the Prince Constantin Brancoveanu |
|---|---|---|---|
| *Goal* | Pr: Material | Circ: Location (time) | Actor |

| *[which]* | *[is]* considered | one of the best examples of "Brancovean" style, |
|---|---|---|
| *Identified / Token* | Pr: Causative | Identifier / Value |

| *[which]* | *[is]* known | for the purity of architectural details and richness of details, for its religious composition, ex – voto portraits and ornamental painting |
|---|---|---|
| *Phenomenon* | Pr: Mental (cognition) | Circ: Cause (reason) |

### 2.1.2. The Dacian Fortresses of the Orastie Mountains in the commercial corpus

## *Logical analysis*

α (1i) ( Alternatively you can visit the six Dacian fortresses from the Orastie Mountains,

=β (1ii) built in the style of murus dacicus, in the period from the first century BC to the first century AD as protection from the conquering Romans .

1 (2i) The six fortresses form the defensive system of Decebalus

+2 (2ii) and were declared World Heritage by ' UNESCO .)

## *Experiential, interpersonal and textual analyses*

(1i) Alternatively you can visit the six Dacian fortresses from the Orastie Mountains, (1ii) built in the style of murus dacicus, in the period from the first century BC to the first century AD as protection from the conquering Romans .

| Alternatively | you | can | visit | the six Dacian fortresses from the Orastie Mountains |
|---|---|---|---|---|
| Adjunct: conjunctive | Subject | Finite | Predicator | Complement |
| | MOOD | | RESIDUE | |
| - | Actor | - | Pr: Material | Goal |
| textual | experiential | | | |
| THEME | | RHEME | | |

(1ii) built in the style of murus dacicus, in the period from the first century BC to the first century AD as protection from the conquering Romans – dependent clauses, not part of Interpersonal and Textual analyses.

| *[which]* | *[were]* built | in the style of murus dacicus, | in the period from the first century BC to the first century AD | as protection from the conquering Romans |
|---|---|---|---|---|
| *Goal* | Pr: Material | Circ: Manner (comparison) | Circ: Extent (time) | Circ: Role (guise) |

(2i) The six fortresses form the defensive system of Decebalus (2ii) and were declared World Heritage by ' UNESCO .

| The six fortresses | form | | the defensive system of Decebalus |
|---|---|---|---|
| Subject | Finite '(*present*) | *form*' Predicator | Complement |
| MOOD | | RESIDUE | |
| Identified / Token | Pr: Relational (identifying - intensive) | | Identifier / Value |
| experiential | RHEME | | |
| THEME | | | |

| and | *[the six fortresses]* | were | declared | World Heritage | by ' UNESCO |
|---|---|---|---|---|---|
| (Conjunction) | *[Subject]* | Finite | Predicator | Complement | Adjunct: circ |
| | MOOD | | RESIDUE | | |
| - | *[Identified/ Token]* | - | Pr: Causative | Identifier / Value | Assigner |
| textual | experiential | | | RHEME | |
| THEME | | | | | |

## 2.1.3. Sighisoara in the commercial corpus

### *Logical analysis*

α (1i) We continue to Sighisoara, the "fortified city" among the very few in Europe,
=β (1ii) which retains its medieval centre on the top of the hill.
α (2i) Here was also born Vlad the Impaler,
=β (2ii) better known as Count Dracula.
α (3i) There are several defensive towers [[that surround the city]],
=β (3ii) named after the trades of their builders: the Tailors' Tower, the Shoemakers' Tower, the Rope Makers' Tower, the Clock Tower etc
CL. SIMPLEX (4) Dinner in the house [[where Count Vlad was born]]/or an intimate restaurant medieval style and accommodation in Sighisoara in the citadel.

### *Experiential, interpersonal and textual analyses*

(1i) We continue to Sighisoara, the "fortified city" among the very few in Europe, (1ii) which retains its medieval centre on the top of the hill.

| We | continue | | to Sighisoara, the "fortified city" among the very few in Europe |
|---|---|---|---|
| Subject | Finite '(*present*) | *continue*' Predicator | Adjunct: circ |
| MOOD | | RESIDUE | |
| Actor | Pr: Material | | Circ: Location (place) |
| experiential | | | |
| THEME | RHEME | | |

(1ii) which retains its medieval centre on the top of the hill – dependent clause, not part of Interpersonal and Textual analyses.

| which | retains | its medieval centre | on the top of the hill. |
|---|---|---|---|
| Carrier | Pr: Relational (attributive - intensive) | Attribute | Circ: Location (place) |

(2i) Here was also born Vlad the Impaler, (2ii) better known as Count Dracula.

| Here | *[it]* | was | also | born | Vlad the Impaler |
|---|---|---|---|---|---|
| Adjunct: circ | [Sub-] | Finite | Adjunct: conjunctive | Predicator | -ject |
| RESIDUE | MO- | | | | -OD |
| Circ: Location (place) | *[Go-]* | Pr: Mate- | - | -rial | -al |
| experiential | | | | | |
| THEME | RHEME | | | | |

(2ii) better known as Count Dracula – dependent clause, not part of Interpersonal and Textual analyses.

| *[which]* | *[is]* | better | known | as Count Dracula |
|---|---|---|---|---|
| *Identified/ Value* | Pr: Caus- | - | -ative | Identifier / Token |

(3i) There are several defensive towers [[that surround the city]], (3ii) named after the trades of their builders: the Tailors' Tower, the Shoemakers' Tower, the Rope Makers' Tower, the Clock Tower etc

| There | are | | several defensive towers [[that surround the city]] |
|---|---|---|---|
| Subject | Finite '(*present*) | *be*' Predicator | Complement |
| | MOOD | RESIDUE | |
| | Pr: Existential | | Existent |
| ex | periential | | |
| | THEME | RHEME | |

(3ii) named after the trades of their builders: the Tailors' Tower, the Shoemakers' Tower, the Rope Makers' Tower, the Clock Tower etc – – dependent clause, not part of Interpersonal and Textual analyses.

| *[which]* | *[are]* named | after the trades of their builders: | the Tailors' Tower, the Shoemakers' Tower, the Rope Makers' Tower, the Clock Tower etc |
|---|---|---|---|
| *Identified/ Value* | Pr: Causative | Circ: Manner (comparison) | Identifier / Token |

(4) Dinner in the house [[where Count Vlad was born]]/or an intimate restaurant medieval style and accommodation in Sighisoara in the citadel.

| Dinner in the house [[where Count Vlad was born]] /or an intimate restaurant medieval style and accommodation in Sighisoara in the citadel | *[are* | *provided]* |
|---|---|---|
| Subject | *[Finite '(present)* | *provide' Predicator]* |
| MOOD | | *RESIDUE* |
| Identifier / Token: possessed | - | *[Pr: Relational (identifying-possessive)]* |
| experiential | | |
| THEME | RHEME | |

## 2.2. Spanish set of commercial webpages

### 2.2.1. The Monastery of El Escorial in the commercial corpus

*Logical analysis*

| | |
|---|---|
| xβ | (1i) After picking you up from your hotel in Madrid, |
| α | (1ii) we will make our way to El Escorial |
| xγ α | (1iii) to visit The Royal Monastery of San Lorenzo El Real |
| =β | (1iv) built by King Philip the 2nd. |
| 1 | (2i) The Renaissance complex combines a palace and monastery, |
| +2 | (2ii) and features a wonderful collection of art. |
| 1 | (3i) We will tour the complex, including the Pantheon of Kings and basilica, |
| +2 α | (3ii) and hear the history of Spain |
| xβ | (3iii) as we wander this great complex. |

*Experiential, interpersonal and textual analyses*

(1i) After picking you up from your hotel in Madrid, (1ii) we will make our way to El Escorial (1iii) to visit The Royal Monastery of San Lorenzo El Real (1iv) built by King Philip the 2nd.

<table>
<tr><td rowspan="4">After picking you up from your hotel in Madrid</td><td>we</td><td>will</td><td>make our way</td><td>to El Escorial</td></tr>
<tr><td>Subject</td><td>Finite</td><td>Predicator</td><td>Adjunct: circ</td></tr>
<tr><td colspan="2">MOOD</td><td colspan="2">RESIDUE</td></tr>
<tr><td>Actor</td><td>-</td><td>Pr: Material</td><td>Circ: Location (place)</td></tr>
<tr><td>experiential</td><td colspan="4" rowspan="2">RHEME</td></tr>
<tr><td>THEME</td></tr>
</table>

(1i) After picking you up from your hotel in Madrid – dependent clause, not part of Interpersonal and Textual analyses.

| After | picking | you | up | from your hotel in Madrid |
|---|---|---|---|---|
| - | Pr: Mate- | Goal | -rial | Circ: Location (place) |

(1iii) *to visit The Royal Monastery of San Lorenzo El Real,* (1iv) *built by King Philip the 2nd* – – dependent clauses, not part of Interpersonal and Textual analyses.

| to visit | The Royal Monastery of San Lorenzo El Real |
|---|---|
| Pr: Material | Goal |

| *[which]* | *[was]* built | by King Philip the 2nd |
|---|---|---|
| *Goal* | Pr: Material | Actor |

(2i) The Renaissance complex combines a palace and monastery, (2ii) and features a wonderful collection of art.

<table>
<tr><td>The Renaissance complex</td><td colspan="2">combines</td><td>a palace and monastery</td></tr>
<tr><td>Subject</td><td>Finite ‘(present)</td><td>combine’ Predicator</td><td>Complement</td></tr>
<tr><td colspan="2">MOOD</td><td colspan="2">RESIDUE</td></tr>
<tr><td>Carrier: possessor</td><td colspan="2">Pr: Relational (attributive-possessive)</td><td>Attribute: possessed</td></tr>
<tr><td>experiential</td><td colspan="3" rowspan="2">RHEME</td></tr>
<tr><td>THEME</td></tr>
</table>

<table>
<tr><td>and</td><td>[The Renaissance complex]</td><td colspan="2">features</td><td>a wonderful collection of art</td></tr>
<tr><td rowspan="2">(Conjunction)</td><td>[Subject]</td><td>Finite ‘(present)</td><td>feature’ Predicator</td><td>Complement</td></tr>
<tr><td colspan="2">MOOD</td><td colspan="2">RESIDUE</td></tr>
<tr><td>-</td><td>[Carrier: possessor]</td><td colspan="2">Pr: Relational (attributive-possessive)</td><td>Attribute: possessed</td></tr>
<tr><td>textual</td><td colspan="2">experiential</td><td colspan="2" rowspan="2">RHEME</td></tr>
<tr><td colspan="3">THEME</td></tr>
</table>

(3i) We will tour the complex, including the Pantheon of Kings and basilica, (3ii) and hear the history of Spain (4iii) as we wander this great complex.

<table>
<tr><td>We</td><td>will</td><td>tour</td><td>the complex, including the Pantheon of Kings and basilica</td></tr>
<tr><td>Subject</td><td>Finite</td><td>Predicator</td><td>Complement</td></tr>
<tr><td colspan="2">MOOD</td><td colspan="2">RESIDUE</td></tr>
<tr><td>Actor</td><td>-</td><td>Pr: Material</td><td>Goal</td></tr>
<tr><td>experiential</td><td colspan="3" rowspan="2">RHEME</td></tr>
<tr><td>THEME</td></tr>
</table>

<table>
<tr><td>and</td><td>[we]</td><td>[will]</td><td>hear</td><td>the history of Spain</td></tr>
<tr><td rowspan="2">(Conjunction)</td><td>[Subject]</td><td>[Finite]</td><td>hear’ Predicator</td><td>Complement</td></tr>
<tr><td colspan="2">[MOOD]</td><td colspan="2">RESIDUE</td></tr>
<tr><td>-</td><td>Senser</td><td>-</td><td>Pr: Mental (perception)</td><td>Phenomenon</td></tr>
<tr><td>textual</td><td colspan="3">experiential</td><td rowspan="2">RHEME</td></tr>
<tr><td colspan="4">THEME</td></tr>
</table>

(3iii) as we wander this great complex – dependent clause, not part of Interpersonal and Textual analyses.

| as | we | wander | this great complex |
|---|---|---|---|
| - | Actor | Pr: Material | Range |

## 2.2.2. The Alhambra in the commercial corpus

### *Logical analysis*

α (1i) We will pick you up in the morning for a transfer to Granada
xβ (1ii) to visit the mighty Alhambra Palaces.
α (2i) Discover a maze of magnificent halls and intimate courtyards
=β (2ii) decorated by rows of elegant arches, bubbling fountains and splendidly carved decorations.
α (3i) See the Palace of Charles the 5th, an outstanding example of Spanish Renaissance architecture, and the Alcazaba fortress with its Torre de la Vela tower
=β (3ii) offering spectacular views of Granada.
α (4i) Please note
'β 1 (4ii) entry is 18 Euros per person (extra)
+2 α (4iii) and bookings in advance is a MUST –
xβ (4iv) there will not be tickets available on the day!
CL. SIMPLEX (5) Continue your visit to the Generalife, a royal place of leisure and recreation with beautiful exotic gardens, stunning water features and the lingering aroma of jasmine [[to remind you of a grand Muslim past]].

### *Experiential, interpersonal and textual analyses*

(1i) We will pick you up in the morning for a transfer to Granada (1ii) to visit the mighty Alhambra Palaces.

| We | will | pick | you | up | in the morning | for a transfer to Granada |
|---|---|---|---|---|---|---|
| Subject | Finite | Predi- | Complement | -cator | Adjunct: circ | Adjunct: circ |
| MOOD | | RESIDUE | | | | |
| Actor | - | Pr: Mate- | Goal | -rial | Circ: Location (time) | Circ: Cause (purpose) |
| experiential | RHEME | | | | | |
| THEME | | | | | | |

(1ii) to visit the mighty Alhambra Palaces – dependent clause, not part of Interpersonal and Textual analyses.

| to visit | the mighty Alhambra Palaces |
|---|---|
| Pr: Material | Goal |

(2i) Discover a maze of magnificent halls and intimate courtyards (2ii) decorated by rows of elegant arches, bubbling fountains and splendidly carved decorations.

| Discover | a maze of magnificent halls and intimate courtyards |
|---|---|
| Predicator | Complement |
| RESIDUE | |
| Pr: Material | Goal |
| experiential | RHEME |
| THEME | |

(2ii) decorated by rows of elegant arches, bubbling fountains and splendidly carved decorations – dependent clause, not part of Interpersonal and Textual analyses.

| *[which]* | *[are]* decorated | by rows of elegant arches, bubbling fountains and splendidly carved decorations |
|---|---|---|
| *Goal* | Pr: Material | Actor |

(3i) See the Palace of Charles the 5th, an outstanding example of Spanish Renaissance architecture, and the Alcazaba fortress with its Torre de la Vela tower (3ii) offering spectacular views of Granada.

| See | the Palace of Charles the 5th, an outstanding example of Spanish Renaissance architecture, and the Alcazaba fortress with its Torre de la Vela tower |
|---|---|
| Predicator | Complement |
| RESIDUE | |
| Pr: Mental (perception) | Phenomenon |
| experiential | RHEME |
| THEME | |

(3ii) *offering spectacular views of Granada* – dependent clause, not part of Interpersonal and Textual analyses.

| *[which]* | *[is]* offering | spectacular views of Granada |
|---|---|---|
| *Identified/ Token: possessor* | Pr: Relational (identifying-possessive) | Identifier/ Value: possessed |

(4i) Please note (4ii) entry is 18 Euros per person (extra) (4iii) and bookings in advance is a MUST – (4iv) there will not be tickets available on the day!

| Please | note |
|---|---|
| Adjunct: comment | Predicator |
| MOOD | RESIDUE |
| - | Pr: Mental (cognition) |

| interpersonal | experiential |
|---|---|
| THEME | |

(4ii) entry is 18 Euros per person (extra), (4iii) and bookings in advance is a MUST – (4iv) there will not be tickets available on the day – dependent clauses, not part of Interpersonal and Textual analyses.

| entry | is | 18 Euros per person (extra) |
|---|---|---|
| Identified / Token | Pr: Relational (identifying - intensive) | Identifier / Value |

| and | bookings in advance | is | a MUST |
|---|---|---|---|
| - | Carrier | Pr: Relational (attributive - intensive) | Attribute |

| there | will not be | tickets available | on the day |
|---|---|---|---|
| | Pr: Existential | Existent | Circ: Location (time) |

(5) Continue your visit to the Generalife, a royal place of leisure and recreation with beautiful exotic gardens, stunning water features and the lingering aroma of jasmine [[to remind you of a grand Muslim past]].

| Continue | your visit | to the Generalife, a royal place of leisure and recreation with beautiful exotic gardens, stunning water features and the lingering aroma of jasmine[[to remind you of a grand Muslim past]] |
|---|---|---|
| Predicator | Complement | Adjunct: circ |
| RESIDUE | | |
| Pr: Material | Goal | Circ: Location (place) |
| experiential | | |
| THEME | | RHEME |

## 2.2.3. Santiago de Compostela in the commercial corpus

### *Logical analysis*

CL. SIMPLEX (1) The trip to Santiago de Compostela visits the beautiful city and its main attraction the towering cathedral.

CL. SIMPLEX (2) This magical city is a must see for many tourists [[visiting Galicia]] and a welcomed site for the many pilgrims [[ending their Camino de Santiago]].

CL. SIMPLEX (3) Santiago was founded around the beginning of the 5th century not long after the collapse of the Roman Empire.

CL. SIMPLEX (4) Santiago became famous with the discovery of the the remains of the Apostle St. James in the early 9th century.

| | |
|---|---|
| 1 | (5i) The Plaza Obradoiro is [[where the main entrance to the cathedral is situated]], |
| +2 α | (5ii) opposite is the Raxoi Palace |
| =β | (5iii) which is now the town hall. |
| 1 | (6i) Santiago de Compostela's historic quarter is full of architecture and monuments [[dating from the Romanesque to Baroque and Neo Classical periods]] |
| +2 | (6ii) and almost all are of an impressive grandeur. |
| 1 | (7i) This city is very impressive |
| +2 α | (7ii) and can also be combined with a visit to Vigo |
| xβ | (7iii) if time permits. |

## *Experiential, interpersonal and textual analyses*

(1) The trip to Santiago de Compostela visits the beautiful city and its main attraction the towering cathedral.

| The trip to Santiago de Compostela | visits | | the beautiful city and its main attraction the towering cathedral |
|---|---|---|---|
| Subject | Finite '(*present*) | *visit*' Predicator | Complement |
| MOOD | | RESIDUE | |
| Actor | Pr: Material | | Goal |
| experiential | | | |
| THEME | RHEME | | |

(2) This magical city is a must see for many tourists [[visiting Galicia]] and a welcomed site for the many pilgrims [[ending their Camino de Santiago]].

| This magical city | is | | a must see and a welcomed site | for many tourists [[visiting Galicia]] for the many pilgrims[[ending their Camino de Santiago]] |
|---|---|---|---|---|
| Subject | Finite '(*present*) | Predicator *be*' | Complements | Adjuncts: circ |
| MOOD | | RESIDUE | | |
| Carrier | Pr: Relational (attributive-intensive) | | Attributes | Attributors |
| experiential | | | | |
| THEME | | | RHEME | |

(3) Santiago was founded around the beginning of the 5th century not long after the collapse of the Roman Empire.

| Santiago | was | founded | around the beginning of the 5th century not long after the collapse of the Roman Empire |
|---|---|---|---|
| Subject | Finite | Predicator | Adjunct: circ |

| MOOD | | RESIDUE | |
|---|---|---|---|
| Goal | - | Pr: Material | Circ: Location (time) |
| experiential | | | |
| THEME | RHEME | | |

(4) Santiago became famous with the discovery of the the remains of the Apostle St. James in the early 9th century.

| Santiago | became | | famous | with the discovery of the the remains of the Apostle St. James | in the early 9th century |
|---|---|---|---|---|---|
| Subject | Finite '(*past*) | Predicator *become*' | Complement | Adjunct: circ | Adjunct: circ |
| MOOD | | RESIDUE | | | |
| Carrier | Pr: Relational (attributive-intensive) | | Attribute | Circ: Manner (means) | Circ: Location (time) |
| experiential | | | | | |
| THEME | | | | RHEME | |

(5i) The Plaza Obradoiro is [[where the main entrance to the cathedral is situated]], (5ii) opposite is the Raxoi Palace (5iii) which is now the town hall.

| The Plaza Obradoiro | is | | [[where the main entrance to the cathedral is situated]] |
|---|---|---|---|
| Subject | Finite '(*present*) | *be*' Predicator | Complement |
| MOOD | | RESIDUE | |
| Identified / Token | Pr: Relational (identifying - circumstantial) | | Identifier / Value |
| experiential | RHEME | | |
| THEME | | | |

| opposite | is | | the Raxoi Palace |
|---|---|---|---|
| Subject | Finite '(*present*) | *be*' Predicator | Complement |
| | MOOD | RESIDUE | |
| Identified / Value | Pr: Relational (identifying - circumstantial) | | Identifier / Token |
| experiential | RHEME | | |
| THEME | | | |

(5iii) which is now the town hall – dependent clause, not part of Interpersonal and Textual analyses.

| which | is | now | the town hall |
|---|---|---|---|
| Identified / Token | Pr: Relational (identifying - intensive) | Circ: Location (time) | Identifier / Value |

(6i) Santiago de Compostela's historic quarter is full of architecture and monuments [[dating from the Romanesque to Baroque and Neo Classical periods]] (6ii) and almost all are of an impressive grandeur.

| Santiago de Compostela's historic quarter | is | | full of architecture and monuments[[dating from the Romanesque to Baroque and Neo Classical periods]] |
|---|---|---|---|
| Subject | Finite '(*present*) | *be*' Predicator | Complement |
| MOOD | | RESIDUE | |
| Carrier | Pr: Relational (attributive - intensive) | | Attribute |
| experiential | | | |
| THEME | | | RHEME |

| and | almost all | are | | of an impressive grandeur |
|---|---|---|---|---|
| (Conjunction) | Subject | Finite '(*present*) | *be*' Predicator | Complement |
| | | MOOD | RESIDUE | |
| - | Carrier | Pr: Relational (attributive - intensive) | | Attribute |
| textual | experiential | RHEME | | |
| THEME | | | | |

(7i) This city is very impressive (7ii) and can also be combined with a visit to Vigo (7iii) if time permits.

| This city | is | | very impressive |
|---|---|---|---|
| Subject | Finite '(*present*) | *be*' Predicator | Complement |
| | MOOD | RESIDUE | |
| Carrier | Pr: Relational (attributive - intensive) | | Attribute |
| experiential | RHEME | | |
| THEME | | | |

| and | *[this city]* | can | also | be combined with | a visit to Vigo |
|---|---|---|---|---|---|
| (Conjunction) | *[Subject]* | Finite | Adjunct: | Predicator | Complement |

<table>
<tr><td></td><td colspan="2">MOOD</td><td>conjunctive</td><td colspan="2">RESIDUE</td></tr>
<tr><td>-</td><td>[Identified/ Value: possessor]</td><td>-</td><td>-</td><td>Pr: Relational (identifying - possessive)</td><td>Identifier/Token: possessed</td></tr>
<tr><td>textual</td><td colspan="4">experiential</td><td rowspan="2">RHEME</td></tr>
<tr><td colspan="5">THEME</td></tr>
</table>

(7iii) if time permits – dependent clause, not part of Interpersonal and Textual analyses.

| if | time | permits |
|---|---|---|
| - | Actor | Pr: Material |

## 2.3. British set of commercial webpages

### 2.3.1. Canterbury Cathedral in the commercial corpus

*Logical analysis*

xβ (1i) Traveling through Kent, the county [[known as the 'Garden of England']],
α (1ii) we make our way to Canterbury
xγ (1iii) to visit the Cathedral.
CL. SIMPLEX (2) This magnificent Cathedral is the most important church within the worldwide Anglican faith.
1 (3i) The central 'Bell Harry Tower' dates back to 1498,
+2 (3ii) and the crypt to the 11th Century.
1 (4i) It is here [[where your guide will tell the story of the shocking murder of Archbishop Thomas Beckett in 1170]]
+2 (4ii) and there will also be time [[to explore the narrow streets of Canterbury]].
CL. SIMPLEX (5) There will be an opportunity for lunch in Canterbury.

*Experiential, interpersonal and textual analyses*

(1i) Traveling through Kent, the county [[known as the 'Garden of England']], (1ii) we make our way to Canterbury (1iii) to visit the Cathedral.

<table>
<tr><td rowspan="3">Traveling through Kent, the county [[known as the 'Garden of England']]</td><td>we</td><td colspan="2">make our way</td><td>to Canterbury</td></tr>
<tr><td>Subject</td><td>Finite '(present)</td><td>make one's way' Predicator</td><td>Adjunct: circ</td></tr>
<tr><td colspan="2">MOOD</td><td colspan="2">RESIDUE</td></tr>
<tr><td>-</td><td>Actor</td><td colspan="2">Pr: Material</td><td>Circ: Location (place)</td></tr>
<tr><td>experiential</td><td colspan="4" rowspan="2">RHEME</td></tr>
<tr><td>THEME</td></tr>
</table>

(1i) Traveling through Kent, the county [[known as the 'Garden of England']] – dependent clause, not part of Interpersonal and Textual analyses.

| Traveling | through Kent, the county |
|---|---|
| Pr: Material | Circ: Location (place) |

(1iii) *to visit the Cathedral* – dependent clause, not part of Interpersonal and Textual analyses.

| to visit | the Cathedral |
|---|---|
| Pr: Material | Goal |

(2) This magnificent Cathedral is the most important church within the worldwide Anglican faith.

<table>
<tr><td>This magnificent Cathedral</td><td colspan="2">is</td><td>the most important church within the worldwide Anglican faith</td></tr>
<tr><td>Subject</td><td>Finite ‘(present)</td><td>be’ Predicator</td><td>Complement</td></tr>
<tr><td colspan="2">MOOD</td><td colspan="2">RESIDUE</td></tr>
<tr><td>Identified/ Token</td><td colspan="2">Pr: Relational (identifying - intensive)</td><td>Identifier/ Value</td></tr>
<tr><td>experiential</td><td colspan="3" rowspan="2">RHEME</td></tr>
<tr><td>THEME</td></tr>
</table>

(3i) The central 'Bell Harry Tower' dates back to 1498, (3ii) and the crypt to the 11th Century.

<table>
<tr><td>The central 'Bell Harry Tower'</td><td colspan="2">dates back</td><td>to 1498</td></tr>
<tr><td>Subject</td><td>Finite ‘(present)</td><td>date back’ Predicator</td><td>Complement</td></tr>
<tr><td colspan="2">MOOD</td><td colspan="2">RESIDUE</td></tr>
<tr><td>Carrier</td><td colspan="2">Pr: Relational (attributive-circumstantial)</td><td>Attribute</td></tr>
<tr><td>experiential</td><td colspan="3" rowspan="2">RHEME</td></tr>
<tr><td>THEME</td></tr>
</table>

<table>
<tr><td>and</td><td>the crypt</td><td colspan="2">[dates back]</td><td>to the 11th Century</td></tr>
<tr><td rowspan="2">(Conjunction)</td><td>Subject</td><td>[Finite ‘(present)]</td><td>[Predicator date back’]</td><td>Complement</td></tr>
<tr><td></td><td>MOOD</td><td colspan="2">RESIDUE</td></tr>
<tr><td>-</td><td>Carrier</td><td colspan="2">[Pr: Relational (attributive - circumstantial)]</td><td>Attribute</td></tr>
<tr><td>textual</td><td>experiential</td><td colspan="3" rowspan="2">RHEME</td></tr>
<tr><td colspan="2">THEME</td></tr>
</table>

(4i) It is here [[where your guide will tell the story of the shocking murder of Archbishop Thomas Beckett in 1170]] (4ii) and there will also be time [to explore the narrow streets of Canterbury].

| It | is | | here | [[where your guide will tell the story of the shocking murder of Archbishop Thomas Beckett in 1170]] |
|---|---|---|---|---|
| Subj- | Finite '(*present*) | *be*' Predicator | Complement | -ect |
| MOOD | | RESIDUE | | |
| Identi- | Pr: Relational (identifying - circumstantial) | | Identifier / Token | -fied / Value |
| experiential | | | | RHEME |
| THEME | | | | |

| and | there | will | also | be | time [to explore the narrow streets of Canterbury] |
|---|---|---|---|---|---|
| (Conjunction) | Subject | Finite: mod | Adjunct: conjunctive | Predicator | Complement |
| | MOOD | | | RESIDUE | |
| - | | - | - | Pr: Existential | Existent |
| textual | experiential | | | | RHEME |
| | THEME | | | | |

(5) There will be an opportunity for lunch in Canterbury.

| There | will | be | an opportunity for lunch | in Canterbury |
|---|---|---|---|---|
| Subject | Finite: mod | Predicator | Complement | Adjunct: circ |
| MOOD | | RESIDUE | | |
| | - | Pr: Existential | Existent | Circ: Location (place) |
| experiential | | | RHEME | |
| THEME | | | | |

## 2.3.2. The Tower of London in the commercial corpus

### *Logical analysis*

=β 1 (1i) Founded by William the Conqueror in 1066-7
+2 (1ii) and enlarged by successive sovereigns,

α (1iii) the Tower of London is one of the world's most famous and spectacular fortresses.
CL. SIMPLEX (2) Over the past 1000 years it has been a Royal Palace, an armoury and a place of imprisonment and execution.
α (3i) The Beefeaters
<=β> (3ii) who guard the Tower
α (3i) will regale you with stories of its past.
CL. SIMPLEX (4) We will visit the Crown Jewels, including the magnificent solid-gold crown [[used at the coronation of Queen Elizabeth II]], the enormous Cullinan diamonds and the extraordinary Koh-i-Noor.

## *Experiential, interpersonal and textual analyses*

(1i) Founded by William the Conqueror in 1066-7 (1ii) and enlarged by successive sovereigns, (1iii) the Tower of London is one of the world's most famous and spectacular fortresses.

| Founded by William the Conqueror in 10667 and enlarged by successive sovereigns | the Tower of London | is | | one of the world's most famous and spectacular fortresses |
|---|---|---|---|---|
| | Subject | Finite '(*present*) | *be*' Predicator | Complement |
| | | MOOD | RESIDUE | |
| | Identified/ Token | Pr: Relational (identifying-intensive) | | Identifier/ Value |
| experiential | | RHEME | | |
| THEME | | | | |

(1i) Founded by William the Conqueror in 1066-7- – dependent clause, not part of Interpersonal and Textual analyses.

| *[which]* | *[was]* Founded | by William the Conqueror | in 1066-7 |
|---|---|---|---|
| *[Goal]* | Pr: Material | Actor | Circ: Location (time) |

(1ii) and enlarged by successive sovereigns

| and | *[which]* | *[was]* enlarged | by successive sovereigns |
|---|---|---|---|
| - | *[Goal]* | Pr: Material | Actor |

(2) Over the past 1000 years it has been a Royal Palace, an armoury and a place of imprisonment and execution.

| Over the past 1000 years | it | has | been | a Royal Palace, an armoury and a place of imprisonment and execution |
|---|---|---|---|---|
| Adjunct: circ | Subject | Finite | Predicator | Complement |
| RESIDUE | MOOD | | | |

| Circ: Extent (time) | Carrier | - | Pr: Relational (attributive-intensive) | Attribute |
|---|---|---|---|---|
| experiential | RHEME | | | |
| THEME | | | | |

(3i) The Beefeaters (3ii) who guard the Tower (3i) will regale you with stories of its past.

| The Beefeaters <<//who guard the Tower//>> | will | regale | you | with stories of its past |
|---|---|---|---|---|
| Subject | Finite | Predicator | Complement | Complement |
| MOOD | | RESIDUE | | |
| Actor | - | Pr: Material | Beneficiary | Goal |
| experiential | RHEME | | | |
| THEME | | | | |

(3ii) who guard the Tower – dependent clause, not part of Interpersonal and Textual analyses.

| who | guard | the Tower |
|---|---|---|
| Actor | Pr: Material | Goal |

(4) We will visit the Crown Jewels, including the magnificent solid-gold crown [[used at the coronation of Queen Elizabeth II]], the enormous Cullinan diamonds and the extraordinary Koh-i-Noor.

| We | will | visit | the Crown Jewels, including the magnificent solid-gold crown [[used at the coronation of Queen Elizabeth II]], the enormous Cullinan diamonds and the extraordinary Koh-i-Noor |
|---|---|---|---|
| Subject | Finite | Predicator | Complement |
| MOOD | | RESIDUE | |
| Actor | - | Pr: Material | Goal |
| experiential | RHEME | | |
| THEME | | | |

## 2.3.3. Edinburgh in the commercial corpus

### *Logical analysis*

CL. SIMPLEX (1) The train from London's King Cross Station arrives at the Royal City of Edinburgh at around 11.30am.

$\alpha$ (2i) Right by the station you board the open-top sightseeing bus

$=\beta$ (2ii) where you'll get a bird's-eye view of this majestic city!

CL. SIMPLEX (3) The hop-on hop-off ticket allows you the freedom [[to leave and re-join the bus as often as you like]].

CL. SIMPLEX (4) You will see the Old Town quarter, the Scotch Whisky Heritage Centre, the gloriously intricate Scott Monument, the Palace of Holyrood House and the brand new Scottish Parliament building.

α (5i) You might want
'β! 1 (5ii) to wander through the cobbled city centre streets
+2 α (5iii) or stroll along Princes Street
+β (5iv) checking out the tartan, whisky and shortbreads [[that have made Scotland famous]]!

CL. SIMPLEX (6) Your tour includes tickets to Edinburgh Castle.

α (7i) The train back to London leaves Edinburgh in the late afternoon
+β (7ii) returning to London's King's Cross at around 10:30pm.

## *Experiential, interpersonal and textual analyses*

(1) The train from London's King Cross Station arrives at the Royal City of Edinburgh at around 11.30am.

| The train from London's King Cross Station | arrives | | at the Royal City of Edinburgh | at around 11.30am |
|---|---|---|---|---|
| Subject | Finite '(*present*) | Predicator *arrive*' | Adjunct: circ | Adjunct: circ |
| MOOD | | RESIDUE | | |
| Actor | Pr: Material | | Circ: Location (place) | Circ: Location (time) |
| experiential | | | | |
| THEME | | RHEME | | |

(2i) Right by the station you board the open-top sightseeing bus (2ii) where you'll get a bird's-eye view of this majestic city!

| Right by the station | you | board | | the open-top sightseeing bus |
|---|---|---|---|---|
| Adjunct: circ | Subject | Finite '(*present*) | Predicator *board*' | Complement |
| RESIDUE | MOOD | | | |
| Circ: Location (place) | Actor | Pr: Material | | Range |
| experiential | | | | |
| THEME | RHEME | | | |

(2ii) where you'll get a bird's-eye view of this majestic city – dependent clause, not part of Interpersonal and Textual analyses.

| where | you | 'll get a bird's-eye view of | this majestic city |
|---|---|---|---|
| Circ: Location (place) | Senser | Pr: Mental (perception) | Phenomenon |

(3) The hop-on hop-off ticket allows you the freedom [[to leave and re-join the bus as often as you like]].

| The hop-on hop-off ticket | allows | | you | the freedom [[to leave and re-join the bus as often as you like]] |
|---|---|---|---|---|
| Subject | Finite '(*present*) | Predicator *allow*' | Complement | Complement |
| MOOD | | RESIDUE | | |
| Actor | Pr: Material | | Beneficiary | Goal |
| experiential | | | | |
| THEME | RHEME | | | |

(4) You will see the Old Town quarter, the Scotch Whisky Heritage Centre, the gloriously intricate Scott Monument, the Palace of Holyrood House and the brand new Scottish Parliament building.

| You | will | see | the Old Town quarter, the Scotch Whisky Heritage Centre, the gloriously intricate Scott Monument, the Palace of Holyrood House and the brand new Scottish Parliament building |
|---|---|---|---|
| Subject | Finite | Predicator | Complement |
| MOOD | | RESIDUE | |
| Senser | - | Pr: Mental (perception) | Phenomenon |
| experiential | | | |
| THEME | | | RHEME |

(5i) You might want (5ii) to wander through the cobbled city centre streets (5iii) or stroll along Princes Street (5$_{iv}$) checking out the tartan, whisky and shortbreads [[that have made Scotland famous]]!

| You | might | want |
|---|---|---|
| Subject | Finite | Predicator |
| MOOD | | RESIDUE |
| Senser | - | Pr: Mental (affection) |
| experiential | | RHEME |

| THEME | |
|---|---|

$_{(5ii)}$ to wander through the cobbled city centre streets $_{(5iii)}$ or stroll along Princes Street $_{(5iv)}$ checking out the tartan, whisky and shortbreads [[that have made Scotland famous]] – dependent clauses, not part of Interpersonal and Textual analyses.

| to wander | through the cobbled city centre streets |
|---|---|
| Pr: Material | Circ: Location (place) |

| or | stroll | along Princes Street |
|---|---|---|
| - | Pr: Material | Circ: Location (place) |

| checking out | the tartan, whisky and shortbreads |
|---|---|
| Pr: Material | Goal |

$_{(6)}$ Your tour includes tickets to Edinburgh Castle.

<table>
<tr><td>Your tour</td><td colspan="2">includes</td><td>tickets to Edinburgh Castle</td></tr>
<tr><td>Subject</td><td>Finite ‘(present)</td><td>include’Predicator</td><td>Complement</td></tr>
<tr><td colspan="2">MOOD</td><td colspan="2">RESIDUE</td></tr>
<tr><td>Identified/ Token: possessor</td><td colspan="2">Pr: Relational (identifying-possessive)</td><td>Identifier/ Value: possessed</td></tr>
<tr><td>experiential</td><td colspan="3" rowspan="2">RHEME</td></tr>
<tr><td>THEME</td></tr>
</table>

$_{(7i)}$ The train back to London leaves Edinburgh in the late afternoon $_{(7ii)}$ returning to London's King's Cross at around 10:30pm.

<table>
<tr><td>The train back to London</td><td colspan="2">leaves</td><td>Edinburgh</td><td>in the late afternoon</td></tr>
<tr><td>Subject</td><td>Finite ‘(present)</td><td>Predicator leave’</td><td>Adjunct: circ</td><td>Adjunct: circ</td></tr>
<tr><td colspan="2">MOOD</td><td colspan="3">RESIDUE</td></tr>
<tr><td>Actor</td><td colspan="2">Pr: Material</td><td>Circ: Location (place)</td><td>Circ: Location (time)</td></tr>
<tr><td>experiential</td><td colspan="4" rowspan="2">RHEME</td></tr>
<tr><td>THEME</td></tr>
</table>

$_{(7ii)}$ returning to London's King's Cross at around 10:30pm – dependent clause, not part of Interpersonal and Textual analyses.

| returning | to London's King's Cross | at around 10:30pm |
|---|---|---|
| Pr: Material | Circ: Location (place) | Circ: Location (time) |

# BIBLIOGRAPHY

## Literature Consulted

Aaker, D. 1995. *Building Strong Brands*. New York: The Free Press.

Adler, J. 1989. "Origins of Sightseeing". *Annals of Tourism Research* 16:7-29.

Alexander, J. 2003. *The Meanings of Social Life: A Cultural Sociology*. Oxford: OUP.

Andersen, T., and M. Boeriis. 2012. "Relationship/Participant Focus in Multimodal Market Communication". *Hermes–Journal of Language and Communication in Business* 48:75-94.

Anholt, S. 2009. "Why National Image Matter". In *Handbook on Tourism Destinations Branding*, by WTO and ETC, ix-xvi. Madrid: WTO.

Antelmi, D. 2011. "Guías Turísticas, Intertextualidad y Memoria Discursiva: Las Guías de Italia en Lengua Francesa". In *La Lengua del Turismo. Géneros Discursivos y Terminología*, edited by M. Calvi and G. Mapelli, 75-92. Bern: Peter Lang.

Antelmi, D., and F. Santulli. 2012. "Travellers' Memories: The Image of Places from Literature to Blog Chatter". *Pasos* 10(4):13-24.

Anthonissen, C. 2003. "Interaction between Visual and Verbal Communication: Changing Patterns in the Printed Media". In *Critical Discourse Analysis: Theory and Interdisciplinarity*, edited by G. Weiss and R. Wodak, 297-312. New York: Palgrave Macmillan.

Archer, B., C. Cooper and L. Ruhanen. 2005. "The Positive and Negative Impacts of Tourism". In *Global Tourism* (3rd ed.), edited by W. Theobald, 79-103. USA: Elsevier.

Ares Ares, A. 2011. "La Deíxis y la Modalización Discursiva en los Itinerarios de Viajes Periodísticos". In *La Lengua del Turismo. Géneros Discursivos y Terminología*, edited by M. Calvi and G. Mapelli, 131-152. Bern: Peter Lang.

Arús, J., E. Bárcena and P. Rodríguez-Arancón. forthcoming. "Fostering Intercultural Competence through Contextualized Texts in EFL Settings". In *Actas del Congreso Internacional MIAC1O: Textual Analysis in Cross-cultural and Intercultural Communication/ Análisis Textual en la Comunicación Intercultural,* edited by I. Elorza and O. Carbonell. Salamanca: Ediciones Universidad de Salamanca.

Ashworth, G., and J. Tunbridge. 2000. *The Tourist-Historic City: Retrospect and Prospect on Managing the Heritage City.* Elsevier: London.

Babu, S., S. Mishra and B. Parida, eds. *Tourism Development Revisited. Concepts, Issues and Paradigms*. New Delhi: Response.

Baldry, A, ed. 2000. *Multimodality and Multimediality in the Distance Learning Age*. Campobasso: Palladino Editore.

Banks, D. 2002. "Systemic Functional Linguistics as a Model for Text Analysis". *Asp* Varia: 35-36.

Bargiela-Chiappini, F. 2005. "In Memory of the Business Letter: Multimedia, Genres and Social Action in a Banking Website". In *Genre Variation in Business Letters*, edited by P. Gillaerts and M. Gotti, 99-122. Bern: Peter Lang.

Bargiela-Chiappini, F., C. Nickerson and B. Planken. 2007. *Business Discourse*. Basingstoke: Palgrave.

Barker, C., and D. Galasinski. 2001. *Cultural Studies and Discourse Analysis. A Dialogue on Language and Identity.* London: Sage.

Barnard, A., and J. Spenser, eds. 1996. *Encyclopaedia of Social and Cultural Anthropology*. Oxon: Routledge.

Barthes, R. 1977. *Image-Music-Text.* London: Fontana.

Bartlett, T. 2002. "How to Create a Tourism Image for a Country?". In *Promotion of the Tourist Image of European Destinations on Competitive International Markets*, by WTO and ETC, 41-46. Madrid: WTO.

Bateman, J. 2008. *Multimodality and Genre: A Foundation for the Systematic Analysis of Multimodal Documents*. London: Palgrave Macmillan.

—. 2014. "Genre in the Age of Multimodality: Some Conceptual Refinements for Practical Analysis". In *Evolution in Genres: Emergence, Variation, Multimodality*, edited by P. Evangelisti-Allori, V. Bhatia and J. Bateman, 237-270. Frankfurt am Main: Peter Lang.

Bateman, J., and J. Delin. 2001. "Contrasting Instructions: from Grammar to Layout". Paper presented at the 2nd International CoLLaTE Colloquium *Contrastive Analysis and Linguistic Theory*, Ghent, Belgium. September.

Becker, B., and J. Wehner. 2001. "Electronic Networks and Civil Society: Reflections on Structural Changes in the Public Sphere". In *Culture, Technology, Communication. Towards an Intercultural Global Village,* edited by C. Ess, 67- 86. USA: State University of New York Press.

Bemard, H. 1988. *Research Methods in Cultural Anthropology*. California: Sage.

Bernstein, B. 1971. *Class, Codes and Control*. London: Routledge and Kegan Paul.

Besnier, N. 2004. "Diversity, Hierarchy, and Modernity in Pacific Island Communities". In *A Companion to Linguistic Anthropology*, edited by A. Duranti, 95-120. Malden: Blackwell.

Bhatia, V. 2004. *Worlds of Written Discourse*. London: Continuum.

Blommaert, J. 2011. "Pragmatics and Discourse". In *The Cambridge Handbook of Sociolinguistics*, edited by R. Mesthrie, 122-137. Cambridge: CUP.

Bloor, M., and T. Bloor. 2007. *The Practice of Critical Discourse Analysis: An Introduction*. London: Hodder Education.

Bolaños Medina, A., M. Rodríguez Medina, L. Bolaños Medina and L. Losada García. 2005. "Analysing Digital Genres: Function and Functionality in Corporate Websites of Computer Hardware". *IBÉRICA* 9:123-147.

Bosch Abarca, E. 2001. "Soportes de Promoción en la Comunicación Turística". In *Discourse Analysis and Terminology in Languages for Specific Purposes,* edited by J. Palmer, S. Posteguillo and I. Fortanet, 325-334. Castello de la Plana: Universitat de Jaume I.

Bugnot, M. 2006. "Función Apelativa y Recursos Hiperbólicos en la Traducción de los Folletos Turísticos". *Çédille. Revista de estudios franceses* 2:21-38.

Buhalis, D. 1998. "Strategic Use of Information Technologies in the Tourism Industry". *Tourism Management* 19(5):409-421.

Buliç, N. 2002. "Image Building and Branding Policy: How to Ensure Sustainable Image Promotion". In *Promotion of the Tourist Image of European Destinations on Competitive International Markets*, by WTO and ETC, 47-54. Madrid: WTO.

Butler, R. 1998. "Tartan Mythology: The Traditional Tourist Image of Scotland". In *Destinations: Cultural Landscape of Tourism,* edited by G. Ringer, 121–139. London: Routledge.

Butler, J., and S. Boyd, eds. 2000. *Tourism in National Parks: Issues and Implications*. West Sussex: John Wiley and Sons, Ltd.

Calvi, M. 2000. *Il Linguaggio Spagnolo del Turismo*. Viareggio: Baroni.

—. 2006. *Lengua y Comunicación en el Español del Turismo*. Madrid: Arco Libros.

—. 2010. "Los Géneros Discursivos en la Lengua del Turismo: Una Propuesta de Clasificación". *Ibérica* 19:9-32.

—. 2011. "Pautas de Análisis para los Géneros del Turismo". In *La Lengua del Turismo. Géneros Discursivos y Terminología*, edited by M. Calvi and G. Mapelli, 19-46. Bern: Peter Lang.

Calvi, M., and M. Bonomi. 2008. “El Lenguaje del Turismo: de los Textos Especializados a la Comunidad del Viajero”. In *La Comunicación Especializada*, edited by C. Navarro, R. Rodríguez Abella, F. dalle Pezze and R. Miotti, 181-202. Bern: Peter Lang.

Calvi, M., M. Bordonaba Zabalza, G. Mapelli and J. Santos López, eds. 2009. *Las Lenguas de Especialidad en Español.* Roma: Carocci.

Calvi, M., and G. Mapelli. 2010. “La Presencia de Términos Culturales en las Páginas Web de Turismo”. In *Nuevos Caminos del Hispanismo.* Actas del XVI Congreso de la Asociación Internacional de Hispanistas (París, 9-13 de julio de 2007), edited by P. Civil and F. Crémoux, 43-51. Madrid: Iberoamericana.

Calvi, M., and G. Mapelli. 2011. “Introduction”. In *La Lengua del Turismo. Géneros Discursivos y Terminología*, edited by M. Calvi and G. Mapelli, 9-18. Bern: Peter Lang.

Calvi, M., G. Mapelli and J. Santos López, eds. 2008. *Lingue, Culture, Economia. Comunicazione e Pratiche Discorsive.* Milano: Franco Angeli.

Carbaugh, D. 2007. “Cultural Discourse Analysis: Communication Practices and Intercultural Encounters”. *Journal of Intercultural Communication Research* 36(3):167-182.

Cardon, P. 2008. “A Critique of Hall’s Contexting Model: A Meta-Analysis of Literature on Intercultural Business and Technical Communication”. *Journal of Technical and Business Communication* 22(4):399-428.

Cazes, G., and F. Potier. 1996. *Le Tourisme Urbain.* Paris: Presses Universitaires de France.

Chacko, H. 1997. “Positioning a Tourism Destination to Gain a Competitive Edge”. *Asia Pacific Journal of Tourism Research.* Accessed January 15, 2014. http://www.hotel-online.com/Trends /AsiaPacificJournal/ PositionDestination.html.

Ciutacu, S. 2009. “Global English into Local Dutch”. In *Romanian Journal of English Studies* 6, edited by L. Frenţiu, 316-323. Timişoara: Editura Universităţii de Vest.

Clyne, M. 1994. *Inter-cultural Communication at Work: Cultural Values in Discourse.* Cambridge: CUP.

Cogno, E., and G. Dall'Ara. 2001. *Comunicazione e Tecnica Pubblicitaria nel Turismo.* Milano: Franco Angeli.

Confer, J., and D. Kerstetter. 2000. “Past Perfect: Explorations of Heritage Tourism”. *Parks and Recreation* 35(2):28-33.

Conrady, R., and M. Buck, eds. 2010. *Trends and Issues in Global Tourism 2010.* Berlin: Springer.

Cook, G. 2001. *The Discourse of Advertising* (2nd ed.). London: Routledge.

—. 2008. "Advertisements and Public Relations". In *Handbook of Communication in the Public Sphere*, edited by R. Wodak and V. Koller, 113-130. Berlin: Mouton de Gruyer.

Coupland, N. 2011. "The Sociolinguistics of Style". In *The Cambridge Handbook of Sociolinguistics,* edited by R. Mesthrie, 138-157. Cambridge: CUP.

Crişan, R. 2013. "Tourism Destination Slogans–Persuasive or Manipulative?". In *The Proceedings of the European Integration–Between Tradition and Modernity Congress,* vol. 5, 943-948. Târgu-Mureş: Editura Universităţii "Petru Maior".

"Cross Cultural Business Management". 2014. Accessed June 18. http://www.scribd.com/doc/7008216/CrossCultural-Business-Management.

Crystal, D. 2004. *Language and the Internet*. Cambridge: CUP.

Cyr, D., C. Bonanni, J. Bowes and J. Ilsever. 2005. "Beyond Trust: Website Design Preferences across Cultures". *Journal of Global Information Management* 13(4):24–52.

Dahl, S. 2004. "Intercultural Research: the Current State of Knowledge". Middlesex University Bussiness School Discussion Paper. No. 26, Middlesex.

Danesi, M. 2004. *Messages, Signs, and Meanings. A Basic Textbook in Semiotics and Communication* (3rd ed.). Toronto: Canadian Scholars' Press Inc.

Daneš, F. 1974. "Functional Sentence Perspective and the Organization of the Text". In *Papers on Functional Sentence Perspective*, edited by F. Daneš, 106-128. Prague: Academic.

Danet, B., and S. Herring. 2008. "Multilingualism on the Internet". In *Handbook of Language and Communication: Diversity and Change,* edited by M. Hellinger and A. Pauwels, 553-595. Berlin: Mouton de Gruyter.

Dann, G. 2005. "Nostalgia in the Noughties". In *Global Tourism* (3rd ed.), edited by W. Theobald, 32-51. USA: Elsevier.

Dejica, D. 2004. "On Discourse Structure in Translation: the Concepts of Theme and Rheme". In *Romanian Journal of English Studies,* edited by L. Frenţiu, 47-56. Timişoara: Editura Mirton.

—. 2005. "Towards a New Model for the Identification of Thematic Information in Discourse". In *Comunicare profesională şi traductologie,* edited by R. Superceanu and D. Dejica, 103-111. Timişoara: Universitatea Politehnica.

—. 2006. "Pragmatic versus Syntactic Identification of Thematic Information in Discourse". *Buletinul Științific al UPT, Seria Limbi Moderne* 5(1/2):55-61.

—. 2010. *Thematic Management and Information Distribution in Translation*. Timişoara: Editura Politehnica.

Delin, J. 2000. *The Language of Everyday Life: An Introduction*. London: Sage.

de Cillia, R., M. Reisigl and R. Wodak. 1999. "The Discursive Construction of National Identities". *Discourse and Society* 10(2):149-173.

de Mooij, M. 2004. "Translating Advertising: Painting the Tip of an Iceberg". *The Translator* 10(2): 179-198.

—. 2005. *Global Marketing and Advertising: Understanding Cultural Paradoxes*. London: Sage.

de Mooij, M., and G. Hofstede. 2010. "The Hofstede Model: Applications to Global Branding and Advertising Strategy and Research". *International Journal of Advertising* 29(1):85-110.

Djonov, E. 2005. "Analysing the Organisation of Information in Websites: From Hypermedia Design to Systemic Functional Hypermedia Discourse Analysis". Phd diss., University of New South Wales, Australia.

Downing, A., and P. Locke. 2006. *English Grammar: A University Course* (2nd ed.). Oxon: Routledge.

Dumitrescu, M. 2009. *A Course in Intercultural Business Communication*. The Academy of Economic Studies, Bucharest.

Duranti, A. 2004. *A Companion to Linguistic Anthropology*. Malden: Blackwell.

Dyer, G. 1982. *Advertising as Communication*. London: Methuen & Co. Ltd.

Dwyer, L. 2005. "Trends Underpinning Global Tourism in the Coming Decade". In *Global Tourism* (3rd ed.), edited by W. Theobald, 529-545. USA: Elsevier.

Eggins, S. 1994, 2004. *An Introduction to Systemic Functional Linguistics*. London: Pinter.

Eggins, S., and J.R. Martin. 1997. "Genres and Register of Discourse". In *Discourse as Structure and Process* (vol. 1), edited by T. van Dijk, 230-256. London: Sage Publications Ltd.

Evans, M., J. Fox and R. Johnson. 1995. "Identifying Competitive Strategies for Successful Tourism Destination Development". *Journal of Hospitality and Leisure Marketing* 3(1):37-45.

Faiola, A., and S. Matei. 2005. "Cultural Cognitive Style and Web Design: Beyond a Behavioral Inquiry into Computer-Mediated Communication". *Journal of Computer-Mediated Communication* 11(1): 375-394.

Fernández Cavia, J., and A. Huertas. 2009. "City Brands and their Communication through Web Sites: Identification of Problems and Proposals for Improvement". In *Information Communication Technologies and City Marketing: Digital Opportunities for Cities around the World*, edited by M. Gascó Hernández and T. Torres-Coronas, 26-49. Hershey: Information Science Reference.

Fontaine, L. 2006. "Where Do 'We' Fit in? Linguistic Inclusion and Exclusion in a Virtual Community". In *Beyond Misunderstanding. The Linguistic Reconstruction of Intercultural Communication*, edited by K. Bührig and J. ten Thije, 319-356. Amsterdam: Benjamins.

Fontaine, L., and Y. Kodratoff. 2002. "Comparaison du Rôle de la Progression Thématique et de la Texture conceptuelle chez des Scientifiques Anglophones et Francophones s'exprimant en Anglais". *Special Issue ASp, la revue du GERAS,* 37-38:59-83. (English translation).

Förnas, G. 1995. *Cultural Theory and Late Modernity***.** London: Sage.

Francesconi, S. 2014. *Reading Tourism Texts: A Multimodal Analysis*. Bristol: Channel View Publications, Limited.

Francis, G., and A. Kramer Dahl. 1991. "From Clinical Report to Clinical Story: Two Ways of Writing about a Medical Case". In *Functional and Systemic Linguistics: Approaches and Uses*, edited by E. Ventola, 339-368. Berlin: Mounton de Gruyter.

Fries, P. 1983. "On the Status of Theme in English: Arguments from Discourse". *Micro and Macro Connexity of Text* 6(1):1-38.

—. 1995. "Themes, Methods of Development, and Texts". In *On Subject and Theme*, edited by R. Hasan and P. Fries, 317-359. Amsterdam: John Benjamins Publishing Company.

Garcia Álvarez, L. 2006. "The Discourse of Turespaña's New Advertising Campaign 'Spain Marks'". In *Discourse and Enterprise. Communication, Business, Management and Other Professional Fields*, edited by F. Ramallo, A. Lorenzo and X. Rodríguez, 71-85. Munich: Lincom Europa.

Garrod, B. 2008. "Exploring Place Perception: A Photo-Based Analysis". *Annals of Tourism Research* 35(2):381-401.

—. 2009. "Understanding the Relationship between Tourism Destination Imagery and Tourist Photography". *Journal of Travel Research* 47(3): 346-358.

Garzone, G. 2002. "Describing E-commerce Communication. Which Models and Categories for Text Analysis?". *Textus* XV (2):279-296.

—. 2008. "Promozione Turistica e Identità: il Caso dei Portali Web di Italia e Spagna". In *Lingue e Culture nella Comunicazione Economica e Commerciale,* edited by M. Calvi, G. Mapelli and L. Santos López, 121-143. Milano: FrancoAngeli.

—. 2009. "Identity in Tourist Communication on the Internet: Italy's and Spain's Websites Contrasted". In *Identities across Media and Modes: Discursive Perspectives*, edited by G. Garzone and P. Catenaccio, 29-58. Bern: Peter Lang.

George, B. 2008. "Holiday Attachment. The Construct and its Measurement". In *Tourism Development Revisited. Concepts, Issues and Paradigms*, edited by S., Babu, S. Mishra and B. Parida, 306-328. New Delhi: Response.

Giacomarra, M. 2006. *Turismo e Comunicazione. Strategie di Costruzione del Prodotto Turistico*. Palermo: Sellerio Editore.

Giordana, F. 2004. *La Comunicazione del Turismo tra Immagine, Immaginario e Immaginazione*. Milan: Franco Angeli.

Gotti, M. 1991. *I Linguaggi Specialistici: Caratteristiche Linguistiche e Criteri Pragmatici*. Firenze: La Nuova Italia.

—. 2008. *Investigating Specialized Discourse*. Bern: Peter Lang.

Graham, B., G. Ashworth and J. Tunbridge. 2000. *Geography of Heritage: Power, Culture and Economy*. London: Arnold.

Greenbaum, S., and G. Nelson. 2002. *An Introduction to English Grammar* (2nd ed.). London: Pearson Education Limited.

Guillén Nieto, V. 2007. "La Comunicación Intercultural en los Negocios". In *Las Lenguas Profesionales y Academicas*, edited by E. Varó, J. Martínez and F. Ramos, 93-103. Barcelona: Editorial Ariel.

Gudykunst, W. 2005. *Theorizing about Intercultural Communication*. London: Sage.

Gudykunst, W., S. Ting-Toomey and E. Chua. 1988. *Culture and Interpersonal Communication*. London: Sage.

Gumperz, J., and J. Cook-Gumperz. 2008. "Discourse, Cultural Diversity and Communication: A Linguistic Anthropological Perspective". In *Handbook of Intercultural Communication*, edited by H. Kotthoff and H. Spencer-Oatey, 13-31. Berlin: Mounton de Gruyer.

Hall, E. 1976, 1997. *Beyond Culture*. New York: Doubleday.

—. 2000. "Context and Meaning". In *Intercultural Communication: A Reader* (9th ed.), edited by L. Samovar and R. Porter, 34-43. Belmont: Wadsworth Publishing Co.

Hall, E., and M. Hall. 1990. *Understanding Cultural Differences*. Yarmouth: Intercultural Press Inc.

Hall, S. 1994. "Cultural Identity and Diaspora". In *Colonial Discourse and Post-colonial Theory: A Reader*, edited by P. Williams and L. Chrisman, 392-401. London: Harvester Wheatsheaf.

Halliday, M.A.K. 1978. *Language as Social Semiotic. The Social Interpretation of Language and Meaning*. London: Edward Arnold.

—. 1985, 1994. *An Introduction to Functional Grammar*. London: Hodder Arnold.

—. 1989. *Spoken and Written Language.* Oxford: OUP.

Halliday, M.A.K., and C. Matthiessen. 2004. *An Introduction to Functional Grammar* (3rd ed.). London: Hodder Arnold.

Harms, E. 2010. "Sustainable Tourism: From Nice to Have to Need to Have". In *Trends and Issues in Global Tourism 2010*, edited by R. Conrady and M. Buck, 111-116. Berlin: Springer.

Held, G. 2004. "L'annuncio Pubblicitario di Destinazione. Osservazioni su un Tipo di Testo Multimodale nella Stampa Odierna". In *Generi, Architetture e Forme Testuali*, edited by P. D'Achille, 257-277. Firenze: Cesati.

Hemelryk Donald, S., and J. Gammack. 2007. *Tourism and the Branded City. Film and Identity on the Pacific Rim*. Aldershot: Ashgate.

Henríquez Jiménez, S. 1997. "El Lenguaje Turístico al Servicio de la Ilustración Impresa". In *Lingüística Aplicada en su Contexto Académico*, edited by J. Piqué and J.A. Besó, 396-400. Valencia: Nau Llibres.

Herbert, D., ed. 1995. *Heritage, Tourism and Society*. New York: Mansell.

Herring, S.C. 2003. "Computer-mediated Discourse". In *The Handbook of Discourse Analysis*, edited by D. Schiffrin, D. Tannen and H. Hamilton, 612-634. Malden: Wiley-Blackwell.

Hiippala, T. 2007. "Helsinki: A Multisemiotic Analysis of Tourist Brochures". Master diss., University of Helsinki.

—. 2012. "The Localisation of Advertising Print Media as a Multimodal Process". In *Multimodal Texts from around the World: Linguistic and Cultural Insights,* edited by W. Bowcher, 97-122. London: Palgrave Macmillan.

—. 2013. "Modelling the Structure of a Multimodal Artifact". Academic diss., University of Helsinki.

Hofstede, G. 1984. *Culture's Consequences*: *International Differences in Work-Related Values*. Beverly Hills: Sage.

—. 1991. *Cultures and Organizations—Software of the Mind*. New York: McGraw Hill.

—. 2001. *Culture's Consequences, Comparing Values, Behaviors, Institutions, and Organizations across Nations*. Thousand Oaks: Sage Publications.

Hofstede, G., and G.J. Hofstede. 2005. *Cultures and Organizations: Software of the Mind* (2nd ed.). USA: McGraw-Hill.

Hofstede, G., P. Pedersen and G.J. Hofstede. 2002. *Exploring Culture: Exercises, Stories and Synthetic Cultures*. USA: Intercultural Press.

Holloway, J. 2004. *Marketing for Tourism*. Essex: Pearson Education,

House, J. 2007. "What Is an 'Intercultural Speaker'?". In *Intercultural Language Use and Language Learning*, edited by E. Alcón Soler and M. Safont Jordà, 7-21. The Netherlands: Springer.

House, R., P. Hanges, M. Javidan, P. Dorfman and V. Gupta, eds. 2004. *Culture, Leadership, and Organizations*. Thousand Oaks: Sage.

Hu, J., K. Shima, R. Oehlmann, J. Zhao, Y. Takemura and K. Matsumoto. 2004. "An Empirical Study of Audience Impressions of B2C Web Pages in Japan, China and the UK". *Electronic Commerce Research and Applications* 3:176–189.

Hughes, H., and D. Allen. 2005. "Cultural Tourism in Central and Eastern Europe: The Views of 'Induced Image Formation Agents'". *Tourism Management* 26:173-183.

Huizingh, E. 2000. "The Content and Design of Web Sites: An Empirical Study". *Information & Management* 37(3):123-134.

Iedema, R. 2001. "Analysing Film and Television: a Social Semiotic Account of *Hospital: an Unhealthy Business*". In *Handbook of Visual Analysis,* edited by T. van Leeuwen and C. Jewitt, 183-204. London: Sage.

Jacobs, M., and N. Hanrahan, eds. 2005. *The Blackwell Companion to the Sociology of Culture*. Malden: Blackwell Publishing Ltd.

Jameson, F., and M. Miyoshi. 1998. *Cultures of Globalization*. London: Duke University Press.

Janoschka, A. 2004. *Web Advertising: New Forms of Communication on the Internet*. Amsterdam: John Benjamins Publishing.

Jansen-Verbeke, M. 2010. "Transformation from Historic Cityscapes to Urban Tourismscapes. A Discussion Note". *Rivista di Scienze del Turismo* 2:31-49.

Jansen-Verbeke, M., and E. Lievois. 2002. "Analysing Heritage Resources for Urban Tourism in European Cities". In *Contemporary Issues in Tourism Development*, edited by D. Pearce and R. Butler, 81-107. London: Routledge.

Jeong, M. 2002. "Evaluating Value-Added Lodging Web Sites from Customers' Perspectives". *International Journal of Hospitality & Tourism Administration* 3(1):49–60.

Jewitt, C. 2002. "The Move from Page to Screen: The Multimodal Reshaping of School English". *Visual Communication* 1(2):171-196.

—. 2004. "Multimodality and New Communication Technologies". In *Discourse and Technology: Multimodal Discourse Analysis*, edited by P. Le Vine and R. Scollon, 182-195. Washington: Georgetown University Press.

—. 2006. *Technology, Literacy and Learning: A Multimodal Approach*. London: Routledge.

Jewitt, C., ed. 2009. *The Routledge Handbook of Multimodal Analysis*. London: Routledge.

Jewitt, C., and R. Oyama. 2001. "Visual Meaning: a Social Semiotic Approach". In *Handbook of Visual Analysis*, edited by T. van Leeuwen and C. Jewitt, 134-157. London: Sage.

Jokela, S. 2011. "Building a Façade for Finland: Helsinki in Tourism Imagery". *The Geographical Review* 101:53-70.

Jones, M. 2007. "Hofstede–Culturally Questionable?". Paper presented at *the Oxford Business & Economics Conference*, Oxford, UK, June 24-26.

Juan González, P. 2000. "Análisis Contrastivo del Lenguaje de los Folletos Turísticos en Ingles y en Español". In *Proceedings of X Congresso Luso/Espanhol de Linguas Aplicadas as Ciencias e as Tecnologias*, edited by A. Cabral, H. Freire, M. Coelho and S. Oliveira, 38-53. Portalegre: Escola Superior de Tecnologia e Gestao.

IZT, and DWIF. 2003. *Neue IuK-Technologien und ihre Relevanz für die Wettbewerbsfähigkeit touristischer Destinationen. Trends, Daten und Fakten im internationalen Vergleich*. Berlin: IZT. Accessed March 15, 2014. https://www.izt.de/fileadmin/downloads/pdf/IZT_WB56.pdf .

Kaltenbacher, M. 2006. "A Seminar on Intercultural Awareness and Literature". In *Coherence of Principles, Cohesion of Competences. Exploring Theories and Designing Materials for Teacher Education*, edited by A. Fenner and D. Newby, 170-174. Strasbourg: Council of Europe Publishing.

Kemmerling-Clack, J. 1999. "Cultural Tourism: An Overview of Impact, Visitors and Case Studies". In *Navigating Global Waters–30th Annual Conference Proceedings, Travel and Tourism Research Association*, edited by R. Moisey, N. Nickerson and D. Klenosky, 154-159. Boise, Idaho.

Kluckhohn, F., and F. Strodtbeck. 1961. *Variations in Value Orientations*. Evanston, Ill.: Row, Peterson.

Kok, K. 2004. "Multisemiotic Mediation in Hypertexts". In *Multimodal Discourse Analysis: Systemic Functional Perspectives*, edited by K. O'Halloran, 131-159. London: Continuum.

Kostelnick, C. 1995. "Cultural Adaptation and Information Design: Two Contrasting Views". *IEEE Transactions on Professional Communication* 38(4):182-96.

Kostelnick, C., and M. Hassett. 2003. *Shaping Information: The Rhetoric of Visual Conventions*. Carbondale: Southern Illinois University Press.

Kotler, P., and D. Gertner. 2002. "Country as Brand, Product, and Beyond: A Place Marketing and Brand Management Perspectives". *Journal of Brand Management* 9:62-82.

Kotthoff, H., and H. Spencer-Oatey, eds. 2008. *Handbook of Intercultural Communication*. Berlin: Mounton de Gruyer.

Kress, G. 1989. *Linguistic Processes in Sociocultural Practice* (2nd ed.). Oxford: OUP.

—. 2003. *Literacy in the New Media Age*. London: Routledge.

—. 2010. *Multimodality: A Social Semiotic Approach to Contemporary Communication*. UK: Taylor & Francis.

Kress, G., and T. van Leeuwen. 1996, 2006. *Reading Images: The Grammar of Visual Design*. London: Routledge.

Kress, G., and T. van Leeuwen. 2001. *Multimodal Discourse. The Modes and Media of Contemporary Communication*. London: Arnold.

Lawes, R. 2002. "Demystifying Semiotics: Some Key Questions Answered". *International Journal of Market Research* 44(3):251-264.

Leech, G. 1996. "Foreword: the Spoken English Corpus in its Context". In *Working with Speech: Perspectives on Research into the Lancaster/IBM Spoken English Corpus,* edited by G. Knowles, A. Wichmann and P. Alderson, ix-xii. London: Longman.

Lehtonen, M. 2000. *The Cultural Analysis of Texts*. London: Sage.

Lemke, J. 1998. "Multiplying Meaning: Visual and Verbal Semiotics in Scientific Text". In *Reading Science*, edited by J.R. Martin and R. Veel, 87–113. London: Routledge.

—. 2002. "Travels in Hypermodality". *Visual Communication* 1(3):299-325.

Lewis, R.D. 2004. "Communicating Cultural Diversity in International Tourism". In *Observations on International Tourism Communications. Report from the First World Conference on Tourism Communications,* by WTO-OMT, 125-132. Madrid: WTO-OMT.

Light, A. 2003. "Culture and Usability: Will Design Patterns ease Problems of Context?". *Usability News*. Accessed July 1, 2014. http://www.usabilitynews.com/news/article1185.asp.

Light, D. 2006. "Romania: National Identity, Tourism Promotion and European Integration". In *Tourism in the New Europe: The Challenges and Opportunities of EU Enlargement*, edited by D. Hall, M. Smith and B. Marciszewska, 256-269. Oxfordshire: Cabi.

Light, D., C. Young and M. Czepczyński. 2009. "Heritage Tourism in Central and Eastern Europe". In *Cultural Heritage and Tourism in the Developing World. A Regional Perspective*, edited by D.J. Timothy and G. Nyaupane, 224-245. London: Routledge.

Lipman, G. 2008. "Global Trends in the Tourism and Travel Industry". In *WTO World Tourism Conference–Tourism Success Stories and Shooting Stars*, by WTO, 19-25. Madrid: WTO.

Lister, M., and L. Wells. 2001. "Seeing Beyond Belief: Cultural Studies as an Approach to Analysing the Visual". In *Handbook of Visual Analysis*, edited by T. van Leeuwen and C. Jewitt, 61-92. London: Sage.

Lombardi Vallauri, E. 1995. "A Simple Test for Theme and Rheme in the Clause Complex". *Language Sciences* 17(4):357-378.

Londero, R. 2006. "Traducir la Publicidad para el Turismo: Referencias Culturales en Anuncios Españoles e Italianos". In *Nuevas Tendencias en el Discurso de Especialidad*, edited by M. Calvi and L. Chierichetti, 249-271. Bern: Peter Lang.

Machin, D. 2004. "Building the World's Visual Language: The Increasing Global Importance of Images Banks". *Visual Communication* 3:316-336.

Macleod, D. 2004. *Tourism, Globalization, and Cultural Change: An Island Community Perspective*. Clevedon: Channel View Publications.

Maiorani, A. 2009. *The Matrix Phenomenon: A Linguistic and Multimodal Análisis*. Germany: VDM Verlag Dr. Müller.

Majó, J., and N. Galí. 2002. "Internet en la Información Turística". In *Actas IV Congreso "Turismo y Tecnologías de la Información y las Comunicaciones"*, Malaga, 397-409.

Manoliu–Manea, M. 1994. *Discourse and Pragmatic Constraints on Grammatical Choices: A Grammar of Surprises*. Amsterdam: Elsevier.

Mapelli, G., and J. Santos López. 2010. "Estudio Comparado de las Caracteristicas Discursivas de la Guia Turistica". In *Viaggiare con la Parola*, edited by E. Liverani and J. Canals, 89-102. Milano: Franco Angeli.

Mapelli, G., and S. Piccioni. 2011. "Taxonomia de los Textos Turísticos: Factores Lingüísticos y Factores Culturales". In *La Lengua del Turismo. Géneros Discursivos y Terminología*, edited by M. Calvi and G. Mapelli, 47-74. Bern: Peter Lang.

Marcus, A., and E. Gould. 2000. "Crosscurrents: Cultural Dimensions and Global Web User-interface Design". *Interactions* 7(4):32-46.

Marcussen, C. 2006. "Trends in European Internet Distribution of Travel and Tourism Services" (7th annual version). Accessed May 5, 2014. http://axses-innkeeper.com/news06-apr-trendsinEu-dist.htm.

Mariottini, L. 2011. "Las Páginas Web de Turismo. ¿Género Móvil o Modelo Mental?". In *Il Discorso del Turismo. Aspetti Linguistici e Varietà Testuali*, edited by E. Liverani and J. Canals, 97-126. Trento: Tangram.

—. 2012. "*I need Spain*. Análisis Pragmático de la Campaña de Promoción Turística 2010". *Pasos* 10(4):105-113.

Martin, J.R. 1992. *English Text-systems and Structure*. Philadelphia: John Benjamins.

Martin, J.R., and D. Rose. 2008. *Genre Relations: Mapping Culture*. London: Equinox.

Martinec, R. 2000. "Types of Process in Action". *Semiotica* 130(3/4): 243-268.

—. 2001. "Interpersonal Resources in Action". *Semiotica*, 135(1/4):117-145.

Matsumoto, D., and L. Juang. 2007. *Culture and Psychology* (4th ed.). Wadsworf: Cengage Learning.

Matthiessen, C. 2007. "The Multimodal Page: A Systemic Functional Exploration". In *New Directions in the Analysis of Multimodal Discourse*, edited by T. Royce and W. Bowcher, 1-63. London: Lawrence Erlbaum Associates, Publishers.

Matthiessen, C., and M.A.K. Halliday. 2009. "Systemic Functional Grammar: A First Step into the Theory". Accessed July 1. http://minerva.ling.mq.edu.au/resource/VirtuallLibrary/Publications/sfg_firststep/SF G%20intro%20New.html.

McCabe, A. 1999. "Theme and Thematic Pattern in Spanish and English History Texts". PhD. diss., Aston University.

McKean, J., D. Johnson and R. Walsh. 1995. "Valuing Time in Travel Cost Demand Analysis: An Empirical Investigation". *Land Economics* 71(1):96-105.

McKercher, B. 1998a. "The Effect of Market Access on Destination Choice". *Journal of Travel Research* 37(1):39-47.

—. 1998b. *The Business of Nature-Based Tourism*. Melbourne: Hospitality Press.

McKercher, B., and H. du Cros. 2002. *Cultural Tourism: The Partnership between Tourism and Cultural Heritage Management*. New York: The Haworth Hospitality Press.

McSweeney, B. 2002. "Hofstede's Model of National Cultural Differences and their Consequences: A Triumph of Faith–a Failure of Analysis". *Human Relations* 55(1):89-118.

Mena, M. 2008. "International Tourism and Developing Economies". In *Tourism Development Revisited. Concepts, Issues and Paradigms*, edited by S. Babu, S. Mishra and B. Parida, 198-213. New Delhi: Response.

Meyer, C. 2009. *Introducing English Linguistics*. Cambridge: CUP.

Mich, L., M. Franch and G. Cilione. 2003. "The 2QCV3Q Quality Model for the Analysis of Web Site Requirements". *Journal of Web Engineering* 2(1&2):105-127.

Miller. M. 2011. *The Ultimate Web Marketing Guide*. Indianapolis: Pearson Education, Inc.

Mirzoeff, N. 1999. *An Introduction to Visual Culture*. London: Routledge.

Mithun, M. 2004. "The Value of Linguistic Diversity: Viewing Other Worlds through North American Indian Languages". In *A Companion to Linguistic Anthropology*, edited by A. Duranti, 121-140. Oxford: Blackwell's.

Mocini, R. 2005. "The Verbal Discourse of Tourist Brochures". *AnnalSS* 5:153-164.

—. 2009. "La Comunicazione Turistica: Strategie Promozionali e Traduttive". PhD diss., University of Sassari.

Moilanen, T., and S. Rainisto. 2009. *How to Brand Nations, Cities and Destinations. A Planning Book for a Place Branding*. Great Britain: Palgrave Macmillan.

Molina, A., and A. Esteban. 2006. "Tourism Brochures. Usefulness and Image". *Annals of Tourism Research* 33(4):1036-1056.

Molina, C., and M. Romano. 2012. "JUST Revisited: Panchronic and Contrastive Insights". *IJES* 12(1):17-36.

Mongkholjuck, C. 2008. "A Genre Analysis of Tourist Attraction Leaflet Produced and Distributed in Thailand in 2004". PhD diss., Kasetsart University

Montes Fernández, A. 2006. "El Lenguaje de la Publicidad". In *Las Lenguas Profesionales y Académicas*, edited by E. Varó, J. Martínez and F. Ramos, 219-232. Barcelona: Editorial Ariel.

Montiel Torres, M. 2002. "Promoción Turística en Internet: las TICs como Herramientas de Divulgación e Información. Casos Prácticos". In *IV Congreso "Turismo y Tecnologías de la Información y las Comunicaciones"*, Malaga, 537-549.

Morgan, M. 2005. "Quality and Sustainability in Established Destinations: Who Pays?". In *Global Tourism* (3rd ed.), edited by W. Theobald, 346-361. USA: Elsevier.

Morgan, N., and A. Pritchard. 1998. *Tourism Promotion and Power: Creating Images, Creating Identities*. Chichester: John Wiley and Sons.

Morgan, N., and A. Pritchard. 2000. *Advertising in Tourism and Leisure*. Oxford: Butterworth-Heinemann.

Moscovici, S. 1981. "On Social Representations". In *Social Cognition. Perspectives on Everyday Understanding*, edited by J. Forgas, 181-209. London: Academic Press.

—. 1998. "Social Consciousness and its History". *Culture and Psychology* 4(3):411-433.

Moya Guijarro, A.J. 2003. "Thematic and Topical Structuring in Three Subgenres. A Contrastive Study". *Miscelánea: A Journal of English and American Studies* 27:131-154.

—. 2006. "On Pragmatic Functions and their Correlation with Syntactic Functions: A Functionalist Perspective". *Atlantis* 28(1):9-28.

—. 2013a. "Textual and Compositional Choices in Hotel Brochures". In *Choice in Language: Applications in Text Analysis*, edited by G. O'Grady, L. Fontaine and T. Bartlett, 301-322, London: Equinox.

—. 2013b. "Visual Metonymy in Children's Picture Book". *Review of Cognitive Linguistics*: 11(2): 336-352.

—. 2014. *A multimodal Analysis of Picture Books for Children. A Systemic Functional Study*. London: Equinox

Moya, Guijarro A.J., and J.M. González Lanza. 2014. "An Interpersonal Study of the Leading Hotels of the World. A Systemic-Functional Social-Semiotic Approach". In *Theory and Practice in Functional-Cognitive Space*, edited by Mª. Gómez-González, F.J. Ruiz de Mendoza Ibáñez and F. Gonzálvez-García, 85-106. Amsterdam: John Benjamins.

Moya Guijarro, A.J., and M. Pinar Sanz. 2007. "La Interacción Texto/Imagen en el Cuento Ilustrado. Un Análisis Multimodal". *Revista OCNOS* 3:21-38.

Murcia, S., and M. O'Donnell. 2003. "Advice in Instructional Texts: A Comparison between English and Spanish". *Proceedings of the 3rd*

*International Contrastive Linguistics Conference*, Compostela, Spain, October 2003.

Myers, G. *Words in Ads*. Oxon: Hodder Education Publishers.

Nardon, L., and R. Steers. 2009. "The Culture Theory Jungle: Divergence and Convergence in Models of National Culture". In *Cambridge Handbook of Culture, Organizations, and Work*, edited by R. Bhagat and R. Steers, 3-22. Cambridge: CUP.

Navarro, C., and R. Miotti. 2011. "La Combinación Preferente en los Sitios Web de los Lugares Patrimonio de la UNESCO Españoles e Italianos". In *La Lengua del Turismo. Géneros Discursivos y Terminología*, edited by M. Calvi and G. Mapelli, 315-334. Bern: Peter Lang.

Neuliep, J. 2006. *Intercultural Communication* (3rd ed.). London: Sage Publications.

Nielsen, J. 2000. *Designing Web Usability: The Practice of Simplicity*. Indianopolis: New Riders Publishers.

Nijman, J. 1999. "Cultural Globalization and the Identity of Place: The Reconstruction of Amsterdam". *Ecumene* 6(2):146-164.

O'Donnell, M. 1997. "Variable-Length On-line Document Generation". *Proceedings of the 6th European Workshop on Natural Language Generation*, Gerhard-Mercator University, Duisburg, Germany, March 24-26.

OECD. 2009. *The Impact of Culture on Tourism*. Paris: OECD Publishing.

O'Halloran, K. 2011. "Multimodal Discourse Analysis". In *Continuum Companion to Discourse Analysis*, edited by K. Hyland and B. Paltridge, 120-137. US: Continuum International Publishing Group.

O'Halloran, K., S. Tan, B. Smith and A. Podlasov. 2009. "Multimodal Discourse: Critical Analysis within an Interactive Software Environment". *Critical Discourse Studies* 8(2):109-125.

O'Halloran, K., S. Tan, B. Smith, and A. Podlasov. 2010. "Challenges in Designing Digital Interfaces for the Study of Multimodal Phenomena". *Information Design Journal* 18:2-21.

Olins, W. 2003. *On Brand*. London: Thames & Hudson.

OMT. 1999. *Promoción de Destinos Turísticos en el Ciberespacio–Retos del Marketing Electrónico*. Madrid: OMT.

—. 2001. *Comercio Electrónico y Turismo: Guía Práctica Para Destinos Y Empresas*. Madrid: OMT.

—. 2002. *Promotion of the Tourist Image of European Destinations on Competitive Markets*. Madrid: OMT.

—. 2003. *Tendencias de los Mercados Turísticos 2003–Panorama Mundial y Actualidad del Turismo*. Madrid: OMT.

—. 2005a. *Tendencias de los Mercados Turísticos 2005–Panorama Mundial y Actualidad del Turismo*. Madrid: OMT.

—. 2005b. *Evaluación y Optimización de los Sitios Web–El Servicio "Destination web watch"*. Madrid: OMT

—. 2008. *Tendencias de los Mercados Turísticos 2006–Panorama Mundial y Actualidad del Turismo*. Madrid: OMT.

—. 2009. *Sustainable Tourism Management at World Heritage Sites–Enhancing Interagency and Stakeholder Coordination for Joint Action*. Madrid: OMT.

—. 2011. *Panorama OMT del Turismo Internacional, edición 2011*. Madrid: OMT.

—. 2013. *Panorama OMT del Turismo Internacional, edición 2013*. Madrid: OMT.

—. 2014. *Panorama OMT del Turismo Internacional, edición 2014*. Madrid: OMT.

O'Toole, M. 1994. *The Language of Displayed Art*. Madison: Fairleigh Dickinson University Press.

Oyama, R. 1999. "Visual Semiotics in a Cross-Cultural Perspective: A Study of Visual Images in Japanese and Selected British Advertisements". PhD. diss., University of London.

Palmer, J. 2002. "Web Site Usability, Design, and Performance Metrics". *Information Systems Research* 13(2):151-167.

Peace Corps. 2011. *Culture Matters: The Peace Corps Cross-Cultural Workbook*. USA: Peace Corps Information Collection and Exchange.

Perandrea, V. 2011. "Il Turismo Online: Strategie Linguistiche di Alcuni Siti Web Spanioli che Publicizzano la Sardegna". Graduation diss., University of Sassari.

Pérez Vázquez, M. 2011. "Verbos de Percepción Sensible e Intelectual en las Guías". In *La Lengua del Turismo. Géneros Discursivos y Terminología*, edited by M. Calvi and G. Mapelli, 295-313. Bern: Peter Lang.

Peterson B. 2004. *Cultural Intelligence: A Guide to Working with People from Other Cultures*. USA: Intercultural Press.

Pierini, P. 2007. "Quality in Web Translation: An Investigation into UK and Italian Tourism Web Sites". *The Journal of Specialised Translation* 8:85-103.

—. 2008. "A Warm Welcome Guaranteed–Aspetti dell'Inglese nei Siti degli Enti Nazionali per il Turismo". *Studi Linguistici e Filologici Online* 6:163-202.

Pinar Sanz, M. 2006. "Political Advertising Discourse. A Critical Discourse Analysis Approach to Ellection Campaigns". In *Discourse and Enterprise. Communication, Business, Management and other Professional Fields*, edited by F. Ramallo, A. Lorenzo and X. Rodríguez, 135-151. Munich: Lincom Europa.

Piñanes Leal, J. 2004. "'Spain Marks'–Presentación de la Campaña Promocional". In *Observations on International Tourism Communications. Report from the First World Conference on Tourism Communications,* by WTO-OMT, 91-96. Madrid: WTO-OMT.

Plog, S. 2005. "Targeting Segments: More Important than Ever in the Travel Industry". In *Global Tourism* (3rd ed.), edited by W. Theobald, 271-293. USA: Elsevier.

Poon, A. 1993. *Tourism, Technology and Competitive Strategies.* Wallingford: CAB International.

—. 2010. "Best Practice Destination Management: Lessons from the Leaders". In *Trends and Issues in Global Tourism 2010*, edited by R. Conrady and M. Buck, 159-171. Berlin: Springer.

Poria, Y., R. Butler and D. Airey. 2004. "Links between Tourists, Heritage, and Reasons for Visiting Heritage Sites". *Journal of Travel Research* 43:19-28.

Precedo Ledo, A., A. Revilla Bonín and A. Míguez Iglesias. 2007. "El Turismo Cultural como Factor Estratégico de Desarrollo: el Camino de Santiago". *Estudios Geográficos* 68(262): 205-234.

Prentice, R., A. Davies and A. Beeho. 1997. "Seeking Generic Motivations for Visiting and not Visiting Museums and Like Cultural Attractions". *Museum Management and Curatorship* 16(1):45-70.

Pyka, D., and R. Freitag. 2010. "Overview of World Tourism 2009". In *Trends and Issues in Global Tourism 2010*, edited by R. Conrady and M. Buck, 3-10. Berlin: Springer.

Ramm, W. 2000. "Textual Variation in Travel Guides". In *Discourse and Community: Doing Functional Linguistics*, edited by E. Ventola, 147-167. Tubingen: Gunter Narr Verlag.

Rheem, C. 2010. "What's Next for European Online Travel?". In *Trends and Issues in Global Tourism 2010,* edited by R. Conrady and M. Buck, 299-309. Berlin: Springer.

Richards, G. 1996. "Production and Consumption of Cultural Tourism in Europe". *Annals of Tourism Research* 23:2-11.

—. 2001. "The Development of Cultural Tourism in Europe". In *Cultural Attractions and European Tourism,* edited by G. Richards, 1-27. Wallingford: CABI.

—. 2003. "Nuevas Tendencias del Turismo Cultural?". In *Tendencias de los Mercados Turísticos 2003–Panorama Mundial y Actualidad del Turismo,* by OMT, 143-156. Madrid: OMT.

—. 2007. "Introduction: Global Trends in Cultural Tourism". In *Cultural Tourism: Global and Local Perspectives*, edited by G. Richards, 1-24. London: Hodder Education.

Rodríguez Abella, R. 2011. "La Lengua de la Promoción Turística en el Sitio www.turismodecanarias.com". In *La Lengua del Turismo. Géneros Discursivos y Terminología,* edited by M. Calvi and G. Mapelli, 153-175. Bern: Peter Lang.

Rodríguez Antón, J., and M. Alonso Almeida, eds. 2009. *Nuevas Tendencias y Retos en el Sector Turismo: Un Enfoque Multidisciplinar*. Madrid: Delta Publicaciones.

Rojek, C., and J. Urry, eds. 1997. *Touring Cultures*. London: Routledge.

Rooijakkers, G. 2002. Quoted from an interview in *De Volkskrant*, October 19th 2002.

Rose, G. 2001. *Visual Methodologies. An Introduction to the Interpretation of Visual Materials*. London: Routledge.

Ruiz, M., and A. Saorín. 2000. "Genre Analysis: A Case of Tourist Texts". In *Proceedings of X Congresso Luso/Espanhol de Linguas Aplicadas as Ciencias e as Tecnologias*, edited by A. Cabral, H. Freire, M. Coelho and S. Oliveira, 121-126. Portalegre: Escola Superior de Tecnologia e Gestao.

Royce, T. 1998. "Synergy on the Page: Exploring Intersemiotic Complementarity in Page-based Multimodal Text". *JASFL Occasional Papers* 1(1):25-50.

Russo, P., and S. Boor. 1993. "How Fluent is your Interface? Designing for International Users. Human Factors in Computing Systems." In *Proceedings of INTERCHI '93*, 24-29. Amsterdam: ACM.

Santana Talavera, A. 2003. "Turismo Cultural, Culturas Turísticas". *Horizontes Antropológicos* 9(20):31-57.

Santulli, F. 2010. "La Guida Turistica come Genere: Tratti Costitutivi en Realizzazioni Testuali". *E|C Serie Speciale* 4(6):25-34.

—. 2011. "Imágenes de Italia en las Guías Turísticas Alemanas". In *La Lengua del Turismo. Géneros Discursivos y Terminología*, edited by M. Calvi and G. Mapelli, 93-112. Bern: Peter Lang.

Saorín, A. 2001. "Writing Tourist Leaflets: Some Common Lacks". In *Discourse Analysis and Terminology in Languages for Specific Purposes*, edited by J. Palmer, S. Posteguillo and I. Fortanet, 335-344. Castello de la Plana: Universitat de Jaume I.

Sapir, E. 1929. "The Status of Linguistics as a Science". In *Culture, Language and Personality,* by E. Sapir (1958), edited by D.G. Mandelbaum, 160-166. Berkeley, CA: University of California Press.

Sawhney, M., and E. Prandelli. 2000. "Beyond Customer Knowledge Management: Customers as Knowledge Co-Creators". In *Knowledge Management and Virtual Organisations,* edited by Y. Malhotra, 258-282. Hershey: Idea Group Publishing.

Scarles, C. 2004. "Mediating Landscapes: The Processes and Practices of Image Construction in Tourist Brochures of Scotland". *Tourist Studies* 4(1):43-67.

Schouten, F. 2007. "Cultural Tourism: Between Authenticity and Globalization". In *Cultural Tourism: Global and Local Perspectives*, edited by G. Richards, 25-38. London: Hodder Education.

Schwartz, S. 1992. "Universals in the Content and Structure of Values: Theoretical Advances and Empirical Tests in 20 Countries". *Advances in Experimental Social Psychology* 25:1-65.

—. 1994. "Are There Universals in the Content and Structure of Values?". *Journal of Social Issues* 50:19-45.

Scollon, R., and S. Scollon. 2001. *Intercultural Communication. A Discourse Approach* (2nd ed.). Oxford: Blackwell.

Selwyn, T. 1993. "Peter Pan in South-East Asia: Views from the Brochures". In *Tourism in South-East Asia*, edited by M. Hitchcock, V. King and M. Parnwell, 117–137. London: Routledge.

Sharpley, R. 2006. *Travel and Tourism*. London: Sage Publications.

Shchiglik, C., and S. Barnes. 2004. "Evaluating Website Quality in the Airline Industry". *Journal of Computer Information Systems* 44:17-25.

Sheridan, E. 2001. "Cross-Cultural Web Site Design: Considerations for Developing and Strategies for Validating Locale Appropriate On-line Content". *MultiLingual Computing & Technology* 43, 12(7). Accessed May 20, 2013. http://www.multilingual.com/.

Singh, N. 2005. "Analysing the Cultural Content of Websites: A Cross-National Comparison of China, India, Japan, and US". *International Marketing Review* 23(1):83-97.

Singh, N., G. Fassot, M. Chao and J. Hoffman. 2006. "Understanding International Web Site Usage. A Cross National Study of German, Brazilian, and Taiwanese Online Consumers". *International Marketing Review* 23(1):83-97.

Singh, S., and N. Dalal. 1999. "Web Home Pages as Advertisements". *Communications of the ACM* 42(8):91-98.

Smith, V. 2001. "Tourism Change and Impacts". In *Hosts and Guests Revisited: Tourism Issues of the 21st Century,* edited by V. Smith and M. Brent, 107-121. New York: Cognizant.

Spencer-Oatey, H. 2005. "Rapport Management Theory and Culture". *Intercultural Pragmatics* 2(3):335-346.

—. 2008. *Culturally Speaking: Culture, Communication and Politeness Theory* (2nd ed.). London: Continuum.

Stein, D. 2006. "The Website as a Domain-specific Genre". *Language@Internet 3*, article 6. Accessed May 10, 2014. http://www.languageatinternet.org/articles/2006/374.

Steinecke, A. 2010. "Culture–A Tourist Attraction: Importance–Expectations–Potential". In *Trends and Issues in Global Tourism 2010*, edited by R. Conrady and M. Buck, 185-196. Berlin: Springer.

Steinmetz, T. 2004. "E-Communication in Tourism–the Role of the Internet, Challenges and Opportunities for Tourism". In *Observations on International Tourism Communications. Report from the First World Conference on Tourism Communications,* by WTO-OMT, 243-246. Madrid: WTO-OMT.

Stenglin, M. 2004. "Packaging Curiosities: Towards a Grammar of Three-dimensional Space". PhD. diss., University of Sydney.

Stöckl, H. 2004. "In-between Language and Image in Printed Media". In *Perspectives on Multimodality*, edited by E. Ventola, C. Charles and M. Kaltenbacher, 9-30. Amsterdam: John Benjamins.

Stoian, C.E. 2013a. "Online Promotion of Heritage Cities: A Multimodal Analysis from a Cultural Perspective". *BrandTrends Journal OUT* 2(5):34-44.

—. 2013b. "Tourism and Technology: A Multimodal Analysis of Online Heritage Promotion". *Professional Communication and Translation Studies* 6(1):109-118.

—. 2015. "Meaning in Images: Complexity and Variation across Cultures". In *Meaning Making in Text: Multimodal and Multilingual Functional Perspectives*, edited by S. Starc, C. Jones and A. Maiorani, 152-170. London: Palgrave Macmillan.

—. forthcomming. "The Promotion of Heritage Tourism in Modern Times: A Multimodal Analysis from a Cultural Perspective". In *Proceedings ALT4 Congress*, Belgrade, 12-14 October 2012.

Suan Jiménez, F. 2011. "La Persuasión a través del Metadiscurso Interpersonal en el Genero Pagina Web Institucional de Promoción Turística en Ingles y Español". In *La Lengua del Turismo. Géneros Discursivos y Terminología*, edited by M. Calvi and G. Mapelli, 177-200. Bern: Peter Lang.

Şerbănescu, A. 2007. *Cum Gândesc şi Cum Vorbesc Ceilalţi: Prin Labirintul Culturilor*. Iaşi: Polirom.

Şimon, S. 2014. *The Persuasive Function of Written Advertisements*. Timişoara: Orizonturi Universitare; Cluj-Napoca: Casa Cărţii de Ştiinţă.

Talón, P., L. González and C. Figueroa. 2009. "El Nuevo Entorno de la Comercialización Hotelera: Nuevas Tendencias y la Necesidad de una Nueva Clasificación de los Canales de Distribución". Paper presented at the V Seminario de Otoño *Información socioeconómica turística y promoción de los destinos en la región Mediterránea*. Benissa, 6-7 November.

Theobald, W. 2005. "The Meaning, Scope, and Measurement of Travel and Tourism". In *Global Tourism* (3rd ed.), edited by W. Theobald, 5-24. USA: Elsevier.

Thernborn, G. 2002. "Monumental Europe: The National Years. On the Iconography of European Capital Cities". *Housing, Theory and Society* 19:26-47.

Thibault, P. 1987. "An Interview with Michael Halliday". In *Language Topics: Essays in Honour of Michael Halliday* (vol. 2), edited by R. Steele and T. Threadgold, 601-627. Amsterdam: Benjamins.

—. 2001. "Multimodality and the School Science Textbook". In *Corpora Testuali per Ricerca, Traduzione e Apprendimento Linguistico*, edited by C. Torsello, G. Brunetti, and N. Penello, 293-335. Padova: Unipress.

Thompson, G. 1996, 2004. *Introducing Functional Grammar*. London: Arnold.

Thorlacius, L. 2002. "A Model of Visual, Aesthetic Communication Focusing on Web Sites". *Digital Creativity* 13(2):85-98.

—. 2007. "The Role of Aesthetics in Web Design". *Nordicom Review* 28(1):63-76.

Thurlow, C., and A. Jaworski. 2010. *Tourism Discourse: Language and Global Mobility*. Basingstoke: Palgrave MacMillan.

Timothy, D. 2002. "Tourism and Community Development Issues". In *Tourism and Development. Concepts and Issues*, edited by R. Sharpley and D. Telfer, 149-164. Clevedon: Channel View Publications.

Timothy, D., and S. Boyd. 2002. *Heritage Tourism*. Harlow: Prentice Hall.

Timothy, D., and G. Nyaupane, eds. 2009. *Cultural Heritage and Tourism in the Developing World. A Regional Perspective*. London: Routledge.

Toledo Pereira, D. 2006. "Thematic Choices and the Context of Culture in the Discourse of Museum and Citytour Guides". In *Discourse and Enterprise. Communication, Business, Management and other Professional Fields*, edited by F. Ramallo, A. Lorenzo and X. Rodríguez, 165-181. Munich: Lincom Europa.

Tomlinson, J. 2002. *Globalizare şi Cultură*. Timişoara: Amarcord.

Triandis, H. 1972. *The Analysis of Subjective Culture*. New York: Wiley.

—. 1995. *Individualism and Collectivism. New Directions in Social Psychology*. USA: Westview Press.

Triandis, H., K. Leung, M. Villareal and E. Clack, 1985. "Allocentrie vs. Idiocentric Tendencies: Convergent and Discriminant Validation". *Journal of Research in Personality* 19:395-415.

Trompenaars, F. 1993. *Riding the Waves of Culture: Understanding Cultural Diversity in Business*. London: Economists Books.

Trompenaars, F., and C. Hampden-Turner. 1997, 1998. *Riding the Waves of Culture: Understanding Diversity in Global Business*. New York: Mcgraw Hill.

Tsotra, D., M. Janson and D. Cecez-Kecmanovic. 2004. "Marketing on the Internet: A Semiotic Analysis". In *Proceedings of the Tenth Americas Conference on Information Systems*, New York, August 2004.

UNESCO. 2014. "World Heritage List". Accessed September 7. http://whc.unesco.org/en/list/.

Unsworth, L. 2001. *Teaching Multiliteracies across the Curriculum: Changing Contexts of Text and Image in Classroom Practice*. USA: Open University.

Urry, J. 1990. *The Tourist Gaze: Leisure and Travel in Contemporary Societies*. London: Sage.

—. 2008. "Globalising the Tourist Gaze". In *Tourism Development Revisited. Concepts, Issues and Paradigms*, edited by S. Babu, S. Mishra and B. Parida, 150-160. New Delhi: Response.

Valdeón, R. 2009. "Info-promotional Material Discourse and its Translation: The Case of the Asturian Tourist Board Texts". *Across Languages and Cultures* 10(1):21-47.

Vanderveken, D. 1990. *Meaning and Speech Acts: Formal Semantics of Success and Satisfaction*. Cambridge: CUP.

van Dijk, T. 2009. *Society and Discourse. How Context Controls Text and Talk*. Cambridge: CUP.

van Leeuwen, T. 1999. *Speech, Music, Sound*. Germany: Macmillan.

—. 2005. *Introducing Social Semiosis*. London: Routledge.

—. 2011. *The Language of Colour: An Introduction*. London: Routledge.

Vimonnan, B. 2003. "A Genre-based Analysis of Tourist Leaflets Produced and Distributed in the United States of America". Master diss., Kasetsart University.

Weightman, B. 1987. "Third World Tour Landscapes". *Annals of Tourism Research* 14:227-239.

Whittaker, R. 1995a. "Theme, Processes and the Realization of Meanings in Academic Articles". In *Thematic Development in English Texts*, edited by M. Ghadessy, 105-128. London: Pinter.

—. 1995b. "More than Mode: Writer's Purpose and Choices at Theme". In *Current Issues in Genre Theory,* edited by I. Vázquez and A. Harnero, 83-130. Zaragoza: Mira Editores.

Whorf, B. 1940. "Science and Linguistics". *Technology Review* 42(6):229-31, 247-8.

Wise, J. 2008. *Cultural Globalization. A User's Guide*. Malden: Blackwell Publishing.

Wolfe-Quintero, K., S. Inagaki and H. Kim. 1998. *Second Language Development in Writing: Measures of Fluency, Accuracy and Complexity*. Honolulu: University of Hawaii Press.

WTO, and ETC (World Tourism Organization and the European Travel Commission). 2009. *Handbook on Tourism Destinations Branding*. Madrid: WTO.

WTTC (World Travel and Tourism Council). 2003. "Travel & Tourism: A World of Opportunity". In *The 2003 Travel & Tourism Economic Research*. London: WTTC.

Würtz, E. 2005. "A Cross-cultural Analysis of Websites from High-Context Cultures and Low-Context Cultures". *Journal of Computer-Mediated Communication* 11(1), article 13. Accessed March 30, 2010. http://jcmc.indiana.edu/vol11/issue1/wuertz.html.

Yeoman, I., U. McMahon-Beattie and M. Brown. 2005. "The Authentic Tourist". In *Scotland 2020*, edited by J. Hassan, 160-166. Edinburgh: Scottish Book Trust.

Yui Ling Ip, J. 2008. "Analyzing Tourism Discourse: A Case Study of a Hong Kong Travel Brochure". *LCOM Papers* 1:1-19.

## Websites Analysed

***Institutional websites***

Great Britain: VisitBritain. 2011. http://www.visitbritain.com/en/EN/.
Spain: Spain.info. 2011. http://www.spain.info/.
Romania: Romania Tourism. 2011. http://romaniatourism.com/.

***Commercial websites***

Great Britain: Evan Evans Tours. 2014. http://www.evanevanstours.co.uk/
Spain: Spain Day Tours. 2011. http://www.spaindaytours.com/.
Romania: Source: Ciao Romania. 2012. http://www.ciaoromania.co.uk/.

# INDEX